QUEER DHARMA

Buddha head, stucco, Gandhara period.
4th/5th century C.E.
Courtesy Staatliche Museen zu Berlin—Preussischer Kulturbesitz
Museum für Indische Kunst. Photo by Jürgen Liepe, 1995.

QUEER DHARMA

Voices of Gay Buddhists

Edited by Winston Leyland

Gay Sunshine Press
San Francisco

First Edition 1998

LIBRARY OF CONGRESS CATALOGING-IN-PUBLICATION DATA
Queer Dharma : voices of gay Buddhists / edited by Winston Leyland.
    416 p. ; 23 cm.
    Includes bibliographical references
    ISBN 0-940567-21-0 (cloth : alk. paper).—ISBN 0-940567-22-9 (paper : alk. paper)
    1. Homosexuality—Religious aspects—Buddhism. 2. Gays—Religious life.
I. Leyland, Winston, 1940-
BQ4570.H65Q84   1998   97-27590
294.3'086'64—dc21   CIP

Gay Sunshine Press Inc., P.O. Box 410690, San Francisco, CA 94141
Write for free catalogue of books available, including how to order extra copies of this book.

Table of Contents

III. INTERVIEW

IV. ESSAYS ON CONTEMPORARY BUDDHISM AND HOMOSEXUALITY

V. GAY FICTION ON BUDDHIST THEMES

VI. QUEER DHARMA POETRY

ILLUSTRATIONS

Page 2: Buddha head, stucco, Gandhara period. 4th/5th century C.E. Photo by Jürgen Liepe, 1995. Page 28: Standing Buddha, 2nd century C.E. Gandhara, India. Page 57: Head of Buddha, 2nd century C.E. Gandhara, India. Page 73: Maravijaya Buddha, late 15th–early 16th century. Bronze with traces of gilding, Lan Na style, Thai. Page 90: Woodcut from *Nanshoku ōkagami* (Great Mirror of Male Love) by Ihara Saikaku, 1687. From story, "His Head Shaved on the Path of Dreams." Page 108: Photo courtesy of *Barazoku*. Page 126: Michael Hyman (left) and Bill Shean, 1996. Photo by Robert Zeballos. Page 148: Issan Dorsey Roshi, 1990. Photo by Rob Lee. Page 208: Photo of Maitreyabandhu. Page 222: Jon Bernie. Photo by Steve Savage. Page 230: Steve Lowell, a self-portrait, 1972. Page 268: Top photo: H.H. Dudjom Rinpoche and John Giorno, September, 1973. Bottom photo: Winston Leyland, 1995. Page 293: H.H. Dudjom Rinpoche, photo by Arnaud Desjardins. Page 298: Buddha with condom. Concept/artist: Stuart Sherman. Photo: Don Felton. Page 358: Scene from the *Chigo Kannon engi* scroll, early 14th century. Page 366: Woodcut, "Shuzen was drawing water from a well . . ." Page 370: Woodcuts, (top): ". . . My reverie was disturbed by. . . "; (bottom): "It was a certain high priest . . ." Page 394: Allen Ginsberg, July 1963.

Introduction

Winston Leyland

Shortly after the death of my Guatemalan lover, Manuel, in December 1993 at the age of forty (our relationship had lasted seventeen years), I happened to purchase Sogyal Rinpoche's lucid and luminous volume *The Tibetan Book of Living and Dying*. The clarity and truth of the Dharma, especially as expressed through the teachings of such spiritual masters as His Holiness Dudjom Rinpoche and Dilgo Khyentse Rinpoche helped me immensely to cope with Manuel's death; but more than that it pierced me through and rapidly impelled me to take refuge and to begin practicing within the Tibetan Nyingma tradition, one that had already long attracted me for its obvious spiritual depth; a dear friend of some twenty-odd years (John Giorno) also practices within it.

After moving back to San Francisco in early 1996, I took part in sittings of the Gay Buddhist Fellowship. A book project had been proposed by several members of the group but had not been developed. Upon hearing of this, I proposed that Gay Sunshine Press should research and publish the book as an independent project. *Queer Dharma* is the result of that initiative.

Planning the volume, I decided on a multi-cultural approach: historical essays, fiction, poetry, but with the main emphasis on articles by practitioners from various traditions (Zen, Vipassana, Tibetan, etc.) on the integration of their gay sexuality and Buddhist practice. Articles with this focus comprise almost half of the present book.

The Dharma, of course, is practiced with equal insight by both women and men. But since Gay Sunshine Press has always published and distributed within a gay male context, a decision was made to follow the same approach with *Queer Dharma*. Naturally the book can be read fruitfully by women, just as a companion volume from a lesbian feminist press could be read by men equally with great spiritual profit.

The material published in *Queer Dharma* originates from various sources: some of the historical material and fiction/poetry have appeared in other venues. I was especially fortunate and privileged to obtain the cooperation of four scholars with world-wide preeminence in the specialized field of research on the history of, and relationships between, homosexuality and Buddhism in the early centuries after the Buddha and in Japan of the 16th–17th centuries: Leonard Zwilling, José Ignacio Cabezón, Peter A. Jackson and Paul Gordon Schalow (see their academic credentials in the individual capsule biographies).

All the material (personal accounts and theological essays) in sections two, three and four appear here for the first time in book form, though several pieces have previous publication history in magazines (such as San Francisco's Gay Buddhist Fellowship *Newsletter*). Provenances for all material is provided in the introductions or footnotes.

A few words about the front and back cover graphics of the present book are apropos. When researching historical Buddhist art of high caliber for presentation in this book (see pages 2, 28, 57, 73), I was struck by a crucial fact: through the centuries artists had very often carved their Buddha figures to meet the needs of their own culture, using designs and motifs which would appeal to the Buddhist practitioners who would see them. Thus the Gandhara head on the cover of this book has Graeco-Roman inspiration in its lifelikeness, even though it comes from the area now Afghanistan-Pakistan. So too I became convinced that the art on the covers of a book such as this one should have a gay consciousness, meeting the spiritual/artistic needs of the gay practitioners who will be reading it. I therefore approached San Francisco artist, Stevee Postman, with this in mind. The result is a front cover collage infused with gay consciousness; and the back cover is a gay version of the traditional Tibetan yab yum statue, expressing through sexual union the emptiness of the mind and the fullness of Dharmic wisdom.

I want to thank everyone who helped make this volume possible: first and foremost all the authors/artists who participated in the project with generosity and enthusiasm. Encompassed in their work are a wide range of views and opinions. *Queer Dharma*, however, is not intended in any way as a definitive study of Buddhism and homosexuality, but rather as a tentative, pioneering, probing book encouraging other gay practitioners to express their insights through their writing.

My special thanks to Steve Peskind. His many valuable suggestions helped to fertilize and fructify this book. He is editor of *Heart Lessons from an Epidemic: Buddhist Practice and Living with HIV* (Berkeley: Parallax Press, 1998), which readers will find replete with Dharmic wisdom. Special thanks also to Trebor for his assistance and enthusiasm; to Daishin David Sunseri for directing me to potential writers; to Clint Seiter for his suggestion of the title "Queer Dharma"; and to Tom Moon for the subtitle; to John Giorno for his warm encouragement; to Kobai Scott Whitney for revising and expanding his seminal article "Vast Sky and White Clouds." Allen Ginsberg, whose work I have published often during the past quarter century, died (April 1997) while production of *Queer Dharma* was in its final stages, but his six poems printed herein should give readers insights into his own practice and gay consciousness.

If *Queer Dharma* is well received, I may publish a second, companion volume in the future. Readers with feedback on the present volume or interest in contributing to a subsequent one can write: Winston Leyland, P.O. Box 410690, San Francisco, CA 94141

Short Readers' Note on Buddhism

History tells us that Siddhartha Gautama, who was to become the Buddha, was born a prince in a small kingdom in Northern India [Most recent scholarship assigns the Buddha's death to ca. 385/350 B.C.E., later than previously estimated]. As a boy he lived in great luxury, but as he grew older he became concerned with spiritual questions. When he saw how the majority of people lived, and how all human beings, including himself, would eventually suffer from old age, sickness and death, he resolved to seek out the causes of such suffering. Consequently, at the age of 29, Sidhartha left behind him his kingdom, his wife and his young son to pursue the life of a wandering ascetic in the hopes of realizing nirvana.

Like all wandering mendicants, he sought out teachers, and from each he learned valuable practices and lessons. However, it is said that after six years of a harsh and meager life of renunciation, Siddhartha decided that this path would not in fact lead to his liberation. Subsequently, he ate a regular meal and then resolved to sit below the bodhi tree and not get up until he fully understood the nature of reality. And it was here under the bodhi tree in what is today Bodh Gaya that the former Prince Siddhartha realized the true nature of reality, commonly called enlightenment, becoming henceforth the "Buddha" or "awakened one."

From that time forward the Buddha vowed to share his discovery and to help others achieve the same result. And so for the next 45 years the Buddha traveled northern India as a teacher. His teachings were simple, posited on experiential reality; the three basic facts of human existence are that there is pain and suffering or unsatisfactoriness; that all things are impermanent; and that the idea of an inherently existing self or ego is in fact an illusion. The Four Noble Truths of Buddhism address this view of reality and make up its general foundation: (1) That suffering pervades our life; (2) that there is a cause to this suffering which is in fact our struggle to not accept or avoid that suffering; (3) that the suffering can in fact end; and, (4) that the means to that end is ethical conduct, meditation and mindfulness.

Having left his own extreme ascetic practices behind as counter-productive, he taught a spiritual path emphasizing moderation, neither indulging in luxury nor renouncing all pleasure, what he called the Middle Way. The core teachings of the Middle Way, which make up the eight spokes of the Wheel of the Dharma, provide the basic rules or guidelines for the spiritual practitioner. They are usually expressed in three subsets: Wisdom (right thought, right understanding); Morality (right speech, right action, right livelihood); and Concentration achieved through meditation practice (right effort, right mindfulness, right concentration).

In addition to these new approaches, much of the Buddha's teachings offered a fresh approach to traditional Hindu teachings from which his own spiritual development had emerged. Like Hindu teachers, the Buddha taught that all beings participate in a cycle of birth, death and rebirth. He taught that there is a state known as nirvana that exists beyond the realm of suffering, desire and aversion and that it is in fact a release from the cycles of birth and death. Building on the vedic belief in karma, the Buddha taught what is called the law of dependent origination which states that all phenomena are conditioned by all phenomena that have occurred before, and that present phenomena create what is to follow in the future. Karma can be seen as a web that holds all things and beings which are in fact wholly interdependent upon one another. It is said that the Buddha's time was not a time unlike our own in which many people were dissatisfied with the traditional Hindu religion and many sects and teachers were to be found attempting to reform and add new dimensions to what had become a lethargic and often irrelevant spirituality. The Buddha is arguably the greatest teacher to emerge from this era.

The Buddhist community, known as sangha, was wholly monastic at this time, and unique in that it allowed women monastics, a radical departure from the predominant Hinduism. The sangha formed one of the three parts of the triple jewel, the other two being the Buddha (teacher) and the Dharma (teachings or truth). After the Buddha passed away in his early 80s, his teachings were preserved and carried on by his monks and nuns. A fortuitous historical circumstance greatly aided the early dissemination of the teachings, when some 100 years after the Buddha's death, King Ashoka, who ruled a vast Indian empire, converted to Buddhism. Consequently, Buddhism spread throughout India and into Sri Lanka. At the same time, Buddhists still found themselves persecuted by the Hindu majority, and in addition a schism developed within the Buddhist community itself around this time. This schism grew into what is today the major division between Buddhist schools of thought, namely, the Mahayana and the Theravada.

The differences between the two schools of thought are complicated and developed over many centuries, but the main distinction is that the Theravadan tradition emphasizes the achievement of enlightenment for those who pursue the monastic life and considers this to be the true tradition that existed at the time of the Buddha. The Mahayana, on the other hand, professes that enlightenment can be achieved by anyone in almost any circumstance as long as he practices the teachings. Consistent with this distinction, the Mahayana believe that enlightenment can be spontaneous while the Theravadan tradition emphasizes that it is a gradual process achieved through successive levels of realization. Another example of the differences between the two major schools of thought can be seen in the idea of the Bodhisattva, which in the Theravadan sense means one on the path to enlightenment, while in the Mahayana view the Bodhisattva is one on the path to enlightenment *or* one who has already reached enlightenment but has chosen to remain in the human realm as an act of service in order to help others become awakened. It should also be noted that the Theravadan school bases its teachings on the Pali canon, or the scriptures as translated by the monks of Ceylon, while the Mahayana school uses these as well as additional material not found in the Pali canon.

As monks from these various schools traveled and spread the teachings, Buddhism as a religion became established in nearly all of East Asia. The Theravadan school established monasteries in Thailand and Burma, and eventually reached Cambodia, Malaysia and Sumatra, while the Mahayana teachings spread to Tibet, China and Mongolia, then on to Korea and Japan. Monasteries and temples were also established as far west as Persia (modern day Iran).

The Egyptian gnostic Basilides (2nd cent. C.E.) was influenced by Buddhism, and Bishop Clement of Alexandria (ca. 150–211 C.E.) mentions the Buddha's "extraordinary sanctity" in his *Stromata*. Though there are a few cases of Medieval Christian monks alluding in their writings to Buddhism, the West did not rediscover the Buddha's teachings until well into the 19th century. By the early 20th century, many Europeans were traveling to India and the East, bringing back tales and texts, learning Buddhist practices and opening the doors to a full-scale re-introduction of the teachings. After the Second World War, Zen Buddhism from Japan made an entrance into American culture, and grew rapidly with the publishing of popular books on the subject by D. T. Suzuki, Paul Reps and Englishman Alan Watts, among others. Theravadan Buddhism and the four schools of Tibetan Buddhism (Gelugpa, Nyingma, Sakya, Kagyu) followed, aided in part by young Americans traveling in Asia and living in monasteries as well as by the political persecutions in Tibet and southeast Asia which brought monks and nuns to the U.S. to teach and live. Pure Land Buddhism from China and Nichiren from Japan have also become well-established both by the Asian immigrants who practice them and by teachers who have brought them across the Pacific; they are considered Mahayana but are distinguished by their emphasis on chanting mantras.

In fact, today, Buddhist practice varies widely from one sect to the next and among groups that have grown out of the two major traditions, Theravada and Mahayana. While Tibetan and Pure Land Buddhism are highly devotional and ritualized, Zen Buddhism is markedly spare and simple as is much of Theravadan practice. In both Tibet and Southeast Asia one can find numerous stupas, or monuments, at holy sites, many of which are said to contain actual relics of the historical Buddha. Or in the case of Tibet, relics of particular manifestations of the Buddha, for in the Tibetan tradition, and in much of Mahayana Buddhism, the Buddha or buddha mind is continually manifesting and incarnating through actual human beings, such as high lamas. For instance, the Dalai Lama is considered a human incarnation of Avalokiteshvara, the Buddha of Compassion. Celibacy is another point of departure between the Theravada and Mahayana traditions, for while it is considered a requirement to complete awakening in the Theravadan tradition, this is not the case in the Mahayana tradition.

Meditation practices vary as well. Though concentration practice is common to all sects, this is achieved by various and diverse means. In Tibetan Buddhism you find the use of visualization and mandalas, ceremony and ritual, whereas in Zen or Theravada practice, these would not be employed and an empty mind is emphasized. The emphasis on chanting found in Pure Land and Nichiren practice is very different from Theravadan, Tibetan and Zen practice, which only make use of chanting to complement meditative practices.

Despite their many differences, almost every school of Buddhism is expanding as we approach the end of the second millennia. From Siberia to Peru, one can find teachers, meditation centers and often even monasteries. (For the profound influence Buddhism is exercising on many gay people in the West, see the article "Vast Sky and White Clouds," pp. 15–26 of this anthology.) Like many philosophies, Buddhism has enjoyed times of expansion as well as having endured eras in which persecution, wars and political turmoil have diminished its influence and presence. Almost extinct in its native country of India until recently, Buddhism has enjoyed a resurgence of late due to the fact that it makes no caste distinctions as does Hinduism and so attracts many of India's Untouchables. The nations where Buddhism continues to thrive as a virtual religious majority include Thailand, Burma, Bhutan, Tibet, Sri Lanka, Laos, Cambodia, and Vietnam. Of course in Tibet, Buddhism has been strictly controlled since the Chinese invasion of 1959 and numerous monks and nuns have been persecuted, tortured and killed, while monasteries and stupas have been destroyed. Many refugees and teachers, including the Dalai Lama, who left Tibet to form a government in exile in Dharamsala, India, have traveled over the Himalayas to escape abuse by the Chinese. During the almost 40 years since the Chinese occupation, most of the major Tibetan monasteries have been reestablished in India. In addition to the current persecutions in Tibet, communist governments in China, Mongolia, Vietnam, Cambodia, Laos and North Korea have all created major obstacles to the practice of Buddhism and religion in general. The war in Vietnam and the ensuing political strife in Laos and Cambodia put additional pressure on Buddhist sanghas for several decades and many monks and nuns lost their lives attempting to bring peace and reconciliation through their political activities. As this book goes to press, Burmese monks and nuns are being arrested, persecuted and even killed by the military regime in that country for their efforts to support the democracy movement and work of Nobel Peace Prize Laureate Aung San Suu Kyi.

[compiled by Trebor from various sources]

Vast Sky and White Clouds:
Is There a Gay Buddhism?

Kobai Scott Whitney

The vast sky does not hinder the white clouds from flying. . . .
White clouds fly with no hindrance.
White clouds flying does not hinder the vast sky's flying.
Not hindering others is not hindering self.

—Eihei Dogen

Since the 1980 founding of a group called Maitri by some gay and lesbian Buddhists in San Francisco, the issue of gay people in the American sangha has been a source of concern, irritation, and even humor for many western Buddhists. Maitri gradually evolved into the Gay Buddhist Fellowship (GBF) and a *zendo* (meditation hall) in San Francisco's Castro district. From the work of former-drag-queen-turned-Soto-priest, Issan Dorsey, at that zendo, a hospice—also to be known as Maitri—was founded by the end of the 1980s.

Similar gay/lesbian identified Buddhist groups have surfaced in many metropolitan areas of the U.S. and Canada. These developments have challenged the Buddhist community, and its gay practitioners especially, to think carefully about the meaning or non-meaning, the importance or non-importance, of such specialized practice groups.

To those of us involved in gay Buddhist organizations, the most obvious question is whether there is really a need for such groups. "Gay Buddhists?" many people have reacted, "What next?" Just another only-in-San Francisco phenomenon, another wacky California New Age splinter group. But the persistence and proliferation of such groups in the years since 1980 has proved not only their viability, but also their important place in Euro-American Buddhism.

If, as gay people, our own first impulse in those early years was toward self-questioning, what has been the reaction of the Buddhist community at large?

Mostly raised eyebrows and some mumbling about the dangers of separatism. One letter from a Buddhist cleric arrived at GBF in its first year

---

KOBAI SCOTT WHITNEY (Hawaii), was born in San Jose, CA in 1946. He practices as a Buddhist hermit attached to the Honolulu Diamond Sangha, a mixed Ringai-Sōtō lineage of Zen. The original version of "Vast Sky and White Clouds" was published in 1974 by *Blind Donkey* and was the first work on gay people in the sangha published in the U.S. He is also a contributing editor to *Honolulu Magazine*.

politely advising celibacy for our members. But in reality, the standard reaction from larger sanghas has been one that might be described as liberal caution. Straight Buddhists often seem vaguely hurt at the idea that their own community might not be meeting the needs of gay and lesbian students.

It was not until Robert Aitken Roshi agreed to speak to our original group in San Francisco that we began to feel a sense of legitimacy vis-à-vis the larger Buddhist community. It was at his encouragement that Richard Baker was convinced to commit San Francisco Zen Center to supporting the group's development. SFZC deserves credit for its allocation of resources over the years, including the assignment of unique and talented monks like Issan Dorsey and Philip Whalen to the needs of gay practitioners.

Yet as legitimacy and acceptance increase for gay and lesbian identified practice groups, the questions still need asking: Why is it helpful for gay people to practice together, and what are the special difficulties of individual gay men and lesbian women in larger, "straight" sanghas around the country?

The Issue of Separatism

It is important for gay people to create their own organizations—forms of affiliation that promote positive ways of socializing, encourage self-help, and promote the realization of each member's fullest human maturity. For all too many years, the only gay institutions were the bars and the bathhouses. Fortunately this has changed and there are now gay hiking clubs, choirs, investment clubs and gay chapters of 12-Step organizations like A.A. and Narcotics Anonymous.

If gay people organize to practice Buddhism together, it is not because we desire separation from mainstream Buddhism, but rather because we need the opportunity to share with, and encourage, one another. For gay people to sit together is to enact the exact opposite of the furtive, self-destructive bar scene that was so much a part of our "coming out."

Yet even liberal straight friends of gay people often argue against such associations, saying, "There is no need for this separatism. The world is made up of all kinds of people, you have to learn to get along in the real world." But gay people are all too familiar with the real world—a world that for them has included rejection and suspicion from others, bias in schools and work places, ostracism from family or church, and even, in all too many cases, outright physical attack.

But there are better reasons for gay sangha building. Any group which has been oppressed by a dominant culture feels powerless. The first step out of powerlessness is to organize the individuals who have experienced the oppression. They can then begin to heal themselves, first by sharing their experiences with each other, and later, by feeling the power they *do* have as a group.

What Buddhism Offers

Most lesbian women and gay men have had to conduct the search for identity and spiritual values without the support of religious institutions. Unfortunately, and with few exceptions, occidental religions have provided both the justification and the encouragement for the homophobia so rampant in American society. Gay people have been actively shunned or passively ignored by both fundamentalist and "high church" denominations. Mormons still expel openly gay church members. Gay Catholic priests are told by their bishops that they will be dismissed if they go public with their sexual identity—even if they remain faithful to their vows.

Thus Christianity, at least in its most recent 1,000 years, has not served, accepted, or encouraged gay people in any but the most covert of ways.

Buddhism, on the other hand, seemed silent on the issue of sexual preference, and this helped make it accessible and attractive to gay people. While the third precept condemns the misuse of sex by any Buddhist, what constitutes misuse has usually been interpreted, at least in the West, as misuse of power in a sexual relationship, or as unbalanced attachment (addiction) to sexual activity. The principle of not-harming is also frequently cited for guidance in the practice of the third precept.

Buddhist monks and nuns, as in the West, are expected to be celibate. Japan is the only Buddhist country which allowed their ordained men to marry. That country has also had a long history of homoerotic activity in monasteries, a history that went underground in the Meiji Era (1868–1912), when Judeo/Christian values and behaviors began to have an impact on Japanese public life. From the 10th through the 18th centuries, *nanshoku* (male love) was a frequent subject of folktales and poems, even of enlightenment stories—in several of which the monk's beautiful boy acolyte turns out to be *Kannon*, the Bodhisattva of Compassion, who is testing the hermit's ability to detach from desire. (See *Partings at Dawn, An Anthology of Japanese Gay Literature*, Stephen D. Miller, Ed., Gay Sunshine Press, 1996 and the articles on homosexuality in Japanese Buddhism and translations by Paul Schalow/Margaret Childs elsewhere in the present volume).

Besides avoiding canonical prohibitions, then, gay people coming to Buddhist practice see that the *dharma* (the law, the teaching) holds the promise of a new and more subtle moral insight based on the law of cause and effect, *karma*, and the imperative to compassion with its bottom line, "not harming."

Probably few Westerners enter into Buddhist practice without the same mixture of suffering and curiosity that led the historical Buddha himself toward the bodhi tree. But for gay men and lesbian women, that suffering has sometimes been acute. Buddhism's focus on suffering—as opposed to evil—speaks directly to that intimately experienced pain.

The Pillow of Doubt

During a 1981 talk at the Hartford Street Zen Center, Allen Ginsberg made the comment that "The best approach to being queer is ordinary mind." Ordinary mind is the uncluttered mind of everyday activity, the mind of immediacy that fetches wood and draws the water. Or, in our post-modern world, the mind that drives to work or surfs the internet. It is mind free of judgments like good and evil, us and them, practice now, enlightenment later.

Great Ancestor Dogen said:

> "Everyday mind" means to maintain an everyday mind in this world or in any world. Yesterday goes forth from this moment, and today comes forth from this place. With going the boundless sky goes, with coming the entire earth comes. . . . The moment is already here. Do not doubt it in the least. Even if you should doubt it, this is nothing but everyday mind (p. 91).

Dogen accepts doubt as an integral part of everyday mind, indeed, he sees doubt as essential to practice, and this can be a very encouraging point of view for gay people who have had to experience doubt at such fundamental levels as: "Is death preferable to a life of continual oppression?" "Is there any place for me in a spiritual tradition?" "Am I worthy of the love of others?" "How can I learn to accept myself when even family and church have found it necessary to reject me?"

In good circumstances, this deep questioning engenders an empirical, see-for-oneself attitude which can be a great help to spiritual practice. Accepted as a part of ordinary mind, doubt becomes the pillow on which we sit during meditation. It is absolutely necessary in the Buddhist scheme of things. Doubt, well used, is what will get us to our teachers.

Those of us who were raised Catholic remember the insistence on "taking things on faith" or, when Sister Frank or Father Ernest had talked themselves into a theological corner, their answer of last resort was always: "It's a mystery!" Lesbian and gay reactions against such authoritarian, externally imposed dogma make the more empirical strategy of Buddhism very attractive.

Public Faces, Private Places

One of the most difficult and pervasive issues faced by gay people is the problem of compartmentalization. That is, there are certain times and places where one can be oneself, and other occasions when information about one's identity must be hidden. Usually referred to as "coming out," (as in the question: "Are you out to your parents yet?") the effort to remove the barriers between life-compartments can be a long and unnerving process.

Many realistic gay people find it necessary to behave differently at work than at home, but it may not even be safe to relax at home if someone is visiting who "doesn't know." Many lesbian women and gay men maintain friendships which must be kept in a separate compartment from other relationships where identity information is freely shared.

This "information management" problem generates a great deal of stress, and it is for this reason that gays have encouraged each other to come out, at least to those who are of some emotional importance to them. The more "out" one is, the more social continuity is achieved and the more the walls between private compartments become permeable—relieving the stress of maintaining multiple identities.

Heterosexual American Buddhists may have some inkling of this phenomenon, for as members of an uncommon or exotic religious group, many have had to face the issue of "coming out" as a Buddhist to relatives and friends. Many have recounted the difficulty they had in sitting down with their Jewish or Christian parents to explain why they have become Buddhists—a revelation that can be almost as horrifying to elders as a revelation of same-sex preference. One straight Buddhist acquaintance recounted wearing a Buddhist rosary (*juzu* or *mala*) around her wrist when she went to work one day. The Christian receptionist took one look at it and exclaimed: "Oh, you're one of *those!*"—in a tone of voice that suggested cannibalism or witchcraft.

The political and legal issue of same-sex marriage has arisen as one good example of making the private public, of the attempt to be "out" with our long-term committed relationships. At this writing, much gay enthusiasm has greeted the Hawai'i Circuit Court decision ordering the state to show cause why it should not issue marriage licenses to same-sex couples. Yet the civil approval of same-sex unions will challenge religious groups of all persuasions to take a stand for, or against, this expanded view of marriage. Some Christian fundamentalist groups in Hawai'i and elsewhere have spent considerable time, energy, and attorney fees fighting any liberalization of marriage laws.

This controversy is likely to inflame the electorates of many states for some years to come. And, just like the Christian faith community, different Buddhist sects have different positions on same-sex marriage. Many liberals, like Robert Aitken-Roshi, have said they would gladly perform weddings for same-sex couples from within their sanghas. Other lines of Buddhist tradition, both ethnic and Euro-American, are likely to be adamant in supporting the status quo. Conservative Christian groups are already organizing for ballot initiatives and even constitutional conventions in any state where same-sex unions are likely to get civil approval. Several liberal legislators in the state of Hawai'i have already lost their re-election bids because they publicly supported same-sex unions. "It's the kiss of death politically," one former legislator told the author.

Even in the gay Buddhist community there is controversy on the same-sex marriage issue. Some gay people with heterosexual marriages in their past dismiss the fight for equal civil treatment with a "been there, done that" attitude. They see matrimony as just another oppressive institution of a gay-unfriendly world.

Others are fond of the notion of public marriage and seem attracted to the possibility (if not the glamor and drama) of such ceremonies. Remember that soap opera series almost always put weddings in their plots during ratings sweep week since no one, it seems, can resist the allure of a tux and a gown. Not a few gay priests and ministers have day dreamed about the money-generating possibilities of cranking out same-sex weddings in some tasteful Waikiki chapel.

Liberals and Conservatives

But recent events remind us that not all fundamentalists are Christians (or vice versa, as Dorothy Parker would have added). After an interview in *Tricycle: The Buddhist Review* with Buddhist scholar Jeffrey Hopkins, there was a flurry of venomous letters to the editor making it quite clear that not all Buddhists support the rights of gay men and lesbians. Hopkins' interview, which discussed his own coming out and explored the concept of gay tantric sex, became one of the most controversial pieces ever published by the quarterly. According to the editor-in-chief, the magazine received over 50 anti-gay letters from (presumably Buddhist) subscribers who said, among other things, that "gays have no right to live in the United States."

The Practice of Desire

Gay people involved in Buddhist practice must face some other issues with their teachers and with their practice communities. In particular, full acceptance of self, both at the psychological and the karmic levels, will always be a theme in the training of lesbian women and gay men. Full experience of self at a psychological level is a necessary, if not sufficient, condition for the full experience of realization which includes, oddly enough, the astonishing and paradoxical discovery of "no abiding self."

Gay people tend to focus on their difference from the mainstream society, and the core of that difference is their sexuality. Thus, like it or not, lesbian women and gay men may focus more than others on this crux of their difference; just as African Americans have an elaborate vocabulary for skin color, so too, we tend to focus on gender and sexuality in our folklore, our humor, and our everyday activity.

While this focus is not necessarily "bad" in any moral sense, it can often be viewed as a distraction to spiritual practice. Yet, from a Buddhist perspective, this does not have to be so. Prince Gautama taught that desire and aversion are the twin forces which must be mastered in the process of liberation. Not "overcome," but mastered. Thus desire, attachment, yearning and infatuation are part of the toolbox of a realistic spiritual practice. They are part and parcel of our experience of *dukkha* (suffering, the constant feeling of dissatisfaction or, according to one translator, a sense of "humiliation").

But from a Buddhist perspective, within the guidelines of the precepts, these human impulses are not sins or evil instincts, but rather they are seen as a fundamental part of *samsara*: the daily round of coming and going, dying and being born, desire and satiation. If, as many Buddhist schools maintain, samsara and nirvana are the same; if, as the great 13th century Japanese Ancestor Dogen taught, practice is already enlightenment, then the elements of that practice must encompass all that is human—without the dualistic distinctions of good and evil, the elect versus the damned, or gay versus straight. The sky is big enough for all the clouds to pass.

For gay Buddhists, then, practice would mean the ability to first notice —note, be aware of in detail, the sexual or romantic fantasies that arise from day to day—on the meditation cushion or off. That is all at first. Noticing is the initial skill.

Then there is the experience of accepting desire. And this may be the hidden secret of all movement toward change. Most people find themselves unable to change how they behave until they accept, in detail, how they have been behaving already. From a Buddhist point of view, the craving self is not to be denied; it is to be watched and accepted, just as we are instructed to watch and accept the experience of our breathing during meditation. Monkey mind can swing from one delusive tree to the next, many times per minute, with no help from us. The trick is to watch and accept.

After the watching, comes the taming. Soto Zen teacher Ed Brown once said, "It's okay to pick something up—as long as you can put it back down again." But how many of us, as gay men or lesbian women, can easily put down our dream of a relationship with so-and-so or our fantasy of a roll in the hay with Mr. or Ms. Right? We are often so programmed by our fantasies that we become unaware of their automatic and limiting quality.

Suzuki-Roshi used to comment that the best way to control a cow was to give it plenty of room to graze. It's okay to pick up a fantasy, as long as we can put it back down—as long as we not become driven by it. Practice means skillfully taming our habitual, unconscious foraging through the fields of sexual and romantic fantasy. It means noticing. It means accepting. It means putting the fantasy down and moving on to the next breath.

The Buddhist teaching of equanimity is at odds with the cult of desire within the gay community. It is much easier for us to be kind and helpful and cheerful with someone who attracts us physically, than with someone who does not fit our stereotype of the sexually desirable. If we somehow judge another person to be dumb or ugly or unpleasant, we are unlikely to give them much time or emotional attention. The American sexual marketplace (not just in the gay world) is very clear about who is attractive and who is not. The more we, as gay practitioners, buy into this fleshy consumerism, the more we violate the basic imperative to equanimity. He is not better than she. Blond is not better than brown. Young is not better than old. "Each one is best," as the old Zen refrain goes. Hot day, cold day; each one is a buddha.

Renunciation

Buddhist conduct has always presumed some form of renunciation in the practitioner. For nuns and monks this takes the form of celibacy, poverty, a shaved head, not touching money, and adherence to the rest of the ornate code of the *vinaya*—the several hundred rules and promises that make up the practice of being a monk. This imperative to make spiritual practice a full-time job and a lifetime vocation is similar to monastic and clerical traditions in other world religions.

Renunciation for lay people in Buddhist societies has sometimes been limited to the concept of *dana*, or the generous giving of the food, labor or money required to support the monks and nuns. Dana presumes that the monks and nuns are practicing for the laity. This tradition continues among the ethnic Buddhists of Europe and the Americas, but is more ambiguous within the communities of Western, "converted" Buddhists now flourishing in non-Asian countries. Some of these communities rely on dana in the form of pledges or membership fees. Others have tried a neo-Benedictine solution, attempting to become self-supporting with various businesses whose profits are used to support the sangha.

Donations to a sangha, to the poor, or to other worthy causes is one way to practice non-attachment to money and is a form of renunciation practice that is appropriate for lay Buddhists. The reason this can be an issue for gay practice is that many straight people experience a kind of jealousy of the gay community in regard to money and wealth accumulation. It is sometimes pointed out that gay people do not (often) have children to support or put through college and that their income allows for a great deal of discretionary spending on clothes, fine dining, travel, entertainment and so forth. This observation generally holds true, as corporate advertisers have gleefully discovered. A swift glance at any slick gay publication will confirm the extent of lesbian/gay consumerism.

This odd combination of being sexually radical but financially conventional presents some unique challenges for gay Buddhists. Although he never condemned any individual for their wealth or financial success, Issan Dorsey-Roshi, the late founder of Hartford Street Zen Center in San Francisco, was quite critical of the middle class, consumerist values of the Bay Area gay community he knew in the 1970s and 1980s. Money, he knew, can be trouble. Money can become greed; it can become abusive power; it can become an insulating delusion.

Since gay people often (but not always) have more disposable income than others, it is imperative for us, as Buddhists, to make decisions on how this "extra" money can be used in the light of the Buddhist principles of dana and non-attachment.

Not all Buddhists are nuns or monks, but there is a deep commitment in all the dharma lines to the principle of simplicity and non-attachment to material things. A positive way of stating this principle of renunciation is to use, instead, the word "generosity." This core Buddhist commitment to generosity toward others is very similar to the original intent of the teachings of both Islam and Christianity, and asks that each of us share our money, time and food with each other.

But to help the poor may not be as obvious as donating time or money to the nearest homeless shelter or hospice. When Jesus said, "The poor you will have always with you," he meant something much more important than a mere comment on the imperviousness of social inequality. He meant that in each of our lives there are people who are poor—in money or in spirit or in the simple lack of good looks or witty speech. To treat our fellow gay sangha members with equanimity means to remember this crucial saying of Jesus—or the equally pivotal injunction of *Kannon* to listen to the cries of the world.

Even if you and I get the same amount on our paychecks, there is always some disequilibrium between us, some poverty that causes suffering to one or the other. One of any duo is always older or fatter, dimmer-witted or more homophobic. Equanimity and compassion, exercised within our circle of family, friends, enemies and sangha members—are what bring our meditation practice into the world of human, gay and straight, interaction.

Issan Dorsey-Roshi always stopped to talk to panhandlers on the streets of San Francisco. If he had money on him, he gave it. He never ignored them, never pretended they were not there—as so many of us do. His example of attention to the drunk or the sick or the loony was one of his most powerful teachings to those of us who knew him. His actions were not gay or straight, they were not politically correct or reactionary—they were human and compassionate and, in the deepest sense, Buddhist.

The Great Matter

Buddhism is a matter of life and death. Since HIV/AIDS came on the scene in the early 1980s, this stark approach to dying and living has given Buddhism new poignancy for many gay men and other people with AIDS. Death is the flip side of life, and the historical Buddha taught the principle of "dependent co-arising." In other words, there is no true experience of life without the realization of death, there is no gay without straight, no enlightenment without delusion. The urbane, consumerist, disco/drug gay subculture of the '70s and '80s was shocked into the great matter by an epidemic that, for several years, one should recall, remained unexplained and emphatically lethal. For several years, it also appeared that the epidemic was inexplicably targeted to gay men, leading some religious groups to describe the epidemic as "the wrath of God" sent down to smite the Sodomites.

We now know that HIV/AIDS is not a gay disease and medical science of the late century has now brought all people with AIDS to the point of being able to experience the same triple challenges of sickness, old age and death that sent the historical Shakyamuni searching for the morning star. Immediate death is no longer the only prognosis. Some people with AIDS, it now seems possible, will live through sickness *and* old age before reaching their life's end.

But the epidemic helped many gay men re-examine their values and reassess the skills they had to meet death—or to grieve the deaths of friends or lovers. Buddhist practice helped many of us meet the great matter. Awakening, fully living, is often described in Buddhist tradition as the "great death." Dogen again:

> This is emancipation right here. As emancipation is not a matter of time, it is not concerned with a discussion of a certain moment or instant. Taking up this understanding, make earth, water, wind, and fire your vital activity; make mind, consciousness, and wisdom your great death (p. 138).

Death is why we practice, gay or straight; and, conversely, life is why we practice, gay or straight. Issan Dorsey said "AIDS is not about dying, it's about living" and "AIDS is not the wrath of God, it *is* God." AIDS has brought many gay men to Buddhist practice, and practice has brought many people with AIDS to a fuller experience of their lives.

Mutually arising; two-to-tango; no practicing death without practicing life.

The Narrow Road to the Broader Path

Many years ago, while working with gay men who were recovering from drug and alcohol addictions, I noticed that some refused to go to "straight" AA meetings until they were far along in their recoveries. Others shunned gay AA meetings and insisted on going only to straight, mainstream AA. It was only later in their recoveries that many of the latter group could bring themselves to attend an all-gay meeting.

There are parallels in the approach of gay people to the Buddhist sangha. Some are more comfortable approaching through an all gay group, others start in a mainstream sangha and begin to look elsewhere at a later point in their practice.

One lucky outcome for gay men and lesbian women practicing together has been the experience of what might be called a pan-Buddhist ecumenism. By practicing in a non-sectarian group like the Gay Buddhist Fellowship, many of us got a good education on the depth and breadth of Buddhism, an experience that we never could have had if we had only practiced in our home sangha.

Instead of just experiencing Buddhism as Soto Zen, for instance, we could practice with others who are Thai Theravadan, Tibetan, Korean Zen, Jodo Shinshu, or any other of the myriad sects and lineages of sects that make up the broader universe of Buddhism. Many straight people in discrete dharma lineages have not often had the same chance to experience the dharma in all its diversity.

So, is there a gay Buddhism?

Yes and no. There is no buddha that is only gay, just as there is no dharma, no teaching, that is for gay people alone. Compassion is an imperative for all Buddhists. Generosity is not gay or straight. But there may be such a thing as a gay sangha.

Just as it can be said that there is a Vietnamese or a Burmese Buddhist culture, so too does it make sense that there might be a gay Buddhist culture—and a gay Buddhist sangha. As Buddhists, on our cushions or off, the business of our practice is with each other. When people hang out, they tend to hang with their own culture. This is not good or bad, it is just true. Lesbian women and gay men tend to hang out with their own kind, just as Koreans go to Korean temples and Thai men join Thai monasteries. No difference.

The challenge for each of us, gay or straight, is to let our practice unfold within the daily life and the specific culture of the sangha to which we belong. Gay people sometimes need to practice together. Gay people also need to be able to come out in their mainstream sanghas.

No one can be excluded from the great matter. The Great Vows for All commit each individual and each practicing Mahayana community to the emancipation of all beings. With respect to gay people, this does not mean that Buddhist sanghas need to ''help'' in some way; but rather the issue is whether the practice community can learn openness and non-hindrance of all its members.

The sky is big enough to let all the clouds pass.

I

BUDDHISM AND HOMOSEXUALITY— HISTORICAL ESSAYS

WHEN DID THE BUDDHA LIVE?

Clouds of controversy have swirled around the question of exactly when the historical Buddha actually lived. Until recently there was common agreement on the modified "long chronology," according to which the Buddha's decease (*Parinirvāna*) occurred ca. 483 B.C. when he was aged 80. Theravada tradition assigns it to 544. A symposium on this question, attended by scholars of Buddhist and Indian history from around the world, was held at Göttingen, Germany in 1988. The consensus was more favorable to the "northern short chronology," giving a much later date for the Buddha's life. See essays by various of these scholars in the book *When Did the Buddha Live? The Controversy on the Dating of the Historical Buddha* (Sri Satguru Publications, Delhi, India, 1995).

Professor Heinz Bechert, editor of this book, believes that the Buddha's *Parinirvāna* "may be dated between ca. 400 B.C. and ca. 350 B.C." (Some Japanese and other scholars point to ca. 383 or 368 B.C.). This means that:

1) The Buddha's *Nirvāna* occurred only a few decades before the famous invasion of India by Alexander the Great (327–325 B.C.).

2) He lived in the same century as such renowned Greek philosophers as Plato and Aristotle.

3) Since India was significantly more urbanized by the 4th century, the Buddha was exposed to small or medium-sized cities. According to Professor Georg von Simson (*When Did the Buddha Live?* p. 176), very early Buddhism in India "points to a way of life also for the urban citizens, a way of self control and moral obligations, leading towards a state of bliss transcending finally both worldly life and renunciation of the world." So, too, does it point for us gay urbanites almost 2400 years later!

All this information obviously does not affect the Buddha's profound teachings, but it does give him an added fillip of accessibility.

—Winston Leyland

Standing Buddha, 2nd century C.E.
Gandhara, India
Courtesy: Asian Art Museum of San Francisco
The Avery Brundage Collection

Homosexuality and Buddhism*

José Ignacio Cabezón

L ittle work of a scholarly nature has been done concerning homosexuality and the religious traditions of Asia in general, but there is a
particular scarcity of scholarship in the area of Buddhism and homosexuality. In Gilbert Herdt's recent entry in *The Encyclopedia of Religion*,[1]
for example, the Buddhist tradition is never mentioned. Only recently has
scholarly attention turned to a discussion of this question.[2] Despite recent
advances in the state of scholarship, the present status of research in this
area can be considered only preliminary, and conclusions of a general
theoretical or comparative nature can, at this stage, be considered only
tentative.[3]

JOSÉ IGNACIO CABEZÓN is Associate Professor of Philosophy, Iliff School of Theology, Denver, CO. He has been a student of Tibetan Buddhism for more than two
decades, and has served as translator for H.H. the Dalai Lama. Professor Cabezón
received his Ph.D. in Buddhist Studies from the University of Wisconsin–Madison.
He is author/editor of five books and numerous articles related to Buddhist
philosophy in India and Tibet.

*An earlier version of this essay was presented at Yale University in 1988 at the
Pedagogy and Politics Conference, the second annual meeting sponsored by the
Gay and Lesbian Studies Center. The present version first appeared in Arlene
Swidler, ed., *Homosexuality and World Religions* (Valley Forge, PA: Trinity Press
International, 1993), pp. 81-101.

[1]Gilbert H. Herdt, "Homosexuality," in Mircea Eliade, ed., *The Encyclopedia
of Religion* (New York: Macmillan, 1987), vol. 6, pp. 445-453.

[2]The work of Leonard Zwilling and John Garret Jones in the context of Indian
intellectual/religious history, Paul Schalow, Tsuneo Watanabe, Jun'ichi Iwata, and
Maggie Childs in the field of Japanese literature, and Melvyn Goldstein in the field
of Himalayan anthropology is particularly noteworthy. My *Buddhism, Sexuality,
and Gender* (Albany: SUNY Press, 1992) contains two articles on the subject, one
by Zwilling and one by Schalow. See also Randy P. Conner and Stephen Donaldson, "Buddhism" entry in the *Encyclopedia of Homosexuality* (New York and London: Garland Press, 1990), Vol. I, pp. 168-171.

[3]Both religion and homosexuality clearly exist in socio-cultural contexts. In approaching the subject, therefore, the socio-anthropological perspective cannot be
overlooked. At the same time, it becomes tempting to slip into a methodology in
which the overtly religious attitudes regarding homosexual behavior and orientation are disregarded in favor of a more sociological approach that focuses almost
exclusively on the cultural setting in which religious traditions and homosexual peoples coexist. The assumption here is that traditional societies are religious creatures
and that by analyzing societal attitudes toward the phenomenon of homosexuality, the religious attitudes implicitly emerge. At least one recent general study of
this sort exists. Gilbert Herdt's entry, "Homosexuality," in *The Encyclopedia of
Religion* (see note 1), despite its tremendous breadth of scholarship, takes such a
methodological stance. I opt here for an approach to the problem that considers
religious elements (doctrine, ritual, and institutions) overt and explicit foci in the
analysis.

As with most of the world's major religious traditions, Buddhism has also enunciated views concerning homosexuality. However, the diversity of the Buddhist tradition (diachronically within a single cultural locus and both diachronically and synchronically from one ethnic and cultural region to another) has, at different places and times, led to divergent opinions regarding homosexuality. We find, for example, that between early and late Japanese Buddhism there exists a distinct difference as regards attitudes toward male love, just as there exist tremendous differences in these attitudes between the Buddhism of India and the Buddhism of Japan. Given this fact, it makes no sense to speak of a single Buddhist position as regards same-sex relations. This makes it necessary to be clear concerning the historical period and geographical location being discussed.[4]

Despite the ambivalence concerning homosexuality in Buddhist history, the evidence seems to suggest that as a whole Buddhism has been for the most part neutral on the question of homosexuality. The principal question for Buddhism has not been one of heterosexuality vs. homosexuality but one of sexuality vs. celibacy. In this sense homosexuality, when condemned, is condemned more for being an instance of sexuality than for being *homos* (involving partners of the same sex).[5] The fact that Buddhism has been essentially neutral in this regard does not imply that the *cultures* in which Buddhism arose and flourished have always been neutral. Some, at certain times, have been tolerant of same-sex relations; others have not. However, because of the essential neutrality of the Buddhist tradition in this regard, it has adapted to particular sociocultural norms, so that throughout its history we find a wide gamut of opinions concerning homosexual activity, ranging from condemnation (never to the point of active persecution) to praise. Were Buddhist doctrine not neutral in this regard, it would be difficult to see how such disparate opinions regarding homosexuality could have emerged throughout Buddhist history.

Where condemnation of homosexuality occurs, it is for the most part an-

---

[4]Limiting ourselves in this way, it is questionable whether or not it is possible to make generalizations about Buddhism even at specific times and places. In the end, the only valid statements may be very specific ones concerning individual people or individual texts (or even portions thereof). Still, the very general nature of this essay, in which many different cultures and historical periods are discussed, makes the qualification of our findings at every turn impossible. Hence I have opted for not making the types of qualifications that, though perhaps leading to greater accuracy, might confuse the reader and obscure the broader issues.

[5]Following John Boswell's distinction between the terms "gay person" and "homosexual person," *Christianity, Social Tolerance, and Homosexuality: Gay People in Western Europe from the Beginning of the Christian Era to the Fourteenth Century* (Chicago: University of Chicago Press, 1980), pp. 41–46, I have for the most part used the latter here, for this essay deals predominantly with the phenomenon of same-sex relations in its broadest sense and is not restricted to a discussion of "persons who are conscious of erotic preference for their own gender," Boswell's characterization of the former.

cillary to the general Buddhist critique of sexual desire. Hence, to understand the negative views concerning homosexuality it is first necessary to understand the Buddhist deprecation of sexuality in general. Here a distinction needs to be made between the place of sexuality in the elite/monastic and lay/folk lifestyles. Despite the fact that the Buddha extolled the celibate monastic life as the ideal, it is clear that he was a pragmatist, realizing that such a way of life would be undertaken only by a minority of his followers. Arising as it did from a *kṣatriya* (warrior/ruling caste) social milieu, Buddhism has always extolled, at least at the lay level, the ideal of the successful and aggressive man in the world. This latter ideal, in obvious tension with the former, is of course that of the sexually active and procreative householder. The tension has been characterized variously by different scholars. Stanley Tambiah, in a sociopolitical context, has described it as the tension between "world conqueror" and "world renouncer."[6] Charles Keyes relies on a similar motif as an interpretive tool in his study of the custom of temporary monastic ordination popular among young men in Thailand, in which he shows how this period in the monastic life acts as an initiatory process that "ripens" the young man sexually, making him fit for marriage.[7] Hence, despite the fact that the celibate life has always been held to be supreme *sub specie aeternitatis*, this monastic ideal has always existed alongside a lay paradigm that extolled, at least for men, sexual, military, and social prowess. What is more, despite the lay precepts that prohibit drinking and adultery, as Leonard Zwilling points out, "it has traditionally been the case that only exceptionally pious or aged laypersons are expected to keep all of the precepts. . . . No Buddhist societies require teetotaling . . . and both the Tibetans and Sinhalese, to take two disparate examples, are far more flexible and nonjudgmental on such matters as pre- and extramarital sexuality than are Hindus, or conservative Christians for that matter."[8] What this means, of course, is that there is a flexibility to Buddhist ethics that takes for granted certain practices that are proscribed at the level of theory. Therefore, despite the ideal of monastic celibacy, the Buddhist tradition as it has manifested itself in various societies and times has been tolerant of diverse forms of sexual expression, especially at the lay level, but at times even in the monasteries, as we will see.

It should also be pointed out that this essay deals almost exclusively with

---

[6]Stanley Jeyaraja Tambiah, *World Conqueror and World Renouncer: A Study of Buddhism and Polity in Thailand Against a Historical Background* (Cambridge: Cambridge University Press, 1976).

[7]Charles F. Keyes, "Ambiguous Gender: Male Initiation in a Northern Thai Buddhist Society," in Carolyn Walker Bynum et al., eds., *Gender and Religion: On the Complexity of Symbols* (Boston: Beacon Press, 1986), pp. 66–96.

[8]Leonard Zwilling, "Homosexuality as Seen in Indian Buddhist Texts," in J. I. Cabezón, ed., *Buddhism, Sexuality, and Gender* (Albany: SUNY Press, 1992), pp. 203–214.

male homosexuality, and here particularly in monastic settings. That lesbian relationships existed (and still exist) within Buddhist cultures is something that can hardly be denied. Yet, as in the West, there is a tremendous dearth of information regarding same-sex relations among women.[9] In the end we must conclude that what Judith C. Brown says of medieval European Christian culture rings just as true of the Buddhist case:

> For Europeans had long found it difficult to accept that women could actually be attracted to other women. Their view of human sexuality was phallocentric— women might be attracted to men and men might be attracted to men, but there was nothing in a woman that could long sustain the sexual desires of another woman. In law, in medicine, and in the public mind, sexual relations between women were therefore ignored.[10]

Despite the fact that same-sex relations between women have been almost totally ignored, both in the traditional literature of Buddhism and by modern scholars, we do find references to lesbian acts in the *Vinaya*, the portion of the Buddhist canon devoted to monastic rules and discipline.[11] Moreover, both Louis Crompton and Bret Hinsch, in recent essays, have written of a Chinese play by Li Yu (1611–1680) concerning lesbianism, "Pitying the Fragrant Companion" (*Lian xiangban*). In it a young married woman meets and falls in love with a woman two years her junior in a Buddhist convent. They take vows as lovers before the Buddha image, and after several interesting scenes the play culminates with the married woman's convincing her husband to take her lover into the household as a second wife.[12] Hinsch has also written of the practice of lesbian marriages in a woman's organization that flourished in nineteenth-century Guangzhou known as the "Golden Orchid Association."[13] In a different context, Nancy Schuster Barnes writes of the Buddhist influence on this same movement:

> Scores of women silk workers refused to marry and lived together as laywomen in groups very like Buddhist nuns' communities. These women were able to choose such a way of life because they were economically independent due to their work, and that was not owed to Buddhism; but the pattern of their lives in the community were. The nun's sangha has always provided an important al-

---

[9]For several instances of this in an early Buddhist text, see Zwilling, p. 207.

[10]Judith C. Brown, *Immodest Acts* (New York: Oxford University Press, 1986), p. 6.

[11]Zwilling, p. 207, states that "mutual masturbation among nuns is also reckoned with, but is considered a relatively minor offense and there are far fewer references to homosexuality in the *Bhikkhunīvinaya* than in the *Bhikkhuvinaya*."

[12]Louis Crompton, "Homosexuality in Imperial China" (Paper delivered at the Conference on "Homosexuality: Which Homosexuality?" Amsterdam, 1987, pp. 37–38.) See also Bret Hinsch's entry in *The Encyclopedia of Homosexuality*, s.v. "China," vol. I, pp. 215–220.

[13]See note 12.

ternative lifestyle for women in China and wherever else the order was strong; these modern Chinese women simply adapted the institution further to fit their own preferences.[14]

Apart from these few instances, however, there is very little available information concerning lesbianism in traditional Buddhist tradition.

As in various other religious traditions, Buddhist monastic life (or, as above, institutions modeled thereon) has always provided a religious lifestyle for lesbians and gay men who sought a socially acceptable alternative to marriage.[15] This is not to imply that homosexual activity has always been widely practiced in Buddhist monasteries and convents. Although more research needs to be done on the social structures and the interactions of the ordained in Buddhist monastic institutions, preliminary evidence seems to indicate that, apart from cases like that of Japan (see below), the vow of celibacy has traditionally been taken very seriously both by male and female monastics. Nonetheless, in an institution where such a vow has always been of primary importance[16] and in which the path of least resistance to its being broken has, by the unisex composition of the community, been same-sex relations, it is not surprising that we should find such cases discussed in the monastic literature. This, combined with the fact that Buddhist writings are, almost exclusively, the writings of monks, gives the entire discussion a particularly male monastic slant. Until more work is done on the lay aspects of Buddhism, and on those that deal with women, this lack of research will have to be accepted as a limitation of this or any other such study.[17]

One final point is worth commenting upon before turning to the different traditions. It is useful to keep in mind that the notion of "homosexuality" is a nineteenth-century European one, and we should not expect that either it or its modern evolutes will be either applicable or particularly illuminating as conceptual vehicles for explaining same-sex relations in cultural and historical contexts that are radically different from our own. This being the case, especially when dealing with other cultures, it seems to me

---

[14]Nancy Schuster Barnes, "Buddhism," in Arvind Sharma, ed., *Women in World Religions* (Albany: SUNY Press, 1987), p. 132. See also M. Topley, "Marriage Resistance in Rural Kwangtung," in *Women in Chinese Society* (Stanford: Stanford University Press, 1975).

[15]Regarding the prevalence of homosexual peoples in the Christian clergy in the Early Middle Ages, see Boswell, pp. 187–188.

[16]Breaking the vow of celibacy (or any of the other three major vows) is said to bring defeat (*pārājika*), a state of moral downfall that can be corrected in that same lifetime only by the attainment of *nirvāṇa*, i.e., arhatship. Practically speaking, it often brings with it expulsion from the monastic community.

[17]Melvyn Goldstein states in his "A Study of the Ldab Ldob," *Central Asiatic Journal* 9 (1964): 134, that "among the Tibetan lay population [homosexuality] carries an extremely derogative stigma and is almost unknown." I believe that Goldstein's conclusions must be accepted cautiously, however.

necessary to unpack the Western notion of homosexuality in terms of its component parts. Therefore, even at the risk of sounding banal, it seems wise to stress at the outset the distinction between homosexual desire, a homosexual act, and a conscious self-identification as a person of homosexual orientation. Homosexual desire, for example, is often never consummated in a sexual act (at times remaining "filial"), and for many cultures a homosexual act implies nothing about the "orientation" of the actor. Indeed, in many cultures where homosexual acts occur, there is simply no notion of "homosexual orientation" with which to self-identify; and even in cultures where the notion is operative, when a man takes the active role in homosexual anal intercourse (as the "penetrator"), this often never vitiates the man's status as a normative heterosexual male. Zwilling's studies of the Indian Buddhist texts, for example, have shown that there was recognition of the fact that "socially normative males" could [and did] engage in homosexual acts, without ever being considered, either by themselves or by society, as homosexual in their orientation. In addition, he describes the *paṇḍaka*, a category which, though broader than what we might call "persons of homosexual orientation,"[18] includes within it both some lesbians and some homosexual men. The point is, of course, that we should not expect that the Western conceptual construct "homosexuality" will be a perfect fit when we are dealing with notions operative in other cultures. Indeed, one of the more interesting aspects of comparative and cross-cultural studies of homosexuality is precisely the exploration of the differences in the semantic fields of key terms.

Part of exploring Buddhist views on homosexuality is examining homoerotic and filial feelings that were never consummated in a homosexual encounter. That the Buddhist Order encouraged brotherly feelings among its members can hardly be denied. We often read accounts of monks who had unusually strong filial ties. If the Buddhist tradition is, as I maintain, essentially neutral on the question of homosexuality, this means that it rarely isolates homosexual activity and homoerotic feelings for special critique. On the contrary, we find that in certain instances these are not only condoned, but actually praised.

When homosexuality is condemned, it has less to do with these feelings or actions being *homo*sexual than with their being *sexual*. Of course, because most of our source material on this subject comes from records related to the institution of monasticism, and because Buddhist monks have a vow of strict celibacy, it is not surprising that in these sources homosexuality should be condemned. Because we find in these works a condemna-

---

[18] As regards the morphology of the *paṇḍaka*, Zwilling, p. 204, notes that the temporarily and congenitally impotent, voyeurs, and *castrate* are all included in the category along with "that person who satisfies his sexual desires by fellating another to ejaculation."

tion of sexuality in general,[19] however, we should not take a condemnation of homosexual activity or feelings in such a context as a censure of gay men and women. It is interesting that, in the lay Buddhist context, we find few instances in which homosexuality is explicitly condemned.[20] In both the texts that concern the ethical conduct of the layperson[21] and in the oral commentaries, it is noteworthy that the descriptions of the violation of the lay vow prohibiting sexual misconduct (*kāmamithyācarā*) rarely mention homosexuality as a transgression; nor is this due to lack of material on the subject. The tradition is quite specific in describing what constitutes a violation of this vow. It states that engaging in sexual intercourse at the wrong time (during times of special religious focus, such as the new or full moon, for example) or in the wrong place (in front of an image of the Buddha, for example) are all infractions of the vow. However, as noted by Zwilling,

> Buddhist tradition essentially conceives of sexual misconduct in terms of sexual relations with various types of prohibited women (*agamyā*), and the performance of non-procreative sexual acts. Among the commentators only (two) . . . include men among forbidden sexual objects.[22]

Given the fact that the tradition is quite specific about the nature of these violations and that elsewhere (in the monastic context) it does not shy away from explicitly mentioning homosexuality in regard to the vow of celibacy, we might surmise that the relatively infrequent references to such acts in the discussion of the transgressions of the lay vow prohibiting sexual misconduct are an indication of the fact that it was not widely considered to be a violation. We must keep in mind, however, that we are here arguing from silence.[23]

HOMOSEXUALITY IN FOUR BUDDHIST CULTURES

I have chosen, in the brief survey that follows, to sweep across Asia as Buddhism itself did. Hence, we will examine homosexuality in the culture

---

[19]The faults of engaging in sexual activity in general are described in great detail in the *Śikṣāsamuccaya*, P. L. Vaidya, ed. (Darbhanga: Mithila Institute, 1961), pp. 43–45. I discuss this at length in an unpublished paper, "Women and Illusion: Toward an Aesthetic in Buddhism," read at the 1987 annual meeting of the American Academy of Religion, Boston.

[20]For a variety of interpretations concerning the meaning of the lay vow concerning sexual misconduct, see Holmes Welch, *The Practice of Chinese Buddhism: 1900–1950* (Cambridge: Harvard University Press, 1967), pp. 365–366.

[21]I refer to texts dealing, for example, with the kinds of advice (*śikṣā, bslab bya*) that is to be given to lay people concerning the correct way of keeping the *upāsa(i)ka* vows.

[22]Zwilling, p. 207.

[23]We are here in the same position as Boswell when he tries to characterize Burchard's view of homosexual behavior. See Boswell, p. 206.

of classical Buddhist India, in Chinese Buddhist history, in the Buddhism of medieval Japan, and in Buddhist institutions in early twentieth-century Tibet.[24] We end with some reflections on contemporary North American Buddhist views regarding homosexuality.

India

It is primarily Leonard Zwilling's work with the Buddhist *Vinaya* (monastic discipline) and *Abhidharma* (metaphysics and cosmology), and John Garret Jones' work on the *Jataka* (the stories of the Buddha's previous lives) that allows us to glean Indian Buddhist attitudes toward homosexuality. In exhaustive research concerning the concept of *paṇḍaka*, Zwilling shows that the term refers to those who suffer "from a variety of sexual dysfunctions and variations" and that "all share the common quality of being *napuṃsaka*, 'lacking maleness.' "[25] The term seems to ascribe to *paṇḍaka* more than the mere quality of being attracted to members of the same sex (which in any case was perceived as a possibility even for a man who fulfilled socially normative gender roles), implying, in addition, a certain effeminacy as well. Therefore, when a *paṇḍaka* is characterized as being exceedingly lustful, incapable of following religious discipline (monastic ordination was denied to them), and vacillating in decision making, qualities that have with some frequency been ascribed to women in Buddhist literature, it is fair to suppose that these qualities in a *paṇḍaka* are perceived as arising more from their effeminacy than from their attraction to members of the same sex.[26] In the end, Zwilling concludes that "when homosexual behavior is not ignored in the Indian Buddhist writings it is derogated

---

[24]I have chosen these four as the focus of this study partly because of the availability of scholarly material concerning homosexual relations and attitudes toward homosexuality, and partly because they show the wide and disparate range of opinions concerning the subject in the Buddhist tradition.

[25]Zwilling, p. 205.

[26]In this context it is interesting that a Chinese Buddhist text, dated by Beyer to the seventh century but based, no doubt, on an Indian original, the *Ta-ch'eng tsao-hsiang kung-te ching*, lists eight causes for a woman's being reborn a woman, four causes for a man's being reborn a woman, four causes for a man's being reborn a eunuch (*paṇḍaka?*) [castrating another man, laughing at a monk, transgressing the precepts because of his desire, encouraging others to do the same], four causes for a man's being reborn a hermaphrodite ["uncleanness where there should be reverence," lust for the bodies of other men, self-stimulation, prostitution of himself to other men while in the guise of a woman] and four causes "whereby a man is born with the lusts and desires of a woman, and enjoys being treated as a woman by other men" [despising, slandering, or defaming other men, transvestism, "lewd uncleanness" with his own clanswomen, accepting reverence though unworthy of it]. See S. Beyer, *The Buddhist Experience: Sources and Interpretations* (Belmont, Calif.: Wadsworth Publishing Company, 1974), p. 53.

much to the same degree as comparable heterosexual acts."[27]

Jones has also shown that the *Jataka* literature, a narrative genre depicting the former lives of the Buddha and his companions, is replete with homoerotic sentiments. Despite the fact that it is condemned in the *Vinaya* literature, he considers it significant that there is no direct reference to male homosexuality in the *Nikāya* literature.[28] He thus considers the silence regarding homosexuality in the *Nikāyas* as an implicit affirmation, though he cautions the reader, as I have done, that "arguments from silence are always hazardous." He concludes, in this regard:

> After all, in loving relationships of this kind, there was no temptation to forsake the Order, since both parties were equally committed to it; there was no possibility of producing children and, in consequence, becoming saddled with just those cares and responsibilities one had joined the Order to escape; on the other hand, there was the possibility, since both were committed to the same teaching and the same training, of keeping the mutual attachment within reasonable bounds and ensuring that it did not hinder what each considered to be more important objectives.[29]

What is perhaps more significant than the silence of the *Nikāyas* is the eloquence of the *Jatakas*. Here, in explanation of the Buddha's close ties to his disciple and attendant, Ānanda, the texts depict a variety of past-life scenarios that are touching and at times homoerotically suggestive. In one of these the Buddha and Ānanda are depicted as two deer who "always went about together . . . ruminating and cuddling together, very happy, head to head, nozzle to nozzle, horn to horn."[30] In another, they are the two handsome young sons of Brahmin parents who refuse to marry so that they may remain with each other, and in yet another a serpent king falls in love with Ānanda. He "encircled the ascetic with snakes folds, and embraced him, with his great hood upon his head; and there he lay a little, till his affection was satisfied."[31] Jones concludes:

> In what is said about friendship in the Jatakas it is fairly clear that a good deal of homosexual emotion is operating. . . . When one remembers the enormous amount that is said in warning of the dangers of heterosexual relationships . . . it is quite remarkable that there is not one word of warning of the dangers of a homosexual relationship.[32]

---

[27]Zwilling, p. 209.

[28]Together with the *Vinaya* and *Abhidharma*, the *Nikāya* is the third section of the Buddhist canon, the *tripiṭaka*.

[29]John Garret Jones, *Tales and Teachings of the Buddha: The Jataka Stories in Relation to the Pali Canon* (London: George Allen Unwin, 1979), pp. 79–80.

[30]Ibid., p. 107.

[31]Ibid., p. 114.

[32]Ibid., pp.113, 115.

What we witness in the Indian context, then, is a certain ambivalence. Where homosexual acts are condemned, they are condemned either for being transgressions of the monastic vow of celibacy or, in the case of the *paṇḍaka*, because it involves men taking on the culturally prescribed role of women through their sexual passivity. At the same time, in the Indian texts there are many "eloquent silences," to use a term of Jones, and in the *Jatakas* even instances of eloquent prose that suggest an acceptance, and occasionally even a eulogy, of homoerotic feelings and, if Jones is right, even of homosexual acts.

China

This same posture—a neutrality that emerges as ambivalence—seems to have characterized the attitude toward homosexuality in China as well.[33] However, very little work has been done on Chinese *Buddhist* attitudes toward homosexuality or on its existence in monastic settings during Imperial times. If, as stated by Louis Crompton, it is the case that the Chinese "perceptions of homosexuality were primarily aesthetic, literary and anecdotal, not moral, social, religious or scientific," then scriptural and other data on which to base our investigation of Chinese Buddhist attitudes toward homosexuality may not be forthcoming. Be that as it may, we know that at the very least both Confucianism and Taoism were neutral on the question of same-sex relations[34] and that, especially during Han times, it became the norm for emperors to have male lovers from all levels of Chinese society.[35] If the basic Buddhist stance toward homosexuality is, as I maintain, a neutral one, then we might expect, given the general cultural acceptance of homosexual love in classical China, that this same attitude would have been equally applicable to Chinese Buddhism, and that those who felt sexual attraction to members of their own sex might very easily have turned to Buddhist monasticism as a religious possibility that was compatible with their sexual preferences, whether or not these were ever physically expressed.

Holmes Welch, in his classic study *The Practice of Chinese Buddhism: 1900–1950*, concludes his section on "Sexual Activity" by stating that "it

---

[33]Crompton, p. 28.

[34]Giovanni Vitiello suggests in a recent essay that Taoism may have even encouraged male love, because the equal exchange of semen in male homosexual relations preserves the essential life force of both partners. See his essay in M. Stemmeler and J. I. Cabezón, eds., *Religion, Homosexuality, and Literature*, proceedings of the Gay Men's Issues in Religion section of the American Academy of Religion (Las Colinas, TX: Monument Press, 1992), pp. 95–102.

[35] Crompton, p. 36.

seems likely that the Monks of China were able to adjust themselves more easily to continence than their counterparts in Europe.''[36] Although one of his informants, an ex-monk, claims to have seen homosexual activity in the monastery, when pressed for details what he describes seems to have been, according to Welch, filial relationships (primarily between older and younger monks). Most of Welch's informants, however, characterized homosexual attraction as "low taste" (*hsia-liu*) and claimed that it was rare. This apparently hostile attitude seems to be a recent phenomenon in Chinese history, however. Hinsch has suggested several factors—influence from the Christian West among them—to explain why in the twentieth century the Chinese attitude toward homosexuality has changed from one of relative tolerance to one of open hostility.[37]

Although we do not know the extent to which homosexual activity existed in Chinese Buddhist monastic institutions, there is a legend that the founder of the Japanese Shingon sect, Kūkai (774–835), brought the practice of homosexuality with him from China. Whether or not the legend has any basis in fact,[38] it is clear from subsequent literature that this was viewed as one of Kūkai's many accomplishments,[39] enhancing his status as a religious figure.[40] This implies, of course, that basic Japanese attitudes toward male love were, by this time, essentially positive.

---

[36]Welch, p. 119. This is similar to the conclusion that Melford E. Spiro comes to in his *Buddhism and Society* (New York: Harper & Row, 1970), pp. 366–368: "By all accounts village monks do in fact comply with the sexual prohibitions, both homosexual and heterosexual, of the Rule," this in the Burmese case. He adds, however: "I was told that homosexuality, too, is not infrequent in the Sinhalese monkhood—between monks and monks, monks and novices, and monks and laymen," though to what extent this is a case of homosexuality as an attribute of the "other" remains to be seen.

[37]This point is also made by Tsuneo Watanabe and Jun'ichi Iwata in the context of Japan. See their *The Love of the Samurai: A Thousand Years of Japanese Homosexuality* (London: GMP Publishers, 1989), chap. 5.

[38]Iwata, pp. 31–34, finds textual references to homosexual relationships prior to the time of Kūkai, though from the context it seems that the earlier culture seems to have been less tolerant of homosexuality. The truth of the Kūkai legend then may lie not in the fact that he introduced homosexuality into Japan, but in that Kūkai's introduction of pederasty into Japanese monasticism legitimated male love.

[39]Contrast this to the case of the Englishman, William Rufus (king of England from 1087–1100), whose chroniclers "charge him with addiction to sins of the flesh and claim that he introduced into England sins which had not previously been common" (homosexuality predominant among them); see Boswell, p. 209. Here we find a case in which the attribution of the introduction of the practice to a foreigner is used as a means of condemning it.

[40]Paul Gordon Schalow, "Kūkai and the Tradition of Male Love in Japanese Buddhism," in J. I. Cabezón, ed., *Buddhism, Sexuality, and Gender* (Albany: SUNY Press, 1992), pp. 215–230.

Japan

Though Buddhist attitudes toward homosexuality can in general be said to be neutral, the exception seems to be Japan, where it was extolled and praised as a secret and mysterious practice that was the greatest source of sexual pleasure available to man. From the fourteenth century on, we find a wide variety of literature devoted to the theme of male love in which the usual pattern is for an older monk to take a young temple acolyte (*chigo*) as a lover.[41] Maggie Childs has written of a short story attributed to the fourteenth century called *Chigo Kannon engi*, in which the bodhisattva of compassion, Kannon, rewards a particularly fervent practitioner with a beautiful young male lover (later revealed to be Kannon herself) [See text of this story on p. 359 of the present anthology].[42] This genre of literature, called *chigo monogatari*, describes love affairs between an elder monk and *chigo* and often ends in the tragic death of one of the lovers, whereupon the survivor assiduously pursues a religious life dedicated to praying for the lost lover. Moreover, Paul Schalow has discussed the *Kōbō Daishi ikkan no sho*, a short text said to have been revealed by Kūkai to a monk as a boon for his prayers, in which techniques for seducing a *chigo* and the various positions for anal intercourse are described in detail.[43] The love of the *chigo* eventually gives way to *shudō* (literally, the "way of the young man") as the *samurai* pederastic ideal. Even in this more secular setting, however, we find the ideal of the love of boys still legitimized in Buddhist religious terms. Hence, *Inu tsurezure*, a seventeenth-century text, states:

> If you pray for happiness in future life, you must learn the teaching of the Buddha. If you learn the teaching of the Buddha and expect to achieve Awakening, you will surely practice *shudō*. For this way is truly like that of true Awakening, in that we may give ourselves wholly to it.[44]

In addition to a variety of homoerotic poetry that begins in the seventeenth century with Kitamura Kigin's *Iwatsusuji*, perhaps the most important and extensive work on the subject is the seventeenth-century work by Ihara Saikaku, *The Great Mirror of Male Love* (*Nanshoku ōkagami*). Here the structure of the work is one in which "the norm is the unabashed and enthusiastic enjoyment of male homosexual love, as if it were somehow outside the confines of Buddhist stricture."[45]

---

[41]See Watanabe and Iwata, chap. 2.

[42]Maggie C. Childs, "Chigo Monogatari," *Monumenta Nipponica*, vol. 35, no. 2, pp. 127–151 (1978); and also her "Sexuality and Salvation" (Paper delivered at the annual meeting of the Association for Asian Studies, Boston, 1978).

[43]Schalow, "The Priestly Tradition," pp. 218–220.

[44]Watanabe and Iwata, p. 113.

[45]Paul Gordon Schalow, *The Great Mirror of Male Love by Ihara Saikaku* (Stanford: Stanford University Press, 1989).

Japanese Buddhism (at least in the periods described above) is thus the exception to the rule. Instead of a guarded neutrality, the literature described above uses a variety of techniques to enhance the status of the homosexual love affair. Its origins are made sacred by its association with Kūkai and with the holy land of China. Moreover, the position of the *chigo* is legitimized by his portrayal as a boon for religious devotion, as a cause for his lover's returning to religious practice (after the *chigo*'s death), and by his identification with the figure of various heavenly beings and bodhisattvas. The reasons for this shift to the positive in the Japanese case are difficult to determine. A traditional view, expressed by one leading classical scholar—namely, that "since relations between the sexes are forbidden by Buddha, priests of the law, being made neither of stone nor wood, entered the way of homosexual love as an outlet for their feelings"[46] explains neither why homosexual relations should have attained the status they did only in Japanese Buddhism nor why the literature described above overlaps with the period in which the celibate monastic ideal was being discarded in favor of a married priesthood. Only further historical and literary research will be able to shed light on this question.

Tibet

In Tibet the practice of homosexuality seems to have been confined almost exclusively to the "working monks" of the larger monasteries. The *lDab ldob*, as they were called, were a fraternity of young monks (predominantly under the age of forty) who prided themselves on their abilities as fighters and athletes, participating regularly in inter- as well as intramural competitions. Either unwilling or unable to devote themselves to the rigorous academic curriculum of the monasteries, they took upon themselves the burden of the day-to-day tasks that kept the monastery functioning: "[We *lDab ldobs*] are the outer wall, [the other monks] the inner treasure."[47] Goldstein has written of the homosexual practices of the *lDab ldob*, which apparently included not only the seduction, but, if he is right, even the abduction of boys (and even, in rare cases, of adults) from the community for sexual purposes.[48] Because the monastic discipline defines the type of sexual intercourse that brings expulsion (*pārājika*) as penetration of the

---

[46]Schalow, "The Priestly Tradition," p. 222.

[47]Goldstein, p. 136.

[48]If, as Boswell states, "no charge against a minority seems to be more damaging than the claim that they pose a threat of some sort to the children of the majority," (*Christianity*, p. 273), then we must question whether or not such accounts are accurate or are manifestations of intolerance. For other cases of the charge of child stealing as a means of derogating minority groups (e.g., Gypsies, Muslims, and Jews) in Europe, see Boswell, *Christianity*, pp. 273, 283.

mouth or anus (of either sex) or of the vagina, it seems that the *lDab ldob* lived up to the letter, if not the spirit, of the law by engaging in a form of intercourse in which stimulation was achieved by insertion of the penis between the legs of the partner from behind.[49] It should be stated, however, that Goldstein's research was based on information gathered from only five informants, most of them lay persons. Although the fact of homosexual activity among the *lDab ldob* can hardly be denied, the details, especially concerning the abduction of youths, have been challenged.[50] In any case, it is clear that despite the Tibetan perception that the *lDab ldob* had a proclivity for same sex partners, the *lDab ldobs* as a whole were held in very high esteem both by the law and monastic population.[51] Hence, if the *lDab ldobs'* homosexuality was considered "sinful," as Goldstein suggests, it must have been perceived as only marginally so, for it was something that was overshadowed by other qualities that in the end tipped public opinion in their favor.*

* * *

Gilbert Herdt has described a morphology for homosexual activity. "It has been demonstrated," he says, "that there are three forms of the cultural structuring of homosexual activities and organization the world over."[52] These he defines as (1) age-structured homosexuality, in which there is a substantial age gap between the partners, (2) gender-reversed homosexuality, in which at least one of the partners adopts the sex roles of the opposite gender, and (3) role-specialized homosexuality, in which a person's "social or religious role" legitimizes his or her homosexual activity. Though the elder monk/*chigo* relationship may be subsumed in the first of Herdt's categories, the work of Schalow, Childs, Watanabe, and Iwata makes it clear that even in the Japanese case not all such relationships involve substantial age differences. These and other examples that fail to fit the pattern suggested by Herdt imply that his categories may not be as universal as he supposes. In any case, it seems far too early to postulate universal morphologies for homosexual behavior, especially when its manifestations throughout Asian societies have yet to be fully explored.[53]

Rita Gross mentions in a recent article that homosexuality is openly prac-

---

[49]Goldstein, p. 134.

[50]My own sources, who would not deny that homosexual activity existed, not only among the *lDab ldob* but among other monks as well, stated that they were unaware of the abduction scenarios described by Goldstein and his informants.

[51]Goldstein, p. 134.

*See also John Giorno's comments on gay sex in Tibetan monasteries, p. 281 of the present anthology.

[52]Herdt, p. 446.

[53]A comment by Boswell in *Christianity*, p. 28, also casts doubt on Herdt's morphology, even as it applies to the clearest case that of the Greeks.

ticed in Western Buddhist communities.[54] This is true. To my knowledge, no North American Buddhist institution has ever marginalized its lay homosexual constituency, nor have any ever impeded the full participation of lay homosexual men and women by, for example, requiring their abstinence. To my knowledge, no gay Westerner has ever been denied Buddhist ordination because of his or her sexual orientation. North American Buddhists have, of course, been as susceptible as their non-Buddhist counterparts to homophobia, especially as it has emerged in the wake of the AIDS crisis, but many Buddhists have also been at the forefront of responding to this crisis. In San Francisco, for example, one of the first (and, according to some sources, *the* first) AIDS hospices was started by a Zen Buddhist group.[55]

CONCLUSIONS

In our brief survey of Buddhist attitudes toward homosexuality throughout selected regions and distinct periods of Asian history, there emerge the conclusions that (1) Buddhist doctrine is essentially neutral on the question of homosexuality (at least as neutral as it is in regard to heterosexual relations) and that (2) this has made Buddhism flexible in its accommodating to the mores and societal attitudes of the different cultural areas to which it spread. It is possible, given the dearth of scholarship in this area, that a different pattern may emerge in the future: that in Buddhist societies cases of persecution or widespread discrimination against gay or lesbian people may find their way to the surface. I doubt that we will find this to be the case, however. Instead, I suspect that as more research of a scholarly nature is done, this pattern of basic neutrality will be firmly established as the essential Buddhist view toward homosexuality. If so, then Buddhism will join the ranks of other major religions of Asia in its essential tolerance of the variety of human sexual expression.

BIBLIOGRAPHY

Barnes, Nancy Schuster. 1987. "Buddhism." In *Women in World Religion*, edited by Arvind Sharma, 132. Albany: SUNY Press.
Beyer, S. 1974. *The Buddhist Experience: Sources and Interpretations*. Belmont, Calif.: Wadsworth Publishing Company.

---

[54]Rita Gross, "The Householder and the World Renunciant: Two Modes of Sexual Expression in Buddhism," *Journal of Ecumenical Studies* 22, no. 1 (Winter 1985): 83.

[55]See, for example, Tensho David Schneider, "Accidents and Calculations: The Emergence of Three AIDS Hospices," *Tricycle: The Buddhist Review*, vol. 1 (Spring 1992): 78–83.

Boswell, John. 1980. *Christianity, Social Tolerance, and Homosexuality: Gay People in Western Europe from the Beginning of the Christian Era to the Fourteenth Century*. Chicago: University of Chicago Press.

Brown, Judith C. 1986. *Immodest Acts*. New York: Oxford University Press.

Cabezón, José Ignacio. 1987. "Women and Illusion: Toward an Aesthetic in Buddhism." Paper delivered at the annual meeting of the American Academy of Religion, Boston.

———. 1992. *Buddhism, Sexuality, and Gender*. Albany: SUNY Press.

Childs, Maggie C. 1978. "Chigo Monogatari." *Monumenta Nipponica*.

———. 1978. "Sexuality and Salvation." Paper delivered at the annual meeting of the Association for Asian Studies, Boston.

Conner, Randy P. and Stephen Donaldson. 1990. "Buddhism." In *Encyclopedia of Homosexuality*. New York and London: Garland Press.

Crompton, Louis. 1987. "Homosexuality in Imperial China." Paper delivered at the Conference on "Homosexuality: Which Homosexuality?" Amsterdam.

Encyclopedia of Homosexuality. 1990.

Goldstein, Melvyn. 1964. "A Study of the Ldab Ldob." *Central Asiatic Journal* 9:134.

Gross, Rita. 1985. "The Householder and the World Renunciant: Two Modes of Sexual Expression in Buddhism." *Journal of Ecumenical Studies* 22, 1:83.

Herdt, Gilbert H. 1987. "Homosexuality." In *The Encyclopedia of Religion*, edited by Mircea Eliade, 6:445–453. New York: Macmillan.

Jones, John Garret. 1979. *Tales and Teachings of the Buddha: The Jataka Stories in Relation to the Pali Canon*. London: George Allen & Unwin.

Keyes, Charles F. 1986. "Ambiguous Gender: Male Initiation in a Northern Thai Buddhist Society." In *Gender and Religion : On the Complexity of Symbols*, edited by Carolyn Walker Bynum et al., 66–96. Boston: Beacon Press.

Schalow, Paul Gordon. 1989. *The Great Mirror of Male Love by Ihara Saikaku*. Stanford: Stanford University Press.

———. 1992. "The Priestly Tradition of Homosexual Love in Japanese Buddhism." In *Buddhism, Sexuality, and Gender*, edited by J. I. Cabezón, 215–230. Albany: SUNY Press.

Schneider, Tensho David. 1992. "Accidents and Calculations: The Emergence of Three AIDS Hospices." *Tricycle: The Buddhist Review*, 78–83.

Spiro, Melford E. 1970. *Buddhism and Society*. New York: Harper & Row.

Stemmeler, M., and J. I. Cabezón, eds. n.d. 1992. *Religion, Homosexuality, and Literature*. Las Colinas, TX: Monument Press.

Tambiah, Stanley Jeyaraja. 1976. *World Conqueror and World Renouncer: A Study of Buddhism and Polity in Thailand Against a Historical Background*. Cambridge: Cambridge University Press.

Topley, M. 1975. "Marriage Resistance in Rural Kwangtung." In *Women in Chinese Society*. Stanford: Stanford University Press.

Vaidya, P. L., ed. 1961. *Śikṣāsamuccaya*. Darbhanga: Mithila Institute.

Watanabe, Tsuneo, and Jun'ichi, Iwata. 1989. *The Love of the Samurai: A Thousand Years of Japanese Homosexuality*. London: GMP Publishers.

Welch, Holmes. 1967. *The Practice of Chinese Buddhism: 1900–1950*. Cambridge: Harvard University Press.

Zwilling, Leonard. 1991. "Homosexuality as Seen in Indian Buddhist Texts." In *Buddhism, Sexuality, and Gender*, edited by J. I. Cabezón, 203–214. Albany: SUNY Press.

Avoidance and Exclusion:
Same-Sex Sexuality in Indian Buddhism

Leonard Zwilling

One of the things about Buddhism which has made it so attractive to gay men and lesbians in the West is its seeming indifference to homosexuality. In my opinion, this has less to do with Buddhism and more to do with the fact that Western dharma teachers tend to be liberal or progressive in their own thinking, and that Asian teachers have come from cultures in which homosexual relations for the most part tend to evoke little more than mild disapproval. When we look at Indian Buddhism, the source from which all of the present varieties of the religion have developed, the picture that emerges is quite different from what we might expect.

The focus will be on sexual relations between persons who would usually be identified as male by sex, although not always by gender; what we mean by this will be explained below. That the emphasis is on male sexuality is because that is what was of greatest concern to the authors of our most important sources, the treatises on monastic discipline (*vinaya*) and doctrinal theory (*abhidharma*). These texts, of course, provide a rather limited perspective from which to view the subject, but one which can be widened by drawing upon other genres of Buddhist literature, or other Indian religious and philosophical traditions. Since female sexuality is treated only incidentally in these sources, we have decided to pass over it here. Although the Buddha, rather reluctantly, authorized the foundation of an order of nuns, sexual relations between women were not an integral part of the social fabric in the way that male same-sex relations were, and so did not concern the authors of the *vinaya* to the same degree. Nor shall we concern ourselves with homoerotic emotion. To those persons who chose to live the householder's life Buddha often recommended the social virtues, especially good friendship, as conducive to general happiness. That there was more than a little of homoerotic emotion involved in good friendship can be seen in some of the *Jātakas*, or stories of the previous lives of the Buddha, and for those who are interested, a reference to this subject will be found in the suggested readings at the end of this article. "Particular friendships" were as strongly discouraged among Buddhist monks as they were among their

LEONARD ZWILLING (Madison, WI) was born in 1945, has been a student of Buddhism since 1965, and has published widely on Indological and Buddhological subjects. He is a world-recognized scholar on Indian Buddhism during its first centuries. His most recent work (with Michael Sweet) is: "Like a City Ablaze: The Third Sex and the Creation of Sexuality in Jain Religious Literature" in *Journal of the History of Sexuality* (Jan. 1996).

Christian counterparts and were the subject of a well known admonition by the Buddha in the *Puggalappasādasutta*.

Before taking up the Indian Buddhist attitude towards male same-sex behavior, it is necessary to have some idea of how this was conceptualized by the society in which Buddhism emerged and developed. Ancient Indian society was thoroughly patriarchal and male potency was considered of very high value; one of the means by which a man might attain high social status was through his potency and its loss was greatly feared. Anxiety over the loss of potency can be seen in the hymns, charms, and prayers of the *Atharva Veda* and the sacrifices of the *Brāhmaṇas* dedicated to its preservation, augmentation, restoration, or destruction in others. It is in these texts belonging to the eighth to sixth centuries B.C.E. that we get our first view of men who did not fulfill the most important male gender role of all, that of procreator. While some of these "impotent men" (*klība, paṇḍaka*) were otherwise normative males who happened to be sterile or impotent, there were other non-procreators who were associated with transgender behavior such as wearing long hair (perhaps in braids), which was already regarded as a characteristic marker of women, the adoption of women's ornaments, and dancing, which was an activity otherwise restricted solely to women. Such persons were considered to be "neither male nor female" (*napuṃsaka*) inasmuch as they were biological males and hence not female, but inasmuch as they incorporated characteristics belonging to females, they could not, strictly speaking, be considered male. Needless to say, the social position of such radical transgressors of male gender norms was very low, and we find them linked together with other despised members of society like the slut (*puṃścalī*) and the wastrel, and associated with sin (*pāpman*).

By the second century B.C.E. such transgendered males were recognized by the dominant Brahmanical society as a genuine third sex (*tṛtīyāprakṛti*) having a purely biological causation like maleness and femaleness. This same view was also propounded at about the same time by the Jains who, along with the Buddhists, were the major rival to Brahmanical ideology. As we shall see, the Buddhists never formally accepted the existence of a third sex, although in their treatment of the gender variant male they did so for all intents and purposes.

In the texts in which the transgendered male first appears there is nothing explicit concerning his sexuality, and this is true even in those works where the third sex concept is advanced; this aspect is revealed primarily in Jain and Buddhist literature.

It is clear from those sources that the transgendered male was, as a sexual object (*maithunāśraya*), strictly the passive partner in sexual relations with gender normative males and that this relationship was commercial, that is, transgendered males supported themselves through prostitution. For Indian society, sexual relations between a gender normative male and a transgendered male would not have been considered homosexual, but by definition, sexual relations between members of two different sexes. Thus, the "elevation" of the feminized male to separate sex status can be regarded as the institutionalization of an indigenous homosexuality, one that was fully congruent with patriarchal heterosexuality. While this indigenous homosexuality evoked a general disapproval similar to that of female prostitution, it was without any real consequences, at least so far as the gender normative *activo* (penetrator) was concerned. This was not so for the *passivo*, or transgendered male, who was "despised by the world (*lokaparibhūta*)."

In addition to the socially sanctioned indigenous homosexuality, sexual relations between gender normative males did not go unnoticed, and they were, in fact, legislated against in both religious and civil law (see the *Manusmṛti* and *Arthaśāstra*) although the penalties were exceedingly slight, such as a purificatory bath and a small fine. According to the famous *Kāmasūtra* of Vātsyāyana (c. third century C.E.) such behavior was characteristic of sophisticated urban men, which suggests that bisexuality, or from the Indian perspective, "trisexuality," since such men were also the clients of the *passivo* (receptor) prostitutes, was the norm for a certain segment of society. It was also recognized that there were otherwise normative men who engaged in homosexual relations but whose sexuality was like that of the transgendered male, that is, they were *passivos*, and these persons were subject to the same kind of opprobrium visited upon their transgendered brothers. To sum up, we can say that ancient Indian society recognized three different forms of homosexual relations; between two normative males, between a normative male and a transgendered male, and a normative male and a "butch" *passivo*. Broadly speaking, homosexual relations *per se* in ancient Indian society while certainly disapproved of, did not inspire the kind of wrath and condemnation we are familiar with in connection with the attitude of the three great monotheisms, keeping in mind that such benignity did not extend to the *passivo*, especially when transgendered, who continued to evoke feelings of disgust and repugnance.

So far as the Buddhists are concerned, it really cannot be said that their attitude differed much from that of Indian society at large. It should be kept in mind that in those first centuries when Buddhism was still making its way and was still largely a religion of monks, it depended almost entirely on the support of the general population for its continued existence. Consequently, the order could not allow behavior that might bring it into disrepute or raise doubts about its integrity. When we examine the *vinaya*, the rules and regulations which govern monastic life, it is clear that the motive behind many of its restrictions, and the disciplinary rules in general, is simply public opinion, and such is the case with the more important regulations concerning homosexual relations.

Homosexual activity in the community of monks did not go unobserved and was undoubtedly not at all uncommon. In the *Sphuṭārtha*, a fifth century C.E. textbook of monastic law for novices, the author, in explaining how one must not deviate from the *vinaya* because of a divergent precedent, offers as the example the monk who points out that in a certain monastery the monks are sexually intimate with each other and asks why should the monks here not do likewise? The *vinaya* itself presents a number of vignettes of homoerotic behavior, such as the monk who can't help having an orgasm while massaging his preceptor's back in the steam room, and there are regulations such as those against a preceptor "boarding" two novices after the youths were found to have had sexual relations with each other, and the rule forbidding two nuns to share the same coverlet. However, it is in the regulation against the ordination of the *passivo* that the Buddhist attitude towards some kinds of sexually transgressive behavior is revealed as well as the shaping of that attitude by public opinion. As the account in the *Mahāvagga* of the Theravāda tradition puts it:

> Now at that time a certain [*paṇḍaka*] came to have gone forth among the monks. Having approached a number of young monks, he spoke thus: "Come, venerable ones, defile me." (*etha, mam ayasmanto dusetha*). The monks refused, saying: "Be off, [*paṇḍaka*], depart, [*paṇḍaka*]! What do we have to do with that?" Refused by the monks, having approached a number of large, husky novices, he spoke thus: "Come, your reverences, defile me." The novices refused, saying: "Be off [*paṇḍaka*], depart, [*paṇḍaka*]! What do we have to do with that?" Refused by the novices, having approached mahouts and grooms, he spoke thus: "Come, sirs, defile me." The mahouts and grooms defiled him. These . . . spread it about saying: "These recluses, sons of the Sakyans are [*paṇḍakas*], and those of them who are not [*paṇḍakas*], defile [*paṇḍakas*]. Thus they are all unchaste." Monks heard these mahouts and grooms who . . . spread it about. Then those monks told this matter to the Lord. He said: "Monks, if a [*paṇḍaka*] is not ordained, he should not be ordained; if he is ordained, he should be expelled." (Adapted from I. B. Horner, *Book of the Discipline*, Vol. 4, pp. 108–109).

In the *vinaya*, *paṇḍakas*, or *passivos*, are considered in the same light as common prostitutes, widows, and grown up unmarried girls, that is, as hyperlibidinous, and hence a danger to the chastity of monks so that the opportunities for interactions between monks and *paṇḍakas* were severely restricted. For example, it is an offense for a monk to sit or sleep in a place where a *paṇḍaka* is present, or having entered upon the rainy season retreat a monk must leave that place if he is made an offer of food, goods, and the like by a *paṇḍaka*, just as he must when made an offer by a common prostitute, widow, or unmarried grown up girl. (Incidentally, all of these women were permitted ordination.) Here again, the need to preserve the public's good opinion is the operative factor in such proscriptions; as the Buddha points out in the *Ussaṅgitasutta*, if a monk associates with *passivos*, widows, etc., he will be thought of as depraved and mistrusted and, by extension, the order. In viewing the *paṇḍaka* as a threat to the chastity of monks he is ascribed not only the behavior, but also the psychological characteristics of those stereotypically "bad" women. As the fifth century C.E. commentator Buddhaghosa puts it, *passivos* are full of defiling passions, their lusts are unquenchable, and they are dominated by their libido and are as promiscuous as common prostitutes, widows, and grown up unmarried girls. An important consequence of the injunction to monks to avoid the company of *paṇḍakas* would have been the limitation of their access to the dharma since they could not be taught by monks (at least not without a chaperone present!) and they would have been without the opportunity to give alms or otherwise make donations to the order and hence to "make merit" in order to improve their situation in the next life. We shall have more to say on the matter of restrictions to the practice of dharma by *passivos* when we look at the traditions of Northern Buddhism.

And what of the *activo*? There are four offenses for which a monk may be expelled from the order; the first is indulgence in sexual intercourse, which is understood as the intentional procurement of an orgasm by penetrating any of the orifices of a man (including one's own), woman, *paṇḍaka* or animal. The normative male in Indian society was a penetrator and hence no distinction is made here between the sex, or species, of the sexual object penetrated. So far as other sexual offenses are concerned, for example, mutual masturbation, such acts may require a formal meeting of the *saṅgha*, or penance of some kind, but the malefactors are not expelled, and the same is true for rubbing against another's body, sitting in a concealed place suitable for sexual activity, and so forth. In general there is a hierarchy of severity in all these offenses; those committed with women are the most serious, with *paṇḍakas*, less serious, and those committed by males with other males (or animals), least serious of all.

As for lay sexual morality, marriage is assumed and abstention from sexual misconduct (*kāmesu micchacara*), the third of the five precepts which comprise the minimal lay morality, was originally conceived of as the avoidance of adultery. In the later commentarial tradition of c. fifth century C.E., this was expanded to include the condemnation of all non-procreative sexual acts, and of other men as sexual partners.

Turning to other Buddhist traditions, the situation is essentially no different than that represented by the Theravāda, but there has been a shift from an exclusionary ethic based to a large degree on a pragmatic acceptance of societal attitudes, to a theological rationalization which made such exclusion the natural consequence of the psychological makeup of the *passivo* himself. We have already seen an example of this kind of thinking in the comments of Buddhaghosa on the hyperlibidinousness of the *passivo* mentioned above.

This shift can best be illustrated by the story of the circumstances behind the non-ordination of the *passivo* according to the *vinaya* of the Mūlasarvāstivāda school, the version of the monastic code adopted and still adhered to in Tibet.

> The Lord was dwelling in Śrāvasti in the Jeta Grove, in the pleasure garden of Anāthapiṇḍada. In Śrāvasti there was a Brahmin who took a wife . . . and after eight or nine months there was born a *paṇḍaka*, one who resembles a male but is neither male nor female. He grew up. When playing with other adolescents he exposed his genitals to them and they asked him: "What are you?" and he replied, "I am a *paṇḍaka*." They said: "You are a Brahmin and it's not right that you should bring disrepute upon your house, so stop behaving that way." They told his parents: "You must stop that *paṇḍaka* from behaving like that," so his parents said to him: "*Paṇḍaka*, we are Brahmins and it's not right that you should bring disrepute upon our house, so stop behaving that way." But although they tried to dissuade him he didn't stop. Once, he went to the Jeta Grove and saw many young monks there and thought, "If I take ordination among them then they can act the man on me and I can act the woman for them." So he went up to a monk and said: "Noble Sir, I seek ordination." "Have you your parent's permission?" "No." "Then go and ask your parents." He went to his parents and said: "Parents, I seek ordination." Since he'd proved to be an affliction to his parents they thought, "How nice it would be to be rid of him," so they said: "*Paṇḍaka*, we give you permission." So he went up to the monks and said: "Noble Sirs, my parents have given me permission and I request ordination" and they ordained him. However he exposed his genitals to the monks and they asked him, "You're a *paṇḍaka*, aren't you?" "Yes," he said. So the monks told the Lord who said to the monks: "Monks, a person who is a *paṇḍaka* lacks the capacity for spiritual growth in the religion and discipline; therefore, monks, you should expel from this religion and discipline the person who is a *paṇḍaka*. Whoever comes seeking ordination should be asked, 'Are you not a *paṇḍaka*?' Whoever ordains without asking is guilty of an offense."

Here we find some significant differences from the account in the Pali *vinaya*; there is no appeal to public opinion, and the Buddha establishes the rule that for a monk to ordain a person without asking him whether or not he is a *paṇḍaka* is to make the ordainer guilty of an infraction of monastic law. In the ordination procedure as described in the Pali *vinaya*, it was sufficient merely to ask the candidate: "Are you a man?" but in this later text, and in similar texts belonging to other Sanskritic traditions, the Buddha requires not only that the candidate be asked whether he is a man, but also whether he is impotent, a *passivo*, a hermaphrodite, sexless, suffering from various genital abnormalities, and so forth. Nor was the candidate's word to be accepted at face value, for the Buddha also requires that the candidate's genitals be examined surreptitiously. Note, too, that making the question a negative: "Are you not a *paṇḍaka*?" turns it into an accusation, a common interrogation technique for smoking out secrets which a person might wish to conceal.

Is it possible to account for this hardening of the Buddhist attitude towards the *passivo*? It may perhaps have had something to do with the fact that by the time of the redaction of the *Mūlasarvāstivādavinaya*, perhaps around the second century C.E., Buddhism as a social institution had reached a state of complexity far beyond the circumstances reflected in the Pali texts. Buddhism by now extended over virtually the entire subcontinent, as far as Iran to the West and deep into Central Asia, and its followers included peoples of numerous cultural and linguistic backgrounds. This new, abstract rationalization for excluding the *passivo* may in fact represent an attempt to disassociate the ban from its original culturally-bound moorings and to universalize it, by cloaking it in theological terms. In addition Buddhism was now receiving royal patronage in many places and was centered in large monastic complexes of great wealth; the attendant complexity of the order's new situation would have been expressed in the exercise of greater control over institutional life, including sexuality. Thus the abstract rejection of the *passivo* from the perspective of these innovations: the proliferation of sexual categories, the examination of the candidate's genitals, and the accusatory form of the question, may in part have been a response to historical and social factors.

As we shall see, the theological rationalization of the *passivo's* unacceptability for monkhood was also to have practical consequences for his ability to practice the dharma, just as the earlier public relations based rejection had. But first it was necessary to enlist the aid of the "schoolmen" to place the Buddha's proscription on a sound intellectual footing. For this we shall turn to the *Abhidharmakośa*, the great fifth century C.E. *summa* of Buddhist philosophy by Vasubandhu.

To begin with, Buddhism recognizes the existence of only two sexes, unlike its Brahmanical and Jain contemporaries for whom gender variant persons such as the *paṇḍaka* were members of a separate, third sex. The Buddhist position is grounded in scripture, specifically in the *Agaññasutta*, often referred to as the Buddhist "Genesis." Here, Buddha teaches that at the beginning of a world cycle beings are sexless, but as they become progressively coarser maleness and femaleness emerge. According to the *Saṃyogasutta* this maleness and femaleness comprise not only the primary and secondary sex markers which distinguish the sexes physically, but also much of what we would consider to be culturally-conditioned gender attributes such as behavior, deportment, speech, dress, interests, and occupation. In the essentialist-constructionist debate over gender, the Buddhists would land in the extreme right wing of the essentialist camp, in that for them biological sex and gender roles are inextricably bound up with each other. How then was one to account for such persons as the *passivo*, given that the Buddhists could not avail themselves of the expedient of a third sex? According to Vasubandhu, in the process of rebirth, the intermediate being who enters the womb has all its required faculties including either maleness or femaleness, that is, it enters the womb only as a male or female, but the embryo in the course of its development may become a *paṇḍaka*, and for this to occur the embryo's original sexuality had to have been defective, though in what way we are not told. Since Vasubandhu does not limit this transformation into *paṇḍaka*-hood to the embryo of one sex or the other, this raises the question of whether or not there are actually two sorts of *paṇḍaka*, the feminized male, and the masculinized female? To this, the answer is yes, and the *vinaya* does, in fact, recognize such a female-*paṇḍaka*, the *itthipaṇḍaka*, who, like her male counterpart, is similarly denied ordination. Unfortunately, we hear nothing more about her in Buddhist literature. It would be tempting to see in her the *nārīsaṇḍā* (with which *itthipaṇḍaka* is virtually synonymous) or lesbian, of the traditional Indian medical system (*āyurveda*).

Of the three emotional/psychological poisons which Buddhists strive to conquer, desire, that is, preeminently sexual desire, is the central one that must be overcome by the aspirant to enlightenment. Hence persons of damaged sexuality like the *passivo*, the impotent man, and the hermaphrodite, are ipso facto incapable of practicing the religious path. According to Vasubandhu it is those three alone among human beings who are incapable of the self restraint necessary for the practice of the religious life. We have already seen that the Pali tradition considered that the *passivo* possessed the defilements (*kleśa*) of both of the sexes to an extreme degree, and the Sanskritic tradition concurred with this, but Vasubandhu additionally points out that the *paṇḍaka* also lacks the careful consideration necessary to combat these defilements. In addition, *passivos* are without a strong sense of either the modesty or the shame which would keep them from wrongdoing. But, paradoxically, the *passivo*'s intention to sin is weak so he is also incapable of the indiscipline which one must check in order to advance in the religious life. This incapacity for indiscipline even extends to the mortal sin of parenticide because the parents of a *passivo*, Vasubandhu points out, having produced a defective child, have little affection for him (see the above *Mūlasarvāstivāda* account), so that the *passivo* in turn, does not develop the strong emotional bond with his parents necessary for the commission of such a sin.

The practical implications of all of this for the *passivo* as a dharma practitioner are spelled out in the *Abhidharmasamuccaya*, which is purported to be by Vasubandhu's brother, Asaṅga. Not only is the *passivo* unacceptable as a monk, he is barred even from being a lay follower (*upāsaka*) because he is considered unfit to associate with or serve members of the order. However, Asaṅga, perhaps reflecting a broader Mahāyāna perspective, seems to allow him to take up the practice of a layman (so far as he would be able to do so without being able to associate with the community of monks) although without receiving formal recognition as such.

As for men who have sex with men (or with *paṇḍaka*), we have seen that from the point of view of monastic law, they are treated no differently from men who have sex with women. This is not to say that such relations were not disapproved of by Buddhism outside of a monastic context. We have already pointed out the addition of men as forbidden sexual objects within the context of the third precept. The practice of homosexual relations was clearly regarded as a sign of societal decadence and decay. In his commentary to the *Cakkavattisutta*, Buddhaghosa, in a passage reminiscent of Romans 1:26, takes "wrong conduct," the reason given in the *sutta* for the decreasing life span of human beings attendant on their increasing corporeality and sinfulness, to mean "the sexual desire of men for men and women for women." In this, Buddhaghosa was echoing the opinion of his times; such views were also expressed, for example, in the *Mahābhārata*.

Homosexuality is also condemned in the *Saddharmasmṛtyupasthānasūtra* which describes the hellish torments awaiting men who have sex with men. In the "Crowded Hell" they are attracted to a man on fire who incinerates them in his embrace; in the "Screaming Hell" their bodies are smashed to atoms by the winds of hell, the bodies are then reconstituted only to be attacked by adamantine rats that eat their genitals. And in a rare reference to pederasty, the pederast in hell sees boys being swept away in the Acid River who cry out to him to save them and he, driven by his lust, plunges in after them.

Thus far, all the texts we have examined have belonged to the earlier Buddhist traditions of which the Theravāda is the sole surviving school. What then of the Mahāyāna, one might ask? Are we to expect a change of attitude befitting its self proclaimed loftier ethic of universal compassion and its goal of universal emancipation? Mahāyāna literature takes virtually no cognizance of the kinds of issues we have thus far presented. The special bodhisattva ethics which are treated at length in such works as the *Bodhisattvapiṭakasūtra* or the *Bodhisattvabhūmi* and are directed to the bodhisattva-monk, require adherence to the *vinaya*, including its sexual code, while the sexual ethic for the lay-bodhisattva is the familiar abstention from adultery. As the *Ugradattaparipṛcchāsūtra* puts it; "Therefore a man must cease from the fulfilling of passion and lust, contented with his own wife, free from desire for his neighbor's," to which, as we have already remarked, other texts added abstention from all non-procreative sexual acts and other males as sexual objects. The attitude of the Mayāyāna toward homosexual behavior in general, and toward the *passivo* in particular, does not really differ in any way from that of the so-called Hīnayāna. In this, Buddhism remained faithful to societal attitudes as well as its own fundamental principle that sexual desire is the single most destructive threat to the moral purification necessary to advance on the path.

SUGGESTED READINGS

For an earlier view of some of the material discussed above see my "Homosexuality As Seen in Indian Buddhist Texts" in *Buddhism, Sexuality and Gender*, ed. by José Ignacio Cabezón, State University of New York Press, 1992, pp. 203-214. For the perspective of the traditional Indian medical system and of Jainism on some of the issues discussed in this paper, see Michael J. Sweet and Leonard Zwilling, "The First Medicalization: The taxonomy and etiology of queerness in classical Indian medicine," *Journal of the History of Sexuality* 3, 4 (1993), pp. 590-607 and Leonard Zwilling and Michael J. Sweet, " 'Like a City Ablaze': The third sex and the creation of sexuality in Jain religious literature," *Journal of the History of Sexuality* 6, 3 (1996), pp. 359-384. An examination of the conception of the third sex in ancient India by the same authors under the title, "The Evolution of Third Sex Constructs in Ancient India: A Study in Ambiguity" is forthcoming in *Empowerment: Gender Constructs in Indian Religion and Society*, edited by Julia Leslie, Oxford University Press. For those interested in surveying some of the sources referred to in our article there is a complete translation of the Buddhist monastic code (*vinaya*) of the Theravāda school by I. B. Horner in 6 volumes under the title *The Book of the Discipline* and a complete English translation by Leo Pruden of Vasubandhu's *Abhidharmakośa*. An excellent treatment of Buddhist ethics and morality from the perspective of the *Jātaka* tales including a good discussion of the homoerotic element in friendship is to be found in *Tales and Teachings of the Buddha* by John Garrett Jones, published by George Allen & Unwin. A sound general introduction to Buddhist ethics from a Theravāda perspective is H Saddhatissa's *Buddhist Ethics* published by George Braziller. Anyone with a serious interest in Indian Buddhist literature, doctrine and history should consult A. K. Warder's excellent one volume survey, *Indian Buddhism*.

Male Homosexuality and Transgenderism in the Thai Buddhist Tradition

Peter A. Jackson

I. INTRODUCTION

In the early to mid 1980s the official Thai response to the spread of HIV infection in that country was characterised by denial and silence. It was only in the latter years of the decade that the threat HIV/AIDS posed to public health in Thailand was formally acknowledged by government and public health officials and that public education campaigns began to be formulated and implemented. As in many other countries, the initial responses of many public figures in Thailand to the recognition of the serious issues posed by the rapid spread of HIV/AIDS were informed more by prejudice and fear of seropositive people than by reasoned consideration of the evidence on modes of infection. In this period homosexual men and female prostitutes were widely condemned as sources of AIDS and threats to public health by many Thai journalists, politicians, public health officials, Buddhist monks and other public figures.[1]

In my 1995 book *Dear Uncle Go: Male Homosexuality in Thailand* I argued that popular Western perceptions of a general tolerance of homosex-

---

PETER ANTHONY JACKSON Ph.D. (Melbourne, Australia) was born in Sydney in 1956 and is currently Research Fellow in Thai History at the Australian National University, Canberra. His books include *Buddhadasa: A Buddhist Thinker for the Modern World* (1988), *Buddhism, Legitimation and Conflict: The Political Functions of Urban Thai Buddhism* (1989), and *Dear Uncle Go: Male Homosexuality in Thailand* (1995).

An earlier version of this article was presented at a conference in London, England in 1993.

[1] Thanks to Eric Allyn and Ross McMurtrie for their valuable comments on earlier versions of this article. Pali is the classical language of the Theravada Buddhist tradition of Thailand, Sri Lanka, Burma, Laos and Cambodia and in this article I use the Pali rather than the Sanskrit forms of Buddhist terms, e.g. *kamma* instead of *karma*, *nibbana* instead of *nirvana*, etc. Note also that Thailand uses the Buddhist Era (B.E.) calendar and all Thai language publications are dated according to this system, which begins with the traditionally ascribed year of the Buddha's death or *parinibbana* in 543 B.C. To calculate the Christian Era year from the Buddhist Era year subtract 543, e.g. B.E. 2540 = A.D. 1997. In this article I also follow the Thai system of referring to authors by their first names rather than by their surnames. In Thailand lists of Thai persons' names are always arranged alphabetically by first name rather than by surname, a practice that follows from the fact that family names were only introduced universally in the early decades of the twentieth century. However, Thais also respect Western custom and list the names of non-Thai persons alphabetically by surname.

uality in Thailand are to an extent inaccurate. While there are no legal or formal sanctions against homosexuality in Thailand, a wide range of cultural sanctions operate to stigmatise Thai homosexual men and women. These anti-homosexual sanctions are diffused throughout Thai society rather than being focussed in any clearly definable institution or set of homophobic practices, as has historically been the case in most Western societies.

However, this situation changed somewhat in the late 1980s. The initial "shock-horror" response to AIDS provided a focus for the previously diffuse anti-homosexual sentiments as homosexual men were publicly labelled as the "source" or "origin" (Thai : *tonhet*) of HIV infection in Thailand. A number of Buddhist writers were involved in this stigmatisation of homosexual men, drawing on Buddhist teachings to construct arguments against homosexuality that contributed to the fear and angst surrounding much public discussion of HIV/AIDS in the country in the late 1980s.

In this article I consider the background to some Thai Buddhists' anti-homosexual arguments by reviewing scriptural and doctrinal references to homoeroticism in the Thai Buddhist tradition. I begin by describing accounts of male homoeroticism in the Thai language translation of the *Tipitaka*, the canonical scriptures of Theravada Buddhism, noting, firstly, divergences in ethical judgments made on homosexuality in the canon and, secondly, similarities between scriptural descriptions of *pandaka* (Thai: *bandor*) and the popular Thai notion of the *kathoey* (transvestite, transsexual, male homosexual). Ethical attitudes presented in the canon are reproduced in many contemporary Thai Buddhist commentators' discussions of homosexuality and an appreciation of the ancient scriptural accounts is important in understanding views on homosexuality that are now represented as being sanctioned by religious authority.

I then consider traditional Thai accounts which propose that homosexuality arises as a kammic consequence of violating Buddhist proscriptions against heterosexual misconduct. These kammic accounts describe homosexuality as a congenital condition which cannot be altered, at least in a homosexual person's current lifetime, and have been linked with calls for compassion and understanding from the non-homosexual populace.

Lastly, I mention more recent Thai Buddhist accounts from the late 1980s that described homosexuality as a wilful violation of "natural" (hetero)sexual conduct resulting from lack of ethical control over sexual impulses. These accounts presented homosexuality as antithetical to Buddhist ideals of self-control and were associated with vehement anti-homosexual rhetoric and vociferous attacks on male homosexual behaviour as the purported origin of HIV/AIDS.

Head of Buddha, 2nd century C.E.
Gandhara, India
Courtesy: Asian Art Museum of San Francisco
The Avery Brundage Collection

2. REFERENCES TO MALE HOMOSEXUALITY IN THE THERAVADA SCRIPTURES

The Pali canon of Theravada Buddhism contains numerous references to sexual behaviour that today would be identified as homoerotic and to individuals who would be called homosexual and transvestites. However, as would be expected of a series of texts composed over two milennia ago in a non-European culture, sexual categories found in the Pali canon do not match contemporary notions of homosexuality or of homosexual people. Most notably, the canon does not clearly distinguish between homosexuality from cross-gender behaviour such as transvestism. Nevertheless, while not being given a single, distinctive name, male-male sex is referred to in many places in the *Vinayapitaka*,[2] the monastic code of conduct, being listed amongst the many explicitly described forms of sexual activity which are proscribed for monks. As Leonard Zwilling (1992:203) states, we

> should not expect any term with the precise connotation of *homosexuality* to appear in Buddhist literature. However, homosexual behaviour stemming from an apparent disposition to seek sexual gratification through relations with members of one's own sex in preference to the other did not go unnoticed . . .

Indeed, careful exegesis of the references in the *Vinayapitaka* can provide us with insights into early Buddhist attitudes towards homoeroticism. It is important, however, that Theravada Buddhist accounts of homosexuality are understood in the context of the religion's general disdain of sexuality and distrust of sensual enjoyment. It is also important to keep in mind that Buddhism began as an order of celibate male renunciates, the *sangha*, and that the *Vinaya* is predominantly a clerical not a lay code of conduct.

Theravada Buddhism's Anti-Sex Attitude

In Buddhism all forms of sexuality and desire must be transcended in order to attain the religious goal of *nibbana*, literally, the extinction of suffering. The first section of the *Tipitaka*,[3] the *Parajika Kandha* of the *Vinayapitaka*, provides detailed guidelines on the practice of clerical celibacy in

---

[2]Zwilling (1992:208) notes that there are no explicit references to homosexuality in the *Suttapitaka*, the collection of the Buddha's sermons or discourses.

[3]I refer to the Thai translation of the *Tipitaka* in this article because the selection of Thai terms used to translate Pali often reflects Thai cultural values, providing insight into the translators' views and preconceptions. For example, the Pali term *pandaka* is sometimes translated directly by the equivalent Thai technical term *bandor*, while at other times it is translated by the colloquial term *kathoey*. All translations in this paper are my own.

the form of often explicit examples of the types of sexual misconduct which lead to "spiritual defeat" (*parajika*) and automatic expulsion from the *sangha*. To quote an often repeated formula in this section of the *Vinaya*, "Whichever monk has sexual intercourse is *parajika*, a defeated one, and will not find communion [in the *sangha*]" (*Vinaya*, Vol. 1, p. 27, *passim*). The definition of sexual intercourse (*methunadhamma*) given in the *Vinaya* reflects the strong distaste for sex within the early Buddhist tradition,

> That which is called *methunadhamma* is explained as: the *dhamma* of an unrighteous man (*asattapurisa*), the conduct of the common people, the manners of the low, *dhamma* which is evil and crude, *dhamma* whose end is but water, an activity which should be hidden, the *dhamma* which couples should perform together. (*Vinaya*, Vol. 1, p. 49)

The precision with which monks' conduct is monitored is shown in the canonical definition of "perform" in the expression "to perform sexual intercourse," which is described as a monk inserting his penis into a vagina, mouth, anus, etc. "even if only as far as the width of a sesame seed" (*Vinaya*, Vol. 1, p. 49).

The extreme imagery evoked in the Buddha's denunciation of a monk who was found to have kept and trained a female monkey to have sex with him, denunciation whose core descriptions of hell are repeated in the condemnation of several other forms of clerical sexual misconduct, graphically portrays the kammic consequences that were believed to follow from a monk's violation of his vow of celibacy or *brahmacariya*,

> Behold O worthless man (*moghapurisa*), the penis you insert into the mouth of a poisonous snake is yet better than the penis you insert into the vagina of a female monkey. It is not good. The penis you insert into the mouth of a cobra is yet better than the penis you insert into the vagina of a female monkey. It is not good. The penis you insert into a pit of blazing coals is yet better than the penis you insert into the vagina of a female monkey. It is not good.

> For what reason do I say the mentioned points are better? Because the man who inserts his penis into the mouth of a poisonous snake, and so on, even if he dies or suffers to the point of death because of that action . . . , after death and the dissolution of his body will not enter the state of loss and woe (*apaya*), the states of unhappiness (*duggati*), the place of suffering (*vinipata*), hell (*naraka*). As for the man who inserts his penis into the vagina of a female monkey, after death and the dissolution of his body, he will enter the state of loss and woe, the states of unhappiness, the place of suffering, hell (*Vinaya*, Vol. 1, p. 29).

According to the canon, sexual misconduct (*kamesu micchacara*) should be avoided by the pious laity as well as by monks and nuns. On early Buddhist attitudes to lay sexuality, Zwilling (1992:207) observes,

Buddhist tradition essentially conceives of sexual misconduct in terms of sexual relations with various types of prohibited women (*agamya*) and the performance of non-procreative sexual acts. Among the commentators only Buddhaghosa[4] and the anonymous author of the commentary to the *Abhidharmasamuccaya* include men among forbidden sexual objects.

In Thailand lay sexual misconduct (*kamesu micchacara*) has traditionally been glossed as *phit mia khon eun*, "violating another person's wife," or as *phit phua-mia khon eun*, "violating another person's spouse (husband or wife)." Homosexual activity between laypersons has traditionally fallen outside the scope of kammically significant sexual misconduct in Thailand.

Most contemporary Thai Buddhist writers follow early Buddhist attitudes and describe sex as extremely distasteful, even for the laity. One Thai writer on Buddhism, Isaramuni, equates sexuality with *tanha* (Thai: *khwam-yak*—craving or desire) and *raga* (Thai: *kamnat*—sexual lust), which are the antithesis of the Buddhist ideal of dispassionate equanimity (Isaramuni 1989:4). And while the *Vinaya* in general details an explicitly clerical code of conduct, similar anti-sex attitudes are now expressed in many Thai Buddhist writers' discussions of lay sexual ethics. In a discourse on married life *Phra* Buddhadasa,[5] an influential reformist thinker, calls reproduction "an activity that is distasteful, dirty and tiring" (Buddhadasa 1987:24) and says that sexual desire is a defilement (Pali: *kilesa*) that arises from ignorance (Pali: *avijja*), which Buddhist doctrine generally describes as the source of human suffering. *Phra* Buddhadasa says that in the past people were "employed" or "engaged" (Thai: *jang*) by nature in the "work" (Thai: *ngan*) of reproducing the species, but people now "cheat" nature by using contraception and having sex without being engaged in the work of reproduction. He maintains that this "cheating," i.e. engaging in sex for pleasure rather than reproduction, is "paid back" because it causes problems such as nervous disorders, madness and physical deformities (ibid.:25).

Phra Buddhadasa calls on laypeople to be mindful and establish spiritually informed intelligence (Pali: *sati-panna*) and to have sex only for reproduction. Furthermore, he maintains that the highest ideal in marriage is to live together without sex, describing the solitary life dedicated to the achievement of *nibbana* as a higher ideal than married life (ibid.:35). Indeed, *Phra* Buddhadasa maintains that marriage is a stage of life for those

---

[4]Zwilling (1992:209) notes that in his commentary on the *Cakkavattisutta* of the *Digha Nikaya*, Buddhaghosa takes the expression "wrong conduct" (*miccha-dhamma*), the cause of humanity's progressive degeneration in Buddhist legend, as meaning "the sexual desire of men for men and women for women." However, the Pali canon itself does not suggest this reading.

[5]*Phra* is an honorific Thai title for monks or *bhikkhu*.

who have not yet realised absolute truth, saying that once the inherent transience and unsatisfactoriness of the world is understood there will be no more desire for sex. He provides an example from the *Tipitaka* (no source cited) of ten year old children in the Buddha's time becoming *arahants*, perfected beings who have achieved *nibbana*, and maintains that this would be possible today if children were educated in Buddhist principles and led to see the truth revealed by Buddhism. *Phra* Buddhadasa adds that as adults such children would have no interest in sex because of their high spiritual status (ibid.:36–37).

Significantly, contemporary Thai Buddhist views on laypersons' sexual behaviour are often more proscriptive and extreme than attitudes reflect in the Pali canon or in traditional or popular Thai accounts of Buddhist doctrine and ethics. *Phra* Buddhadasa's work has been especially influential among educated and middle class Thai Buddhists. However, his views on sexuality are at variance with Thai Buddhism's traditional distinction between lay and clerical ethical conduct. The ethical extremism of *Phra* Buddhadasa and other contemporary Buddhist reformists in Thailand such as *Phra* Phothirak results from a clericalising trend whereby ethical demands traditionally made only of monks are now increasingly also being required of laypersons. The much publicised asceticism and celibacy of the prominent political figure and strict Buddhist, Major-General Chamlong Srimuang, epitomises the monastic regimen that some contemporary reform movements within Thai Buddhism (e.g. Santi Asoke) require of their devout lay followers.

Heterosexuality and Homosexuality as Equivalent Defilements

In the context of Buddhism's general anti-sex attitude, the *Vinayapitaka* often describes homosexuality in terms that place it on a par with heterosexuality. But this ethical equivalence is negative, with heterosexuality and homosexuality being described as equally repugnant sources of suffering and as constituting equivalent violations of clerical celibacy. The *Vinaya* identifies not two but four gender types, proscribing monks from having sexual relations with any of these four. The four gender types are male, female, *ubhatobyanjanaka* and *pandaka*. The latter two Pali terms are used to refer to different things in different sections of the canon and I attempt to define them precisely in the next section. But broadly it can be said that ubhatobyanjanaka[6] refers to hermaphrodites, while

---

[6]Pali: *ubhato*—Two-fold, double; *byanjana*—A sign or mark (of gender, etc.); *ka*—Derivative-forming suffix.

pandaka[7] refers to male transvestites and homosexuals. The *Vinaya* lists those sexual activities with men, women, *pandaka* and *ubhatobyanjanaka* that entail spiritual defeat and a monk's automatic expulsion from the order. These proscribed sexual activities are:

1. Anal, vaginal or oral intercourse with a female human, non-human (i.e. an immaterial being) or animal;
2. Anal, vaginal or oral intercourse with an *ubhatobyanjanaka* human, non-human or animal;
3. Anal or oral intercourse[8] with a *pandaka* human, non-human or animal; and
4. Anal or oral intercourse with a male human, non-human or animal.

Considering proscribed sexual activities with each gender type in detail, the *Vinaya* then lists twenty-seven types of sexual intercourse with a human female which entail spiritual defeat. These are: anal, vaginal and oral sex with a waking or sleeping woman, a drunk woman, a mentally deranged woman or a woman with a nervous disorder, an intellectually deficient woman, a dead woman, a dead woman whose body has not yet been eaten by animals and a woman whose body has been gnawed at by animals (*Vinaya*, Vol. 1, pp. 53–69). These same examples of proscribed sexual conduct are then repeated for the three other gender categories, with vaginal sex being deleted from the lists of proscribed sexual acts between monks and *pandaka* and males.

Together with bestiality (see "The Case of the Female Monkey," *Vinaya*, vol. 1, p. 27), necrophilia (see "The Two Cases of Open Sores [in Dead Bodies]," *Vinaya*, Vol. 1, pp. 221–222) and sex with inanimate objects (see "The Case of the Moulded Image," *Vinaya*, Vol. 1, p. 222 and "The Case of the Wooden Doll," *Vinaya*, Vol. 1, p. 222), the *Vinaya* also proscribes a range of homoerotic or strictly speaking autoerotic forms of sexual activity such as auto-fellatio (see "The Case of the Nimble-backed Monk,"

---

[7]It is possible that *pandaka* is derived from the Pali term *anda*, which variously means "egg" or "testicles," and may originally have had the sense of male reproductive deficiency or incapacity. Monier-Williams (n.d.:580) defines the cognate Sanskrit terms *pandra* and *pandraka* as "eunuch or impotent man." Zwilling (1992:204) says that the term is of obscure origin and may ultimately be derived from *apa + anda + ka*, "without testicles." He adds, however, that this should not be taken literally as meaning that a *pandaka* was necessarily a eunuch but, rather, should "be interpreted metaphorically as we do in English when it is said of a weak or pusillanimous person that he (or she) 'has no balls.' " Zwilling adds that the term *pandaka* used in the canon could not have meant a eunuch because, with the exception of the congenitally impotent, accounts of *pandaka* describe a man who is capable of "either erection, ejaculation, or the experience of sexual pleasure."

[8]The fact that vaginal intercourse is not listed as a possibility for *pandaka* indicates that they are biologically male.

Vinaya, Vol. 1, p. 221) and auto-sodomy (see "The Case of the Monk with a Long Penis," *Vinaya*, Vol. 1, p. 221).

In the *Vinaya*'s listings of proscribed sexual activities, sex between monks and the various categories of women, hermaphrodites, transvestites, men, dead bodies, animals and inanimate objects are all described in equivalent terms, none being presented as any more morally reprehensible than any other and all entailing spiritual defeat, although sex with inanimate objects was regarded as a lesser infraction entailing penance but not expulsion from the *sangha*. However, elsewhere in the *Vinaya* and in other sections of the *Tipitaka* it is made clear that *ubhatobyanjanaka* and *pandaka* are spiritually and ritually inferior to men, often being compared with women and criminals. But before reviewing these scriptural references I first consider in detail the definitions of the Pali terms *ubhatobyanjanaka* and *pandaka* and their relationship to the Thai notion of *kathoey*.

Defining Ubhatobyanjanaka, Pandaka *and* Kathoey

The Pali Text Society *Pali-English Dictionary* defines *ubhatobyanjanaka* as "Having the characteristics of both sexes, hermaphrodite" (Rhys Davids 1975:154) and the reformist Thai Buddhist writer *Phra* Ratchaworamuni[9] provides a similar definition in his *Dictionary of Buddhist Teachings*, namely, "Beings with the genital organs of both sexes" (Ratchaworamuni 1984:435). Khamhuno, author of a weekly newsmagazine column on Buddhist affairs, has defined *ubhatobyanjanaka* in Thai as *kathoey thae* or "true *kathoeys*" (Khamhuno 1989:37), that is, hermaphrodites. However, Bunmi Methangkun, head of the traditionalist Abhidhamma Foundation, indicates that psychological as well as physiological factors are involved when, following the *Abhidhammapitaka* (no reference cited),[10] he describes two types of hermaphrodites, namely, female (Pali: *itthi-ubhatobyanjanaka*) and male (Pali: *purisa-ubhatobyanjanaka*). According to Bunmi, an *itthi-ubhatobyanjanaka* is physically female, including having normal female genitals, but when physically attracted to another woman,

> her previously female mind disappears and changes instead into the mind of a man, and at the same time male genitals appear while her female genitals disappear and she is able to have sexual intercourse with that woman. (Note: "to disappear" here does not mean that she does not have [female genitals any more].) (Bunmi 1986:238)

---

[9]*Phra* Ratchaworamuni (Pali: Rajavaramuni) is the former ecclesiastical title of the monk *Phra* Prayut Payutto. His current ecclesiastical title is *Phra* Thepwethi (Pali: Devavedhi).

[10]Zwilling (1992:206) cites Buddhaghosa as providing an account of *ubhatobyanjanaka* in his *Abhidharmakos'a* that is almost identical to that provided by Bunmi.

A *purisa-ubhatobyanjanaka* is the opposite of the above, that is, someone who is physiologically male but when sexually attracted to another man loses his masculinity and takes on the mental characteristics and physical features of a woman so that he is able to have heterosexual relations with the man who arouses him (Bunmi 1986:238–239).[11] Bunmi goes on to say that male and female hermaphrodites are primarily distinguishable as follows,

> An *itthi-ubhatobyanjanaka* person is herself able to become pregnant to a man and can also make another woman pregnant but a *purisa-ubhatobyanjanaka* person cannot himself become pregnant even though he can make a woman pregnant. (Bunmi 1986:239).

In an interesting precursor to the modern distinction between sexual orientation and biological sex, Buddhaghosa describes the hermaphroditism of the *ubhatobyanjanaka* as arising from a dissonance between the masculine and feminine "power" (*indriya*) of an individual and their sexual organs (*byanjana*). He describes masculine and feminine behaviours as respectively arising from the "power of masculinity" (*purusindriya*) and the "power of femininity" (*itthindriya*). However, he maintains that these powers are not the cause of the male and female sexual organs and goes on to describe *ubhatobyanjanaka* as persons with the body of one gender but the "power" of the other. As Zwilling correctly observes (1992:206), in this account Buddhaghosa does not in fact describe hermaphroditism but rather bisexuality or homosexuality.

A famous scriptural example of such a sex-changing *ubhatobyanjanaka* is the case of a wealthy man named after his home town of Soreyya that is recorded in the *Dhammapadatthakatha*, the commentary on the *Dhammapada*. The Sri Lankan scholar Malalasekera summarises the Soreyya legend as follows,

> Once when he [Soreyya] and a friend with a large retinue were driving out of the city to bathe, he saw Maha Kaccayana [a prominent disciple of the Buddha] adjusting his robe before entering the city for alms. Soreyya saw the Elder's body, and wished that he could make him his wife or that his wife's body might become in colour like the Elder's. Immediately Soreyya turned into a woman and, hiding from his companions, went with a caravan bound for Takkasila. Arriving at Takkasila, he became the wife of the Treasurer of that city and had two sons. He already had two sons in Soreyya, born to him before his transformation. Some time after, he saw his former friend driving in a carriage through Takkasila and, sending a slave-woman to him, invited him to the house and entertained him. The friend was unable to recognise him till he revealed the truth. Thereupon they both returned to Soreyya and invited Maha Kaccayana to a

---

[11]The popular American science-fiction and fantasy writer, Ursula Le Guin, describes a planet inhabited by such beings in her award winning novel *The Left Hand of Darkness*.

meal. Soreyya fell at his feet, confessed his fault, and asked for forgiveness. When the Elder pardoned him he once more became a man. He entered the order under the Elder and went with him to Savitthi. There people having heard of his story worried him with questions. He therefore retired into solitude and, developing insight, became an *arahant*. Before that when people asked him which of his children he loved best he would say, "Those to whom I gave birth while a woman," but after attaining arahantship he would say, "My affections are set on no one" (Malalasekera 1960:1311–1312).

Definitions of *pandaka* are more diverse than those provided for *ubhatobyanjanaka*. The *Pali English Dictionary* defines a *pandaka* as "A eunuch, weakling" (Rhys Davids 1975:404), while the Thai translation of the *Vinaya* provides the definition, "a *kathoey*, a castrated man or eunuch" (*Vinaya*, Vol. 1, p. 768).[12] Suchip Punyanuphap, author of a comprehensive Thai language summary of the forty-five volumes of the *Tipitaka*, equates *pandaka* with *kathoey* and defines both in behavioural and psychological rather than physiological terms as, "a person who takes pleasure in having relations with a man while feeling that they are like a woman" (Suchip 1982:224n). Khamhuno says that *pandaka* are people who have abnormal sexual feelings, whether homosexual, sado-masochistic, etc., while *ubhatobyanjanaka* denotes physical *kathoeys*, i.e. hermaphrodites (Khamhuno 1989:37). Bunmi says that a *pandaka* is "a person who has a deficiency in the signs of masculinity [for men] or femininity [for women] (Bunmi 1986:235)[13] and goes on to describe five types of *pandaka* identi-

---

[12]This gloss is provided in a list of terms written either by the Thai translators of the *Tipitaka* or the editorial team and was not part of the original scripture.

[13]According to Zwilling (1992:205), *pandaka* refers to men who "lack maleness," not to women, denoting a man who "fails to meet the normative sex role expectations for an adult male." This male-focussed orientation of the term could perhaps be expected to follow if, as Zwilling suggests, the derivation of the term is indeed "without testicles." The Pali Text Society *Pali-English Dictionary* does refer to a feminine derivative form of *pandaka*, *itthipandika*, as occurring in the *Vinaya* (Rhys Davids 1975:404), but Bunmi's extension of the term to denote women who fail to meet the normative sex role expectations for an adult woman is perhaps not strictly canonical and may be influenced by the common tendency to translate *pandaka* into Thai as *kathoey*. While in common Thai usage *kathoey* usually denotes a nonnormative male, the term is occasionally used to denote a non-normative female and Thai dictionaries usually do not assign a determinate gender, whether male or female, to the term. The Royal Institute Thai language dictionary (1982:72) defines a *kathoey* as "A person who has both male and female genitals; a person whose mind (psychology) and behaviour are the opposite of their [biological] sex." In his *Photjananukrom Thai* (Thai dictionary) Manit Manitcharoen (1983:70) explicitly defines *kathoey* as denoting either a man or a woman and also attempts to correct popular Thai misconceptions with his definition, "Homosexuals or the sexually perverted are not *kathoeys*. The characteristic of a *kathoey* is someone who crossdresses (*lakka-phet*), a male who likes to act and dress like a woman and has a mind like a woman, or a female who likes to act and dress like a man and who has a mind like a man."

fied in the *Abhidhammapitaka* (no reference cited).[14] However, only one of these five types matches his own definition of showing deficiencies in either masculinity or femininity. The five types of *pandaka* Bunmi lists are:

1. *asittakapandaka*—A man who gains sexual satisfaction from performing oral sex on another man and from ingesting his semen, or who only becomes sexually aroused after having ingested another man's semen (ibid.:235–236).
2. *ussuyapandaka*—A voyeur, a man or woman who gains sexual satisfaction merely from watching a man and a woman having sex (ibid.:236).
3. *opakkamikapandaka*—Eunuchs, that is, castrated men lacking complete sexual organs. Unlike the other four types of *pandaka* Bunmi describes, these men attain their condition after birth and are not born as *pandaka* (ibid.:236).[15]
4. *pakkhapandaka*—People who by the force of past misdeeds become sexually aroused in parallel with the phases of the moon, either becoming sexually aroused during the two week period of the waning moon (Pali: *kalapakkha*) and ceasing to be sexually aroused during the fortnight of the waxing moon (Pali: *junhapakkha*) or, conversely, becoming sexually aroused during the period of the waxing moon and ceasing to be sexually aroused during the period of the waning moon (ibid.: 236).[16]
5. *napumsakapandaka* (also sometimes called simply *napumsaka*)—A person with no clearly defined genitals, whether male or female, having only a urinary tract (ibid.:237). Another definition of a *napumsaka* given by Bunmi is, "a [male] person who is not able to engage in activities like a man" (ibid.:239). Elsewhere Bunmi adds that *napumsaka-pandaka* are born without any genital organs as punishment for having castrated animals in a past life (ibid.:267).[17]

Bunmi also notes that "lower level" spirits such as *thewada* (Pali: *devata*) and *pretasurakai* (Pali: *preta-asurakaya*), which he collectively calls

[14]Zwilling (1992:204) traces these five types of *pandaka* to Buddhaghosa's *Samantapasadika*, Asanga's *Abhidharmasamuccaya* and Yas'omitra's commentary to the *Abhidharmakos'a*, adding that a similar list occurs in Hindu brahmanical medical and legal treatises.

[15]Zwilling (1992:204) says that this type of *pandaka* "attains ejaculation through some special effort or artifice." Bunmi's description of *opakkamika* as eunuchs appears to follow another type of *pandaka* that Zwilling says is identified by Yas'omitra, the *lunapandaka*, which implies a man who has been intentionally castrated.

[16]Zwilling (1992:204) cites Buddhaghosa as saying that a *pakkhapandaka* "becomes temporarily impotent for fourteen 'black days' of the month but regains his potency during the fourteen 'white days,' that is, from the new to the full moon."

[17]According to Zwilling (1992:204) Buddhaghosa describes a *napumsaka* as "one who is congenitally impotent."

phi-sang-thewada, can also be *kathoeys*, in this case using the Thai term *kathoey* to include both the Pali categories of *pandaka* and *ubhatobyanjanaka* (ibid.:255).

Contemporary Thai accounts of *ubhatobyanjanaka* and *pandaka* are complicated by the tendency of authors to identify both these groups as *kathoeys* and to use this Thai term interchangeably with the Pali terms. Different Thai authors use the term *kathoey* to refer to at least four distinct conditions covering a diverse range of physical, psychological and emotional phenomena that are now usually separated out into biological sex (hermaphroditism), psychological gender (transvestism and transsexualism) and sexuality (homosexuality). Originally *kathoey* appears to have referred to true hermaphrodites. However, it has come to be used more broadly to refer to people who are believed to possess or take on physical, behavioural or attitudinal characteristics generally ascribed to the opposite sex. The complex of phenomena referred to by the term *kathoey* reflects Thai cultural norms of masculinity and femininity and notions of appropriate sex roles, gender behaviour and sexuality. *Kathoey* denotes a type of person not simply a type of behaviour and in different contexts can include one or more of the following groups:

1. Hermaphrodites (Pali: *ubhatobyanjanaka*; Thai: *kathoey thae* or "true *kathoeys*"): that is, people who to a greater or lesser degree are either born with or at some time after birth naturally develop physical characteristics of both sexes. Hermaphrodites also include people born without any clearly determinable sex (Pali: *napumsakapandaka*).
2. Transvestites and Transsexuals (Pali: *pandaka, itthi- & purisa-ubhatobyanjanaka*; Thai: *kathoey thiam* or "pseudo-*kathoeys*"): that is, people who are physically male or female but prefer either to dress and behave as a member of the opposite sex or, in the case of transsexuals, to undergo hormone treatment and/or surgery in order to change their body to more closely approximate the physical features of a person of the opposite sex. In the Pali canon transsexualism is described as a spontaneous change of sex caused purely by psychological factors and not requiring medical intervention.
3. Homosexuals (Pali: *pandaka*; Thai: variously, *kathoey*, *gay*, *tut*, etc. for men; *kathoey*, *tom*, *dee*, etc., for women): that is, people who are physically male or female and are sexually attracted to people of their own sex.

The term *kathoey* includes homosexuals because in Thailand homosexuality, on the model of hermaphroditism, is popularly regarded as resulting from a psychological mixing of genders. That is, within the Thai cultural context a male homosexual is commonly regarded as having a woman's mind and a woman's sexual desires and a lesbian is regarded as having a man's mind and a man's sexual desires. The blending of genders denoted in the term *kathoey* may thus be solely physical, solely an imputed psychological mixing, or a combination of both.

The Thai term *kathoey* is derivationally unrelated to the Pali scriptural terms it is commonly used to translate, suggesting an indigenous pre-Buddhist conception of abnormal gender/sexuality. The Thai peoples adopted Theravada Buddhism around the eleventh and twelfth centuries of the Christian era. But whether or not Buddhism has been instrumental in influencing the development of the popular Thai notion, a very similar mixing of physical and psychological sex, gender behaviours and sexuality occurs both in the Pali terms *pandaka* and in the Thai term *kathoey*. Both terms are parts of conceptual schemas in which people regarded as exhibiting physiological or culturally ascribed features of the opposite sex are categorised together. If Buddhism was not the source of the popular Thai conception of *kathoey* then at the very least it has reinforced a markedly similar pre-existing Thai cultural concept.

Several points emerge from the diversity of definitions for *ubhatobyanjanaka*, *pandaka* and *kathoey*:

Firstly, the mix of sexual and gender phenomena denoted by the terms *ubhatobyanjanaka*, *pandaka* and *kathoey* are lumped together because in both the canonical Buddhist and traditional Thai views they represented an assumed continuum of sex/gender imbalance, from the solely physical (hermaphroditism) to the psycho-physical (transvestism, transsexualism) and the solely psychological (homosexuality).

Secondly, what further united the diverse physiological, psychological and behavioural categories brought together under these terms is the assumption, detailed further below, that all have a common kammic origin in heterosexual misconduct in a past life. Indeed, the issue of the origin of homosexuality dominates contemporary discussions of the topic by Thai Buddhist commentators and, as described in detail in the following sections, this has important implications for Buddhist ethical pronouncements on homosexuality.

Thirdly, *ubhatobyanjanaka* and *pandaka* denote types of people rather than types of behaviour and are primarily gender categories—denoting assumed deficiencies or aberrations in masculinity or femininity—rather than categories that denote sexuality. This is shown by the fact that the *Vinaya* in places refers to homosexual behaviour between monks who are not identified as being either *ubhatobyanjanaka* or *pandaka*. That is, homosexuality is not the central defining feature of these two categories. But having said this, it is still the case that the aberrant gender of *ubhatobyanjanaka* and *pandaka* people is generally assumed to imply that they engage in homosexual behaviour.

The traditional sense of the Thai term *kathoey* also appears to have focussed primarily on assumed gender aberration as defining a type of person and only secondarily on homosexual behaviour. However, the diffuseness of many contemporary Thai discussions of *pandaka* appears to result not only from the diverse range of phenomena referred to by the term in the Pali scriptures but also from a recent shift from assumed gender imbalance to homosexuality as the defining characteristic of a *kathoey* individual. This recent semantic shift in Thailand—to regard homosexual behaviour as much as cross-gender attributes as defining some persons' individuality—is still in process and older, gender-focussed readings of the term *kathoey* co-exist with the newer emphasis on sexuality. Nevertheless, the extent of the semantic shift that has taken place in the past two or three decades can be seen from the fact that *kathoey* is now commonly used by heterosexuals as a derogatory term for any homosexual man even when that man is not effeminate and does not cross-dress.[18]

This shift in the sense of *kathoey*, together with the common tendency to use this word to translate the Pali term *pandaka*, leads many contemporary Thai commentators to read the Buddhist scriptures as referring to "homosexuals" in the modern sense of the term. For example, in his article "Gays Appear in *Sangha* Circles" Khamhuno uses the Pali, Thai and English terms *pandaka*, *bandor* and *gay* interchangeably to mean homosexual men (Khamhuno 1989:37). This represents an important shift in the reading of the term *pandaka*. Many ethical judgments made of *pandaka* in the *Vinaya* (see below) relate primarily to the transgression of ascribed gender roles for men and women. However, when *kathoey* is understood to mean "homosexual" or "gay" and *pandaka* is translated by *kathoey* then scriptural judgments on *pandaka* are read as referring to homosexuality or gayness whether or not these are associated with cross-gender behaviour. In other words, early Buddhist pronouncements on one phenomenon—cross-gender behaviour—are now widely read in Thailand as referring to another, distinct phenomenon—homosexuality or gayness.

Attitudes to Pandaka *and* Ubhatobyanjanaka *in the* Tipitaka

It is difficult to discern a single distinct ethical position on homosexual behaviour in the Pali canon. The *Vinaya* proscribes all intentional sexual activity for monks and in this regard makes no distinction between hetero-

---

[18]For example, in 1988 the prominent Thai social critic, Sulak Sivaraksa, criticised the administrative style of former Prime Minister, General Prem Tinsulanonda, in playing one wing of the Thai military off against another in order to remain in power, as being like that of a eunuch (Thai: *khanthi*) and a *kathoey* (Sulak 2531:125). General Prem has never married and is rumoured to be homosexual but as a career soldier, Korean War veteran and former head of the Thai Army he could not be described as matching the traditional Thai conception of an effeminate, cross-dressing *kathoey*.

sexual or homosexual activity. There are some cases in the *Vinaya* where *ubhatobyanjanaka* and *pandaka* are regarded tolerantly, being treated no differently from other people. Yet there are also other cases where they appear to be discriminated against. However, it is not always easy to determine whether it is these individuals' cross-gender behaviour or their homosexuality which is tolerated or criticised in the different references, as the two issues of gender and sexuality were not conceptually distinguished in the canon. But given the tendency of some contemporary Thai authors to read these references as in fact making judgments on homosexuality it is important that they be considered in some detail in order to understand the impact of religious teachings on attitudes today.

The *Vinaya* does not appear to contain any explicit ethical pronouncements on the behaviour of lay *pandaka* or *ubhatobyanjanaka*. Furthermore, the Theravada scriptures and related commentary literature are not consistent in their ethical judgments of *pandaka* and *ubhatobyanjanaka* within the *sangha*, recording attitudes varying from the accepting and compassionate to the unaccepting and discriminatory. What appears to determine the Buddha's described attitude in different cases is not the individual *pandaka's* or *ubhatobyanjanaka's* different gender or sexual interests as such, but rather how openly he/she reveals his/her difference and whether their condition was known before they were ordained into the *sangha* or was only discovered after ordination. In general, the Buddha was more tolerant of *pandaka* and *ubhatobyanjanaka* who were less open about their difference and whose condition was only discovered after ordination.

Furthermore, canonical attitudes to *pandaka* in particular appear to have developed over time as the Buddha attempted to ensure that the newly formed *sangha* remained respectable in the eyes of the public of his time. As reported in the canon, attitudes to *pandaka* in the *sangha* developed in response to incidents of public criticism as much as in response to any application of general ethical principles. In trying to avoid being seen as disreputable in the eyes of lay society in ancient India, the early *sangha* appears to have absorbed, codified and institutionalised prevailing antagonistic attitudes to *pandaka*. As Richard Gombrich notes,

> Whenever the Buddha is represented as disapproving of something, he says that it is not conducive to increasing the number of believers. He then pronounces a rule, for which he gives a stock list of ten reasons. They can be summarised as the protection and convenience of the Sangha, the moral purity of its members, increase in the number of believers and the good of non-believers. This, we might say, epitomises the Buddhist view (at least in the Theravada tradition) of how Buddhism relates to society. Nor is this empty rhetoric: the occasions for promulgating rules are frequently lay dissatisfaction (Gombrich 1988:90).

In following sections I detail how attitudes recorded in the canon prefigure contemporary Thai Buddhist accounts of homosexuality on at least two main counts. Firstly, canonical divergences permit a variety of contemporary accounts of homosexuality—ranging from the compassionate if condescending to the discriminatory—to be presented as authoritative Buddhist pronouncements on the issue. Secondly, the Buddha's own social pragmatism on the issue of the *sangha's* treatment of *pandaka* and *ubhatobyanjanaka* monks parallels inconsistencies in the writings of some modern reformist Thai Buddhist thinkers who have developed progressive and compassionate analyses of social issues such as poverty and the impact of rapid social change on village life but who remain steadfastly antagonistic on the issue of homosexuality.

Instances of Scriptural Tolerance of Pandaka

There are a number of scriptural examples of *pandaka* and *ubhatobyanjanaka* being tolerated within the *sangha*, in some cases becoming honoured members of the order respected for their high levels of spiritual attainment. The *Vinaya* describes cases of ordained monks changing gender and taking on the physical characteristics of women and, conversely, of ordained nuns changing gender to take on the physical characteristics of men. When these cases were brought to the Buddha's attention he is reported as saying that he had approved their ordinations and they had maintained the rainy season retreat (Pali: *vassa*, Thai: *phansa*) of the *sangha*, that is, they had demonstrated their worthiness as members of the *sangha*. He then gives permission for the monk who became a woman to live with the order of nuns and follow the nuns' code of conduct, and for the nun who became a man to live with the order of monks and follow the monks' code of conduct (*Vinaya*, Vol. 1, p. 220). Commenting on this liberal pronouncement, Bunmi laments, "But in the present time who will be the judge if a monk changes into a woman? There are no longer any nuns for such a person to go and live with" (Bunmi 1986:255). That is, given that the order of Theravada Buddhist nuns fell into decay in early medieval India and for technical reasons cannot be reconstituted in modern Thailand,[19] it is no longer possible for the Buddha's liberal pronouncement to be followed.

The commentary literature also contains a number of legends and stories of *pandaka* and *ubhatobyanjanaka* being accepted within the *sangha*. The previously described account of Soreyya is a case in point. In particular, the scriptural claim that Soreyya ultimately attained arahantship would appear to contradict the view held by some contemporary Thai

---

[19]According to the conservative Theravada tradition followed in Thailand, only a congregation that includes nuns correctly ordained according to that tradition has the authority to ordain another woman as a nun. With no correctly ordained Theravada nuns to be found in any modern country, it is impossible for the female *sangha* to be reconstituted.

Buddhists that homosexuals are constitutionally incapable of achieving *nibbana* or other high spiritual attainments. Bunmi for one opposes this view and provides scriptural support for a compassionate and accepting stance on homosexuality by citing scriptural references to spiritually eminent and respected *pandaka* and by equating *pandaka* with *kathoey*, which he in turn identifies with gay or homosexual. Bunmi refers to the *Abhidhammapitaka* (no reference cited) as stating that Ananda, the Buddha's first cousin and personal attendant, had been born as a *kathoey* in many previous lives (Bunmi 1986:261). Prasok, a newspaper columnist writing on Buddhism,[20] also refers to this scriptural account, saying,

> In previous existences *Phra* Ananda, the Buddha's personal attendant, had been a gay or *kathoey* for many hundreds of lives. In his last life he was born as a full man who was ordained and was successful in achieving arahantship three months after the Buddha attained *nibbana*. The reason he was born a *kathoey* was because in a previous life he had committed the sin of adultery. This led to him stewing in hell for tens of thousands of years. After he was freed from hell a portion of his old *kamma* still remained and led to him being reborn as a *kathoey* for many hundreds of lives (Prasok 1989:10).

Malalasekera cites the *Dhammapadatthakatha*, the *Dhammapada* Commentary, which describes Ananda's various previous existences, as the source of this story and gives the following apparently bowdlerised summary,

> When Ananda was born as a blacksmith he sinned with the wife of another man. As a result he suffered in hell for a long time and was born for fourteen existences as someone's wife,[21] and it was seven existences more before his evil deed was exhausted (Malalasekera 1960:267–268).

The case of Vakkali noted by the lay Buddhist author and academic, Sathienpong Wannapok, provides further evidence of the non-canonicity of the contemporary Thai view that homosexuals are incapable of following the Buddha's teachings or of achieving the "fruits of the path." In his article, "When Gays See the *Dhamma*," Sathienpong relates his version of the Vakkali legend to provide scriptural support for the position that gay men can achieve enlightenment by renouncing their sexual desire in the same way as heterosexuals and that homosexuals and heterosexuals are no different spiritually. Sathienpong begins by noting that in the commentaries on the *Tipitaka* (no reference cited) those who saw the Buddha and subsequently developed faith in his teachings are divided into four categories:

---

[20]I thank Dr. Louis Gabaude for pointing out that Prasok and Khamhuno are pen names of the same author.

[21]Note that being born female is here represented as kammic punishment for a man's sexual misconduct in a previous life.

Maravijaya Buddha, late 15th–early 16th century
Bronze with traces of gilding, Lan Na style, Thai
Courtesy: Asian Art Museum of San Francisco
The Avery Brundage Collection

1. *rupapamanika* (variously spelt *rupappamanika*)—literally "measuring [significance] by form," that is, those who developed faith because of attraction to the Buddha's impressive physical appearance, including his "radiant coppery complexion" (Sathienpong 1987:59).
2. *ghosapamanika* (variously spelt *ghosappamanika*)—those who were impressed by the Buddha's voice and developed faith.
3. *lukhapamanika* (variously spelt *lukhappamanika*)—those who were impressed by the simplicity of the Buddha's way of life and so developed faith.
4. *dhammapamanika* (variously spelt *dhammappamanika*)—those who were impressed by the Buddha's teachings and consequently developed faith.

Sathienpong says many men in the *rupapamanika* category were so taken by the Buddha's physical appearance that their attraction to his "handsomeness" was the prime reason they gave up their worldly lives to follow the *sangha's* ascetic practices, adding that in modern terms men in this category would be called gay. Significantly, men described as *rupapamanika* are not otherwise described as being *ubhatobyanjanaka* or *pandaka*. That is, *rupapamanika* denotes a man with no deficiency in his masculine characteristics who was attracted to the Buddha's physical appearance and became an ordained monk.

In the version of the legend related by Sathienpong,[22] Vakkali was the son of a Brahmin from Savitthi and was so impressed by the Buddha's physical appearance that he sought ordination. But after being ordained he did not undertake the normal monastic activities, instead spending his time following the Buddha everywhere so that he could look at him. One day when Vakkali was staring unblinkingly at the Buddha, the Buddha castigated him, asking what he was looking for "in this stinking rotten body? Anyone who sees the *dhamma* has seen the Buddha and anyone who has seen the Buddha has seen the *dhamma*" (Sathienpong 1987:60). The Buddha then ordered Vakkali out of his presence. Vakkali was so shattered by this command that he attempted to kill himself by jumping off a mountain. But *deva* or spiritual beings informed the Buddha of Vakkali's dejection and he quickly went to the monk's aid in time to save him from committing suicide. With an extremely brief exposition of the *dhamma*, "The eyes see *dhamma*," the Buddha gave Vakkali the insight he needed in order to attain enlightenment and he immediately attained arahantship.

---

[22]The Vakkali story is recounted in a number of texts and has several versions. Malalasekera's (1960:799–800) useful summary of the different versions is included at the end of this article.

Instances of Scriptural Discrimination Against
Pandaka *and* Ubhatobyanjanaka

The scriptures describe the Buddha as expressing a compassionate attitude towards people who began to show cross-gender characteristics after ordination and to those who, while attracted to members of the same sex, were regarded as being physiologically and behaviourally true to the then prevailing cultural notions of masculinity. However, the Buddha opposed accepting into the *sangha* those who openly expressed cross-gender features at the time they presented for ordination. Volume Four of the *Vinaya* recounts a story of a *pandaka* who violated the clerical vow of celibacy and whose bad example led to a comprehensive ban on the ordination of *pandaka*. This story is interesting on a number of counts and I reproduce it in full below.

The Story of the Prohibition of the Ordination of *Pandaka*

At that time a *pandaka* had been ordained in a residence of monks. He went to the young monks and encouraged them thus, "Come all of you and assault[23] me." The monks spoke aggressively, "*Pandaka*, you will surely be ruined. *Pandaka*, you will surely be [spiritually] destroyed. Of what benefit will it be?" Having been spoken to aggressively by the monks, he went to some large, stout novices and encouraged them thus, "Come all of you and assault me." The novices spoke aggressively, "*Pandaka*, you will surely be ruined. *Pandaka*, you will surely be destroyed. Of what benefit will it be?" Having been spoken to aggressively by the novices, the *pandaka* went to men who tend elephants and horses and spoke to them thus, "Come all of you and assault me."[24] The men who tend elephants and horses assaulted him and then publicly blamed, rebuked and criticised [the *sangha*], saying, "A *samana* of the lineage of the son of the Sakyas is a *pandaka* and these *samanas*, even those who are not *pandakas* themselves, assault the ordained *pandakas*. When such is the case these *samanas* are not practising *brahmacariya* (celibacy)." The monks heard the men who tend elephants and who tend horses blaming, rebuking and criticising thus and informed the Blessed One of the matter.

The Blessed One then ordered the monks, "Behold monks, a *pandaka* is one

---

[23]The Pali term here is *dusetha*, which variously means "To spoil, ruin; to injure, hurt; to defile, pollute; to defame" (Rhys Davids, 1975:328). Zwilling (1992:207) prefers "to defile." However, the Thai language version translated here renders *dusetha* as *prathutsarai*, a term that means "to harm, injure or assault." The Thai translators appear to have understood the text as describing the *pandaka* as calling on the young monks to perform anal sex on him, and their choice of the Thai term *prathutsarai* appears to reflect an assumption that anal sex is associated with suffering assault.

[24]The laymen that the *pandaka* monk incited to have sex with him would not have been breaching the clerical code of celibacy and so the use of the term *prathutsarai* here should probably be interpreted as "to assault" rather than "to commit an offence," presumably referring more to the assumed violence (to manhood?) of the homosexual act than to the violation of a code of conduct.

who is not to be ordained. Monks should not give them ordination and those who have been ordained must be made to disrobe" (*Vinaya*, Vol. 4, pp. 141–142).*

This story shows the Buddha's concern to uphold the public image of the *sangha* and his wish that his followers should not be seen to violate commonly accepted standards of behaviour.[25] A number of cultural assumptions underlie the elements of this story and the Buddha's concluding pronouncement. Firstly, the fact that the *pandaka* monk is described as approaching in succession "young monks," "large, stout novices" and a presumably coarse group of "men who tend elephants and horses," reflects a conjuncture of notions about types of sexually attractive men still found in sections of both Thai and Western homosexual subcultures today. Secondly, while the individual monk in question violated *sangha* discipline, the Buddha betrays an assumption that *all pandaka* are likewise unsuited to monastic life when he prohibits any further ordinations of *pandaka* and orders those already in the *sangha* to be expelled. *Kathoeys* are often regarded in a similar way in Thailand today, commonly being stereotyped as untrustworthy prostitutes with hyperactive sex drives. These contemporary Thai stereotypes of *kathoeys* have precedents in descriptions of *pandaka* in Pali. Zwilling (1992:205) notes that the view of *pandaka* as "lascivious, shameless, unfilial and vacillating" was reflected in early Buddhist literature,

> According to Buddhaghosa *pandakas* are full of defiling passions (*ussanakilesa*); their lusts are unquenchable (*avapasantaparilaha*); and they are dominated by their libido (*parilahavegabhibhuta*) and the desire for lovers just like prostitutes (*vesiya*) and coarse young girls (*thulakumarika*) (*Samantapasadika* III, p. 1042). Thus the *pandaka* . . . was considered in some degree to share the behaviour and psychological characteristics of the stereotypical "bad" woman.

It might be contended that what the Buddha's ban on the ordination of *pandaka* reflects is concern about the disruptive effect of effeminate transvestite homosexuals in an order of celibate, predominantly heterosexual

---

*EDITOR'S NOTE: This passage is also quoted by Leonard Zwilling in his earlier article in this book (see p. 48), but different versions are used. Leonard Zwilling cites the Pali Text Society version, while Peter Jackson in the present article has translated the Thai language version into English. So both quotes come from different sources and reflect slightly different textual versions of the quote.

[25] Buddhism, the middle path, has always been concerned with the maintenance of social order and since the Buddha's time the *sangha* has never claimed to provide a universal vehicle for the spiritual liberation of all individuals in society, explicitly excluding those who are considered to reflect badly on the monkhood in terms of prevailing social norms and attitudes. *Pandaka* are one of the groups excluded from ordination into the *sangha* and given the still common Thai conflation of *pandaka/kathoey*/homosexual/gay, homosexual men are also regarded as being excluded from the *sangha*.

monks. However, the above piece emphasises homosexuality, indeed passive homosexual sex, as the violation and source of disruption. What the above-quoted section of the *Vinaya* suggests is a conflation of passive homosexual sex with demasculinisation, i.e. being a *pandaka*. Leaving aside the ethical misconduct of the individual *pandaka* monk, what the Buddha's subsequent comprehensive ban on the ordination of *pandaka* indicates is a concern to exclude non-masculine men from the *sangha*. The ban also shows that a characteristic regarded as defining a man as non-masculine or a *pandaka* is a preference for certain types of homosexual sex. These same attitudes remain prevalent in Thailand today. A man who is known to be the receptive partner in anal sex may be labelled a *kathoey*, i.e. non-masculine, even if he is not effeminate or a transvestite, but the inserter in anal sex rarely suffers such stigmatisation. The above-cited scriptural references to penetrative homosexual sex (i.e. *methunadhamma* defined in "masculine" or penetrative terms), while proscriptive, do not imply that the men who engaged in such sexual behaviour with the *pandaka* monk jeopardised their masculinity. In other words, the canon appears to inscribe attitudes to male-male sex and masculinity that parallel views widely held in contemporary Thailand.

The ban on the ordination of *pandaka* or *kathoeys* has continued until today. In 1989 Khamhuno reported a meeting of the Mahatherasamakhom or *Sangha* Council, the supreme governing body of the Thai *sangha*, at which the matter of "sexually perverted (*wiparit thang phet*) persons being ordained as monks" was raised (Khamhuno 1989:37). The *Sangha* Council discussed the matter after news reports of the ordination of a *kathoey* and local criticism of the abbot who permitted the ordination. In reporting the Council's meeting, Khamhuno reaffirmed the Buddha's edict that *pandaka* should not be ordained, writing, "In fact, the *Vinaya* and the laws of the Mahatherasamakhom clearly specify that people who are *kathoeys* or *pandaka* are prohibited from being ordained," adding that *pandaka* and *ubhatobyanjanaka* are also prohibited from being ordained as novices (ibid.).

Khamhuno comments that when a man presents for ordination he is ceremonially asked a number of questions in Pali by the ordaining preceptor. Among these is the question, *purisosi*—"You are a man, are you not?" The ordinand is then expected to answer with the affirmative expression, *amabhante*. Khamhuno says that this question is meant to determine whether the ordinand is in fact a man, not a person with two genders (*ubhatobyanjanaka*) or a *kathoey* (*pandaka*), and justifies the ban on gays in the *sangha* on the basis of having to prevent people who can bring the order into disrepute from being ordained.[26] By equating gays with *kathoeys* and

---

[26]Other authorities cite a different origin for the ceremonial ordination question *purisosi*, referring to the Buddhist legend of a *naga* or serpent disguising itself as a man in order to obtain ordination into the *sangha*.

hermaphrodites and affirming the ban on their ordination, Khamhuno indicates that the crux of the prohibition on their ordination is, as suggested above, the expression of inappropriate or inadequate masculinity. The ordination question, "You are a man, are you not?" thus refers to more than biological male sex, also including the culturally defined gender notion of masculinity. In other words, the ordination question could be translated as "You are a 'real' man, are you not?"

That deficient masculinity lies at the core of the notion of *pandaka* (and also of *kathoey*), and is the basis of discriminatory attitudes towards this group in the Buddhist scriptures, is further demonstrated in sections of the *Vinaya* where *pandaka* are described as having a spiritually inferior status to men. For example, Volume Four specifies that if a monk is ill on the day when the *patimokkha*, the two hundred and twenty seven clerical rules of conduct, are ritually recited and he is unable to join in the ceremony he may declare his moral purity, that is, the fact that he has not violated the clerical code during the past fortnight, to another monk. This second monk may then convey the ill monk's affirmation to the assembly of monks at that monastery. But if the monk to whom the ill monk makes his affirmation has some stigma attaching to him then the affirmation is invalidated and must be made again to another, ritually pure monk. The specified types of stigma that invalidate an affirmation of moral purity include: the fact that a purported monk is only a novice (i.e. not fully ordained into the order), if the monk is mentally deranged, a murderer, a non-human (i.e. a spirit) posing as a human or if the monk is a *pandaka* (*Vinaya*, Vol. 4, pp. 194–195). That is, according to the *Vinaya*, *pandaka*, along with murderers, the mentally deranged, non-humans, etc., are spiritually defective and lack the ritual authority required in order to convey an ill monk's affirmation of moral purity to the assembly of monks.

Furthermore, in the section of the *Vinaya* dealing with ceremonial seating arrangements for monks. The Buddha permits monks to sit together with other monks in a specified arrangement but explicitly prohibits them from sitting together with *pandaka*, women and *ubhatobyanjanaka*, indicating that he considered it spiritually inappropriate for monks to sit with members of these three non-masculine groups (*Vinaya*, Vol. 7, p. 84).

3. CONTEMPORARY THAI VIEWS ON HOMOSEXUALITY

Scriptural attitudes to *pandaka* and *ubhatobyanjanaka* are not uniform and depending on which sections of the *Tipitaka* are referred to or emphasised can lead to differing ethical positions on homosexuality, some compassionate and others invidious. Indeed, two broad schools of thought on homosexuality are current among contemporary Thai Buddhist writers, one accepting, the other unaccepting. The key factor differentiating the divergent stances is the author's conceptualisation of the origin of homosexuality. Those who maintain that homosexuality is a condition which is outside the conscious control of homosexuals and has its origins in past misdeeds take a liberal stance, while those who maintain that it is a wilful violation of ethical and natural principles take an antagonistic position.

Kammic Accounts of the Origins of Homosexuality

Bunmi has provided a detailed exposition of the traditional kammic explanation of homosexuality and the ethical corollaries of this account. Like most contemporary Thai Buddhist authors, Bunmi translates *pandaka* into Thai as *kathoey*, which he appears to understand in its more traditional sense of primarily denoting an assumed gender imbalance and only secondarily denoting homosexuality. In places he uses the terms *rak-ruam-phet* (homosexuality) and "gay" when he wishes to focus more on sexuality than gender, but in general Bunmi does not distinguish being homosexual from being a *kathoey*, conflating sexuality with gender.

Bunmi lists a number of types of sexual misconduct in a past life that can lead a person to engage in homosexual activity in their current life. These misdeeds include committing adultery, being a prostitute, sexually interfering with one's children or being sexually irresponsible, such as a man not caring for a woman who becomes pregnant by him (Bunmi 1986:120–121). Bunmi emphasises that the strength of old *kamma* (Thai: *kam kao*) generated by such transgressions cannot be counteracted and its consequences have to be accepted,

> Even if brought up well in this life or born into a high family or as the child of royalty, no matter how prestigious their background, they [people who committed sexual offences in a past life] will not be able to stop themselves from becoming mixed up in sexual matters from an early age. No matter how much their parents criticise them and no matter how much they are instructed, they will still easily act wrongly with regard to sex and will not see it as dangerous but rather as something ordinary (ibid.:121).

Criticising popular Thai ideas on the origins of homosexuality, Bunmi denies that being a *kathoey* is caused by raising a boy with girls or by raising a girl with boys, maintaining that individuals in the categories of human beings, animals and "lower level spirits" (*phi-sang-thewada*) are born as *kathoeys* because of causal factors in their past lives (ibid.:39–41). Buddhist views that being a *pandaka/kathoey* is a type of stigma that marks a person as deficient are clearly shown by Bunmi's note that the *Abhidhammapitaka* (no reference cited) lists the kammic causes of being born with a disability. He maintains that being a *kathoey* is included in this list of disabilities along with being born or becoming physically disabled, being mute, mad, blind, deaf and intellectually disabled (ibid.:265). The Buddha prescribed that people with any of these disabilities, plus those with serious illnesses and diseases, should be barred from ordination.

Bunmi maintains that sex-determined *kamma* is of two types, that which manifests from birth and leads to hermaphroditism and that which manifests after birth and leads to transvestism, transsexualism and homosexuality (ibid.:287). He says those who are born hermaphrodites cannot attain *nibbana* in this life but those who become *kathoeys* after birth can attain *nibbana* if they apply their discriminating intelligence (Thai: *panya*) to the task of spiritual liberation (ibid.:294). Bunmi also says that *kathoeys* tend to be born in societies in which sexual misconduct is prevalent because such societies provide appropriate environments for them to expend their kammic debts (ibid.:301).

Significantly, Bunmi maintains that actions and desires which have an involuntary cause in the kammic consequences of past sexual misconduct do not themselves accrue any future kammic consequences. They are the outworking of past *kamma*, not sources for the accumulation of future *kamma*. According to Bunmi, homosexual activity and the desire to engage in homosexual activity fall into this category and are not sinful and do not accrue kammic consequences. In a similar vein, he says that,

> Changing one's sex is not sinful (Pali: *ducarita*). Consequently the intention to change one's sex cannot have any ill kammic consequences. But sexual misconduct (Thai: *phit-kam*) is sinful and can lead to consequences in a subsequent birth (ibid.:306).

In Bunmi's account the only sexual activities that accumulate future kammic consequences are traditionally sanctioned forms of heterosexual misconduct. Bunmi says that sexual misconduct with a member of the opposite sex has kammic consequences because, "it is like stealing, because the person responsible for that person has not given their permission" (ibid.:308). Bunmi does not explicitly refer to female *kathoeys* and his examples of sexual misconduct that lead to being born a *kathoey* are moral infractions committed by men. His use of a proprietary simile, comparing adultery to theft, appears to reflect a view of women as men's property. It is also noteworthy that in Thai the words used to describe the results of a wife or child being sexually interfered with are very similar to the terms used to describe the results of being robbed. Bunmi describes both robbery and adultery as *kert sia hai*—"causing a loss or damage (to wealth, reputation, etc.)" (ibid.).

The sexual activities that Bunmi says Buddhism classes as sins are precisely those which in traditional Thai society, and presumably also in ancient India, were regarded as dishonouring and sullying the female victims and their male relatives or spouses, namely, adultery, rape and sex with a girl who has not been given in marriage. In this cultural context two men having sex does not cause any equivalent damage or loss (Thai: *sia hai*), except perhaps to their reputations as "real men" should they be discovered. But when a man is cuckolded or his wife is raped then his property has been interfered with and, in Bunmi's words, an action equivalent to a theft has occurred. Similarly, having sex with a girl who has not been given in marriage, that is, ceremonially handed over from her father to her husband, is also to interfere with a man's traditional property, in this case his daughter, and may make the young woman difficult to marry off.

There is therefore a close relationship between, on the one hand, those sexual activities which Buddhist teachings proscribe for lay people and which are interpreted as incurring kammic debts and, on the other hand, the traditional sexual mores and gender roles of Asian societies. A range of physical gender imbalances and sexual activities and inclinations which slip outside these traditional norms are considered to have a neutral kammic impact and are not regarded as evil or sinful. Significantly, it is violations of tabus and mores relating to potentially reproductive sexual behaviour which are proscribed in Bunmi's traditionalist Buddhist account, while behaviours and conditions without reproductive consequences, including homosexuality, are not regarded as sinful. However, this situation changes markedly in some more recent Thai Buddhist interpretations, which identify homosexual behaviour as most definitely sinful.

Compassion for Homosexuals in Traditional Thai Buddhist Accounts

Prasok is another writer who says that *kamma* is the root cause of homosexuality but he also believes that the Buddhist principle of *anicca* or impermanence plays a causal role. Prasok calls homosexuality one of the "perversities of nature" (*khwam-wiparit khorng thammachat*) and compares homosexuals to calves born with five legs, saying they are strange but still part of natural processes. He maintains that because of the play of the principle of impermanence the factors determining masculinity and femininity are incomplete or mixed in some individuals, leading to physical and psycho-sexual differences. Prasok's views lead him to adopt a compassionate if condescending view of homosexual people when he writes, "I am not criticising anyone [i.e. homosexuals] at all because I see that this proceeds according to the outworking of each individual's old *kamma*" (Prasok 1989:10).

Prasok adds that in a previous birth all people who are now *kathoeys* have had to climb the spike tree of hell (Thai: *ton-ngiw*). After committing sexual sins they were reborn in hell where they were chased by vicious beasts, their only escape being to climb a tree with spikes in its trunks and branches which pierced their limbs and bodies as they clambered up it. Prasok says these people suffered great torment and cried out "Oh! Oh! I've learnt my lesson," and because of the suffering *kathoeys* have purportedly endured in hell he feels in no position to condemn them, adding that you cannot criticise people because of their *kamma*.

Bunmi's view on the kammic origins of homosexuality and being a *kathoey* lead him to a similar compassionate but condescending stance. Bunmi says,

> Society in Thailand and in almost every other country in the world does not really accept *kathoeys*. This is because they do not know the real truth about the causes of becoming a *kathoey*, which are extremely pitiable (Bunmi 1986:42).
>
> People who study and understand the *Abhidhamma* will not laugh at or ridicule *kathoeys* . . . but rather will sympathise with them and feel sorry for them and find ways to help them to the extent that they can be helped. They will point out the ways of dealing more intelligently with life's problems so that *kathoeys* don't repeat their old mistakes that will lead to great sadness and sorrow in the future (ibid.:40).

Bunmi comments that Thai people generally laugh at *kathoeys* but they do not know that "those who laugh at and ridicule *kathoeys* were themselves *kathoeys* in a past life" (ibid.:251). Bunmi claims that in some past life everyone has been born a *kathoey* because everyone has been guilty of sexual misconduct at some point in their multitude of previous existences. He maintains,

> If they studied the causes of being a *kathoey*, the life of the mind, . . . all those who like to laugh at and ridicule *kathoeys* would not be able to laugh any more. Because the very people who laugh at *kathoeys* were themselves once *kathoeys*. Absolutely everyone without exception has been a *kathoey* because we have gone through innumerable cycles of birth and death, and we don't know how many times we have been *kathoeys* in past lives or how many more times we may be *kathoeys* in the future (ibid.:258).

Bunmi here is arguing that *kathoeys* should be treated with tolerance and compassion, Buddhist virtues regarded as meritorious, and he points out that contemporary Thai society often fails to reflect the ethics of its ostensible Buddhist heritage in the case of *kathoeys* and gays. But while compassionate, Bunmi's views do not lead to full acceptance of transvestism or homosexuality because he holds up *kathoeys* as examples of what happens to people who breach codes of sexual conduct. Even compassionate Buddhist interpreters still regard being homosexual or a *kathoey* as a condition inherently defined by suffering, citing the lack of acceptance, social opprobrium and the ensuing problems these people suffer. It is the perceived suffering of *kathoeys* and homosexuals that leads traditionalist Buddhist interpreters such as Bunmi and Prasok to regard this variety of sexuality as the *kammic* consequence of past sexual misdeeds. These interpreters do not consider the possibility that the suffering endured by homosexuals may not be inherent in their sexuality but rather may result from the intolerant social environment in which they live. Following the kammic account of the cause of homosexuality, the suffering of homosexuals can only be endured, not ameliorated, because it is interpreted as resulting from the individuals' own past misdeeds and will continue until the *kammic* consequences of those misdeeds have been expunged. Bunmi and Prasok construe homosexuals' suffering as a reminder and a moral lesson on the unfortunate consequences of sexual misconduct. *Kathoeys* may be pitiable and worthy of sympathy but in the kammic account they are still the products of immorality, albeit in a past life, and in an ideal cosmos populated only by moral people they would cease to exist.

AIDS and Anti-Homosexual Intolerance in Thailand

The kammic account of the origins of homosexuality is not the only Buddhist interpretation current in Thailand. Since the arrival of HIV/AIDS in Thailand in the mid-1980s a number of Buddhist writers have presented strongly anti-homosexual views. These more recent critical positions consider homosexuality to be a conscious violation of sexual mores and therefore ethically reprehensible. As in the West, which I suspect to be the source of many of the more extreme anti-homosexual arguments presented in Thailand in recent years, HIV/AIDS has led to the foregrounding of subcurrents of homophobia in Thai culture and society.

The critics continue to conflate gender and sexuality issues, interpreting homosexuality as a consequence of gender imbalance or perversion. However, in the light of the focus on male homosexual activity as a mode of transmission of HIV infection during the early years of the pandemic, Thai Buddhist critics concentrated more on the sexuality of people identified as *kathoeys* than on these persons' assumed gender imbalance. It is interesting that this inversion of the traditional structuring of ideas of gender and sexuality in the notion of the *kathoey*, placing homosexuality rather than gender at the focus of the concept, was associated with a shift in Buddhist attitudes from relative tolerance to condemnation of homosexuality. AIDS thus had an important cultural impact in Thailand, contributing to shifts in the understanding of what constitutes a *kathoey* and leading to increased stigmatisation of male homosexuality.

4. CONCLUSION

Buddhism is a complex tradition and there is no single canonical or scripturally sanctioned position on homosexuality. Rather, the Pali scriptures contain a number of divergent trends which different interpreters can use to develop views on homosexuality that range from the sympathetic to the antagonistic. Whether an interpreter adopts a sympathetic or a critical stance depends on whether he or she regards the cause of homosexuality as lying outside the individual, in old *kamma* build up in a previous life, or in the individual's own supposedly immoral conduct.

It is interesting that the latter, intolerant view is the more recent and, paradoxically, is presented by some authors who are otherwise identified as progressive. Buddhist authors like *Phra* Ratchaworamuni are generally concerned to reform Thai Buddhism by uprooting institutional corruption, demythologising traditional Buddhist metaphysics and making the *sangha* a purer and more effective cultural vehicle for transmitting traditional values in the contemporary world. As in the West, public panic about AIDS and latent fears about homosexuality combined in Thailand in the 1980s to produce an increasingly explicit intolerance of homosexuality in some quarters. But AIDS alone does not explain the vehemence of the recent Buddhist attacks on homosexuality. In my 1989 book *Buddhism, Legitimation and Conflict: The Political Functions of Urban Thai Buddhism* I described how reformist interpretations of Buddhism have been associated with a de-emphasis on *kamma* as an explanation for why society and people are the way they are. This has opened the way for the development of an interventionist Buddhist social theory in Thailand which focuses more on people's capacity to change their circumstances than on the extent to which their current life conditions are kammically pre-determined. From an ethical standpoint, interventionist and politically progressive Buddhist theories place more emphasis on individuals' responsibility for their own future. However, in the context of the AIDS panic in the second half of the 1980s and a widespread if previously diffuse anti-homosexual sentiment in Thailand, the new reformist accounts of Buddhism fostered the development of a more focussed anti-homosexual polemic.

Reformist and modernist trends in Thai Buddhism are often regarded as politically progressive because of their opposition to the historical alignment of the *sangha* with the authoritarian centralised state and military dictatorship. On the other hand, traditional metaphysical views of Buddhism which emphasise the assumed determining power of *kamma* are criticised by reformists as intellectually backward and politically conservative. Paradoxically, however, the reformist, politically progressive interpretations of Buddhism are often linked with a strident moralism and a vehement anti-homosexual stance unprecedented in recent Thai history. While, on the other hand, the conservative traditionalists who still believe in the determining power of *kamma* take a more *laissez faire* approach to issues such as homosexuality.

Thailand in the second half of the 1980s thus provided an interesting example of how changing intellectual and social conditions can bring a previously neglected area of social and cultural life to prominence and invest it with new meanings and significance. Thai history in the 1980s also shows that political progressivism, intellectual modernisation and ethical liberalism are not necessarily related trends and can move independently and at different rates. Indeed, the very factors which lead to perceived political progress and expanded socio-economic opportunities for some sectors can simultaneously lead to regressive and discriminatory developments in other spheres which restrict and deny opportunities to other sectors of society.

Nevertheless, the impact of Buddhist authors' anti-homosexual rhetoric appears to have been relatively small. To a large measure this has been because the 1980s issue of homosexual men as the purported source of AIDS has all but been forgotten in the 1990s as the magnitude of the problem of heterosexual transmission of HIV in Thailand has become apparent.[27] The vehement anti-homosexual rhetoric in Thailand in the second half of the 1980s has not led to any noticeable increase in publicly expressed intolerance or discrimination against male homosexuals beyond that which already existed. Paradoxically, the brief period of public anxiety about homosexual men as vectors of HIV/AIDS and the associated religiously authorised criticisms of *kathoeys* may in fact have contributed to the consolidation of gay identity among increasing numbers of Thai homosexual men, and not only because of the public prominence given to homosexuality.

There has been considerable discussion among Western gay/lesbian analysts about the historical shift in Western societies from viewing homosexuality as a behaviour to a defining characteristic of a type of person, i.e. the homosexual (see Halperin 1990). The changing relative emphases on gender and sexuality in the notion of *kathoey* appear to be leading to a similar shift in Thailand. When the class of people identified as *kathoeys* were primarily defined by their assumed gender imbalance then homosexuality was viewed as a behaviour that "men" as well as *kathoeys* may engage in. But as *kathoeys* have come to be defined more by their sexuality then the idea of the homosexual as a class of person has also gained currency in Thailand. This change is reflected in the already noted heterosexual use of

---

[27]Chris Lyttleton (1995) notes that, at least in many rural areas of Thailand, officially sponsored safe sex education programs conducted in the early 1990s have all but ignored unprotected homosexual sex as a risk activity, focussing almost solely on heterosexual sex. This further demonstrates the marginal nature of homosexuality in Thailand. In the early years of the pandemic homosexual men were isolated and stigmatised as the supposed source of HIV infection. But as the heterosexual population has become threatened in Thailand homosexual men, who are at just as great a risk of infection as heterosexual men, have tended to be ignored in the official safe sex campaigns.

the term *kathoey* to refer derogatorily to homosexual men and the idea that even though a gay man may look like a "man," he is really a *kathoey* underneath.

There is no doubt that Western notions of the homosexual as a type of person have influenced Thai conceptions of sexuality. However, in Thailand the notions of homosexual personhood and gay identity have developed from a specifically Thai base. The pre-existing notion of the *kathoey* as a type of person defined by their unconventional gender/sexuality has provided an indigenous foundation for the development of new sexual identities that often appear to mirror those in the West. The view of some Thai critics that gayness in Thailand results from corrupting Western influences or mimicking of Western "sexual fashions" (see Sulak 1984:121) is therefore mistaken, but so is the perception of many Western visitors to Thailand that gay identity there is an exact mirror of Western sexualities.

Despite their discriminatory character, the fact that the Buddhist-based diatribes published in the light of HIV/AIDS focussed on homosexual men's unconventional sexuality rather than their ascribed cross-gender behaviour contributed to the consolidation of notions of homosexual identity in Thailand. In the 1990s Thai homosexual men tend to be defined as much if not more by their sexuality as by their assumed breach of gender norms, and one unintended consequence of the 1980s criticisms may be the firmer establishment of homosexuality and gayness as acknowledged focuses of sexual and social existence in Thailand.

APPENDIX

Malalasekera's interesting summary of the legends surrounding Vakkali *Thera* (Malalasekera 1960:799-800) is reproduced in full below.

"He belonged to a brahmin family of Savatthi and became proficient in the three Vedas. After he once saw the Buddha he could never tire of looking at him, and followed him about. In order to be closer to him he became a monk, and spent all his time, apart from meals and bathing, in contemplating the Buddha's person. One day the Buddha said to him, 'The sight of my foul body is useless; he who sees the Dhamma, he it is that seeth me' (*yo kho dhammam passati so mam passati; yo mam passati so dhammam passati*).[28] But even then Vakkali would not leave the Buddha till, on the last day of the rains, the Buddha commanded him to depart. Greatly grieved, Vakkali sought the precipices of Gijjhakuta. The Buddha, aware of this, appeared before him and uttered a stanza; then stretching out his hand, he said: 'Come monk.'[29] Filled with joy, Vakkali rose in the air pon-

---

[28]cp. *Itivuttaka*, (P.T.S.) section 92.
[29]The Buddha is often quoted in the canon as using this brief expression to accept monks into the *sangha*.

dering the Buddha's words and realised arahantship.[30]

"According to the *Theragatha* Commentary,[31] when Vakkali was dismissed by the Buddha he lived on Gijjhakuta, practising meditation, but could not attain insight because of his emotional nature (*saddha*). The Buddha then gave him a special exercise, but neither could he achieve this and, from lack of food, he suffered from cramp. The Buddha visited him and uttered a verse to encourage him. Vakkali spoke four verses[32] in reply and, conjuring up insight, won arahantship. Later, in the assembly of monks the Buddha declared him foremost among those of implicit faith (*saddhadhimuttanam*).[33] In the *Parayanavagga*[34] the Buddha is represented as holding Vakkali up to Pingiya as an example of one who won emancipation through faith.

"The *Samyutta* account[35] gives more details and differs in some respects from the above. There, Vakkali fell ill while on his way to visit the Buddha at Rajagaha, and was carried in a litter to a potter's shed in Rajagaha. There, at his request, the Buddha visited him and comforted him. He questioned Vakkali, who assured him that he had no cause to reprove him with regard to morals (*silato*); his only worry was that he had not been able to see the Buddha earlier. The Buddha told him that seeing the Dhamma was equivalent to seeing him, and because Vakkali had realised the Dhamma, there would be no hereafter for him. After the Buddha had left, Vakkali asked his attendants to take him to Kalasila on Isigili. The Buddha was on Gijjhakuta and was told by two *devas* that Vakkali was about to 'obtain release.' The Buddha send [sic] word to him: 'Fear not, Vakkali, your dying will not be evil.' Vakkali rose from his bed to receive the Buddha's message, and sending word to the Buddha that he had no desire or love for the body or the other *khandhas* [aggregates or factors making up human existence], he drew a knife and killed himself. The Buddha went to see his body, and declared that he had obtained nibbana and that *Mara's* attempts to find the consciousness of Vakkali would prove fruitless.

---

[30]*Manorathapurani, Anguttara* Commentary (S.H.B.) i. 140f.; the *Apadana* account (*Apadana* ii. 465f.) is similar. It says that the Buddha spoke to him from the foot of the rock. Vakkali jumped down to meet the Buddha, a depth of many cubits, but he alighted unhurt. It was on this occasion that the Buddha declared his eminence among those of implicit faith; also *Dhammapadatthakatha* iv. 118f. The *Dhammapadatthakatha* reports three verses uttered by the Buddha in which he assures Vakkali that he will help him and look after him.

[31]*Theragatha* Commentary (S.H.B.), i. 420.

[32]These are included in *Theragatha*, vss. 350–354.

[33]cp. *Anguttara Nikaya* (P.T.S.) i. 25; also *Divyavadana* (ed. Cowell & Neill, Cambridge) 49 and *Sammoha-Vinodani, Vibhanga* Commentary (P.T.S.) 276; *Visuddhimagga* (P.T.S.) i. 129.

[34]*Sutta Nipata* (P.T.S.) vs. 1146.

[35]*Samyutta Nikaya* (P.T.S.) iii. 119 ff.; *Saratthappakasini, Samyutta* Commentary ii. 229.

"The Commentary adds that Vakkali was conceited and blind to his remaining faults. He thought he was a *khinasava* [one whose mind is freed from mental obsessions], and that he might rid himself of bodily pains by death. However, the stab with the knife caused him such pain that at the moment of dying he realised his *puthujana* [worldly, unliberated] state and, putting forth great effort, attained arahantship.

"His resolve to become chief among the *saddhadhimuttas* had been made in the time of the Padumuttara Buddha, when he saw a monk also named Vakkali similarly honoured by the Buddha."[36]

EDITOR'S NOTE: There is some overlap between the historical sections of this article and that by Leonard Zwilling (pp. 45–54 of the present book). Both scholars summarize the Theravada Buddhist scriptural references to male homosexuality. The coverage by Peter Jackson in the present article is done in a longer, more technical and comprehensive way, relating more to the contemporary Thai reading of the Pali Sources. Leonard Zwilling's coverage is briefer; he focuses on the original Pali rendering and the ancient Indian context.

REFERENCES

Buddhist Scriptures

Phra Traipidok Chabap Luang (The Tipitaka, Official Royal Edition), Department of Religious Affairs, Ministry of Education, Bangkok, 4th Printing, 2525 (1982).

Other Books

(Phra) Buddhadasa *Bhikkhu, Chiwit Khu (Life As a Couple)*, Sukhaphap Jai Printers, Bangkok, 2530 (1987).
Bunmi Methangkun, *Khon Pen Kathoey Dai Yang-rai (How Can People Be Kathoeys?)*, Abhidhamma Foundation, Bangkok, 2529 (1986).
Gombrich, Richard, *Theravada Buddhism, A Social History from Ancient Benares to Modern Colombo*, Routledge & Kegan Paul, London, 1988.
Halperin, David M., *One Hundred Years of Homosexuality and Other Essays on Greek Love*, Routledge, New York, 1990.
Isaramuni, *Withi Porng-kan Rok Et (The Method to Protect Against AIDS)*, Isaramuni Pointing the Way Series Vol. 34, Work to Revive the *Dhamma* for the Return of Ethics and the Supramundane, Liang Chiang Press, Bangkok, 2532 (1989).
Jackson, Peter A., *Buddhadasa: A Buddhist Thinker for the Modern World*, the Siam Society, Bangkok, 1988.

---

[36]*Apadana* (P.T.S.) ii. 465f.; *Manorathapurani, Anguttara* Commentary (S.H.B.) i. 140.

———, *Buddhism, Legitimation and Conflict: the Political Functions of Urban Thai Buddhism*, Institute of Southeast Asian Studies, Singapore, 1989.

———. *Dear Uncle Go: Male Homosexuality in Thailand*, Bua Luang Books, Bangkok, 1995.

Khamhuno (pseud.), "Gay Prakot Nai Wongkan Song (Gays Appear in *Sangha* Circles)," "Sangkhom Satsana (Religion and Society Column)," *Siam Rath Sutsapda (Siam Rath Weekly)*, Vol. 36, No. 22, 18 November 2532 (1989), pp. 37–38.

Lyttleton,Chris, "Storm Warnings: Responding to Messages of Danger in Isan," in *Thai Sexuality in the Age of AIDS: The Australian Journal of Anthropology*, 1995, 6:3, pp. 178–196.

Malalasekera, G.P., *Dictionary of Pali Proper Names* (2 Vols.), Luzac & Co. for the Pali Text Society, London, 1960.

Manit Manitcharoen, *Photjananukrom Thai* (Thai dictionary), Ruam-san, Bangkok, 2526 (1983).

Monier-Williams, Monier, *A Sanskrit-English Dictionary*, Oriental Publishers, New Delhi, n.d.

(*Phra*) Phadet Thattajiwo *Bhikkhu, Waksin Porng-kan Rok Ee (A Vaccine to Protect Against AIDS)*, Thammakay Foundation, Pathumthani, 2530a (1987).

———, *Luang Phor Torp Panha (Reverend Father Responds to Problems)*, Thammakay Foundation, Pathumthani, 2530b (1987).

Prasok (pseud.), "Khang Wat (Beside the Monastery Column)," *Siam Rath* (daily newspaper), Bangkok, 2 March 2532 (1989), p. 10.

Ratchabanditayasathan (Royal Institute), *Photjananukrom Chabap Ratchabanditayasathan* (Royal Institute Edition Dictionary), Bangkok, 2525 (1982).

(*Phra*) Ratchaworamuni (current ecclesiastical title *Phra* Thepwethi), *Photjananukrom Phutthasat Chabap Pramuan-sap (A Dictionary of Buddhist Teachings, Compiled Edition)*, Mahachulalongkorn Ratchawitthayalai, Bangkok, 2527 (1984).

Rhys Davids, T. W. & William Stede (eds.), *Pali-English Dictionary*, Oriental Books Reprint Corporation, New Delhi, 1975.

Sathienpong Wannapok, "Meua Gay Morng-hen Tham (When Gays See *Dhamma*)" in *Suan-thang Nipphan (Passing [in Opposite Directions] on the Way to Nibbana)*, Chor-mafai Publishers, Bangkok, 2530 (1987), pp. 59–62.

Sulak Sivaraksa, *Lork-khrap S. Siwarak (Unmasking S. Sivaraksa)*, Reuan Kaew Printers, Bangkok, 2527 (1984).

———. *Lork-khrap Watthanatham Thai (Unmasking Thai Culture)*, Suksit Siam, Bangkok, 2531 (1988).

Suchip Punyanuphap, *Phra Traipidok Samrap Prachachon (The Tipitaka for the People)*, Mahamakut Ratchawitthayalai, Bangkok, 2525 (1982).

Zwilling, Leonard, "Homosexuality as Seen in Indian Buddhist Texts," in José Ignacio Cabezón (ed.), *Buddhism, Sexuality, and Gender*, State University of New York Press, New York, 1992.

From *Nanshoku ōkagami* (Great Mirror of Male Love) by Ihara Saikaku, 1687. A handsome youth, Tamura Sannojō, takes the hand of his suitor Maruo Kan'emon as they exchange vows of undying love. The buck and doe in the background are symbols of devotion between lovers, since it was believed that deer mated for life. From story, ''His Head Shaved on the Path of Dreams.''

The Legend of Kūkai and the Tradition of Male Love in Japanese Buddhism

Paul Gordon Schalow

A popular legend in Japan stated that male homosexual love (*nanshoku*) was introduced to Japan from China in the ninth century by Kūkai (774–835), founder of the True Word (*Shingon*) sect of esoteric Buddhism. This legend cannot be taken as fact, of course. The introduction of a uniquely "priestly" mode of male homosexual practice may have been accomplished in the eighth and ninth centuries during Kūkai's lifetime, but it is safe to conclude that Kūkai played no more role in its introduction than to serve as a focus for attribution of the phenomenon.[1] The legend's significance lies, rather, in the purpose it served in the lives of Buddhist believers and in how it was given new meaning for secular society in the seventeenth century. To clarify the scope of the Kūkai legend, this article will examine four texts in which the legend appears: *Kōbō daishi ikkan no sho* (1598, *Kōbō Daishi's Book*),[2] *Inu tsurezure* (1619; 1653, *A Mongrel "Essays in Idleness"*),[3] *Iwatsutsuji* (1667, *Wild Azaleas*) by Kita-

---

PAUL GORDON SCHALOW was born in St. Louis, Mo. in 1952. He earned a Ph.D. in Japanese literature from Harvard University in 1985 and now teaches Japanese at Rutgers University, N.J. His publications include a study and translation of Ihara Saikaku's *The Great Mirror of Male Love* (Stanford University Press 1990). See footnotes for the original provenances of these translations.

[1] By the fifteenth century, orthodox Shingon Buddhism was plagued with numerous "heresies," of which this may be one. Speaking of the Tachikawa School, which preached sex between men and women as the only means of obtaining Buddhahood and gaining the Way, the Shingon priest Yūkai (1345–1416) said, "Many secret manuals and texts of this heretical school were in circulation, often called 'oral transmission of the secrets of esoteric doctrine.' To this day there are ignorant people who study such works and believe them to possess the loftiest thoughts. In truth they are neither exoteric nor esoteric, but merely so many stones wrapped in jade. . . . Many people studied these teachings, but they did not meet with divine favor, and for the most part both the teachings and the men have perished." R. Tsunoda, et. al., eds. *Sources of Japanese Tradition* (New York: Columbia University Press, 1958), p. 169.

[2] Excerpts of *Kōbō Daishi's Book* were translated for this article from the unannotated printed version of *Kōbō Daishi ikkan no sho* in Okada Yasushi, ed., *Kinsei shomin bunka kenkyūkai*, no. 13, *Nanshoku bunken tokushū* (Tokyo: Oranda Shobo, 1952), pp. 14–23.

[3] Excerpts of *A Mongrel "Essays in Idleness"* were translated for this article from the unannotated printed version of *Inu tsurezure* in Asakura Haruhiko, ed., *Kanazōshi shūsei*, vol. 4 (Tokyo: Tokyodo Shuppan, 1983), pp. 5–26.

mura Kigin,[4] and *Nanshoku ōkagami* (1687, *The Great Mirror of Male Love*) by Ihara Saikaku.[5] These texts will show that the Kūkai legend affirmed same-sex relations between men and boys in seventeenth century Japan, both in the spiritual world of temples and monasteries and in the secular world of samurai and merchants.

Kūkai transmitted the Buddhist esoteric tradition to Japan in 806 after his return from China, where he studied for almost two years under the Chinese master Hui-kuo (764–805). It was customary in True Word Buddhism for the mysteries of the faith to be transmitted orally from master to pupil, rather than in book form, and this meant that the relationship between master and disciple was of greatest importance. By the time Kūkai founded the True Word temple complex on Mt. Kōya in 816, his remarkable spiritual powers had already attracted a large number of disciples and made him the subject of legend even before his death there in 835.

During his lifetime, Kūkai made great contributions to the life and culture of Heian Japan through major civil engineering projects, his mastery and teaching of Chinese scholarship, and his original writings on Buddhist doctrine. In recognition of his contributions and the continued spiritual hold he exerted on Japanese believers, the imperial court conferred on him the posthumous title of Kōbō Daishi ("Great Teacher Transmitting the Dharma") in 921. In the centuries after Kūkai's death, the name Kōbō Daishi became associated with several important cultural, social, and historical developments that occurred during his lifetime and in which he may have played a role. In aggregate, the legends constituted a religious construct called Kōbō Daishi worship.[6] Among the legends in that religious invention was one that he introduced male homosexual love to Japan.[7] It is not known when this legend first developed, but a poem in Chinese by Ikkyū (1394–1481) is the first evidence we have of it. "Monju, the holy one, first opened this path; Kōbō of Kongō then revived it. Without male and female, its pleasures are like an endless circle; men shout with pleasure

---

[4]Excerpts of *Wild Azaleas* were translated for this article from the unannotated printed version of *Iwatsutsuji* in Asakura Haruhiko, ed., *Kanazōshi shūsei*, vol. 5 (Tokyo: Tokyodo Shuppan, 1984), pp. 351–369. A full translation of "Wild Azaleas" appears in Stephen D. Miller, ed., *Partings at Dawn: An Anthology of Japanese Gay Literature* (San Francisco: Gay Sunshine Press, 1996), pp. 103–124.

[5]A complete translation of *Nanshoku ōkagami* by Ihara Saikaku appears in P. G. Schalow, trans., *The Great Mirror of Male Love* (Stanford, Calif.: Stanford University Press, 1990).

[6]Described in J. Kitagawa, "Master and Saviour" in *On Understanding Japanese Religion* (Princeton, N.J.: Princeton University Press, 1987), pp. 182–202.

[7]The legend's appearance may have been related to another legend claiming that Kūkai was so holy he never lusted for a woman his entire life (*isshō fubon*). In the popular mind, the fact that Kūkai felt no lust for women meant that he simply preferred boys.

when they attain entrance.''[8] Far from detracting from his reputation as the object of Kōbō Daishi worship, this legend, like others, enhanced Kūkai's stature and apparently was thought of as compatible with his other spiritual and secular accomplishments.

KŌBŌ DAISHI'S BOOK

One of the earliest surviving manuscripts—dated 1598—to state a connection between Kūkai and male love is *Kōbō Daishi's Book*. The use of Kūkai's posthumous name in the title indicates that the connection was already well established, and that *Kōbō Daishi* is used largely as a byword for male love. The preface of the brief work describes how a layman goes into seclusion to pray to Kōbō Daishi for instruction in "the mysteries of loving boys in Japan" (*nihon shudō no gokui*). On the seventeenth day of the man's austerities, Kōbō Daishi appears and agrees to present him with a one-volume book explaining the love of boys, the basics of which "even monkeys in the hills and fields can comprehend." The text speaks of the "mysteries" of loving boys, implying a connection with the esoteric mysteries of True Word Buddhism. The fact that the preface identifies the book as personally transmitted by Kōbō Daishi substantiates the primary importance of the relationship between master and pupil in True Word Buddhism and, in a sense, legitimizes the book's contents.

Kōbō Daishi's Book, divided into three sections, claims to reveal secret teachings regarding the love of boys. The first section describes hand positions used by young acolytes to communicate their feelings to priests; the second section advises priests on how to evaluate an acolyte's emotions by observing him closely; and the final section describes methods of anal intercourse. The categories—hand positions, observations and penetration—bear a close resemblance to the four classes of Indian *tantras* associated with looking, touching, embrace, and penetration.

Part One

Part One decodes ten hand signals. The concern with positions of the hands and their meaning mimics, and possibly parodies, the holy hand positions (*mudrā*) that were an integral part of True Word teaching and religious

---

[8]The poem is quoted in *Inu-tsurezure* (1619; 1653) in Asakura Haruhiko, ed. *Kana-zōshi shūsei*, vol. 4 (Tokyo: Tokyodo Shuppan, 1983), p. 12. Monju (*Mañjuśrī*) generally is considered the deity of wisdom. His connection with boy love in Japan derives from the fact that the bodhisattva's name in Japanese, Monju shiri, contains a homophone for the word ass (*shiri*). Kūkai is referred to as "Kōbō of Kongō" after the name of his main temple on Mt. Kōya, Kongōbu-ji.

practice. Priests and acolytes communicated their sexual feelings in the esoteric idiom of hand positions.

1. If an acolyte clenches his fingers—from the index finger to the little finger[9]—it means "You are the only one I love."
2. If an acolyte clenches both hands completely except for one thumb,[10] it means "I acknowledge your love and will make myself yours to do with as you please."
3. If an acolyte touches the index and middle finger to his thumb,[11] it means he wants to see you.
4. If an acolyte flips the tassle of his fan, it is an invitation to visit.
5. If an acolyte forms a circle with the index finger and thumb on both hands, it means "Tonight." If he uses the middle finger, it means "Tomorrow night." And if he uses the ring finger, it means "Some other time."[12]
6. If an acolyte touches the middle finger and ring finger to his thumb on both hands, it is an invitation to come visit.
7. If an acolyte touches the ring finger and little finger to his thumb, it means he wants to tell you something but cannot because people are watching; he'll try again the next night.
8. If something will prevent his coming as promised, he will touch the ring finger to his thumb on both hands.[13]
9. If an acolyte touches the index and little fingers to his thumb, it means he will come again tomorrow night.
10. If an acolyte tugs at your sleeve, it means he definitely wants you to visit.

---

[9]This resembles the clenched fists of the *kongō ken-in mudrā*. "The right hand (Buddha) symbolizes Sentient Beings in whom intelligence of the Buddha exists in a perfect state, and the left hand (Beings) rings the bell in order to disperse illusion and error." E. D. Saunders, *Mudrā: A Study of Symbolic Gestures in Japanese Buddhist Sculpture* (Princeton, N.J.: Princeton University Press, 1960), p. 114.

[10]This *mudrā* resembles the folded hands of the outer bonds fist, *gebaku ken-in*, and suggests a frankly sexual interpretation of its spiritual meaning: "*dai yoku* (great avidity), indicates the love of Vairocana for all Beings, a love, which, in man, is represented by the limited desire for affection: in Kongōsattva (Vajrasattva, the Bodhisattva who emanates from Vairocana), this love is translated by an Avidity (*yoku*) to love all Beings at the same time. Thus in Shingon ritual, the *gebaku ken-in*, emblematic of Great Avidity, symbolizes the Heart and the Compassion of the Buddha." Ibid., p. 120.

[11]This *mudrā* is vaguely like the *tembōrin-in mudrā* of the turning wheel of the law. "In the Japanese Esoteric sects, making the mudrā, accompanied by the right ritual words, may for the celebrant take the place 'of all sermons, for no predication is more perfect than the Law.'" Ibid., p. 100.

[12]These are three variations on the Amida *Mudrā*, a form of the *an-i-in mudrā* of appeasement. See Ibid., pp. 73–74. The remaining *mudrā* in 6–10 do not resemble any commonly known hand positions in Japanese Buddhism.

[13]This *mudrā* resembles the circle formed by the ring finger and thumb in 5. The meanings seem to be similar.

Part Two

Part Two instructs priests on seven ways to observe an acolyte so they can tell whether he is ready for lovemaking; and, if he is not, how to arouse him and make him ready. Several of the instructions are accompanied by twenty-one syllable Japanese poems (*waka*) that illustrate the lesson. The most important quality a priest looks for in an acolyte is *nasake*, an empathetic sensitivity to love. When a boy possesses this sensitivity, seduction is hardly necessary; without it, the task of seduction is difficult, at best.

1. After an acolyte has spoken, observe him carefully. The acolyte who speaks quietly is sensitive to love. To such a boy, show your sincerity by being somewhat shy. Make your interest in him clear by leaning against his lap. When you remove his robes, calm him by explaining exactly what you will be doing.

> White snow on a mountain peak
> turns to pure water on the rocks
> and finally flows down.

   As this poem illustrates, snow on even the highest mountain peak is destined to melt and flow downward. Likewise, no matter how lacking in sensitivity to the mysteries of love an acolyte may be, he can be made yours if you approach him right.

2. An acolyte may be very beautiful but insensitive to love. Such a boy must be dealt with aggressively. Stroke his penis, massage his chest, and then gradually move your hand to the area of his ass. By then he'll be ready for you to strip off his robe and seduce him without a word.

> I gaze up at the distant top of a cedar tree;
> the wind blows strong
> and even the cedar bends.

   The poem illustrates that even a proud heart will yield if the effort is strong enough.

3. It is best to deal gently, not aggressively, with a gentle-hearted acolyte. Quietly put him at ease, and then penetrate him.

> I gaze up at the quiet moon at Isobé
> and my heart, too, grows calm.

4. If an acolyte practices martial arts, be sure to praise his swordsmanship. Then tell him some warrior tales. Things will proceed naturally from there.

Before snow accumulates,
it is shaken off the branches;
in a windy pine, snow breaks no limbs.

As this poem illustrates, if snow is shaken off a pine before it has a chance to build up, it will not accumulate to the breaking point. Likewise, an acolyte's resistance should not be allowed to accumulate but be met as it comes; this is the only way to success.

5. If an acolyte is known to like birds, talk about birds—even if you hate them—act as if you shared his interest. To an acolyte who likes to study, talk about his studies. After he opens up, you can do what you will with him.
6. The greatest pleasure is to proceed without resistance with an acolyte who possesses a great sensitivity to love.
7. If an acolyte is too shy to show himself to you, delay by plucking the hairs of your nose and then try again.[14]

Part Three

Part Three concerns final consummation of the seduction in the form of anal intercourse with the acolyte. Seven positions are described in the idiom of tantric meditation postures; the sexual positions are given names evocative of those used in Buddhist texts to describe postures for meditation.

1. There is a method called *skylark rising*. The ass is raised in the air like a skylark rising in the sky. Insertion is painless.
2. Always keep "cut plums" on hand in case you want to attempt insertion without saliva.
3. There is a method called *turned-up-soles*. Place the acolyte's legs on your shoulders and penetrate him from the front.
4. There is a method called *reverse drop*. Insertion is from above the turtle's tail, and should be accomplished gradually.
5. There is a method called *summer moat*. Press the boy's ass to the moat of your belly as you enter. The method is painless, even for a young acolyte.
6. There is a method called *dry insertion*. Moisten only slightly with saliva, then penetrate. The method causes severe pain.
7. The method for initiation is called *tearing the hole*. In this method, a man with a large penis penetrates in one thrust without lubrication. The method causes severe pain.

---

[14]The sense here is obscure.

Conclusion

In the conclusion, the author attributes the teachings in *Kōbō Daishi's Book* to Kūkai himself, conveyed to him as a reward for his religious devotion. That attribution is the central legitimizing fact of the book. The postscript to the main manuscript consists of three popular beliefs about boy love that have parallels in beliefs about women: that women with small mouths were amorous, and that facial features gave clues to the shape of a woman's genitals.

> I received this book of secret teachings from the founder of boy love in Japan, Kōbō Daishi, under the condition that I not show it to anyone. Signed Mitsuo Sadatomo, a hermit in Satsuma Fief.
>
> 1. An acolyte with a tiny mouth is best. They say that those with large mouths do not have tight asses.
> 2. It is best if the ass is slightly reddish in color. A dull ass may contain feces.
> 3. One look at a boy's face will tell you what his ass looks like.
>
> I have taken the liberty of adding the above three lines. Submitted with humble respect by Mitsuo Sadatomo, in the third year of Keichō [1598], third month, a felicitous day.

Kōbō Daishi's Book bears the date 1598, well before the Genroku era (1688–1703) when books on sexuality were tinged with irony. Although not meant to be read ironically, the book nevertheless foreshadows the more modern Genroku approach to sex in the playfulness that comes through in certain passages. One such passage appears in the book's introduction: "The love of boys began in olden times when Kōbō Daishi made a vow of love with Wen Zhou. Sentient Being (*shujō*) refers to a man and boy who fall in love with each other, become fast friends, and make a vow of brotherly love; the phenomenon is recorded in many books. Because Kōbō Daishi began the practice of this way of love, it has been preserved all these years and continues to the present day in both Japan and abroad."

Sentient Beings (*shujō*) is a proper Buddhist term referring to all living things, but here it is defined as the love of boys (*shudō*). The confusion of the two terms may have been meant to elicit a laugh from the book's readers. If that is the case, what necessitated this linguistic inventiveness? The use of religious language and symbols in *Kōbō Daishi's Book* may represent not just religious heterodoxy but a challenge directed at a society defined by Confucian ethical constructs that discouraged sexual activity as socially disruptive in all but its most conventional forms.

A MONGREL "ESSAYS IN IDLENESS"

The title of the vernacular prose text known as *A Mongrel "Essays in Idleness"* makes reference to a very famous 14th-century collection of writings on philosophical and aesthetic matters called *Essays in Idleness* (*Tsurezure-gusa*; tr. Donald Keene, 1967) by Yoshida Kenkō (ca. 1283–ca. 1352). *Essays in Idleness* was one of the most highly admired and widely imitated examples of classical prose in the Japanese language, and it continued to exert its influence on the structure and style of numerous vernacular prose texts (*kana-zōshi*) throughout the Edo period (1600–1868). The fact that our text calls itself a "mongrel" *Essays in Idleness* (*Inu tsurezure*; *inu* means dog in Japanese) suggests that our text is consciously situated outside of the high courtly tradition to which the original *Essays in Idleness* belonged, and is more in tune with the marginal world of unorthodox discourses such as comic linked verse (*haikai*) and vernacular prose that flourished in Japan's urban centers in the 17th century.

A Mongrel "Essays in Idleness" is not a parody of the classical text, however. It is a serious and admiring attempt to apply the aesthetics and philosophy of the original work to the experience of male love in the early years of the 17th century. The author is a man of advanced years who reflects on his experience as a lover of youths (and as one beloved of other men in his own youth) in the same nostalgic and sentimental manner employed by the 14th-century Yoshida Kenkō. The author's reflections on the love of youths are imbued with an awareness of Buddhist thought, and in several sections he reveals his familiarity with the legend of Kūkai as the originator of male love in Japan. The first of these is in chapter eight, the relevant portion of which is translated here.

> Love reveals itself in different ways appropriate to every area of human experience, but nowhere is it expressed as deeply as in the way of boy love. A single night of love, even when the pleasure lasts but the briefest of moments, is enough to make memories that will be with a man until the day he dies. The pen is inadequate to express the nature of a love so deep. Even poetry fails. Boy love was apparently unknown in the period of the Nara emperors [Nara was the capital of Japan from 645–794], but the story has been passed down from generation to generation that Kūkai introduced it to our country, and that when Narihira was still a youth going by the name Mandara, Kūkai loved him and made him his disciple.

The association of Kūkai, who died at his Shingon temple complex on Mt. Kōya in 835, with Ariwara no Narihira, who was born in the new capital of Heian in 825, is historically utterly implausible. It has force as legend, however, because of Narihira's reputation as a man of extraordinary physical beauty. The legend of Narihira was developed in part in the 10th-century literary work *Tales of Ise*, and was picked up and developed further by numerous writers in subsequent centuries, sometimes in relation to male love. *A Mongrel "Essays in Idleness"* reveals, then, the intersection of two legends: that Kūkai introduced male love to Japan, and that Narihira was beloved by men in his youth, and loved youths as a man. The conflation of the two legends suggests that the author of our text was not so much interested in recording historical fact but in creating an aura of legitimacy for male love through reference to the hallowed names of Kūkai and Narihira.

Chapter thirteen of *A Mongrel "Essays in Idleness,"* translated here in full, tells of events on Mt. Kōya that indirectly conjure the validating image of Kūkai with regard to male love.

> Women are strictly forbidden from entering Mt. Kōya. Not even female plants will grow there, and no female birds or animals are to be found within its precincts. I have heard that dogs, too, practice boy love on the mountain. When one male dog is in love with another, it will save some of the food given to it by the monks to share with it later. This was told me by someone who had observed such cases with his own eyes. Such devotion between male dogs is exemplary. I wonder if even mankind is capable of a devotion so true.

It is tempting for us to read the above passage about "boy love" between male dogs as ironic, but the author and his contemporary readers probably saw in it genuine evidence that nature (at least as nature manifested itself in the specially charged environment of Mt. Kōya) exhibited examples of their way of love. The passage may have struck them as humorous, but its purpose was to suggest the ubiquity and legitimacy of male love, a love that linked all species of plant, bird, and animal with humankind in the special zone blessed by Kūkai and known as the temple complex of Mt. Kōya.

WILD AZALEAS

Wild Azaleas was the first collection of homoerotic poetry and prose in Japan, compiled in 1667 by Kitamura Kigin (1624–1705), scholar and adviser to the ruling Tokugawa shoguns. Most of the poems in the collection are addressed by priests to their acolyte lovers. The title comes from the opening poem, thought to be the first homoerotic poem in Japan, which appeared originally as an anonymous love poem in the tenth-century imperial anthology, *Kokinshū*.[15]

> My stony silence
> recalls the wild azaleas
> of Mt. Tokiwa:
> you cannot know of my love—
> but how I long to meet you!

[15]Translated in H. C. McCullough, *Kokin Wakashū: The First Imperial Anthology of Japanese Poetry* (Stanford, Calif.: Stanford University Press, 1985), p. 115.

Kigin attributes this anonymous poem to Shinga Sōzu, one of Kūkai's ten major disciples who carried on the True Word tradition after Kūkai's death. Kigin's attribution is based on a fourteenth century commentary by Kitabatake Chikafusa (1293–1354), *Kokinshū-chū*, containing oral traditions about *Kokinshū* from the Nijō and Fujiwara court families and other sources. It is generally recognized that many anonymous poems in Japan's imperial anthologies were listed as such to conceal the identity of the poet. It therefore is a remote possibility that Kigin's attribution is based on knowledge of the true circumstances of the poem's composition. Far more likely, however, is the possibility that the poem's connection with Shinga Sōzu was a later invention.

Preface

Kigin's preface to *Wild Azaleas* is of great interest for the insight it provides into the way the connection between Buddhism and male love was conceptualized by at least one seventeenth century scholar.

> To take pleasure in a beautiful woman has been in the nature of men's hearts since the age of male and female gods, but for a man to take pleasure in the beauty of another man goes against nature. Nevertheless, as relations between the sexes were forbidden by the Buddha, priests of the law—being made of neither stone nor wood—had no recourse but to practice the love of boys as an outlet for their feelings. Just as the waters that plummet and flow below the pass at Tsukubané form the deep pools of the Mino River, so this form of love proved to be deeper than the love between men and women. It afflicts the heart of aristocrat and warrior alike. Even the mountain dwellers who cut brushwood have learned of its pleasures. This form of love is rarely celebrated in Japanese poetry, however. Perhaps the first poem to do so was the one in *Kokinshū* by Kūkai's disciple, Shinga. This poem made the nature of male love apparent to the world, like a tassle of pampas grass waving in the wind, so that even the uninitiated learned of its existence.

For our purposes, the most interesting point made in the preface is the connection between the supposed origins of male homosexuality in Japan and the Buddha's injunction forbidding priests to have sexual relations with women. It gives evidence of a generous view of human sexual need in the Japanese religious tradition, that "need"—in the unnatural situation where relations with the opposite sex are forbidden—supersedes the "natural" legitimacy of male and female relations. Whether physical necessity is enough to explain why priests became enamoured of boys is an issue that will be discussed in the following section, where Saikaku's stories suggest that more is involved in the love of boys rather than just deprivation. By the seventeenth century, men may have entered the Buddhist priesthood because they were predisposed to the love of boys, the complete reverse of Kigin's vision.

THE GREAT MIRROR OF MALE LOVE

Ihara Saikaku (1624–1693) was known for most of his life as a poet of comic linked verse (*haikai*), but in the last ten years of his life he turned to prose and became Japan's first commercial writer. His works are now ranked among the classics of Japanese literature. In 1687, he published a book called *The Great Mirror of Male Love*, a collection of forty short stories idealizing romantic relations between men and boys in samurai and merchant class circles. The introductory chapter of the book recounts the history of male love in Japan. Because Saikaku's purpose was to entertain his readership, he was inventive in his account. At one point he makes reference to the Kūkai legend: "Kōbō Daishi did not preach the profound pleasures of this love outside the monasteries because he feared the extinction of humankind. No doubt he foresaw the popularity of boy love in these last days of the law."[16]

Saikaku took the legend of Kūkai and made it relevant outside the Buddhist tradition by claiming that Kūkai originally suppressed knowledge of male love except in Japan's monasteries and temples because the time was not yet ripe for universal dissemination of its secrets; he foresaw that male love would gain followers and be better suited to the "last days of the law" (*mappō*), the period of degeneration and decline heralding the end of the world, when the impending extinction of humankind made sexual procreation a moot issue. What more fitting form of sexuality for a doomed age—Saikaku seems to suggest—than nonprocreative love between men and boys? Saikaku's readership must have enjoyed the bold humor of this claim.

The Great Mirror of Male Love contains several detailed depictions of Buddhist priests and monks involved in homosexual relations with boys. The second story in the collection, "The ABCs of Boy Love" (1.2), is the story of Daikichi and Shinnosuké, two boys who "were always side by side, inseparable as two trees grafted together or a pair of one-winged birds. When the boys later reached their peak of youthful beauty, men and women, clergy and layman alike, were all smitten with the handsome youths. The two were the cause of a thousand sorrows, a hundred illnesses, and untold deaths from lovesickness."[17] The narrative continues with a brief but fascinating passage about the effect of their beauty on a certain Buddhist monk.

---

[16]Schalow, *The Great Mirror of Male Love*, p. 56.
[17]Ibid., p. 61.

At about this time, there lived in the far reaches of Shishigatani a Buddhist ascetic who was over eighty years old. They say that from the moment he chanced to see these two splendid boys, his concentration on future salvation failed him and the good deeds he had accumulated in previous incarnations went to naught. News of the priest's feelings reached the boys. Not sure which of them the old gentleman had his heart set on, both went to his crude abode for a visit. Predictably, he found it impossible to dispense with either cherry blossoms or fall foliage. Thus, he satisfied with both of them the love he had harbored from spring through autumn.

The next day, both boys paid another visit to the priest, for there was something they had neglected to tell him, but he was nowhere to be found. They discovered only a poem, dated the previous day, tied to a forked branch of bamboo:

> Here are travel weeds
> Tear-stained like my faithless heart
> Torn between the two;
> I shall cut my earthly ties
> And hide myself away in bamboo leaves.

Of what was this old priest ashamed? Long ago, the priest Shinga Sōjō wrote:

> Memories of love revive,
> Like wild azaleas bursting into bloom
> On Mt. Tokiwa;
> My stony silence only shows
> How desperately I want you!

The boys took the bamboo branch and had a skilled artisan make it into a pair of flutes.[18]

The juxtaposition of these two poems and the implication of guilt suggests an interpretation of their meaning. The first poem represents the parting words of an old monk who consummated his love for the boys, whereas the second poem is by a priest who denied himself even the expression of his love in words. There is deliberate ambiguity in the line "torn between the two" in the first poem; does it refer to the choice between two boys, or the choice between earthly and spiritual concerns? The poem states that the conflict has caused the monk to vow to sever his ties with the world—a vow first made when he originally took the tonsure—and live in seclusion. It implies that he was ashamed by his failure to concentrate on spiritual concerns. But that failure ultimately led to the renewal of his vow and represents a triumph of sorts. The positive outcome is typical of the literary tradition of Acolyte Tales (*chigo monogatari*) dating from the Muro-

---

[18]Ibid.

machi period (1392–1568).[19] The old ascetic's faithless heart in the first poem contrasts dramatically with the other priest's faithfulness to his vows in the second poem. Shinga's heart—if the poem is indeed by Shinga Sōjō—burns in silence, unconsummated but guiltless. Ironically, unspoken passion may be the greater sin of the two, for unresolved lust is among the most powerful earthly ties in Buddhism. By sinning, the old priest achieves a spiritual renewal that eludes the second poet. Perhaps that is why Saikaku asks, "Of what was this old priest ashamed?"

In "The Sword That Survived Love's Flames" (3.3), Saikaku's narrative tells the story of two traveling companions on their way to worship at Mt. Kōya, Kūkai's seat of spiritual power. Along the way, they observe the following:

> [A] priest who looked as if he might be in charge of one of Mt. Kōya's temples came by with a young cowherd from one of the temple-owned farm villages. He had obviously tried to disguise the boy as a temple acolyte, but dirt was plainly visible behind the boy's ears. His hair was properly bound up, but it looked reddish and dry. The sleeves of his plain, light-blue hemp robe were far too short; it seemed to be an adult's round-sleeved robe slit under the arms to make him look boyish. He sported a pair of long swords, no doubt consigned to the temple by a parishioner in mourning. The sword guards were too big for the small hilts. The boy slouched under their unaccustomed weight as he walked along in the priest's tow. The men watched them pass, impressed with the priest's ingenuity.[20]

The humor in this passage derives from the priest's not entirely successful attempt to disguise a farmboy as an acolyte so that he can smuggle the boy into his temple quarters. The majority of temple acolytes would have been of samurai or aristocratic birth, making it difficult for a farmboy to resemble them. His hair lacked the luster of a samurai boy's well-groomed and oiled hair; he was unaccustomed to the weight of a sword, something samurai always carried; and as he already was too old to wear the open-vented sleeves of an adolescent boy, slits had to be cut in the sleeves of his own adult robe so he would look like a younger man. Saikaku was writing primarily for an urban merchant-class audience, who would have enjoyed making fun of the Buddhist clergy. The humor is directed not at the priest's taste for boys, which Saikaku's readers shared, but at the duplicity involved in smuggling a young man into the temple for sexual purposes. Saikaku's concern is not to moralize, but to draw attention to the hypocrisy in much of human behavior, and he does so to great effect.

---

[19]For a discussion of Acolyte Tales, see M. H. Childs, "*Chigo Monogatari:* Love Stories or Buddhist Sermons?" *Monumenta Nipponica* 35, no. 2 (Summer 1980): 127–151.

[20]Schalow, *The Great Mirror of Male Love*, p. 139.

Saikaku reserves his most scathing depiction of hypocrisy in the clergy for the latter half of *The Great Mirror of Male Love*, where he deals with boy prostitution in the kabuki theater. Although merchant-class men can properly engage kabuki actors for prostitution without breaking any vows, priests who do so are branded as wayward for their failure to abandon sexual pleasures. In "A Huge Winecup Overflowing with Love" (6.1), Saikaku opens the narrative with biting sarcasm.

> They say that Buddhist priests are "scraps of wood" purged of all feeling, but there is no occupation more pleasant in the world. They can hold parties in their temples whenever they please, their only duties to intone the *sūtras* of their sects and don robes when meeting parishioners. Rather than waste the offerings of the faithful on things without meaning, they use the money to buy the love of young actors, entertainment well suited to the priest's lot.
>
> Even when entertaining boys in their rooms, they never once forget the gravity of their vows and adhere religiously to their vegetarian diet of stewed dumplings and mushrooms, chilled chestnuts with silvervine pickled in miso, and clear soup of sweet seaweed and salted plums. With these delicacies they extend their drinking bouts through the long nights. (How they can drink!) Such sincere devotion to their vows is highly commendable. Just because they do not suffer Buddha's immediate divine punishment does not mean chief priests can go ahead and enjoy the meat of fish and fowl. After all, if priests could indulge in fish and women to their hearts' content, it would be foolish for a man not to take the tonsure![21]

The preceding passage sets a humorous tone in a story about a boy actor, Itō Kodayū. Condemnation of priests for humorous effect is not uncommon in Saikaku's narratives. In an earlier narrative, Saikaku went so far as to blame priests of the wealthy Rinzai sect for inflating the price of boy prostitutes. "Tears in a Paper Shop" (5.1) begins with a brief history of boy prostitution in the kabuki theater, the major features of which are historically accurate, though his comments about priests are difficult to verify.

> [O]ne year wealthy priests assembled in the capital from all over the country to commemorate the 350th anniversary of the death of Zen Master Kanzan, first rector of Myōshin-ji. After the religious services were over, they went sightseeing at the pleasure quarter on the dry riverbed. They fell in love with the handsome youths there, the likes of which they had never seen in the countryside, and began buying them up indiscriminately without a thought for their priestly duties. Any boy with forelocks who had eyes and a nose on his face was guaranteed to be busy all day.
>
> Since that time, boy actors have continued to sell themselves in two shifts, daytime and nighttime. The fee for a boy who was appearing onstage rose to one piece of silver. The priests did not care about the cost, since they had only a short

---

[21]Ibid., pp. 219–220.

time to amuse themselves in the capital. But their extravagance continues to cause untold hardship for the pleasure-seekers of our day.[22]

Saikaku's narrator expresses resentment of the priests for making boy actors too expensive for local men to afford as prostitutes, a perspective that would have appealed to Saikaku's merchant-class readers. The Rinzai sect, of which Kanzan Egen (d. 1359) was a major spiritual leader, was known as a wealthy one, so its priests could have afforded actor's fees more easily than most. Priests from less well-to-do sects often went to extreme lengths to pay for their nights of love. Saikaku records some of their methods in "Love's Flame Kindled by a Flint Seller" (5.3.).

> At his appointments, Sennojō entertained with a slight flush of wine on his cheeks, pale red like maple leaves in autumn. One look could drive a man mad with desire. Wayward priests from Takao, Nanzen-ji, and Tōfuku-ji, not to mention myriad other temples, sometimes sold entire collections of calligraphy passed down for generations in their temples, whereas others cut down and sold whole forests of trees and bamboo under temple jurisdiction, all for the sake of acquiring the love of this boy. Afterwards they were invariably thrown out of their temples with nothing but an umbrella to hide their shame.[23]

If there were those, as the preceding passage suggests, who were driven from Buddhist orders for the sake of boy love, there also were those who joined Buddhist orders for the same reason. One such example appears in "Bamboo Clappers Strike the Hateful Number" (7.4). In the story, a group of young actors and their patrons are on an excursion to pick mushrooms in Fushimi, outside the capital of Kyoto. They come upon an isolated hut in the hills and look inside. It is the home of a recluse monk.

> Inside, the walls were papered at the base with letters from actors. Their signatures had been torn off and discarded. Curious, the boys looked more closely and discovered that each letter concerned matters of love. Each was written in a different hand, the parting messages of kabuki boy actors. The monk who lived there must once have been a man of some means, they thought. He apparently belonged to the Shingon sect, for when they opened the Buddhist altar they found a figure of Kōbō Daishi adorned with chrysanthemums and bush clover, and next to it a picture of a lovely young actor, the object no doubt of this monk's fervent devotion.
>
> When they questioned him, the monk told them about his past. As they suspected, he was devoted body and soul to the way of boy love.
>
> "I was unhappy with my strict father and decided to seclude myself in this mountain hermitage. More than two years have passed, but I have not been able to forget about boy love even in my dreams." The tears of grief he wept were

---

[22]Ibid., p. 190.
[23]Ibid., p. 204.

enough to fade the black dye of his priestly robes. Those who heard it were filled with pity for him.[24]

This passage indicates the strong hold that the legend of Kūkai must have had on the imaginations of both Saikaku and his readers. It suggests that there was a strong positive association between Buddhist tradition, particularly in the True Word sect, and male love. The association of True Word Buddhism with male love stemmed in part from its condemnation of sexual relations with women, in part because of its emphasis on the personal transmission of secret teachings from master to pupil, something that apparently led to strong emotional bonds between priests and their acolytes. Finally, because of the strong Confucian orthodoxy that discouraged overly personal visions of self and society, it was perhaps natural that the esoteric religious tradition and its founder in Japan, Kūkai, be rediscovered and, in a sense, reinvented in the seventeenth century as a social heterodoxy legitimizing the sexuality of men in the urban merchant class. Only further study clarifying the complex blend of social, religious, and sexual issues at play in the Kūkai legend will allow us to answer why this component of the Japanese Buddhist tradition of male love had such an impact on secular life and literature in the seventeenth century.[25]

---

[24] Ibid., p. 268.

[25] An earlier version of this article appeared under the title "Kūkai and the Tradition of Male Love in Japanese Buddhism" in *Buddhism, Sexuality and Gender*, edited by José Ignacio Cabezón (Albany, N.Y.: State University of New York Press, 1992), pp. 215–230.

Spiritual Dimensions of Male Beauty in Japanese Buddhism

Paul Gordon Schalow

MALE LOVE AS THE EXPERIENCE OF BUDDHIST MUTABILITY

During the 17th century in Japan, male writers of the samurai class produced a number of texts on the topic of male homosexual love. Male love as practiced by the samurai involved an adult man's love of a samurai youth. The sexual and emotional relationship conformed to a social construct called *shudô*, "the way of the youth," and 17th-century texts treating *shudô* defined both prescriptively and descriptively the nature of the man-youth relationship. These texts belonged to a genre of colloquial literature called *kana-zôshi*, books written in vernacular Japanese and employing a minimum of classical Chinese characters or locutions. One important characteristic of the genre, no matter what the topic, was that the books were meant to exhort and educate readers in moral behavior and, especially, the Confucian virtues.

The text translated here is unusual because it is Buddhist-inspired. The title is *The Record of Heartfelt Friends* (*Shin'yûki*, 1643).[1] The "heartfelt friend" (*shin'yû*) was the youthful lover in a man-youth relationship, *shin'yû* standing in juxtaposition to *nen'yû* (or *nenja*), the adult partner. The title thus suggests that the lessons contained in the book were primarily intended for the edification of samurai youths. The term "heartfelt friend" was apparently not a familiar one to most people of the day, for when a second edition of the book appeared in 1661, it was retitled *Tales of the Way of the Youth (Shudô monogatari)*, employing the more familiar term *shudô*.[2] In any case, the appearance of a second edition speaks for the book's contemporary importance as a guide to the intricacies of "the way of the youth."

The Record of Heartfelt Friends takes the form of a Buddhist catechism in question/answer format, in which an enlightened master guides youths

---

PAUL GORDON SCHALOW's biographical note can be found on page 91.

[1]*Shin'yûki* is discussed in English briefly in Watanabe Tsuneo and Iwata Jun'ichi, *The Love of the Samurai: A Thousand Years of Japanese Homosexuality* (London: Gay Men's Press, 1989), pp. 110–111, where the title is translated "Book for the friends of the soul"; and in Ihara Saikaku, *The Great Mirror of Male Love* (Stanford: Stanford University Press, 1990), pp. 6–7.

[2]Noma Kôshin, ed. *Kinsei shikidô ron, Nihon shisô taikei* (Tokyo: Iwanami Shoten, 1976), pp. 60 and 379.

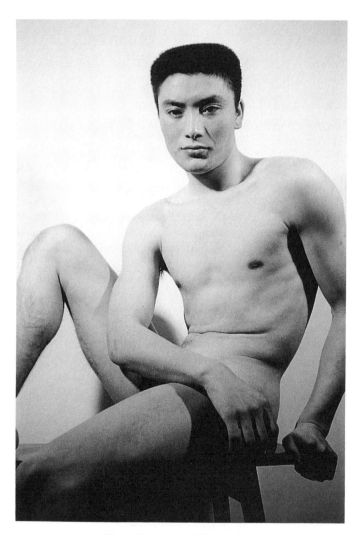

Photo Courtesy of *Barazoku*

in the proper practice of "the way of the youth" by responding to their questions. The master's teachings can be summarized as follows: A man's lust for a youth is an expression of his appreciation of the mutability of adolescent male beauty. A youth's beauty attains metaphysical meaning when he responds to and relieves the lust his beauty generates in a man. The youth's ability to respond to a man is evidence of responsive love (*nasake*). Responsive love exists due to positive karmic virtue accrued from previous lives, and its exercise contributes in turn to "good" karma in the youth's future incarnations. Together, the man's lust and youth's relief of it serve as a form of Buddhist spiritual experience of mutability (*mujô*) and karmic destiny. To cynical modern ears this formula sounds self-serving and manipulative of youths, but to its original readership in the cultural and spiritual milieu of 17th-century Japan, the text represented a sincere explanation of the principles at work in the dynamic of love between man and youth.

DESCRIPTION OF THE CATECHISM, PARTS ONE AND TWO

Part One of *The Record of Heartfelt Friends* begins with the master's soliloquy, describing his retirement from the vulgar world in search of the meaning of human existence. The master identifies the human heart as the source of all suffering and pain, and argues that our lives will only improve if "compassion (*jihi*) and love (*nasake*) are held in the highest regard by all people, from the ruler down to the common man." Buddhist compassion and love are directly equated, in typical syncretic fashion to the five Confucian virtues: brotherhood, righteousness, ceremony, wisdom, and trust.

After thus establishing the preeminence of compassion and love, the master begins instruction on the nature of sexual love. He states that all human beings, male or female, priest or layman, are subject to sexual desire; this is a core truth of the human situation that simply cannot be escaped or denied. Given this fact, the master argues that satisfaction of desire is essential to human mental and emotional health. Those who suffer for the sake of love are described as superior to those who are unable to love, or who determine whom to love on the basis of the status of their would-be lover. To illustrate this last problem, the master introduces the cases of two remarkably handsome young men, one from China named Yü-hsin (dates unknown) and one from Japan named Noritoki (13th century), who lacked compassion and love in their dealings with the men who fell in love with them. In both cases, the cold-hearted youths were killed by the vengeful spirits of the men they spurned.

Here in the text, a question is interjected from a youth who asks why some youths such as Yü-hsin and Noritoki are, despite their physical beauty, incapable of responsive love. The master explains that these youths cannot love because they possess an unresponsive, cold-hearted nature, and he compares them to lovely flowers that lack fragrance. He also states that a youth with physical deformities is born that way as retribution for his unloving ways in a previous incarnation, and warns that handsome but unloving youths will suffer a similar fate.

But the youth questioning the master is not willing to place all of the blame on youths for being unresponsive in love, and suggests that sometimes a boy with the sincerest intentions will be misunderstood by an uncouth, insensitive man and will end up being accused of lacking love. The master dismisses this suggestion as highly unlikely. It is his opinion that such misunderstandings are relatively rare, and that reputations for cold-heartedness are usually deserved by the youths who acquire them.

The young questioner is not content to accept this, however, but responds by shifting the blame for cold-heartedness from youths onto adult men. The master objects to this strategy with a quote (actually, spurious) from Japan's greatest literary masterpiece, *The Tale of Genji*, to the effect that "love given to even the most ill-bred, insensitive man is not wasted," but the youth counters that *The Tale of Genji* is about heterosexual love (the love of women), not about homosexual love (the love of youths), and therefore the quote is inapplicable. The master disagrees vehemently: "If loving women is the only way of love, then how can 'the way of the youth' also be the way of love?" To prove his point, he lists past Chinese and Japanese examples of male love that illustrate the benefits of love between a man and a youth. He concludes that ancient precedent proves that it is proper for a youth to respond to a man's affections, for otherwise his youthful beauty is wasted. Part One concludes with a final injunction to samurai youths to be loving in their dealings with men:

> Evil does not cause evil only for others, neither does love benefit only others. It all circles back to become love directed at oneself. If a man tells you that he loves you, show your mastery of the rectitude of love and avoid error by returning his love, regardless of his status; thus should the heart [of a youth] be trained.

Part Two begins with a description of the flawed characters of some youths, based on seven types of "hearts" that they possess. There is the "merciless heart" of youths who reject a man's advances; the "vacillating heart" of youths who lead a man on but never commit themselves to love him; the "heart lacking Buddha-Nature" of youths who dare to criticize their male lover behind his back; the "heart of the Six Ways," belonging to youths who want to respond but are afraid of what others will say; the "greatly vacillating heart" of youths who make a vow of love with two men; the "thoughtless heart," belonging to youths who inform their lover of an interloper's identity, thus obliging him to engage in a duel to the death with the man; and the "heart calling at the gate," belonging to youths who become attached to a man but do not form a sexual relationship with him. The cure for all these character flaws, according to the master, is simple: "Youths ought to study 'the way' obediently and carefully."

The master then defines the stages of youth as a period of nine years from ages twelve to twenty, divided into three intervals of three years each. These intervals are compared to the three periods of time (*sansei*) codified in Buddhist metaphysics: past, present, and future. In the first stage, to age fifteen, the youth is still a child in need of instruction in "the way." This period is called the past. The next three years are called the present, when a youth's beauty is at its peak and he learns to love through proper training of his heart and mind. The final three years from age eighteen are called the future, when a youth matures and prepares for adulthood by further training himself in manly conduct. The master further develops the idea of karmic retribution for good and evil deeds, firmly placing the bond of man-youth love in the category of good deeds. Nevertheless, the meaning of the bond is primarily in the lesson of life's mutability that it teaches. The master concludes the catechism with a standard litany of Buddhist truth, that life is brief, that every meeting concludes in separation, that every gain leads to eventual loss. The book ends with a poem reiterating the theme that love and compassion alone have the power to redeem an otherwise unredeemably sorrowful existence.

TRANSLATION:
THE RECORD OF HEARTFELT FRIENDS (SHIN'YŪKI, 1643)[3]

Part One

I decided to pursue the way of the retired mountain hermit and spend my time reflecting on the world in which we live. First, it is obvious that the present life is an abode of dreams and illusions. In the course of our lives in this abode of dreams and illusions, the hearts of all people—highborn and lowborn alike—are beset by many unexpected sorrows and joys, and by order and chaos. How difficult it is to perceive the principle underlying this state of constant flux. Order and chaos in the heart originates from whether one's heart achieves intimacy with the hearts of others, or whether it fails to achieve such intimacy; thus, there is no other explanation but that all things proceed from the heart. Is that not what Tu Mu-zi meant when he wrote in *Ode of A-Fang Palace*, "The heart of one man is the heart of all men"?[4] Truly, is it not obvious that the source of grief and joy, order

---

[3]Translation based on the annotated, modern print version of the text in Noma, pp. 7–25. Paragraph breaks follow Noma.

[4]Ode written upon viewing the burned ruins of the imperial palace, built by the First Emperor of Chin.

and chaos in one man's heart is the same for all men? In this regard, it seems to me that if we neglect the teachings of the sages and fail to emphasize compassion and love in our lives, we invite not only the destruction of our households but also certain death. Now, in China there were Chieh of the Hsia Dynasty and King Chou of the Shang Dynasty,[5] and in our country there was Governor Taira no Masatoki,[6] who knew nothing of the way of compassion and love: as a result, they lost their kingdoms and shortly thereafter even lost their lives.

Compassion and love alone ought to be practiced by all people throughout society, from the supreme ruler at the top to the common-folk below. Those who know nothing of compassion are in no way different from dogs and horses. [The five Confucian virtues of] brotherhood, righteousness, ceremony, wisdom, and trust are none other than [Buddhist] compassion and love. Again, it was the Buddha who taught that "He who has love will reach paradise, but the evil man will enter the cycle of rebirth." When you think of it, our bodies do not survive for long in this floating world. We resemble only withered blossoms before the wind, or ice in sunlight. Now, there are examples both in China and in our country, from ancient times to the present day, of poets and songsters who have written of life as "a floating world of dreams" and "a temporary shelter." There is even an old song that goes:

> Even were I to live as long again
> as I have lived till now,
> brief it would be,
> yes, how brief it would be.

This song is so true.

Nevertheless, though we may be enlightened to the brevity of our lives, we continue to mingle with the dust of this profane world, and thus it seems that our hearts are easily tempted into evil. This is because there are two diseases that afflict humankind. Evil has many manifestations, or so they say, but desire and lust is always its source. How can priest or layman, man or woman, rest undisturbed? First, to begin with no one can look at sexual beauty without being captivated by it. Now, then, if the feelings that arise are not satisfied, they torment the body in the form of a thousand griefs and a hundred diseases; some people are even driven to madness. Truly, the hearts of such people must be filled with pain, and therefore it is proper to respond warmly with love. Now, then, there are those who are

[5]The names Chieh and Chou, last rulers of the Hsia and Shang Dynasties respectively, are used as a synonym for tyranny. From *Shi chi*.

[6]Unknown. Possibly a mistaken reference to the regent Taira no Kiyomori, whose political demise and death is the subject of the 13th century *Tale of the Heike (Heike monogatari)*.

incapable of love. And again, there are those who distinguish [whom to love] on the basis of status or wealth. Can this be called brotherhood? I have heard it said that "[A] gentleman makes no distinction on the basis of status or wealth," so, therefore, such youths will experience nothing good beyond the grave.

In general, there are numerous cases in both Japan and China of handsome youths incapable of love. In T'ang China there was a handsome youth named Yü-hsin whose beauty was without equal in the more than four-hundred provinces of T'ang China. Truly, it is said that "those who saw him extinguished their souls, and those who heard news of him bent their ears [for more]." Nevertheless, this youth knew nothing of the way of compassion and love. For this reason, a certain poet wrote *Ode Decrying Coldheartedness* and placed it outside the youth's gate, blaming him on his lack of love. Yü-hsin did not heed the accusation, but continued anew each month and grew worse each day in his evil-hearted, mistaken way. As a result, due—no doubt—to the resentment of innumerable [men], he suddenly went mad in the spring of his sixteenth year and ended up wandering throughout the provinces and villages of the land, exposing himself to ridicule. He finally died in a place called Yang Zhou. Not one [of the men] felt the slightest regret at his death but, on the contrary, rejoiced. "They say that 'resentment can shatter boulders,' so its effect on the human body is only natural." Again, the story has been told for generations and is well known even today that Sô-fun, Lord of Yang Zhou, composed a poem on the occasion of passing Yü-hsin's grave:

> The cold-hearted youth;
> whether right or wrong,
> I feel no sadness seeing Yû-hsin's grave.

In any case, [youths] ought to concentrate exclusively on cultivating compassion and love.

Again, in our own country—was it during the reign of Emperor Kôan? —there was a Lesser Captain of the Left named Noritoki, son of Hino Dainagon Hirotoki. His complexion was like that of a peach blossom awaiting spring, his body like a willow swaying languidly in the breeze, so beautiful that even Mao Shang and Hsi Tzu would have hidden their faces in shame. The emperor favored him above the rest, so his fellow courtiers "waited eagerly for the droppings of the well-fed horse."[7] Everything about Noritoki was so splendid that no man could resist falling in love, from courtiers and nobles all the way down to farmers. Among his admirers was a courtier named Sukéshigé, Middle Captain of the Palace, who

---

[7]An expression indicating others flattered the emperor's favorite in an effort to benefit themselves.

with Noritoki was in attendance to the emperor. Sukéshigé once observed Noritoki up close in the guard's station at the Shishinden Palace, and from that moment he became lovesick and took to his bed. He pondered how [to contact Noritoki], but because he wanted to avoid discovery, he spoke of his feelings to no one. Nevertheless, it is the way of this floating world that feelings unavoidably make themselves known, and [soon] the entire capital was aware of the matter. Sukéshigé thought in his heart, "Well, since my name is the talk of the capital, my feelings must be as obvious as red maple leaves in autumn," and he made up his mind [to confess his love]. He composed a hundred songs in one night and sent them to Noritoki to plead his case, but Noritoki never responded. This was more than Sukéshigé could bear. He soon took to his sickbed, heartbroken, and eventually passed away. His angry spirit would not leave, however, and clung to Noritoki. Noritoki himself took ill and before long, in what was the third week after Sukéshigé's death, he also died.

Question: In any case, if we lack compassion and love, it is clear that there are many cases of retribution of this sort. Particularly in the present day, I have observed many youths, all of whom are equally handsome, like "a single branch of pear blossoms moistened in the spring rain, plum blossoms opening in the snow, or crab-apple blossoms that droop languorously." And yet, there are some youths who lack love. What are we to make of this?

Answer: It is for that reason the *Kokinshû* preface states: "A flower with little fragrance, such is a beauty who lacks love." The comparison may be fitting, but it does not go far enough. A handsome youth who lacks love is mean-spirited, the most undesirable trait in the world. Though there may be large numbers of youths in this floating world, handsome ones are rare and so [they ought to be loving]. Now then, there are those born with physical imperfections due to karma from past lives. These youths, as they reach their prime, will no doubt experience times of shame and moments of sorrow. The emotions generated by their suffering cannot be adequately compared to a mere mountain. As I see it, such youths once possessed great physical beauty in a previous life. As a result, they were desired by many men, but because their hearts were full of evil, the youths failed to comprehend the benefits of love. Finally, their lives came to an end and in the next life they suffered retribution for the seriousness of their sin and were made to endure the suffering of unlimited tortures. In the cycle of rebirth they happened to be reborn as human beings once again but, due to the above obstacle from a past life, were born physically imperfect. Clearly, this is retribution. It goes without saying that a youth so handsome that "a single smile elicits one hundred lusts" yet who lacks a loving heart is lost on the Way of Three Evils. Even if that were not so, is it not the case that he must suffer immediate shame?

Question: But for many youths, it may be a question of rank. What I mean is, imagine that a certain man falls in love with a youth. Then the youth, being exceptional in character, immediately establishes "a relationship of the ox's ear" with the man, and they sign oaths of love. Now then, the lover is also a man of exceptionally tender character, and together they are like Han Yun and Mao Liu. One day, the boy innocently asks, in the course of discussing the qualities of ten varieties of incense, "Please give me a cloth (*kin*) to place under the incense burner." His lover, being of low rank and uncouth, thinks he is referring to gold (*kin*) and later speaks ill of him. "Well now, how crude it is for a youth of his rank to express such greed for gold!" When others hear it, they naturally have no praise for him. He has suffered shame undeservedly. In this regard, I am reminded of Ku Yuan from the kingdom of So who drowned himself in a lake because he was wrongfully accused by his king, though he served his sovereign faithfully. When such uncouth men exist, no matter how much a youth desires to love a man, is he not destined to fail?

Answer: Such cases may exist, but do you suppose there are large numbers of youths in this world as splendid [as Ku Yuan]? Or do you suppose there are large numbers of youths deficient in love? I have given this matter careful thought, and in my experience youths as splendid [as Ku Yuan] are exceedingly rare.

Question: It may be the case that both sides are right, and both are wrong. Be that as it may, do you suppose there are large numbers of male lovers who know the intricacies of "the way of the youth"? Or do you suppose there are large numbers of male lovers who do not know them? In my experience, those who know the intricacies are rare.

Answer: Well, I think it is the Kashiwagi chapter of *The Tale of Genji* where it says that "the way of love defies logic." If you understand that concept, it is only natural that love be given to a man of even the most lowly and uncouth rank.

Question: Is *The Tale of Genji* about "the way of the youth"? I understood that it was Genji's character to love only women. In particular, I have never heard mention of "the way of the youth" in classical times.

Answer: If loving women is the only way of love, then how can "the way of the youth" be the way of love? And how can you say that "the way of the youth" is not talked about in ancient times? Even in olden times in T'ang China, Duke Zhuang of Chêng loved Tzu Tong, Duke Ling of Wei loved Mi-tzu Hsia,[8] King Ai of Wei loved Lord Long Yang,[9] Han [Emperor] Kao Tzu loved Chi Ju, Han Emperor Hui loved Hong Ju. Likewise, Emperor Wu loved Li Yen-nien, Emperor Ai loved Tong Hsian, Emperor

---

[8]Duke Ling of Wei (534–493 B.C.); the relationship is recorded in *Han Fei tzu*. See Bret Hinsch, *Passions of the Cut Sleeve* (Berkeley: University of California Press, 1990), pp. 20–22.

[9]Hinsch, pp. 32–33.

Wen loved Teng T'ong,[10] and Tong P'o loved Chieh Sui.[11]

In our own land, also, in ancient times there was a courtier named Lord Tadashigé of Oku[12] who was the most powerful man in his day. Nevertheless, this man was arrogant and uncouth and knew nothing of the value of love. He despised good deeds and rejoiced over bad ones, practiced evil and avoided good, and was an unspeakably evil man. He had an only son by the name of Prince Shigémitsu. The boy was the opposite of his father in every way, from childhood possessed of a normal heart that rejoiced over good deeds and grieved over evil ones, full of compassion and deeply loving, and now at the age of fourteen he had become a handsome youth whose physical beauty was quite beyond compare. There was in the household a man named Kagémasa, who was remarkably attracted to Prince Shigémitsu's beauty, but due to his own low rank he feared to approach his young lord; try as he might to express his desire to meet, he could not bring himself to speak the words. Thinking that his unhappiness was obvious in the extreme and that his feelings would make themselves known, he merely suffered in silence. Prince Shigémitsu must have heard of the matter, for he immediately made an oath of love with Kagémasa; their lovemaking was "in heaven, two one-winged birds [flying side by side], on earth, two trees with grafted branches," and it goes without saying that the Prince loved him deeply. Nothing could compare with the gratitude in Kagémasa's heart.

A year passed quickly, and since it is the way of this floating world for people to despise the poor and the lowly, when the boy's father, Lord Tadashigé, found out about this matter, he thought "This is the work of that damned Kagémasa," and plotted to have him executed. Kagémasa had no idea of this, but when Prince Shigémitsu heard, he urgently summoned Kagémasa to him and explained the situation. "How I regret this development! Throughout the time of my oath of love with you, you have given me solid advice and loyal service, and your love for me was so great that you would gladly have given your life for me; as a result, I have felt happy and secure. Must I now remain behind in the world and spend my days in lonely sorrow? That you should be executed on my account is especially hard to bear," he said weeping bitterly, distraught that they must say farewell. Kagémasa heard him and said, "I am most grateful for your gracious words. It has been said that 'A samurai dies to prove his loyalty to his lord, but a son does not die to prove his filial piety.' I am but a low-ranking man in my prince's service, and have enjoyed your benevolence and love over and over again for more than a year; I can think of nothing I desire more than to be executed for your sake. If I cannot repay you in this life for the

---

[10]Hinsch, pp. 35–37.

[11]The poet Su Shih (1036–1101), also known as Su Tong P'o, describes his love of Li Chieh Sui in a poem called "The Wind and Water Cave."

[12]Michinoku, the northernmost provinces of Japan making up modern Tôhoku.

kind benevolence you showed me, it will surely be an obstacle to salvation in my next life, and my biggest failing in this one. If I die this very moment, I swear to repay your every kindness, even from the grave.'' He bowed deeply to Prince Shigémitsu and withdrew from his presence, and thereafter acted as if he knew nothing of the matter.

Many men appeared before Lord Tadashigé to receive their sentences of execution. Prince Shigémitsu could not bear it, and again summoned Kagémasa for an audience. ''It seems that you will soon die. Since that is the case, put your life in my hands. Rather than die by the sword of another, let me be the one to slay you so that we may sit side by side on the same lotus leaf in the next world,'' he said, filled with grief, and as he spoke he sank to the floor. Kagémasa's heart was filled with gratitude; he put himself at the mercy of the Prince's sword and, at the age of twenty-five, received his death sentence. Shigémitsu immediately shaved his head and described his feelings in words that he wrote down in great detail and placed next to Kagémasa's corpse; he then set out in search of enlightenment. His parents, who remained behind, were consumed with regret and searched the provinces for their son, but Prince Shigémitsu was nowhere to be found. Overwhelmed by grief, both parents experienced enlightenment. Afterwards, Prince Shigémitsu spent three years engaged in various prayers for the repose of Kagémasa's soul and, at the age of seventeen, jumped to his death. All this occurred because both of his parents were arrogant and uncouth and had no comprehension of the brotherhood and righteousness of love, and thus they lost their only son in this manner. In actual fact, it is said that Monju Bosatsu[13] took human appearance in the form of Prince Shigémitsu. Lord Tadashigé's heart was unenlightened, so Monju took pity on him and, in order to undo his evil deeds and bring him to enlightenment, was born as his son and became the embodiment of the brotherhood and righteousness of love and jumped to his death; just as Monju had hoped, both husband and wife experienced enlightenment and ultimately became river pilots poling the boat of all-wisdom, experiencing true pleasure and escaping from the cycle of rebirth to be reborn in paradise.

The fact that such things occurred in ancient times proves that if a man takes a liking to you, you ought to respond with affection; only then will this floating world of ours function smoothly. It would be wise to ponder this point well. After all, in this floating world that is like a brief dream, here today and gone tomorrow, your peak of youthful beauty lasts but a moment, and you ought not waste even one moment of that beauty while it is yours. There is a poem in Chinese that expresses it this way:

---

[13]*Monju shiri*, was a virtual patron saint of youths loved by men, due to a pun on the name, *shiri* also meaning ''ass.'' Sanskrit: *Mañjú srî bodhisattva*, deity of wisdom.

> Look closely, for youth speeds on;
> Neither can long life be preserved in this world.
> Beauty is not exempt from aging and decay;
> So, love while your looks are fresh.

The period during which men will be attracted to you is but a brief one. Those of you who comprehend the value of love will enter "the special way" in this life, and by avoiding being thought ill of, even if you should die, you will without fail enter the way of truth.

This is exactly what the poem—by Zen master Ikkyû,[14] I think—means when it says,

> Live your life
> looking at the moon
> and gazing at blossoms;
> do not make it a Buddha, or waste it—
> this body of yours.

If we ask what [Ikkyû] meant by writing thus, we see that it is a poem urging all people to train their hearts. "Looking at the moon" means that people with their clouded heart must look to the shining moon for clarity. "Blossoms" are a symbol of those things that you never tire of looking at and that others likewise never tire of looking at. "Gazing at" means that if someone takes a liking to you, on the basis of the benefits of love, you must give him your love and gaze into each other's eyes. "Live your life" means to live life in this uncertain world so as not to be spoken ill of or thought ill of by others. A regular youth of limited intelligence who trains his heart in this way and is well thought of by men in this life will surely enter the way of enlightenment in the next life. "Do not make it a Buddha" means that you must not die having lived your life with an uncommitted heart, being spoken ill of and thought ill of by others. "Or waste it—this body of yours" means that, though someone may have had the rare good-fortune of being born in human form, those in this life who are spoken ill of and thought ill of will surely enter the Path of Three Evils in the next life. This means, if someone fails to enjoy the pleasures of this life, what a waste his life will have been. The entire poem is a command to train yourself in the way of love. Whether highborn or lowborn, poor or rich, old or young, whether bird or beast, none can afford to despise love. And that is not all. An old poem states:

---

[14]Ikkyû Sôjun (1394–1481), a brilliant and eccentric priest, said to have been the illegitimate son of Emperor Go-Komatsu (r. 1392–1412).

> If you cause suffering,
> there will always be retribution;
> no one ever made an enemy
> by being loving.

Evil does not cause evil only for others, neither does love benefit only others. It all circles back to become love directed at oneself. If a man tells you that he loves you, show your mastery of the rectitude of love and avoid error by returning his love, regardless of his status; thus should the heart be trained.

Part Two

Question: All men, being by nature arrogant and uncouth, are ignorant of how to love; at such times, what ought they to do?

Answer: Love is like time: there are some who experience it with knowledge of its way, and others who experience it knowing nothing. To cultivate oneself enough to avoid violating the rules of proper conduct of this floating world does not require a complete grasp of the complexities of the way. Nevertheless, there are those who are completely ignorant of the rules of proper conduct. Among the things they do not know, first and foremost is the failure to distinguish between right and wrong: They use crude language or tell improper stories in front of youths. They lie. They keep silent when they ought to speak out and harbor evil in their hearts without cause. They fail to die when duty requires it and resent others for no reason. They stubbornly refuse to take advice; they alienate people with their pettiness and greed. They are intolerant of social obligations and accuse the innocent of wrong-doing. Though fools, they act as though they know it all. They are unreliable and lacking in cultivation. They forget the obligations they owe and treat their parents with disrespect. They have no compassion or love in their hearts. In general, there are many men of this sort. Their behavior cannot be called proper for a human being. Proper conduct for a human being would be the opposite of each of the items listed above; only then could it be called manly conduct.

To cultivate oneself so as to avoid violating the rules of proper conduct, a youth need not have a complete grasp of the way. Youths need only be obedient in upholding its precepts. For the man in love, depending on the feelings of the youth, his love may turn to joy or it may turn to resentment; thus, some youths distinguish on the basis of high or low rank and use restrained or unrestrained words accordingly. Such actions are caused by what is called a "Merciless Heart," and are a great disgrace. Only by making no distinction between highborn and lowborn and always, in all matters, properly distinguishing right from wrong can love be called a "way."

Sometimes there are youths who, though very handsome, lack a lover. Seeing such a boy, there are occasionally men who fall so deeply in love they are willing to die, but though their feelings are clearly discernible in their eyes, they go on day after day unable to tell the boy how they feel. There are youths who, even when they realize how the man feels, not only refuse to love him, but will criticize the man who loves them. This, too, results from the "Merciless Heart."

Again, there are occasionally youths without lovers who will insist that they have a lover every time they respond to a man's expressions of interest, but when asked for proof they can never provide it. Such an action is caused by what is called a "Vacillating Heart," which is a particularly vulgar condition.

Each of the above problems is the topic of widespread discussion, but there are youths who take no notice whatsoever. No youth, even one who is happy without a lover, should refuse a man who expresses a sincere interest in him. The reason they refuse a man who loves them is because they take his feelings lightly. This man's feelings are the result of karma from a previous life, and once he falls in love his suffering is without respite night and day. No matter how painful the suffering, however, he never thinks ill of the youth. Because he never thinks ill of him, the man considers giving his life for him, and even when gazing at the moon or cherry blossoms, his heart feels no pleasure; it is full of thoughts of the youth. The unbearable suffering he endures cannot be adequately compared to a mountain. Is it possible to justify rejecting a man who is suffering in this way? In general, the human heart can be discerned in a single glance. In particular, the man whose interest is sincere can easily be discerned. Even if the man is an enemy of a youth's father, if the youth judges him to be a man who sincerely loves him, the youth should tell himself that the man picked him out of all the youths in the world because of a karmic bond from a previous life, and be grateful for his loving attention; he should not take the man's feelings lightly, but in all things do everything in his power to please him. If he does so, the man will gladly (as the proverb says) "for a single day of your love, give up one hundred years of life," and the man's happiness will be greater than a mountain. Thereby, he will desire further intimacy. At that time, if the youth somehow finds a way to give himself to the man in a vow of love, so they cultivate their feelings for each other and share three years of intimacy by his side, is it not like a dream within a dream? Not only that, but his good name will live through the ages; but the world being unstable and life brief, it seems that some still think they disgrace themselves if they love a man. There is no misconception as hard to dislodge as this one.

Again, there are occasionally youths with a lover whom they act like they love, but in their hearts they revile him. Such youths possess what is called a "Heart Lacking Buddha-Nature," and are evaluated at the same level as dumb beasts. The reason for this is, once a youth binds himself to a man as his lover, their relationship ought to pattern itself after the relationship between parent and child. That is why, when a boy refers to his lover, he touches his thumb ("parent finger") to his little finger ("child finger"). With a bond as close as that of parent and child, if a child makes light of his parent, can such a youth be called human?

Again, there are youths whose hearts are gentle, but fearing what people might say, they are unable to respond with love. They possess what is called the "Heart of the Six Ways."[15]

Again, sometimes a man will fall in love with a youth who already has a lover, and it reaches the point where they actually meet. When the man cuts his thighs and wrists and vows to kill himself [if the youth refuses him], some youths immediately give their consent. They possess what is called the "Greatly Vacillating Heart." Above all else, it is the single most important precept of "the different way" that once a youth makes a contract with a man, he ought never speak the same vow with another man, even in jest or in his dreams—even for a moment, even if it is a lie, even if the other man actually kills himself.

Sometimes, when a youth who has a lover receives a love letter from another man, he does not consider what is right and wrong, and tells his lover about it. He has what is called a "Thoughtless Heart," which is a tragic waste. No man can idly sit by if he hears that an interloper wants to force himself on the boy he loves. If the lover is kept unaware it need not lead to a confrontation, but being a mere youth, if the youth thoughtlessly tells his lover, it immediately becomes a contest of egos between the lover and the interloper; inevitably in such cases, someone ends up being killed for no reason. Again, a lover ought to constantly train himself to notice such situations without having to be told by someone else. And again, a youth ought to speak freely to his lover regarding questions of proper conduct. It is a mistake, however, to tell the lover something without first considering what is right and wrong.

Even if a youth is approached by a man who is uncouth, he ought not reveal a hint of it to his lover, but should refuse him on the basis of what is right and wrong in love, and if the man is truly, truly ignorant of right and wrong, and threatens to end his life, then the youth ought to write down his thoughts in a final testament and die without regrets. This is what Confucius meant when he said, "It is possible to ask the way in the morning, and be dead by nightfall." The youth's lover who is left behind will be shocked when he hears the news and, gazing at the words in the boy's final testament, will experience true enlightenment and pray for the repose

---

[15]Among the Six Ways of Hell is the way of the hungry ghost, a form of torture in which starving spirits are repeatedly tempted by food, but when they try to eat, the food bursts into flame and is consumed by fire. The analogy is with youths who desire to partake of love with a man but are prevented by scruples.

of the youth's soul for the number of days equivalent to the length of their relationship. And when he reaches the final day of his prayers, in most cases he jumps to his death.

Again, there are times when a youth shares a deep intimacy with a man, but he does not enter the "way of the youth" and the relationship is aborted. This is called "The Heart Calling at the Gate," and deserves punishment as severe as if the youth had incurred the wrath of his father. Taking the preceding points into consideration, youths ought to study "the way" obediently and carefully.

Now, "the way of the youth" lasts for an interval of nine years, from ages twelve to age twenty. That interval is divided into three parts of three years each, which can be likened to the three periods of time: past, present, and future.

The first three years, beginning with age twelve, are the past. During this period the youth is still quite a child, so *shudô* "the way of the youth" is written with the characters *shu* "primary," *dô* "child," and *dô* "way."

The next three years, beginning with age fifteen, can be likened to the present. This is the middle of the nine years of "the way of the youth," when a youth is at his peak. He develops deep respect for the rights and wrongs of love, strives not to go against the way's precepts, and trains himself to apply what he has learned to every aspect of life; unsurpassed in his heart and speech, he is at his peak in this period. For this reason, the word for these three years is written with the characters *koto naru* "being special" and *michi* "way" and is pronounced *shudô*. The meaning of the word "being special" is that the youth is outstanding in both heart and speech.

The next three years from age eighteen can be likened to the future. This is, namely, the interval when "the way of the youth" comes to a conclusion, so training in manly conduct is now added to earlier training in the heart of "the special way," and without wasting a single moment of the precious time remaining to him, the youth must become enlightened in all matters. The reason twenty years customarily represents one generation in human life, and why "the way of the youth" ending in twenty years is referred to as one generation, is all because of this fact. Therefore, the word for these three years is written with the characters for *owaru* "ending" and *michi* "way" and is pronounced *shudô*. In this way, once a youth reaches his twentieth year is it not the case that he will never again possess in this life "the beautiful complexion and figure of a blossom"?

Since the years fly by thus in a moment, for a youth not to love while his beauty is fresh could hardly be appropriate, could it? Some youths may have been born predestined to have only the twenty years mentioned above as their allotted span of life. If such a youth shows no compassion or love and dies at an early age, what will become of him in the world to come? Do not the feelings of tenderness that move a youth to love [a man] remain with him as good deeds after his death? The way this works is, if a youth gives even a little love in his early years, the recipient will remember it for the rest of his life, and likewise others will not forget the debt of gratitude for the love the youth gave long ago, so that never for a moment will he be thought ill of, allowing him to achieve True Buddhahood for his good deeds. But those who show no love in their youth, though they reach adulthood, will plot only evil in their hearts from dawn to dusk. Occasionally, they may put on a show of decency in front of others, but in private they curse and revile blameless men and envy their good deeds. Such people will earn the enmity of everyone they meet, and should they die, the news would be met with rejoicing. Retribution for the grave sin of earning the resentment of others lingers for three cycles of suffering and rebirth.

The Buddha himself taught:

> If for many years
> a man holds evil in his heart,
> and puts on a show of good while cursing the Buddha,
> he earns a boundless burden of sin.[16]

This means that there are both good and evil men living in this world. The hearts of evil men are always resentful of others, but when they meet someone they put on a friendly expression and deceive them with flattering words, while behind their backs they curse and revile good men innocent of any wrongdoing. Such people must bear the burden of a sin too heavy to weigh. Living things, whether human or non-human, are ultimately not divided into good and evil. It is one body that produces good thoughts, and one body that produces evil thoughts, so when we reach the point where we can simply dispense with evil thoughts and train ourselves to have only good thoughts, there we find no division between good and evil. That is why the sutras teach that "The three cycles of suffering and rebirth are based on the heart alone; there is no law outside the law governing the heart."

The heart that gives love is good, and the heart that receives love is also good. But a person who lives twenty years will eventually be beset with the eight sufferings, and he will find that his burden of sin easily grows heavier and becomes harder to relieve. At such a time, our only hope is to become enlightened to the good heart in this temporary dwelling place and to pray for rebirth in paradise. In particular, it is said that "human life is like dew on a morning-glory, here in the morning and gone by nightfall." Moreover, it is clear that life is unpredictable for old and young alike. There is nothing as fleeting as the dwelling place that is this world. For that reason, Li P'o has written:

---

[16]From the *Lotus Sutra*.

> Heaven and earth is a journey home for all things.
> Time is a traveler for a hundred generations.
> This floating world is like a dream;
> How often is pleasure ours to give?

Nevertheless, no one knows what karma he brings from former lives. Perhaps he embraced greed, lived for money, suffered physical pain, and committed serious crimes. People, plants, birds, and beasts all receive, each and every, a life of pleasure or pain determined by karma from past lives. Human beings, however, possess the same body of Buddha nature and are without a doubt capable of achieving Buddhahood through enlightenment in this world. As for the obvious good and evil we see in this world, the good is good from previous lives and the evil is evil from previous lives. Both good and evil are retribution from lives that came before. By observing the present, we can know the future.

In any case, the three cycles of rebirth are filled with suffering. There is no pleasure for any living thing. Our lives in this temporary dwelling place, all phenomena are like a dream. A career is short-lived, and glory comes to an end. We flourish for an hour, and live but an instant. A wife and child become unwelcome bonds, and attachments burden the heart. Lust is the source of suffering, and ambition leads to grief. Where there is life, there is also death. Where there is pleasure, there is also pain. A man in his prime cannot escape decline; those we meet are destined to leave. The body is like a flame before the wind, and life is like dew on the grass. Fleeting is this world, and unreliable are our bodies. "There is no rest in the three worlds of rebirth, like a burning house in which we are trapped." It is exactly as the Buddha teaches. The whole of the law returns to one point:

> The body, the heart.
> If we leave behind
> The darkness of the heart,
> There, is compassion and love.
> The moon at daybreak.

Kan'ei 20 [1643], Eighth Month, an Auspicious Day.[17]

---

[17]The present article appeared originally in *Religion, Homosexuality and Literature*, ed. by Michael L. Stemmeler and José Ignacio Cabezón (Las Colinas: Monument Press, 1992).

II

THE DHARMA AND GAY LIFE IN THE WEST:
PERSONAL ACCOUNTS

Action is being truly observant of your own thoughts, good or bad, looking into the true nature of whatever thoughts may rise, neither tracing the past nor inviting the future, neither allowing any clinging to experiences of joy, nor being overcome by sad situations. In so doing, you try to reach and remain in the state of great equilibrium, where all good and bad, peace and distress, are devoid of true identity.

DUDJOM RINPOCHE

Michael Hyman (left) and Bill Shean, 1996. Photo by Robert Zeballos.

Practicing Together As a Gay Couple

Michael P. Hyman

My oldest remembered experience, felt years before I was aware of any sexuality, is that of a little boy in one of New York's outer boroughs, hurrying many extra blocks out of my way to avoid being bullied or beaten up by the "other" boys. I never knew or asked myself why I should have been so afraid, why I felt so different. Growing up, I couldn't muster the courage to enter the competitive sports that filled "other" boys' lives, and imperceptibly slid into friendships that were mostly with girls, or boys like myself. I spent much of the time alone.

Exile, vulnerability, and fear are the gay man's companions throughout childhood. This sense of differentness encourages withdrawal and a frozen approach to the outside world—actually he is on the edge, on the outside looking in. To sidestep danger and achieve acceptance, he pretends with every expression and gesture that he is somebody else.

And yet, "The privilege of a lifetime is being who you are . . . we must be willing to get rid of the life we've planned, so as to have the life that is waiting for us" . . . Joseph Campbell calls us to pass beyond the gates of hope and fear, to live an authentic life.

Risk? At some point in many of our lives, the impulse to serve the truth mounts and sharpens, as with Joyce's Stephen Dedalus, to the point where loss and danger no longer matter: "I will not serve that in which I no longer believe whether it call itself my home, my fatherland or my church. . . . And I am not afraid to make a mistake, even a great mistake, and perhaps as long as eternity too." He cuts the tether, his moorings, and ventures into uncharted territory.

On a spiritual path, particularly the Buddhist path, gays must make the leap from lives of peculiar deprivation and avoidance to full immersion in the joys and sorrows of their world.

Is there an invitation intrinsic to Buddhism that beckons two gay men or women to a mutual lifelong dance? For that matter, do the words "gay-Buddhist-couple" carry associative significance? Asking this question I eventually came to appreciate the ways in which this path has shaped our lives. When people take Refuge and the Buddhist Precepts, Mahayana and Vajrayana vows in our cases, they step onto paths that affect every moment of the rest of their lives. So serious!? Delicious humor and irony infect "the

MICHAEL C. HYMAN (Sonoma, CA) was born in 1945 and practices Zen Buddhism at the Sonoma Mountain Zen Center, as well as in the Tibetan Shambhala tradition of Chogyam Trungpa Rinpoche. He is a pathologist and writer and lives with his partner, Bill Shean (a Tibetan practitioner), to whom he dedicates the present article.

whole catastrophe,'' as Zorba put it, but it cannot be denied that Buddhists assume a burden of intentionality, shared no doubt by religious practitioners in other traditions as well.

When gay men and women enter committed relationships, they vote themselves an entire set of tensions: These affect where you live, the job you take or the career you follow, the friends you make, the family you keep or lose, the health you risk, the lover you pursue, the politics you choose, and the religion you practice. To assert, as a few do, that homosexuality is a matter only of sexuality may be true for those few, but not for the vast majority who walk about with both eyes open. In mid-America, hardly a waking hour of our lives passes untinged by self-consciousness as gay men. The screen blips continuously forming an unbroken line in our minds so that we are unaware of the separate stimuli: a slight tightening in the back of our necks as the two of us enter the line in the neighborhood bakery for croissants at 8 a.m. (''what are they thinking of us?''); the predictable scan from nearby tables, along with our background anxiety, when we enter a restaurant as the only two men dining together, mooneyed. Make your own list. San Franciscans or New Yorkers might chortle, but in most of America being gay and publicly together is dicey business. Never quite relaxed. Despite lifetimes of worldly accomplishments, rarely shirking involvement, we know the cost. Those who have circumscribed themselves in Key West or Provincetown may claim to have avoided the stigma of queerness, but they have their own list: aging, popularity, physical beauty, etc.

In America it is no longer chic to make fun of blacks, Latinos or Jews, but it is quite all right even, especially, now to bash faggots or fairies. A ''faggot'' is a bundle of kindling wood. In the Middle Ages, homosexuals were used as faggots in place of wood. We are the last, lowest rung on the American ladder, favorite targets of those just above us. The 1996 Republican Convention attempted to paper over its extreme right platform (constitutional amendment against gays in the military) by pounding our ears with calls for ''diversity'' and ''inclusiveness''—no one is to be left out of the American dream—no one will be left behind. Lists of groups were repeated over and over, as if, by repetition, they might convince the voting public that they really mean it. In any case, gays were never mentioned beyond the platform. Never. We are not included. Gays are not part of acceptable diversity. To be gay colors an individual's life in myriad ways and carries significant weight for almost every man or woman. To argue the point seems an oxymoron but there are those who believe that our difficulties arise in proportion to our visibility—lie low and the obstacles disappear. Others feel that ''gay'' only determines the direction of one's penis.

From a purely Buddhist viewpoint, though, homosexuality is our karma —that's all, folks, an entire world of lifestyles, sensitivities, and creative impulses—just another karmic stream. But only a foolish Buddhist would deny or minimize the significance of the imposing forces that shape the life of a gay person. On one level, they are quite empty. At the same time, they are rich and full and demand consideration.

Add the "couple," or the "committed couple," or the "married gay couple." Who are they? For us it began by falling in love, passion predominating. Within a few years our relationship was buoyed by a shared Buddhist vision, a certain way of regarding the world. With time, friendship builds, passion waxes, wanes, waxes again(!), but takes its place among the chemical elements that bind two people who are not so much "in love" as loving each other. Let's face it: the laundry gnaws at the glamour. Long-term intimacy, trust, fun, joy, communication, honesty, and conflict, cook each couple, through and through. We have gone through a one-year separation (and missed each other so much that our planned time apart was progressively whittled down by biweekly visits, etc., until we gave in and moved back together after nine months). We have survived the perilous issue of monogamy. Coming out so late in life, I was reluctant to commit myself totally to this partnership. Bill, having sown his oats over three decades, was quite ready to commit, and understandably insisted that I do so.

Also, a year-and-a-half after my kids left for college, we agreed with great trepidation (and clucking about the wasted money) that I could maintain nearby a separate apartment where I could flee, if I so chose, whenever Bill had his kids for periods of time. He didn't have to worry about my uptightness while coping as a single parent. Wandering through many crises as a father myself, I was too exhausted to repeat the process, and undeniably, something within me, then in my late 40s, said it was time to pay attention to my own life. Understandably, Bill was jealous and fearful that I would have affairs and drift away. He was occasionally angry that I would not assume a full-time parental role again with his teenagers. But it worked out! I did not feel the need to have affairs. The apartment, quiet and simply furnished, facing a park and the mountains, was a fantastic release of the pressure that mushroomed whenever his unruly brood used to show up, with their chaotic schedules and self-absorbed adolescent needs. I had had enough of that. Done it. For the 20% of days that I retreated to my apartment, a healing relaxation justified every penny of the extravagance. Finally we moved to another town and I gave it up, feeling that I could deal with Bill's offspring in defined ways. They had matured some and I had loosened up a little. Bill and I had reconciled our differences and were willing to work with them. Now his kids are growing up; they come and go. Bill and I argue once in a while over family issues, sometimes heatedly, but in general recognize our limitations and adaptability. You come to know the other person.

To be sure, straight couples face a drove of challenges, wading their way through the speed and vulgarity of our times. But gay couples must deal also with most of these, as well as their own. Even so, is a special discourse necessary? At first, we didn't think so. For us, same-sex marriage and commitment are equivalents, as I think they would be for most Buddhists. Neither yet grants us survival or spousal benefits. Marriage "in the eyes of God" is otherwise a so-what for us, although strictly speaking, Buddhism and certainly Shambhala training do not contravene faith in a divine presence. We've been together 12 years. Not an eternity, but long enough to have made the conscious decision that we want to spend the rest of our lives together. We have not had a "marriage" ceremony because we have not gotten around to it. If the qualities of friendship were lacking, no ceremony would supplant them. If the foundation exists, however, ceremony and ritual metaphorically enrich and celebrate our lives. Why not?

When I was married to my wife, we never fought. After the divorce, close friends and family shook their heads in disbelief: "But you never quarreled!" It was true. Resembling the mom and pop of a '50s sitcom, our marriage was lethally flawed by an institutionalized lack of communication, an unwillingness to reveal ourselves. Quite cowardly, in retrospect. We were good friends, had some good times, and tried to be devoted parents. She was a psychologist and a kind person. While outsiders thought we were the perfect couple, I eventually saw that we were passing each other in the night.

Some people can go no further. For others, at a certain age or stage in the marriage, this arrangement becomes not only unsatisfactory but untenable. You gag on it. Cannot do it any more. Not another day of that awful blankness. My realization of the life-death I was living occurred while driving to the kids' soccer fields. Passing an arroyo or dry stream-bed, it suddenly clicked: this is my marriage! When I tried to bring up the matter of our dessicated relationship, she ignored the whole thing, wiping the dishes, never looking my way. A "committed couple," gay or straight, I think, are first and foremost consciously together. They have not necessarily signed in blood a document like The Mayflower Compact, and may or may not be monogamous, but they are aware of the alchemy that brought and keeps them together. As the dynamics shift, so do the reasons for partnership. Many find that they have grown apart, are headed in widely different directions. Others, building a brick wall around them to protect their insularity, suffocate and split.

Gay couples face additional snags. From a sense of panic, AIDS catapulted many into partnerships. Some were committed, but others arose from fear of the disease and were matters of convenience. As the plague spread, attitudes diverged. Some couples virtually went underground to avoid the pain and danger. The resultant isolation drove gays to seek release in extra-marital flings, leading to those "inexplicable" cases of AIDS in 20-year marriages, sometimes causing the death of the innocent partner. Not a few became so deeply enmeshed in the epidemic that from a point of despair, they eschewed any notion of commitment and flocked to the parks, bars and remaining baths. And within some quarters of the gay community, especially the activists, a kind of contempt for gay couples as Uncle Toms has arisen. Skeptics see gay couples merely as pale imitations of suburban straights, so-called "guppies," worthy only of derision. If AIDS is cured, will gay couples fade into history, a quirky anomaly of our times? We really don't know, but my guess is, probably not. As gay couples win grudging acceptance and relax, they will appreciate the nurturing evolution of a strong relationship.

I describe our story at some length only to emphasize its non-linearity. There are many ways to live as a "committed gay couple" and you may not find yours approved or even listed in a self-help book. Buddhist teachings, I feel, resonate with this approach, but with a bit of a twist. In retrospect, having been mostly closeted (as has Bill) for work reasons until quite recently, I believe that the closeted gay couple has a much tougher time of it than those who find it possible to be open with their homosexuality. The issue of "outing" has an unanswerable quality, like abortion. Each of us has a different capacity to ride the winds of change. And sometimes we vastly misjudge them, both the capacity and the winds. How often have you come out to some significant person in your life only to be confronted with a "so what?" Or perhaps she never spoke to you again. The whole thrust of this exploration is the generally resilient and strengthening but unpredictable effect of opening up to the experiences of your life. Two gay people can help (or hinder) each other in the process. Buddhism encourages it, demands it, if you take practice seriously.

But if you are closeted, hiding that huge gay part of what accounts for your personality, your generosity and wickedness, joys and guilt, perhaps your love for the color purple, then you undercut the cultivation of genuineness that surely is the fruition of years of Buddhist practice. Even though we know that that personality is ultimately empty, first you have to get to know it, chew it through and through, until its transparency makes the whole issue moot. You may delude yourself by including within your brick wall many friends and family; ultimately you choke. Everyone lives according to the circumstances of his or her life, which is to say, their karma. The closet gay incorporates into each day the tiniest or most gigantic lies, untruths about himself, his lover, and society, that corrode his sense of integrity. There is no way around this major cause of suffering for the closetee. Defended people tend to be brittle and hard (remember *Boys in the Band*?). If their practice is working, Buddhists notice a kind of softness that develops within themselves, what Trungpa Rinpoche called "the tender heart of sadness." Engaged softness partly results from an authentic life.

A gay couple, truthful and kind with each other, can ameliorate the pain of the closet, but is there any escape from the rub of pretending you are someone else? Contrast that situation with living a Buddhist life of openness. Of course, one answer, the twist mentioned above, is that Buddhism never tells you what to do. There is no Eleventh Precept, "Thou shalt come out of the closet." For some, juggling their lives, experiencing and acknowledging its raw suffering in a conscious way, is exactly their Buddhist path, no less valid than someone who burst out of the closet on a white horse. As the I Ching says, no blame. It all depends on how and why and what significance you attach to it. The closet path is not anti-Buddhist at all, but its compromises often force couples into tortuous choices, years of melancholy and isolation, and accentuate the lines of stress. If they survive, they're probably the stronger for it. Buddhism certainly doesn't promise "happiness" as we in the West know and expect it.

Within the context of American society, gay couples cannot avoid a certain defensiveness in their lives. The more uncloseted you are, the more exposed you become to the blatant hatred around you. Paradoxically, a confident couple in a reasonable environment may pass through this stage, fitting into their community in a relatively quiescent and uneventful way. One cannot overestimate the support that a couple can give each other in this passage. More than your parents, because both of you are gay; more than your friends, because you share each victory and defeat as if they were your own. You become shock absorber for the grief or rage that your lover brings home from some outrage at work. As Buddhists, you know how to work with emotions as practice: acknowledging, neither repressing nor acting out, eventually perceiving their emptiness as the pain or anger fades and passes. Buddhists also learn the nature of displaced emotions and projection. It's all too easy to bring home the fury you feel from some teenager in a jeep who yelled "faggot" at you on the road, and unaccountably erupt at your spouse over nonsense. A gay Buddhist couple who confine their Buddhism to the cushion miss out on the best practice: the juiciness of their lives together.

Ploughing through the obstacles, we, like much of America, have been through periods of therapy: years of it for Bill in his youth, after fleeing homophobic Missouri; me in mid-life after abandonment of the straight marriage, hanging out there on a limb. We have watched friends on antidepressants, seen a few in shock therapy, Jungian therapy, psychoanalysis, primal therapy, etc. During a time when I was very sad, Roshi suggested 108 bows, three times a day. Many devotional Buddhists believe that more intense, ardent practice gets you through these slumps. Others urge a gentle approach. And there are a lot of Buddhist therapists. "Buddhist" is an insufficient credential for a therapist, although a therapist who is Buddhist views the world in a way that may be quite helpful for the right client. In other words, we don't feel there is a single or easy answer to the question of the value of therapy for gay Buddhist couples. We have never been to couple therapy. Both of us are suspicious of therapists who crow over their

Buddhist connections, and of people who equate Buddhist practice as therapy, and of most therapy in general. As individuals, neither of us feels that it significantly diminished the isolation, insecurity and internal homophobia that accompanied our lives as gay men. On the other hand, sometimes therapy can help get you through the night, singly or in couples. And a good Buddhist therapist may be light years ahead of his materialist counterpart, in helping clients work through difficulties, straight or gay.

Before meeting Bill, I had been closeted and married to a woman for 17 years. We had two children. Bill had been "out" and married to a woman for eight years, and also had two kids. During our 12 years the four kids spent every other weekend, holidays, and many other days and nights together with us and each other; we have been their nuclear family in that sense: My younger son, Matt, is a close friend, truly a half-brother, to Bill's son, Andy. Bill's daughter, Margo, a few years younger than the rest, adds a spicy female energy that was missing from my time with Matt and Jordan. Bill and his kids tend to be unruly and spoiled. Me and mine tend to be orderly (repressed, Bill says) and spoiled. All of them are meandering into young adulthood as responsible, decent human beings. These 12 years have shifted some of the focus from their maternal nests, and have forced all six of us to modify significantly the self-centered directions that we enjoyed so much. And finally, endless days on the athletic fields, spaghetti and garlic bread dinners, and evenings watching nerd movies or enduring adolescent wails, have beaten us into the submission of a somewhat peculiar, in other ways very ordinary, American family post-divorce. Any straight family knows this: raising kids, even part-time, consumes much of your time and occupies considerable attention. And that's when all goes well. Frequently it doesn't.

All through this time Bill and I have followed our separate but overlapping Buddhist practices. The immense personal emphasis on children and family more often than not led to postponement of an intended retreat or sesshin. Regular daily practice got shunted around carpools and unscheduled flu. Perhaps this sounds like martyrdom; at times that's how it felt. Most parents are familiar with the sensation of constant giving that defines parenthood, especially when the going gets rough in the teenage years. No one prepared me for that. You give up time, money, effort, energy, youth, lust, and practice among other things. And expect nothing in return. But of course that's exactly what practice is. Sometimes I hated it, felt that my life was all sacrifice, dribbling away. I had come out at 39, left the marriage, in exchange for what? Another marriage? Where was all the gay fun (remember, gay is g-a-y) I was supposed to be having? Uchiyama-Roshi said, "Everything that happens to you is your life." It doesn't affect your life; it is your life. And Buddhist practice fully attends the details of life, in this case being gay fathers committed to our children and to each other. We don't have to fake a grin, to pretend that it's all too wonderful. But we could sometimes grin, acknowledging that things are what they are.

Parenthood is not the typical situation of most gay couples, but it requires emphasis here, because for Bill and I, the Buddhist vision sometimes supplied the glue that held us together, and reciprocally, in between crises we appreciated the crises as our practice. Very good practice. Well, I can say that now, past the eye of the hurricane. The whirlwind of our lives was further accelerated by nearby ex-wives, the necessity for substantial careers and a geographic spread that dictated much commuting (mostly by Bill). We maintained a large house for the mass migrations that came and went. These things are idiosyncratic, not your classic laid-back, two-in-a-nest gay couple spending months at retreats or on RSVP cruises. But everybody has something. We did not have AIDS. We earned enough for vacations here and there. The kids are growing up. All of this is preface to the statement that we did not feel ''special'' as a gay Buddhist couple, in fact hardly had time to think about it.

Bill came out in his twenties, and shortly afterwards became a student of Maezumi-Roshi in L.A. A few years later he recognized his root guru in Chogyam Trungpa Rinpoche, and moved to Boulder where he remained until we met. Currently, he goes to retreats led by Tsultrim Gyatso Rinpoche, but loves Zen sesshin and also follows the Shambhala path. He works with computers, has taught many Buddhist classes, and is a meditation instructor. He has been part of Vajradhatu for about 25 years.

I married young, fleeing a New York Jewish childhood, followed a direct career track through medical school into pathology, where I worked in one hospital for 25 years. The '60s passed me right by. Somehow, the operas of Wagner's Ring Cycle led me to Jung, then to Alan Watts, on to Kapleau-Roshi's books and group, then to *Zen Mind, Beginner's Mind*, and finally (finally?) to my teacher, Jakusho Kwong-Roshi and the Sonoma Mountain Zen Center. Encountering Shambhala Training in Boulder through Bill's connection with the Vidyadhara, I've gone through the levels and attended Warrior Assembly. The Shambhala vision is critical for me, an important balance and appreciation of a relative world that softens the austere Zen leaning towards the absolute. All those black robes.

Each of us has his own practice rooted in distinctly different traditions. Bill's (Tibetan) Vajrayana and Shambhala shrines, replete with symbolic objects, vessels, cloths, candles and tables, resemble a miniature Chartres (in fact, I call it ''the cathedral''). My Zen altar is small and simple, containing incense, candle, a Buddha figure and an offering of flowers or fruit. Each of us hangs photos of teachers or gurus on the wall. Sometimes we share a room, sometimes not. Neither has a problem sitting at the other's shrine or altar. When traveling, we light incense and meditate together, sitting on improvised pillows or cushions. Each has adapted to the other's need for individual or solitary retreats and the absences that these entail. Possessiveness goes. Many Vajrayana practices are secret. Bill does these alone or at feasts with other senior practitioners who have taken abhisheka. Since his vacations have been limited, I've done most sesshins without him.

But we also overlap, see the other point of view. I revere the Dalai Lama, love to read and listen to Joko Beck, and have a connection with the late Kalu Rinpoche stemming from a Kalachakra transmission, early in my Buddhist path, as well as with the late Dilgo Khentsye Rinpoche. Toni Packer's "just attending" approach, eschewing formal Buddhism, also makes sense. I've studied Mind Training and tong-len as taught by Pema Chodren. Bill's extensive background includes all three yanas. If Bill attends sesshin with me, we're allowed to share a tent. I would love to sit a dathun with Bill, or study the Mahayana at Vajradhatu's Rocky Mountain Dharma Center. I've taken the Maitri course on the Buddha families and intend to pursue music, calligraphy, and ikebana, sponsored by the Shambhala Center. My separate shrine includes Trungpa, and Bill's has a photo of Suzuki-Roshi. Both of us understand the dangers of spiritual shopping. We'd rather spend our time practicing than searching for the latest trendy teacher/teaching.

We have been very busy people, with little inclination to investigate the soap operatics of gay Buddhist coupledom. In fact, we both naturally and spontaneously declined to join a nascent gay Buddhist meditation group (incorporating different traditions) in Denver. Our plates were overfull, thank you. Most long-time Buddhists go through cycles in their practice. Enthusiasm comes and goes. "Progress' and plateaus follow one another, are probably superficial observations at best. These bumps are compounded by the complexities of the student-teacher relationship, which seem to have a life of their own. In Bill's case, Rinpoche's death, the illness and death of Osel Tendzin, and the subsequent turmoil in his community sucked a lot of energy into the ether. I have had a number of periods of doubt, enough to "give them a wide meadow" and ride them out. But in general, we have remained steady in our personal and practice commitments, not really questioning the effect each might have on the other.

Survival as a gay couple has proven to be far more difficult than sustaining a Buddhist practice. Our attraction to the Buddhist path was more visceral than cerebral, but who can doubt that tolerance by the "church" tends to lead a homosexual more to Buddhism than to the Assembly of God, or Islam? Or Judaism, in my case? Or midwestern fundamentalism in Bill's? The Third Grave Precept enjoins us against abuse of sexuality. Nothing in Zen or Tibetan Buddhism, to my knowledge, refers to the abomination of men lying with men. What the average Buddhist/Shinto priest in small-town Japan or Korea says to his congregation, I do not know. Buddhist temples in mid-America that cater to Asian-Americans uncomfortably tend to resemble the Catholic Church around the corner. Lots of ornate statues. Lots of prayers to Buddha. But who's to say?

The American Buddhist guidebook is vague on sexual identity and expression. It bears no resemblance to any religious TV channel you might randomly surf. "Vague" is probably better than "tolerant." There is no more reference to homosexuality than there is to God, or to love. But the American Buddhist experience has been anything but vague. In the Vajradhatu of Trungpa's day, gays as singles or couples were open and common, as was bisexual experimentation. The anecdotes are endless and outrageous. While the major Zen sexual scandals have been heterosexual, one gets the impression that this was only the luck of the draw. Baker-Roshi, himself the dharma heir of Suzuki-Roshi, installed Issan Dorsey as abbot of a predominantly gay Hartford St. Zen Center. No one really seems to care about these things. Maybe in Peoria, they do, but most American Buddhist sanghas have permitted broad diversity of membership. I know of no questionnaire that inquires about one's sexuality.

However, prejudice can be strange and subtle. In "Ambivalent Zen," Lawrence Shainberg recounts an episode with Eido-Roshi, walking with him in Greenwich Village, where the master appears to view all those homosexuals on the street as aliens from outer space. Zen Centers tend to be populated by liberals who are mostly but not always free of deep sexual prejudice. There are probably plenty of exceptions and the individual experiences a welcome or rejection according to the variables of time, place, and person. Including the teacher, who may set the tone of the Center.

At the core of Buddhism lies the experience of oneness and emptiness. A true understanding of this side of Buddhism could not possibly support solid prejudice of any kind. From another angle, everything, every single thing, every thumbnail and hangnail, is unique. Every blade of grass, each grain of sand. Indeed no two snowflakes are alike. But isn't it remarkable, when you really think about it , that no two of five billion people are exactly alike? If all things are different, then each has its own value, and cannot be judgmentally compared. Yes, you may prefer pistachios to cashews, and one antique may seem to you better preserved than another—to you! Each thing has its own intrinsic value. No thing (or person) is inherently better or worse than another. Including gays. If Buddhists follow the doctrine behind their faith, then Buddhism is a comfortable place for gay men and women.

While there may be a wide spectrum of response to the arrival of a gay person on the scene, Buddhism does not orchestrate it. For gay Buddhist couples, beyond Vajradhatu and San Francisco, my experience has been one of normal welcome or ho-hum. We are still rather unusual entities, looked at quizzically by some, encouraged by others, openly rejected by very few, and certainly not in the name of Buddhism. Although Buddhism pays no particular attention to sexual identity, it pivots on the essential emptiness of these labels, and resonates with the call of Avalokiteshvara for compassion for sentient beings. Including gay Buddhist couples. Not so special. But also not not special.

Let's face it: not to be rejected feels quite good. That's why there are more gays meditating than rolling in Four Square Bible Churches. Also, we have our own understanding of The First Noble Truth. The horror of AIDS superimposed on timeless homophobia has resulted in profound individual and group awareness of human suffering. Our plight may seduce us to think that our suffering is worse, the worst; are we God's unchosen people? But as Buddhists we know better. We remember Cambodia and Rwanda and just as significantly, the neglected or abused kid down the street, the homeless person we passed on our way to work, or the rich, privileged, lost divorcee who is contemplating suicide. Suffering is the human condition. While appreciating our differentness, all differentness, Buddhism avoids judgment. There is no Original Sin.

So the good news is, we're not evil. The very good news is, we are connected to all things, and the best news is that our suffering is related to our attachments and will diminish when we live the life that doesn't grasp and experiences emptiness/openness on the spot. The bad news is, the good news leaves us rather adrift, without moorings or reference points. This is a critical truth in Buddhism and an unavoidable experience for anyone who stays long enough on the path. It is exactly here where the path, situation, karma, call it what you will, of a gay couple diverges from mainstream straight humanity, and even from our single gay brothers and sisters.

Heterosexuals draw enormous support, continuously and unconsciously, from political and social institutions, religious tradition, and their cultural history. Our current attempts to scale the political barriers to same-sex marriage (or legitimization of our commitment) have met with overwhelming opposition virtually everywhere. On this one President Clinton fell into bed with Newt Gingrich. One state legislature after another panicked at the possibility that they might have to honor a potential decision in our favor by the Hawaii State Supreme Court. Even in San Francisco, local polls tilted away from approval. The vehemence of the fundamentalists is puzzling, as is the suspicion and opposition of the rest of the straight world. Quite clearly, they feel that union between a man and a woman is unique and superior to gay coupling (not just unique, maybe it is, but crucially, superior). Many people would not admit to outright prejudice, but that's exactly what it is. Political enshrinement of the exclusivity of traditional marriage can only formalize its superiority in the eyes of most people, and our inferiority. William Bennett, who wrote the book on virtue (pun intended) penned a column listing the dangers of equivalent status for gay relationships. These included the by-now-familiar charge that we threaten the viability of straight marriage, somehow diluting its potency. We taint it. Doing so well on its own, with a 50% failure rate, marriage comes under attack by throwing gays the crumb of status. We do insist on spousal benefits. Is the financial squeeze at the nub of their contempt? Who believes that? Bennett goes on to suggest that societal approval of gay unions would entice youth into homosexuality (I'm not kidding) and that the "notorious promiscuity" of gays would cause cataclysmic acceleration of heterosexual adultery, again, ruining marriage.

These are not characterizations. As one of those under attack, I have followed this debate closely. The above arguments typify straight America's refusal to grant gay couples the dignity of civil status. It is worth some study. Most encouraging, however, is the fact that the dialogue is happening at all. Limp wrists and sequins abound (and there's nothing wrong with them) but the old gay stereotype is gone for good. Gays and lesbians do not supplicate, we insist on equal treatment as couples. This is new. After the congressional vote, the *San Francisco Chronicle* counseled that patience would carry the day. Be patient. Hell, I'm 51! In our relationship we have worked to develop the dignity that any married couple takes for granted. We are equal to them! Is something wrong? So, there has been a paradigm shift of agenda in America.

By the way, it's not just America. The Puritans founded this theocracy, but if you travel with your eyes open, you notice that homophobia, though much tempered and subtle, is nearly universal. Britain recently confirmed its no-gays-in-the-military law. More interesting is France. Arriving from the airport, you cannot help noticing huge billboards advertising products with near-naked women. On the streets of Paris, a gay man is not stigmatized. One smells an atmosphere of relaxed sexuality and sensuality. But a gay couple who think and act as if they are truly "ensemble" evoke barely cloaked derision. In the provinces, family mystique brings out the most conservative response. Typically French, their contempt is revealed not in stupid laws but by a certain look. Not paranoid. Real. Or in Oaxaca, Mexico, supposedly an area of live-and-let live sophistication where the native Indians understand the love of men for men. In one popular bar, men dance with women while staring at other men. Men may not dance with men. At another bar a knock on the door meets with a look through a peephole before we are allowed in. Men have affairs, perhaps for life, but most of them marry for their families and the Church, also for life. Straight jackets. Denmark recently legitimized gay unions, as did Iceland. Perhaps Scandinavia will lead the way. Below the surface things are not always what they seem. A Norwegian man recently wrote to the British *Gay Times*, acknowledging his country's political progressivism. His main purpose, however, was to inform us of the vitriolic homophobia rampant in Norwegian society as a whole (not surprising in the land of Ibsen). At any rate, it's a mirage to think that freedom lies just beyond our borders.

The gay cause for equal rights and protection is proceeding, albeit unevenly. But gay couples, some defiant, many in the closet, stand alone and on the defensive. We enjoy virtually no political or social standing. Any wife-beating, child-abusing, sociopathic straight couple attains rights the minute they sign the agreement. The various religions not only echo this inequity; they fuel its persistence. Very, very few Christian churches will sanctify homosexual unions—especially galling since so many of the clergy are gay. We have no friend in the Protestant and Catholic traditions or historical doctrines. Yet we "enjoy" the negative spinoff from the immense publicity given to intergenerational sex by repressed priests.

If you could somehow add together all the political, social, and religious hostility to the advent of the upright gay couple, I think it would pale before the absence of a significant gay cultural history. Our culture buttresses straight relationships at every turn. *The Celluloid Closet* poignantly demonstrated the cloying, recondite way in which gay lovers were forced to show their affection by Hollywood rules. A literature, our literature, is just now beginning to develop. Where is the culture that treats the gay person and especially the gay couple, Not As Victim? Not to be pitied. Not as lesser. I don't say "proud," either, because that implies to me an ongoing battle to cast off a sense of inferiority. As their Bible says, "In my Father's house are many rooms." We are another room, painted purple. OK, lavender. A queer room.

A few years ago we saw the Broadway musical, *Falsettos*. Widely acclaimed by gays and straights alike, and so popular it inspired a sequel, this ostensibly sympathetic and supportive play followed the intertwining lives of a gay and straight couple. The gay couple fought incessantly, almost by nature, compared with the straight couple. The latter suffered tepid New Age difficulties. Then one of the gays began his descent into AIDS. Midway, Bill and I literally turned spontaneously to each other and I whispered, "When is this going to change?" I meant the play, which treated the gay couple as cute and pathetic, tuning up the call for pity with an AIDS finale. But I also meant our culture, of which this play was representative. The straight culture mostly hates and ignores us, except in the watering holes of Berkeley and Cambridge where our angst is appreciated. Our own embryonic culture understandably has focused upon AIDS. Sooner or later, cure or no, we will realize that there is more, much more to appreciate from the gay couple than their epitaphs. I honestly do not feel that my life is a tragedy. This is Buddhist practice.

But *They* have a distinct and concrete cultural history, stretching back continuously to The Flintstones. *We* get derivative stories of Hadrian and Antinous, or the lovely but rootless love poems of Sappho. The gay couple basks in the compassion of the Parliament of Iceland and the rumors about mad King Ludwig of Bavaria. The straight couple grows up under the wings of the all-powerful Roman Catholic Church, is encouraged by insurance, taxation, and retirement policies throughout their lives, and is nurtured by the Arthurian romances and *Gone with the Wind*. It goes on and on.

But wait. I just complained about gays being regarded as victims. We are victims of political, social, and religious oppression and we are just beginning to manifest a collective consciousness as a people, a tribe (some of us would still deny such a thing exists). A homosexual is not a victim by nature; we are victims because the straight world treats us, fears us, hates us, as abnormal and threatening. As soon as one uses the language of We and They, a litany of sadness begins. Buddhists should know better, shouldn't we? If the Dalai Lama can say that he doesn't hate the Chinese Communists, are we justified in our resentments? The lesson I learned at the Holocaust Museum was that as soon as human beings are separated into categories for judgmental purposes, the groundwork for horror is laid. Gay Buddhists are caught, in a way, between the loving kindness of a religion that rejects divisiveness, and a vilified sexuality that calls for response and resistance.

The gay Buddhist couple lacks the cushion that, say, a gay Episcopal couple can fall back on. The Episcopals are promised various rewards if they are good, most importantly, heaven. Buddhists are taught to practice with no gaining idea. To think you're going somewhere is not only a delusion, it's counter-productive. The gaining idea takes you away from the here-and-now, to the past and future, neither of which truly exist. Soto Buddhists, at least, are taught just to practice. It seems to me that nowadays the Episcopal Church has become rather popular among gays. It retains the ceremony and ritual of the Catholic Church without the authoritarian repression of the latter. It offers hierarchy and reward. Gays tend to like a bit of color. There aren't many gay Quakers. Similarly, in Buddhism, my impression is that there are many more gay Vajrayana or "Tibetan" Buddhists than there are zennies, possibly for similar reasons.

The United Church of Christ or Congregationalists, Unitarians, and Episcopalians and a few other small Christian groups have developed some degree or another of acceptance, of your "fitting in." Particularly if you don't wear your boa on Sunday. Bruce Bawer's *A Place at the Table* epitomized the call for conservative "normalcy" among gays and the potential rewards that it offers. In these churches polite discussion might engage the clergy and their parishioners on the gay rights movement. Paul Monette's anti-religious (especially anti-Catholic) vitriol dug in at the opposite pole, pointing out the hypocrisy and hopelessness of compromise. At the end of his *Last Watch of the Night*, Monette's shrillness settled into an epiphanic, calm core point: after all, we have attempted, pleaded for, acceptance throughout the ages by church and state, to no avail. Having witnessed society's overall indifference to AIDS, do we need any more proof of the failure of a passive, assimilative approach? From an absolute point of view none of this really matters; from a relative point of view, urgent action is required. So what does the good Buddhist do?

In Buddhism, we are asked to follow a form, various forms, which constitute and support the practice. Everyone is treated alike. Gay couples are treated alike. In so many stories (Nangaku's polishing the tile; the life of

Milarepa) we eventually come to realize that the separation between Self and Other is itself a delusion, a fixed point of view. Everyone brings his/her neurosis to the practice, but in the practice and at the retreat center, personality, rather the cult of personality, is mostly ignored. (It will come up anyway in a thousand ways.) In one sense, this is a relief. In formal practice, no one cares about who you are (your storyline). However, for people who have undergone the most severe internal repression imaginable, who have spent their entire lives pretending to be someone else (straight), a religion that brushes your particularity aside can be a bit of a letdown. Fundamentally, the practice is not to make you a different person, but to become more completely who you are, which is quite good enough. Our lives embody the truth of the Net of Indra. Everything is inter-connected, and illuminates itself and everything else. The death of a mighty king affects a blade of grass a continent away. The teachings neither condemn nor confirm our ideas of our so-called sexual identity. Thus the Buddhist vision offers an enormous, cosmic rubric of support for gays, and (though not especially) for the gay couple, but on the ground level, the day-to-day, working out of our lives, we are pretty much left alone. (However, I would argue, less in Tibetan than in Zen Buddhism. In the Vajrayana, specific and extensive teachings deal with the difficulties of working with human neurosis.)

In the Introductory talks on Taking Refuge, Rinpoche makes clear the point that those who begin this path are not hiding out, running away, building walls, or avoiding conflict. According to him The Refuge Vows include yielding territory, forsaking privacy, a commitment to non-aggression and vulnerability. So the gay Buddhist couple, also, is invited to participate in the adventure of dissolving the cocoon (some of these terms are used more in Buddhist, others more in Shambhala contexts, but all stem from Rinpoche's work and are compatible with each tradition). What does this mean?

In the Kagyu branch of Vajrayana or Tibetan Buddhism, Trungpa Rinpoche and Khentsye Rinpoche wrote one of the great distillations of Buddhism that speaks to all, but, I feel, aims poignantly right at gay hearts:

> Since all things are naked, clear, and free from obscurations, there is nothing to attain or realize;
> The everyday practice is simply to develop a complete acceptance and openness to all situations and emotions;
> And to all people—experiencing totally without reservations and blockages, so that one never withdraws or centralises into oneself.

John Welwood is a psychologist who excerpted from his forthcoming book (*Love and Awakening*) an article, "Partner, Lover, Worthy Opponent" (*Shambhala Sun*, March, 1996, pp. 15–17). According to Welwood, two people who recognize a "soul connection" encourage dormant, undeveloped parts of themselves to come forth and find expression. "We have met our match, someone who won't let us get away with anything that is false or diminishes our being." This can produce "intense, transformative fire." He says our typical reaction is to defend ourselves and dig in—I'm right; he/she's wrong. The partner "threatens to blow our cover," but is actually "doing us a favor." It becomes "sacred combat," an "artful dance. . . . The purpose of the struggle is to soften you." The ego's tendency to seek confirmation is thwarted in an honest relationship.

Welwood applies Buddhist teaching to personal relationships. This view is novel. For most gays (and most straights) a committed relationship implies sunsets on the beach leading to a quiet fireside, a nest of peace. Enough conflict already. What? Prepare for battle? Well, anyone in a long-term relationship is aware that that's how things are, whether you like them or not. Most of us run from it, think it's bad, that conflict is a nasty prognostic sign for a couple. For two people who have chemistry together, warm sunsets do not require conjuring; they happen. But the inevitable difficulties cause most of us to wring our hands or run like rats to our holes. Welwood says, not only are they all right, they are vital to the growth of both people. The entire process is practice and inspires the more formal parts of practice.

Gay Buddhist couples, whipsawed by societal and religious condemnation, can hardly be blamed for reluctance to incorporate marital jousting into their daily lives. From a Buddhist point of view, however, our vulnerability in a sense has given us a "head start," has jolted us way ahead of the pack in our capacity to deal with strife and conflict as practice. Receiving no confirmation or reference point from society or even from our own religion, we are primed to prune each other's ego-feathers albeit with lovingkindness. We have the freedom and joy to be who we are, alone or together. Out there already, we may as well step off the "100 foot flagpole" of Zen—a total immersion into the moments of pain and pleasure of relationship. Unfortunately, it's all too easy to ask someone else to do the courageous thing, to adopt a kamikazi approach to relationships.

Suzuki-Roshi, in *Zen Mind, Beginner's Mind* talks about becoming conscious of the temperature of our practice, to know how hot it can get without producing a smoky fire. The fire should burn completely; no trace. In other words, each of us has a different capacity for intensity of practice, for conflict, for vulnerability. If you're taking the easy way out, avoiding conflict and cocooning, the fire gets smoky. If you leap into the relationship with the idea of resolving all conflicts in the first week, the fire gets smoky. The problem arises when you approach the situation with a fixed or solid idea about how things should go. To rip yourself open, in sesshin after sesshin, might lead to enlightenment or to a complete nervous breakdown. I think the warning holds true, and is very important to recognize, in John Welwood's advice. Has anyone had an easy life? Most gays have not. The students of Trungpa Rinpoche, especially Pema Chodron, have taught us the value of being gentle, with ourselves as well as with others. Non-aggression, Lesson #1, applies to ourselves. If we can't manage it here, how can we express it genuinely elsewhere?

Both of us have taken Refuge Vows: "I take refuge in Buddha, dharma, and sangha." For Bill and me, this means living an intentional life, however meager the results may seem. As two able gay men in the time of the plague, it includes a special responsibility to our gay mahasangha, or the whole gay world. Hitherto, we have been preoccupied with family, ambition, career, and pleasure as well. Now a bit older, we can devote more energy to alleviating the suffering prevalent in the AIDS epidemic, as well as leading deliberate lives in every way. Indra lives! It includes a commitment to formal practice, which we believe is the yin to the yang of ordinary life as practice. As Trungpa saw it, Taking Refuge also acknowledges our essential homelessness, that security is a delusion. Homelessness is the true human condition for all; who knows it better than gay people? But living in the moment also means that home is where you are, that home is everywhere for a practitioner.

"Taking Refuge" might seem paradoxical, since it's anything but a hide-out, but the notion is not unique to Buddhism. Joseph Campbell studied its equivalent in many cultures and religions. He once said that the hero on his journey must enter a forest, really an ancient image, of course, of the hero's unconscious. If he takes some path, the journey is false, doomed to failure. He must enter the dark forest, encountering the unknown and danger, and create his own path, to realize the journey. Homelessness!

As Joseph Campbell put it, the purpose of a relationship is beyond the two people. They exist together for the relationship itself. Campbell's (and Jung's) elaboration of relationships raises interesting and difficult issues for gay couples. He felt that in a relationship men and women re-create the androgyne, the yin of the one fitting into the yang of the other to form a complete whole. Buddhists might prefer to view sexuality as an expression of energy and karma. In *The Tao of Physics*, Fritjof Capra made these notions accessible to the non-physicist and illuminated their link to Buddhism. Although Newtonian physics (fixed laws that govern solid objects) "works" in our commonly seen world for most things at most times, we know that matter, space, and time, even with our limited knowledge, function in ways that are vastly different from classical physics. From the laws of probability (things do not happen exactly) to the notions of space and matter (they are not distinctly separate) we find that our ordinary human way of looking at things is just one viewpoint and does not apply for every situation. In other words, energy and space are closely related, perhaps two different sides of one coin. Oneness is more than New Age jargon.

Although there is no "scientific proof" for it (nor for the mass of accepted Jungian theory), it seems reasonable or at least possible that our maleness and femaleness are a sliding scale, perhaps approximations, not solid features but behavioral manifestations of energy that are unique for each man and woman. In nature one finds an almost infinite variety of sexual expression. Thousands of years of human culture have rigidified or codified the definition and expression of what we call male and female. Most people feel that their sexual identity is quite "fixed" or biological. The rest are considered aberrations. But, to put it bluntly, your penis or vagina are the same "particles" or "waves" of energy/space that are differently arranged. So is Velveeta. Sorry. We are a continuum.

Men and women appear to be quite different from each other and most commonly they feel a desire for a type of activity that leads to more of them. "Men" and "women" presumably fall close to other "men" and "women" on the sliding scale of physical/sexual equipment and desire for each other but our categorizations are convenient ways of correlating approximate aggregates of energy and space to the human storyline. Human history and culture provide an acceptable static, structure for what probably is a not so tidy arrangement of heterosexual function. That is not to say, as many gays like to assert, that most straight men are "closet cases." Who knows how many? And it doesn't matter. But it does matter that our queerness (really a great word when stripped of derogatory associations) is just another point on the sliding scale. Relatively uncommon, rather visible, with occasionally bizarre combinations and manifestations of male/female, but just another color, another room ("in my Father's house are many rooms"), arising from the same ground (or groundlessness) of energy/matter/space. No blame.

Buddhists believe that things have no abiding or fixed substantiality. Impermanence, emptiness, oneness, are another language for referring to energy/space. In the classical Buddhist view, karma, the sum total of all our actions (body, speech and mind) through all our past lives and including the present, incorporating every interaction with other beings, determines our current and future rebirths. Sexuality is just one aspect of that rebirth, one type of arrangement of energy/space. Regarded as karmic energy, sexuality is not problematic.

It might be hard to agree with or grasp these concepts on a macro level. My intended focus is the gay couple. The *Birdcage* stereotypes, like the straight couple, and gay and straight singles, contain within themselves and their relationship if they have one, both a psychological (they chose each other for a good reason) and culturally nurturing matrix which enables them to function in their daily lives with a minimum amount of disturbance related to their sexuality. They have "found" ways of predictably relating to each other and the world(s) in which they live, as well as being comfortable with the defined person who they see in the mirror. But the ordinary gay couple (not complementary butch and femme), more like than unlike each other, love each other and appreciate their queerness, but have a very difficult time figuring out who pushes the cart in the grocery store. This quandary recurs many times a day and extends into almost every facet of their lives. In a sense, they might complete Campbell's androgyne within themselves, but not with each other unless there is a conscious or subconscious, shift in the way their male and female energies in each man (or woman) relate to those in their partner.

Though these conjectures are speculative, I hope you get the point, because I think it happens all the time and is, I suspect, the major reason for the sadly common breakup of gay relationships. "Male" and "female" energies in many gay couples are more additive or redundant than complementary. They have no precedent, no formula, no support or understanding as to how these might momentarily shift. The couple sinks into a rigid pattern that works for neither of them, and each eventually goes his own way. Supposedly seeking "the perfect guy," they really want the completion of the androgyne. Many of us are so hurt from our early lives that we fear, and are unwilling to risk, a shift in our role within the couple. Perhaps it's impossible for some. But some gay couples are able (many without thinking about or being aware of it) to engage each other in this dance. Perhaps this shift is our version of Welwood's "worthy opponent," because friction with gear shift is not unknown. Often it is great fun, containing the unexpected, another leap off the 100 foot pole of Zen. Not knowing who you will be in the next moment. Not needing to know. Here is a major reason for gay couples to enjoy the Buddhist feast on energy, change, impermanence, dance, and sex. Introducing a sense of play in gay sexuality allows our "maleness" and "femaleness" some movement. A dynamic approach enhances the vitality and survival of our relationships.

Perhaps it is their fundamental understanding of energy flux, including sexual, and its underlying insubstantiality, that accounts for the ho-hum response of so many Buddhist teachers, especially Vajrayana (Tibetan) towards homosexuality. For a gay Buddhist couple, though, working (sounds too much like work) with each other's psychosexual resonance is good practice, joyful, and perhaps crucial to their survival as a couple. In so doing, they provide a vision for younger gay (and non-gay) Buddhists (and non-Buddhists) who follow them. It's bodhisattvic, and the heart of intimacy.

Pursuing life together as a gay couple, Buddhist or not, is more than a romantic fling at the state fair. Our failure rate surely exceeds the 50% of straight marriages, for many reasons. The gay couple must share a deep commitment to each other, the relationship itself, and their place in the world, and at the same time manifest the ability to dance over, under, or around the roadblocks thrown in their way. Some of these are internal. If the couple's raison d'etre is escape from suffering, distancing themselves from a hostile world, and crystallization of their patterns of response to each other, i.e., security, they probably face trouble.

Buddhism's inherent appreciation of interdependence, emptiness, change, "not one—not two," and its broad tolerance regarding sex removes judgment from relationships but also pulls away the props—that little twist again! Never told what to do, the gay Buddhist couple is left with the Precepts and the ubiquitous image of Avalokiteshvara (the bodhisattva of kindness or compassion). There are no reference points or doctrinal grounding, no lovely heavenly reward beyond karma, no promise that life will get easier. Contrasted with heterosexual Christian couples, it feels as if both the difficulties and opportunities are enhanced. Buddhism, if you take it seriously, allows a dropping of fixed roles and expectations, resulting in endless work and play. The Buddhist approach is quite a challenge, analogous to raising children: As you go along, it requires you to yield progressively more and more territory, in order to realize your homelessness. As this happens, you experience true intimacy, and not only within the couple. As the clamshell opens, the clam could relax. Not easy, and not for everyone. So, we could cheer up and calm down. Can the gay Buddhist couple "make it"? Trungpa said:

> Whatever occurs in the confused mind is regarded as path; everything is workable. It is a fearless proclamation—the lion's roar.

Anxiety, depression, fatigue—and a great, great joy, holding hands with your lover as you enter Campbell's forest, keeping in mind, however, that each of you is truly alone.

Why should we try? The tasks seem insurmountable. Would we not be better off alone in our apartment with a good dose of Haagen Dazs? Despite 12 years together with Bill and a conscious commitment, these thoughts still waft through my mind on a regular basis, rather parallel to the land-mines that we encounter. Suzuki-Roshi tackled this question in his remarks on the Sandokai. In the third talk on lightness and darkness (relative and absolute), he alludes to difficulties with his wife and the differences between men and women. Men tend to be idealistic; women tend to nag. "Can't live with her, can't live without her." What should one do? Though his situation might seem anachronistic (women tend to nag?) or idiosyncratic, the question is timeless. Suzuki-Roshi's answer was, "better to live with her." Better to work with, hate and enjoy, the continual flash-points of relationship in the relative world than to flee towards some blissful, illusionary imitation of the absolute. After all, those flash-points arise from, are not separate from, the absolute, or emptiness.

For gay Buddhists, entering into a committed relationship is itself a hero's journey. Weaving their ways through Campbell's forest, the two find intimacy in nothing other than their daily triumphs and sorrows. Or as, in *My Dinner with Andre*, Wally finds fulfillment in waking up with his girlfriend Debbie, in their cold flat, to discover his cup of cold coffee on the table, with no cockroach or fly in it. Sharing a life or practice in its fullest sense enriches every moment of the day with exquisite sensitivity. Whatever happens, or whatever you think is happening, as the story goes, bodhisattvas of all kinds and in all disguises rise up along the way to guide you.

On the other hand, forestalling romantic religious euphoria, we should remind ourselves that gay-Buddhist-couple is after all only a string of words, concepts, and feelings—our peculiar string—with no more inherent substance than giant-Himalayan-panda. We are important from one, our, point of view. Spending a lot of time on your point of view can be fun as long as you realize that it's a form of entertainment. Attachment to your point of view—"I am right; they are wrong"—is merely solidification, bricking yourself in.

We are gay, and we may choose to be a twosome and practice Buddhism. Without demeaning the sacrifices or discounting the obstacles, we could regard "gay couple" as a form of practice—no more, no less. In "Nirvana, the Waterfall," (*Zen Mind, Beginner's Mind*), Suzuki-Roshi likens our individual lives to drops of water cascading over the edge of a waterfall, separated by falling but finally rejoining the limitless flow of existence. He says that it is our deepest desire, our nature, to want to return to the waterfall. Looked at in that way, gays are a stream in Suzuki-Roshi's waterfall. One practice is to be a gay Buddhist couple.

Dogen, the founder of Soto Zen in Japan, wrote in the *Bendowa* of 1240 about jijuyu zammai, or the Wholehearted Practice of the Way. That is, to live wholeheartedly. Zazen, or sitting meditation, is one form. Truly being, being completely, a gay Buddhist couple, whatever that means to you and whatever mistakes you make along the way—that is another form. Katagiri-Roshi saw our practice as living amidst a bubbling spring of water that constantly wells up around us. Our practice is to be whoever we are, whatever we are doing, in that moment. To really do that, paraphrasing Dogen Zen-ji, is to study yourself, to know yourself, to lose your self-consciousness, to forget to remember that you are a gay Buddhist couple, and to become enlightened by all things. Enjoy the waterfall!

Issan Dorsey Roshi, 1990. Photo by Rob Lee.

Stories about My Teacher

Daishin David Sunseri

In his early life, my teacher, Issan Dorsey Roshi, was a speed freak, a drag queen, a junkie, a prostitute, an alcoholic and at times a real bitch. My teacher was also a Zen monk, a hospice worker, a friend to homeless people and drug addicts, a loving and compassionate being, and at times a real saint. This dichotomy was actually the foundation for his life and teaching, and was his path to liberation, albeit a somewhat unusual one. In my early life, I was a drug dealer, a marijuana farmer, a male prostitute, an erotic entertainer and at times a stubborn fool. I was also a hospice worker, an advocate for the homeless, a Dharma practitioner, a Zen monk and at times a dedicated student. This dichotomy was also the foundation for my own life and practice, and is my path to liberation, definitely a strange one.

Issan and I were meant to meet one another and to practice together because this is how the Dharma unfolds if each of us is open to all its manifestations. Having a deep understanding of himself, his motivations and his somewhat destructive tendencies, Issan was able to find compassion for his own confused and misdirected spiritual urges, and *then* to have compassion for those of us with similar life experiences. He was not afraid to be himself completely, and because of that, he made it possible for me and many others to fully be ourselves with no apologies. When Issan and I began practicing together, a certain empathy developed between us. We were able to work together with little or no friction because our mutual commitment to the Dharma was firmly grounded in our experience and understanding of the perilous obstacles that plague us all on the path. Our checkered pasts were a wonderful gift that enabled us to have some sense of the extent to which human beings will go to find some pleasure, happiness and peace of mind. Issan's life was a direct and simple expression of the most profound Buddhist teaching. His moment to moment practice of mindfulness was the practice of non-duality, of no separation from activity, of complete interconnectedness and intimate compassion. For me his greatest teaching was himself: he was an actual living manifestation of the Dharma in everyday life.

DAISHIN (Great Heart) DAVID SUNSERI (San Francisco) was born in 1952. He is an ordained Zen monk, a disciple of Issan Dorsey Roshi and has practiced in the Gay/Lesbian Buddhist Community for the last thirteen, as well as working with the sick and dying for twenty years. He is a teacher within San Francisco's Gay Buddhist Fellowship.

THE STORIES

Jail

When Issan and I first began working together, I decided to be completely honest with him about my past, so I spent a lot of time telling him about my experiences as a drug dealer and a male prostitute. He always paid very close attention to what I told him, and rather than being shocked, he was usually quite interested in hearing all the details about my "on the edge" life. In fact, he seemed to really love those parts of me that I found most self-destructive. At one point I described being arrested on various occasions, and spending time in jail. He asked how many times I'd been in prison and I said six or seven times. He brushed aside my response, and mentioned casually that I shouldn't worry about it, and that he'd been behind bars a lot more times than that. We laughed about it for days. He not only understood me, but in some way helped me to see through and let go of those life experiences I thought of as negative.

Speed Freak

Issan worked with a lot of people to help them in any way he could. One time a speed freak friend of his was visiting and I heard loud noises and shouts coming from Issan's room. I ran up the stairs to see what was happening, and a man flew past me almost knocking me down. As I walked into Issan's room, I saw that the place was in shambles. This fellow in a rage had torn the room apart, knocked the Buddha statue on Issan's altar to the floor, smashed his vase of flower offerings, threw papers on his desk all over, and tried to tear down the window shades. The normally neat room was completely trashed. Issan was red-faced and agitated, saying that the man had done all this. He spoke with a lot of emotion and excitement in his voice, but was not angry. He simply stayed at the level of energy the situation warranted. He was excited but not really in any pain about it all. Then we raced downstairs to find the man who had done all this. When he saw us, he panicked and struck Issan, throwing him to the ground. I grabbed at the man, but he hit me, too, and ran out the front door and down the street.

I tried to pick Issan up, and thought we should call the police about the assault. Issan said no, that this person was suffering a great deal and that the attack was just an attempt to relieve the pain. So I asked what we should do. He said, "Let's go clean up my room." So the two of us went up to his room and began to straighten things up. The first thing Issan did was to place the Buddha back on his altar and then to offer incense. As he did this, he began to cry and softly said, "There's so much suffering in the world. We have so much to do." Tears came to my eyes too as we went about cleaning the room. My teacher never spoke negatively about this man; he had always tried to help him. This expression of deep compassion affected me in the most profound way.

Care

Taking care of the details of our daily lives is our practice.
                                        —*Dogen Zenji*

In our Soto Zen tradition mindfulness practice is the moment to moment observation of and attention to what's in front of us. And for Issan taking care of his own life and the lives of those around him was a primary practice; that and daily zazen (meditation). This was a constant and strong expression of Buddha nature for him, and it was apparent in all his actions. On many occasions he would treat me with such attention that it would almost feel embarrassing. Once when I was quite sick in bed with the flu, he made soup for me and brought it to my room, and insisted that I eat the whole bowl. I had a high fever and wasn't able to feed myself. He gently fed me the soup, and then massaged my feet and back. I can recall he held my hand and sang to me until I fell asleep. The last thing I remember him saying to me was, "You have to get well soon. We don't have time for you to be sick. We have to practice together more." He spoke so softly.

On a beautiful spring day in 1988, we had a visit from Dainin Katagiri Roshi, abbot of Minnesota Zen Center, and one of Issan's teachers. Issan was nervous about Roshi's coming, and spent hours preparing for it. We cleaned the meditation hall, placed fresh flowers on the altar, bought special tea cakes that were Katagiri's favorite. When the abbot arrived, Issan was so happy he could barely contain himself. He showed Roshi around the Zen Center, explained his work with the sick and the dying, and enjoyed being with his old teacher. For the few hours Katagiri visited us, Issan treated him with great deference, seeing to all his needs, paying attention to every detail. When it was time for the Roshi to leave, Issan got down on his hands and knees to help Katagiri put on his sandals. This last gesture was a bit too much for me. After the visit was over, I confronted Issan about grovelling to his Zen teacher: that his behavior was demeaning and condescending, and that I didn't think he should treat any person that way, even an important Buddhist teacher. Issan looked at me, and with a sharp tone in his voice, said, "I didn't do it for *him*!" I realized then that all the actions of caring for the Roshi were Issan's practice of mindfulness for himself, and that I had completely misunderstood his behavior. Slowly I began to see this everyday teaching as a central part of my own path.

During one particularly busy time when we were first creating Maitri

Hospice for People with AIDS, Issan told me that he wanted me to do Doku-san (formal practice interview) with him. This is a very structured and somewhat solemn interchange where a Zen practitioner has the opportunity to meet the teacher face-to-face, and ask questions or present his or her own understanding of the Dharma. I entered the room, did the formal prostrations and sat down on a cushion two feet from Issan, facing him. In the candlelight he looked very calm, very settled. He began speaking first, thanking me for all my work on the various projects we were doing. Then he cautioned me to take care of myself. He was worried that I was burning out, that I wouldn't have the energy to continue working so hard. I just sat there, realizing that he was doing as much if not more than I was, and that his concern about me was his first thought. I bowed to him, and told him I was worried about him burning out too. He just said, "I'm a tough old bird. Don't worry about me." As we sat there, I felt an ever greater connection with him, and was so thankful for my life and practice. I expressed my gratitude to him for his commitment to practice and bowed to him. As I was about to leave the room, he leaned over and kissed me on the cheek in the most heartfelt way. I remember his smile vividly.

Part of Issan's and my practice together was expressed in a physical demonstrative way. I felt very close to him and he felt the same, so there was a constant interaction at many levels. He was very easy to touch, and was emotionally and physically very open and accessible. To me this quality was an indication of his deeply compassionate nature. If a person were ready to hear and feel the Dharma in a tangible connected way, Issan was there to manifest it. In all our physical interactions, he never was overtly sexual with me. Mostly being with him and being touched by him felt appropriate and nurturing. In fact, his touch is what I remember most clearly about him.

No Judgment

On one occasion Issan and I were going to visit a man with HIV disease in a Tenderloin hotel. We walked into the seedy lobby of the place and headed for the small elevator. It was a dilapidated old lift, barely able to accommodate two people. As we stepped into it, two large men, apparently bikers, entered the hotel and headed toward the elevator. Issan motioned that we should wait for them. I was concerned about being in a close space with these guys. They both were well over 250 pounds each, dressed in black, with rough tattoos running up and down their arms; one had a knife at his belt. Issan held the door open for them as they got in. We were all crushed together, not able to move. As soon as the elevator started to move, my teacher began to engage the two men. "Hi, my name is Issan." My heart sank. I couldn't believe he was talking to these guys. I remember thinking to myself: *Shut up, Issan! We're going to get hurt. These men are dangerous!* The elevator ride seemed interminable, and the whole while I was lost in my own worry about what was going to happen to us. I was so panicked, I didn't hear a word that was said; I was completely paralyzed by the situation, unable to really be present, feeling fear and anger that my teacher would put us both in danger.

Then the elevator stopped and the two men started to leave. As they did, they both gave Issan a hug, and I could hear them laughing and telling him it was great meeting him. He had actually made friends with the men during our short time together. As they walked away from the elevator, Issan remarked what nice boys they were. I explained my fears to him, what I was experiencing, how I sized up the situation. He laughed and said something about how everyone just needs some attention, to be cared for. I saw Issan's real compassion that day in an elevator, and on numerous other occasions during the time I lived and worked with him.

Another time Issan was going to do his wash at the local laundromat. As he entered the place, he noticed a young man curled up under one of the folding tables and moaning. On looking more closely, Issan saw that the man was covered in his own feces from head to toe. Alarmed, Issan helped him up and brought him back to the Zen Center. I saw them both down the street, and rushed to help. It took a while to clean the man up and to find out who he was. He was new to San Francisco from the Midwest, and was staying with his sister and brother-in-law. When they discovered he was gay and HIV positive, they threw him out of their house. Not having survival skills and being ill with intestinal flu, he had wandered the streets for a few days with severe diarrhea, hadn't eaten anything and became disoriented, eventually passing out under a table at the laundromat. Since the man was confused and upset, Issan and I had a hard time communicating with him. He was frightened and paranoid, and didn't want to see a doctor or leave us. So we tried to take care of him the best we could. We put adult disposable diapers on him, and constantly fed him liquids to keep him hydrated. We were concerned that he had lost so much fluid that the balance in his blood might be affected. Issan kept him in his own room for a few days as he went through many delusional episodes. At times he was coherent, at other times very confused, frustrated and scared. Issan stayed with him through all various mental states and remarked that they reminded him of his own personal delusions. After about a week, the young man began to improve, and eventually agreed to see a doctor. So at that point he went on his way, ready to return to a somewhat more normal life. When he left, Issan remarked to me that he felt so fortunate to be able to help people, and hoped we'd be able to continue to be of service to gay men and lesbians.

Dying

When my teacher was dying, we were able to spend some intimate time together. I would stay by his bed and hold his hand, sometimes just listening to him breathing. It was a great comfort to me to be able to be with him in this way, to watch him as he slept, to be physically close to him and so connected at this special time. Sometimes we would talk quietly about our lives together, about my practice and what he wanted me to do. The things I remember most vividly were the requests he made of me, the things he asked me to do as part of my practice. First, he asked me to continue to work and practice in the gay Buddhist community. He was concerned that gay men and lesbians wouldn't have the opportunities to practice in an open and honest way, out of the closet. He said we all needed as much help as we could get. He also asked me to use the Buddhist name he had given me, and in addition to wear my kesa (monk's robe) for meditation and ceremonies. He mentioned many other things to me, but he was keenly interested in setting up a practice place in a rural setting that would also have a residential hospice connected to it. He felt it would be helpful for dying people to spend the end of their lives in a strong practice environment in a peaceful country place. As he was dying, I recall one very intense moment when the strain was emotionally too much for me, and I began crying. I just blurted out how much I loved him. He looked at me, smiled slightly and said that he loved me too, and that it helped him to know my feelings. The last words he spoke to me were: "Practice hard, do your best, and take care of all beings."

For Issan

What is our practice?
Is it something that can be put
Down on a piece of paper?
My teacher was a fool
And a wise man,
So our practice is both wise and foolish.
My teacher's true nature,
His true name is One Mountain
That does not move
And that is forever crumbling.
And Great Heart falls into the arms
Of One Mountain.
Great Heart, One Mountain
Utter folly
Utter and immense gratitude—

I bow to my Teacher
As he bows to me,
And we meet face to face,
Eyebrow to eyebrow,
Heads touching
Hearts melting
No minds, no bodies, no thoughts—
Just this One Mountain
That becomes Great Peace,
Just this Great Heart
That becomes Bright Courage.
One Mountain, Great Heart,
Great Peace, Bright Courage,
All in the Mind of Buddha.
I offer no bow to my Teacher
And Friend,
Issan Dainei Daiosho—
May his teaching go on and on
And end in this moment.

Home

Downstairs the meditation hall was cold at 5:00 a.m. in the morning, icy floor on my bare feet, cold air coming from the wall and window cracks, cold fog trying to seep into the place. Issan was warm upstairs. He'd just drank hot green tea from his summer tea bowl. He was on the floor, doing his morning exercises, his legs stretching this way and that. He looked like a baby playing, his shaved head shining. He was warming up for meditation, getting his legs and back ready for two hours of sitting still. He moved with a smooth swimming motion, familiar positions he'd taken thousands of times before. Then he stood up and began putting on his robes, finally his kesa (monk's robe). I helped him adjust the folds of it behind where he couldn't reach. The back of his neck and head were so precious to me. I lit two sticks of incense and stood behind him. I could feel his warmth as we walked downstairs into the cold meditation hall. We stopped at Suzuki Roshi's altar; he offered incense, did prostrations, bowed and then moved to the main altar. I walked behind him in the sweep of his robes. We were together alone in this basement zendo, acting out the morning rituals of an ancient tradition. He approached the altar, held his hands together in gassho, signalling me to hand him the stick of incense so he could offer it. He carefully took it from my hands, lightly touching my fingers, and put it to his head. As he placed it in the incense bowl, he looked at me with a small slight smile and said very softly, *"This is your home.* " I could feel chills rise on my body, the hair at the back of my neck stood up, and I shuddered all over. I was so shocked and touched by his words, tears filled my eyes. Then we sat down on our cushions to meditate. Through most of the next two hours of meditation I heard those words resonating deep in me, filling every part of me. I realized then they would be with me for the rest of my life, that this Zen monk so reached into me that I would understand the teaching more fully than ever before. In a cold zendo in early morning, I was finally and completely home. And home was this beautiful and clear Dharma.

When I began practicing with Issan Dorsey, I was not looking for a teacher. In fact, I was much too skeptical of any religious authority to even acknowledge his teaching skills. But I was inexplicably drawn to Issan, and found myself extremely attracted to his strong commitment to practice. Also he was who he said he was. He had incredible integrity.

What surprised me most about my relationship with Issan was how intimate it was; how at times we were like lovers, yet not sexual. He understood me in the most complete and open way, and accepted me fully, virtues and shortcomings in all. He affected me in many ways; not so much by what he said, although he said many things that touched me deeply, but more by who he was, how he conducted his life. His greatest teaching was who he was, and by extension, what he did on a daily basis. He cared for me in every aspect of my life.

When he did prostrations, he did them with such concentration and so fully that it affected me in a way I cannot describe. There was so much teaching in his bow because he did it so completely, as if he was bowing for all of us, that he *was* all of us in some way. Full teaching of all the Buddhas in his bow.

One evening I was waiting with others for a friend of mine who was very late, and I was quite upset about it and expressed it. Issan heard me and walked into the room, looked at me with those sweet eyes, smiled and said, "David is so impatient." He said it as if he was giving me a great compliment, with complete acceptance and warmth. I'll never forget that moment. I've never been so cared for or so loved by anyone as I was by him, and I'm profoundly grateful for that teaching of real wisdom and compassion.

> O, that my monk's robes were wide enough
> to gather up all the suffering people
> in this floating world.
>
> Ryokan

Mindfulness Is Not a Part-Time Job

Dharma Talk by Issan Dorsey Roshi

Someone said to me the other day, "Aren't you always working on something?" Yes, we're always working on something, but hopefully it's not up here in our heads, filled with words to obscure it. I was talking with a friend recently about the phrase, "coming to reside in your breath-mind," and working with the phrase, and how useful it is to me. I thought it was interesting that I'd never *really* heard it before, and was just now beginning to work with it. I realized that I actually just heard it deeply.

This has been with me since I first started practicing. It's a whole way of working with your mind—and I've been thinking a lot about that lately. I hope you won't have to wait for 20 years before you begin to hear how to work with this thing called mind in zazen (meditation).

Now, people who come to practice immediately sit much easier than they did when I first began to sit at Sokoji Temple years ago. I remember everybody sitting with their legs bent up. They'd sit for five minutes, then they'd lie down and moan. But now people come and it's like we already did that part for them. It's as if we have a shared body that has already gone through that preliminary stuff, and people are already able to experience some aspect of zazen practice and how we practice together.

We have to be willing to explore and experiment. First we have to have a sense of humor and a willingness to explore and experiment with our lives and our uncomfortableness. We know that sometimes we can sit for a few minutes, or even a few days, but at some point it gets pretty uncomfortable; and it's uncomfortable for us not to invite our thoughts to tea, and to reside in our breath-mind.

"Don't invite your thoughts to tea" is an expression of Suzuki-roshi's which I've always found useful. You know, these are just words, and we have to remember that every human concept is just delusion. Still, we use words and provisionally talk about our experience. Lately, I have been exploring this way of thinking with a friend who has AIDS dementia; the virus is living in his brain. I'm thinking and working on it and talking with him about it because the virus that is attacking many of us now ends up being in the brain. So is there some way for us to experience that? I don't know yet. My question is: how to be with people who have dementia and how to experience the dementia that we all have now anyway? It's called delusion. Mind is always creating confusion, joy and pain, like and don't

---

ISSAN DORSEY ROSHI, an openly gay man, was a Sōtō Zen monk and teacher in the lineage of Shunryu Suzuki-roshi. He was the first Abbot of Issanji Temple in the Castro district, founded Maitri Hospice, and died of AIDS in 1990.

like, and depression. But there is also a "background mind." This is what my friend and I have been discussing together.

Sometimes when I'm talking about uncomfortableness, I talk about the five fears. One of the five fears is the fear of unusual states of mind. How do we come to have appreciation and respect for this fear and not just some resistance, so that we can enter our fear, allowing these new areas of uncomfortableness? When we can enter each of these new spaces, we can begin to look at truthfulness.

Why do we have to sit? Really there's no reason to sit. If we're completely sincere, then there's no reason to sit. I'm not completely sincere so I have to keep sitting to check. Even if we're involved with unskillful actions, the one quality we should strive for is truthfulness. Truthfulness takes a total commitment to see all aspects of ourselves and our unskillfulness. If we can embrace the totality of ourselves, we can embrace the totality of others and of the world. Our tendency is to think about things before we do them. Even when we see a flower we say, "Oh, what a beautiful flower." "Beautiful flower" is extra. Just look at the flower with no trace.

Suzuki-roshi wrote, "When we practice zazen, our mind is calm and quite simple. But usually our mind is very busy and complicated, and it is difficult to be concentrating on what we are doing." This is because when we act, we think, and this thinking leaves some trace. Our activity is shadowed by some preconceived idea. The traces and notions make our mind very complicated. When we do something with a simple, clear mind, we have no shadows and our activity is strong and straight forward.

So, even with zazen practice, it gets so complicated. We're dissecting every aspect of what's going on, reviewing and comparing. How do we keep it simple and straightforward? How do we come to know this basic truth of practice and Buddhism? The teaching and the rules can and should change according to the situation and the people we're practicing with, but the secret of practice cannot be changed. It's always truth.

We teach ourselves and encourage ourselves by creating this space (the meditation hall) so we can begin looking at our mind. "Don't invite your thoughts to tea." "Where is our breath-mind?" "How do you create background mind?" I used to say: allow this kind of mind to arise. But now I'm saying: *create* background mind.

This practice is simple: watch your breaths and don't invite your thoughts to tea. But not inviting your thoughts to tea doesn't mean to get rid of thinking. That is discrimination. So, there's no reason to get rid of thoughts, but rather to have some blank, non-interfering relationship with them. Don't make your mind blank, but rather, have some blank relationship with the thoughts. Begin to see the space behind and around the thoughts, and shift the seat of your identity out of your thoughts and come to reside in your breath-mind. We develop our intention to reside in our breath-mind by first bringing our attention to "breath as mind," and then by shifting the seat of our identity from our thoughts to our breath.

This all ties in with how we use this space, this laboratory. We should have a willingness to explore with our lives, and this is our laboratory right here—how we use the meditation hall and how we use what happens outside of it. Mindfulness is not a part-time job.

Two Meditations

John R. Killacky

IN MY FATHER'S BED

Recently I was in Chicago visiting my mother and slept in the bed in which my father died last January. Les had been a difficult man—hard working all his life and hard drinking for much of the earlier years. We were never that close—gay sons and their daddies are often like that. Early on I checked out; retreating into my fantasy world leaving him far behind. At his funeral, I found myself listening to my cousins describe family gatherings that I had no recollection of.

He and I were estranged for many years until his cancer diagnosis almost a decade ago. With the urging of my sister, I went home. Greeting me at his door he asked, "Why have you come?" I answered, "Because I'm told you're dying." He let me into his lair and I stayed the weekend. We began to navigate through a lifetime of misperceptions and fear. When things got a little too raw there was always the ever-present television that our attention could meander to (and of course mom was forever ready to play the conciliator).

The next years proved to be both excruciating and extraordinary as we both sought each other's validation, with neither one giving in too much. Displaced anger and pain flared up as we negotiated sometimes as father and son; sometimes man to man. Disappointments and disapproval became tempered with familiarity and recognition of accomplishments by the both of us.

Aspiring middle class Irish Catholic; he married and stayed in the neighborhood. Following in his father's footsteps, he sold cattle at the Chicago Stockyards. When the yards relocated some thirty years ago, he stayed behind with his wife and five children to begin all over again in his forties. He eventually got a political patronage job (as did my mom) working in the Chicago Park District. But he never did speak about this job in his later years; his identity and stories were always from either the Yards or from his army service in the Second World War.

JOHN R. KILLACKY (San Francisco) is Director of San Francisco's Yerba Buena Center for the Arts, writer, filmmaker and twenty-year student of Buddhism. His writing has appeared in *Minneapolis/St. Paul Magazine*, *Inside Arts*, *StarTribune*, *Hungry Mind Review*, *P-form*, *High Performance*, *Shambhala Sun*, *Juice*, *Dance/USA Journal*, *Art Papers*, *Utne Reader*, *Gaze*, *Able-Together*, and *Lavender Lifestyles*; as well as being included in *Out in All Directions, The Almanac of Gay and Lesbian America*.

In the ensuing years, whenever conversations needed to plateau we could always return to his time in France as an Army Warrant Officer with him retelling me stories and pulling out photographs. I never minded for this was a side of the man that I had never listened to in earlier decades. Eventually he told me how hard it was for him with my public opposition to the Viet Nam War in the late sixties.

"Almost as hard as when I found out about you, you know, your personal life." He never did say the words gay or homosexual, but after friends began to die he empathized and wanted me to know that he was sorry. "Everybody shouldn't die so young . . . at least wait until you get to be my age."

At his wake, I listened to stories about a man I knew far too little of. Men and women regaled me with his exploits and gleefully described the fights he would invariably get himself into at the neighborhood bars when the outsider "suits" would come in and try to disrupt. I had only experienced the tormented side of his Irish temper as a child.

People wanted to let me know how much he had meant to them and how he would be missed. I was grateful for their expression since I hadn't known too many of his friends. One man told me that he had known my father for sixty years. I wondered quietly to myself if any of my generation will survive the pandemic long enough to have that lifelong opportunity.

He looked old in his casket. His skin though seemed softer and less weather-beaten than I remembered. Even as a child, I loved playing with his wiry hair and wrinkly furrowed brow; yet now he was cold and waxen. One of his six grandchildren kept trying to wake up from his nap. He wore his herringbone sports jacket and a new shirt and tie. As a Veteran he held his American flag proudly. I cried as I kissed him goodbye.

Some weeks after the funeral, I dreamt that the family was called back to witness his "last breath." As we gathered, the mortician explained that it was a great honor to watch as a departed one passes on and not to worry. There he was again, my father in his casket wearing his herringbone jacket. A wave went through his body and he exhaled, rising into the air and slowly turning over; floating back his clothing was discarded and his body lost all volume and shape. He flattened and disappeared.

I awoke from that dream bewildered, but at peace. I turned on the lights and realized that it was forty-nine days after his real death. Remembering that the Tibetans believe that one enters the "bardo" state for up to seven weeks until you are reborn, I smiled and thought, "He's free now . . . he's gone on."

That dream came back to me vividly again as I recently slept in my father's bed, the bed where he died. I am grateful that I got to know what little I did of him in recent years, both as a person and as a parent. That was a gift for each of us. Good-bye, daddy.

WALKING WITH THE DEAD

A dead man's words: "Go home. The future is crowded." His sister gave me Philip-Dimitri's book, inscribing, "One day I'll probably perform (it)." Holding on to a dead brother.

I too, hold on to the dead. They have become the elements of my reality. I hear Celie's fluid-filled lungs gasping for air as her family healed itself, gathered around her wasted transgendered body. Her daddy only switched pronouns at the very end, pleading to her clouded, unblinking eyes to forgive him. Her quick, shallow breaths are wind in my universe.

Peter's night sweats become water. Entwined in fevers, chills, sweat, piss, shit, tears, cum, and spit; I kissed his cracked lips and held him forever that night. I wish Peter's fluids could help Willie now. I hardly recognized him with his discolored skin, shriveled and shrunken onto his skull. His dehydrated body imploded as we hugged.

My fire still resides in Bill's fever-ridden body on the ice mattress in that hospital. It was too early on to name the disease, so he smoldered and wasted away, an anomaly for the medical students to ponder. I'd nap with him on the frozen bed: "No, I'm not cold, I'm with my friend."

David's ashes are my earth. Defiled at death, his wishes were ignored as the family cremated him before an autopsy could reveal how his lesion-filled brain and lungs could have functioned for so long. I imagine smearing his ashes, warrior-like onto my body, as I rage into the night.

I hold on to all of them. My dead: they are my mandala. Telling their unfinished stories affirms my own life. I walk among them and live.

Grief and the Path to Awakening:

Appreciating What a Gay Sangha Offers

Mark Marion

Hope can neither be affirmed or denied.
Hope is like a path in the countryside.
Originally there was no path.
Yet, as people walk all the time in the same spot,
a way appears.

—Lu Xon

I

In Tibet there is the story of Krisha Gotami, a young woman who had the good fortune to live at the time of the Buddha. When her first child was about a year old, it fell ill and died. Grief stricken and clutching its little body, Krisha Gotami roamed the streets begging anyone she met for a medicine that would restore her child to life.

Some ignored her, others laughed at her, and some thought her mad. But finally she met a wise man who told her that the only person in the world who could perform the miracle she was looking for was the Buddha. So she went to the Buddha, lay the body of her child at his feet, and told him her story.

The Buddha listened with infinite compassion, and then said gently, "There is only one way to heal your affliction. Go down to the city and bring me back a mustard seed from any house in which there has never been a death."

Krisha Gotami felt elated and set off at once for the city. She stopped at the first house she saw and said, "I've been told by the Buddha to fetch a mustard seed from a house that has never known death." "Many people have died in this house," she was told. She went on to the next house. "There have been countless deaths in our family," they said. And so to a third and a fourth house, until she had been all around the city and realized that the Buddha's condition could not be fulfilled.

So she took the body of her child to the burial ground and said goodbye to him for the last time, and then returned to the Buddha. "Did you

MARK MARION (San Francisco) is a psychotherapist, whose Buddhist practice is in the Vipassana tradition. He has written a chapter about coping with multiple loss in the gay community for the book *Gay and Lesbian Mental Health: A Sourcebook for Practitioners* (New York: Haworth Press, 1996). He also participates in the Bay Area's Gay Buddhist Fellowship.

bring the mustard seed?'' he asked. ''No,'' she said, ''I'm beginning to understand the lesson you are trying to teach me. Grief made me blind and I thought that only I had suffered at the hands of death.'' ''Why have you come back?'' asked the Buddha. ''To ask you to teach me the truth,'' she replied, ''of what death is, what might lie behind and beyond death, and what in me, if anything, will not die. The Buddha began to teach her, saying, ''If you want to know the truth of life and death, you must reflect continually on this: there is only one law in the universe that never changes —that all things change and that all things are impermanent. . . . Because pain has now made you ready to learn and your heart is opening to the truth, I will show it to you.''*

The first time I came across the story of Krisha Gotami, I felt the whole of my mind and body becoming still, as only happens when I am hearing something that all my experience tells me is true. I had listened to parts of this story many times before from friends, family, and people I worked with, but I had never truly heard it. But in exploring the meaning of sangha —of a gay sangha—my mind keeps returning to this story again and again.

There is a legacy that we all share as gay men, of separation and of loss, that I believe gives us an affinity for Buddhist practice. A gay sangha is a natural result of this affinity, and offers the opportunity to join with other gay men on a spiritual path. Together we can discover that our life experiences of separation and loss, this shared legacy, is no longer an impediment to fulfillment. It is, instead, a doorway to awakening to fulfillment. Of all the many meanings of the word ''sangha,'' my favorite is simply, ''working together to discover our true nature'' (thanks to GBF member David Sunseri).

Finding Buddhist practice and a gay sangha has been a lifesaver for me that I would not have pursued if not for the separation and loss in my own life. There was a time, about six years ago, when the bottom fell out of my life. Very quickly, dearly held assumptions about who I was and what life was about (in which I had invested my security and sanity) began to crumble.

I was working part-time as the HIV/AIDS counselor/advocate at an East Bay agency. My job was to provide crisis counseling for people with HIV and their family, friends, and lovers. I was also coordinating an HIV-antibody test site and supervising support groups. In addition to all of this, I was maintaining a private practice.

This schedule was demanding, but I thought I was doing OK. I became used to dealing with illness and death in my work, and depended upon my private sense of spirituality to keep things in perspective. I thought that was enough.

---

*The story of Krisha Gotami is paraphrased from *The Tibetan Book of Living and Dying* by Sogyal Rinpoche (Santa Cruz, CA: Rigpa Fellowship, 1992).

But then a sequence of events happened that began to erode what I thought was solid ground. First, I became ill with hepatitis, but since it was not casually contagious, I continued working. My joke about it was that, since I was now jaundiced to a vivid orange from my toes to my eyeballs, I could finally wear all those fashionable earth-tone colors that had previously clashed with my waspish white pallor.

Lame humor only provided me with temporary relief, however, because in the weeks that followed, key members of my biological as well as my "gay family" began dying. Between cancer, heart disease, and AIDS, several people who had been emotional anchors for me were suddenly gone. Although I had lost people before who were close to me, the relentlessness and timing of these deaths cut to the core.

The line between the reality I experienced at work and at home began to blur. Although I recognized I was still one of the lucky ones (my losses paled in comparison to those of most of the people I was working with), still, the cumulative impact was immobilizing.

On the surface, I was handling it well. I mapped out my own grieving process and focused on the positives in my life. For one thing, my lover and I were forging a deeper bond as we went through these losses together. Also, the slowness of my recovery from jaundice brought numerous compliments from surviving friends and family about my "fabulous tan" at one memorial service after another.

But underneath, living had stopped for me. The expanding universe suddenly began contracting, collapsing under the weight of its own gravity, shutting out the light. I wanted my friends and family back. I wanted my life to return to the way it had been. More than anything, I wanted to escape the powerlessness and the lack of control I felt, the sense that the world was no longer a safe or friendly place. Somehow I also wanted to be able to protect my friends and myself from the pain and death that seemed to be everywhere. Like Krisha Gotami, I refused to accept the truth; I was searching for something that would restore life to the way it had been.

It is ironic that loss—while being perhaps the most universal experience of the human condition—can still make each of us feel alone, separate, and uniquely wronged. And like Cleopatra, queen of denial, my royal decree was that the people I loved and needed were not permitted to die and leave me behind.

As a therapist, I frequently reminded my clients that separation and withdrawal are natural ways we react to loss or trauma. They serve as the psyche's internal circuit-breaker, shutting down the power when feelings of loss overwhelm us. But what is a temporary survival instinct can become a permanent condition. Then it ultimately becomes a refusal of life itself.

Somewhere in my own withdrawal and depression, sentiments along the lines of "Physician, heal thyself!" must have pointed me toward Buddhism and GBF. I think I was attracted to Buddhist practice because it deals so honestly with the truth of suffering. There was no sidestepping or sugar coating. There was no running away, but instead, opening to the truth of impermanence. I was not interested in going on the spiritual journey alone—I'd already done enough of that. Nor was I interested in being a part of a community where being gay was spiritually questionable or even just plain different. (I'd done enough of that, too.) So GBF felt like home.

In the time that has passed since the bottom fell out of my life, living for me has been a practice in finding the courage to open to the grief of unacceptable loss. Sometimes I fear the absolute nakedness of it. At such times, I experience a slowing down and contraction. At other times, I feel myself opening up and expanding into the vast emptiness of it. Then I experience a "letting go." In the silence of meditation, I hear the words of the Buddha to Krisha Gotami: "Because pain has now made you ready to learn and your heart is opening to the truth, I will show it to you . . . there is one way and one way only out of Samsara's ceaseless round of birth and death, which is the path of liberation." In either case, to practice together with other gay men who have suffered separation and loss just like me has helped me to rediscover a sense of meaning and hope that I couldn't have found alone.

For me, a gay sangha unites two of the most important components of lasting meaning and genuine hope. One is the sharing of the experiences, gifts, and challenges that come with being gay. The other is practicing together and supporting each other in awakening, and discovering our true nature. In GBF, both of these components are present.

A gay sangha provides us with a home where we can rediscover and deepen our acceptance of ourselves and our ability to trust others. It is also a place where we can use the grief and alienation that have been part of our lives to deepen our practice, and to stimulate questions that can lead us back to our own true nature, questions such as: "What can bring a lasting self acceptance and belonging?" "What, if anything, is real?" "What in me, if anything, will not die?"

As a beginning practitioner I'm not yet at the point where I can view the suffering that happens in my own, or someone else's life, as a wonderful opportunity for spiritual growth. As I heard another GBF member concisely (if politically incorrectly) put it, "Samsara sucks." Especially in the form of AIDS, it is infuriating and horrifying. With more than a decade of unprecedented grief and loss, many of us are very weary. Facing ongoing loss seems to leave few options, for sanity's sake, except either denial or despair.

Buddha offered to Krisha Gotami an alternative, and in the Dharma we are also offered this alternative. What allowed Krisha Gotami to see the alternative was opening to the truth of suffering. For myself, I take the alternative begrudgingly. Even after getting whacked relentlessly over the head by the sledgehammer of suffering, illness, and death, my ego shows itself to be remarkably resilient, and still wanting control.

But this is starting to change for me. A spaciousness is almost imperceptibly opening up around my ego's grasping. It's like the answer a friend gave me when I asked him how life was going for him. He replied, "Considering the enormity of my expectations and the depths of my ingratitude, I have to admit, I'm doing OK." Sometimes I can smile at the ego's expectations and ingratitude.

Through heart-felt dharma talks and discussions at GBF sittings, I am slowly opening to whatever is happening, including aloneness or grief, as well as surrender and joy. I find courage, inspiration, and support within the practice and fellowship of a gay sangha.

Before finding GBF, I often felt like a solo explorer on the spiritual path. Facing the truth of suffering and death alone sometimes was like staring into a dark, bottomless abyss. But in the Buddha, Dharma, and Sangha, I discover what amounts to a new set of eyes with which to gaze into that abyss—a new vision that is radiant, boundless, deathless.

Everything in experience—including the most unpleasant—can be turned back toward our practice. We can allow it to propel us together toward the discovery of our true nature.

II

One memory of early childhood stands out vividly. I am in my backyard, sitting in the grass, feeling effortlessly connected to everything and everyone. It is notable because most of the other memories are not happy, but for this image of a three- or four-year-old sitting alone in the middle of the lawn, feeling a profound sense of serenity and wholeness. It is actually more of a full body experience rather than an image. There is an interconnectedness, a belonging, a sensation of the life force flowing through me and through everything. Everything is fresh, radiant, glowing with life; inside is very quiet, very still . . . wanting nothing.

Most of us have some kind of a sense of this spacious openness and natural connectedness in memory or intuition. Perhaps in the silence of meditation the mind has stopped long enough to reveal this sense of belonging with each other and all things, this trusting, open acceptance of self and others that allows for a feeling of flowing in the world. Or perhaps there has been a moment of rare beauty that has captured the attention so completely that, for an instant, everything but that moment was gone, and yet that moment was everything.

For myself, this experience stands in sharp contrast to the habitual way of living. The world that I recognize is defined by separateness. Much of what is outside of me is the "other," unknown and potentially threatening. This separate "me" is required to be forever vigilant, forever seeking safety and protection. It is a struggle, a constant strategizing for survival, and for control toward the goal of getting what I need to preserve safety. From this perspective, any memory or intuition of natural connectedness and harmony looks hopelessly, laughably naive. "Don't you remember the traumas, the betrayals, the abandonment and violation?" this separate self scolds. "That kind of innocence just makes you all the more easily victimized, a sitting duck!"

The mind continually relives a montage of disappointments, traumas and betrayals that expose the vulnerability of the separate me and the necessity of fear. The images and feelings of abandonment or violation—my suffering—are the justification for this hypervigilance. In fact, my suffering (with the emphasis on "mine") is the cause of the fearfulness, the aggression, the need for control. Survival requires abandonment of the spacious, peaceful openness that I remember from childhood for the cramped closet of safety and protection. If joy in life is lost in the process, then that is just the price of growing up and facing reality. Or is it?

I remember a friend of mine, Dan. He was a very handsome, sweet and courageous man who was living with AIDS. One day he confided in me his own secret dread about his dying. He could deal with almost anything, he said, except blindness or paralysis—becoming "a vegetable," as he put it. The powerlessness, helplessness, absolute dependency brought up on him a terror and aversion that he almost could not describe.

A couple of years later, Dan became ill with a rare opportunistic infection that caused both blindness and complete paralysis. In the last weeks, which were mercifully few, he could neither see, nor move, nor speak, although his mind remained lucid and alert. On the last visit I remember sitting next to his bed, looking into his face, holding his hand. Dan's eyes were alive and searching my face, even as his expression—like his body— was slack and drawn. Somewhere in that moment of meeting his gaze, time seemed to stop. There was nothing to say, nothing that could be said that would help or change anything. The powerlessness and helplessness of the situation was overwhelming. Grief filled both of us. Tears streamed down Dan's frozen, mask-like face.

Somewhere in that moment of meeting each other's eyes and holding the gaze—something inside broke. It was as if in recognition of a moment of unbearable suffering—the separate "me" shattered. I left that day feeling hollow and empty. Any vigilance or defensiveness was gone, replaced by a soft, transparent sorrow.

The struggle for survival that had so dominated my consciousness with its relentless momentum, in one moment derailed and lurched to a halt, its purpose suddenly becoming distant and meaningless.

"There is nothing to protect, no one will survive, there is no safety and everything is completely and utterly out of my control."

That moment of squeezing Dan's hand, of meeting his gaze, was more than I could withstand, more than this separate ''me'' could bear. Somewhere in the space between Dan's eyes and my eyes, the defenses gave way. Any sense of uniqueness or specialness of my personal suffering melted, along with the separateness it engenders. What remains is only the feeling of profound pain and love. Between us was the recognition of defeat, the inevitability of surrender. Defeat in the war for survival of our separate ''I'' or ''me''—a war that we had already lost anyway.

Many of us have had moments, sitting at the bedside of someone who is dying—perhaps alone or sometimes surrounded by friends, family and loved ones—when the presence of loss, the enormity of suffering, has opened our hearts. The sadness, hurt and grief melt our separateness, leaving a tremendous love for the person who is dying and compassion for one another. Then we are experiencing what Krisha Gotami discovered in her futile search for a mustard seed. We are all together in this condition of suffering and impermanence. Not alone, not separate, not unique. The pain of this shared reality brings compassion and an undefended intimacy with each other.

I do not minimize the horror and anguish of loss. Sometimes the pain is so great that we do not feel anything but pain, and in it we seem to be terribly alone. How can anyone forget the sinking feeling of powerlessness to help, the hollow sensation of that last slender thread of hope snapping in two or the deafening sound of the heart breaking? But what Krisha Gotami, in the loneliness of her grief, finally recognized was that the thread of hope that snaps in two is the hope for survival of the separate ''me'' and what breaks in the heart is the hard, angry defense against the truth of suffering.

All that remains, then, is an exquisitely tender awareness of how fragile we are, how priceless every moment is, and how unbearable sorrow exposes a deep and abiding love.

If you feel separate, alone, alienated by the unique devastation over your own loss, then take instruction from the Buddha. Go to your friends and neighbors to collect that mustard seed from someone who has not been touched by grief. You will discover, like Krisha Gotami, that your own unique and personal pain is written on the heart of every other human being.

For myself, since that day, the sense of separateness has returned. The primacy and urgency of the pursuit of safety, protection and control has emerged from the ashes and continues to reassert its ludicrous agenda. But the truth is so simple. Everything dies, and so will I. This separate ''me'' is forever complicating and testing this simple truth, looking for an escape clause. But opening to suffering ever so slowly melts the habitual hard, angry denial that I had so blindly believed could save me. I will never forget the gift that Dan gave me, or ever again look at my childhood experience of oneness with disdain. In meditation I have the opportunity to rediscover this interconnectedness and serenity that I tasted as a little boy. In meditation, I can also watch the desperation of this separate "me" in its struggle to survive and I increasingly notice how heartless and how suffocatingly small that vision can be.

We do not have to fall for the endless complications and tests of the simple truth that everything dies and we will too. Our own personal suffering that has seemed to sustain and justify this separate sense of "me"-ness can instead point toward the path to awakening, if we can recognize that the suffering is not finally our own or personal at all. Opening to grief and loss means letting go, at least for an instant, just long enough to see the futility of the struggle. And then we can stop. In stopping what is revealed is not bleak despair, but instead a connectedness of belonging, of unbearable sorrow that exposes a deep and abiding love. For myself, every moment is an opportunity to choose.

Buddhism, Healing & Gayness: a Personal Journey

Lee Robbins

Buddhism began with suffering and the perception of suffering. The recognition of the constancy and extent of suffering led the Buddha to seek its ending, its ending for self and its ending for others—and the recognition that there is no real difference. And below the suffering came the discovery of an ocean of boundless compassion for suffering.

Watching the intermittent anguish of my friends and my self, I have come to believe that gayness in our society comes with more than its quota of pain. Not solely as a result of social evil, condemnation, hostility, ostracism and actual persecution, but because gay people seem to possess a certain sensitivity to suffering, conceivably a certain attraction to it, perhaps an admiration of our seemingly heroic capacity to bear it, even a compassionate willingness to carry the burden for others, gay and non-gay, as well as ourselves. Many times I've noted how the movie and music images of anguished suffering women attract gay men. Anguished, persecuted, powerless, surviving women, suffering for love. Gayness, despite its ironic title, often seemed to me to be *about* suffering.

Gayness, properly understood from a Buddhist perspective, is but another manifestation of mind having, as all manifestations of mind, no actual separate reality. Yet this facile statement only serves to remind me of an anonymous verse:

> Though I know pain isn't real
> When I sit on a pin,
> I dislike what I fancy I feel.

The story of one personal journey that follows builds from my personal journals over the last decade. Perhaps these experiences, shared here on paper, may make the path a millisecond shorter or a fragment lighter for another.

I grew to adulthood in an agnostic Jewish family, an only child. Mine was an intact nuclear family but one which frequently moved from state to state. Wearing glasses from age 7, good at reading, poor at sports, emotionally reticent, often lonely, longing even then for closeness to other boys.

LEE ROBBINS (San Francisco) was born in 1939 and practices within the Vipassana tradition and the teachings of Stephen Levine. He also participates in the Bay Area's Gay Buddhist Fellowship.

In my agnostic family and secular society, I saw no need for religion, no meaning in spirituality. *Science* seemed more the path and, in the spirit of the times, I spent my high school and early college years preparing to be a nuclear physicist.

In my family, I learned also that a partner relationship was a necessity *and* that relationships don't work. And a more general message: a good person and a good son must be happy. My mother, the dominant figure, constantly said I should do what she told me to achieve success while acknowledging her own discontent. As usual enough in families, I, the son, was to fill the family need which my mother had been unable to attain for herself.

At the time, my father seemed largely irrelevant. [In later years I remarked that my parents had met when my father accidentally knocked down my mother while skating at an ice rink—and that was the last time he was the top in the relationship.] Not until his eighties did I become conscious that my father had been quite central to what tranquillity and sanity I possessed, that his quiet and distance were also strength and acceptance.

In short, my mother taught that not only is suffering inevitable but it was my sacred family duty to find a way out of this inevitable failure. Perhaps this was the first half of the Buddha's message that life is impermanence and suffering without his discovery of the ending of suffering. Perhaps it was simply the impetus for my own path.

In my teen years, still neither sexual nor spiritual, I remained ignorant of both practices. My mother frequently pointed out my brightness and drew the moral that this gift made it even more incumbent upon me to achieve success and happiness. The ambiguity lay in the meaning of success which seemed sometimes to refer to serving others and sometimes to mean monetary security. In any case, she informed me, college was essential.

Eager to attain my mother's approval and fulfill my family destiny, when she instructed that to go to college I needed a scholarship and that to get a scholarship I needed good grades, I went in one semester from C's in the 7th grade to A's in the 8th, and continued this through the end of high school.

Graduating Harvard on a scholarship, going on to another Ivy League college on a fellowship, I thought that, with intelligence and sufficient hard work, I would be able to maintain control over my life and finally achieve an end to suffering. Grandiose dreams arose that I would achieve this not only for myself and my family but for all the world—perhaps as a scientist finding means to end the world's pain.

Considerable joy was mixed in, friendships, achievements, experiences from skiing to travel. Things seemed to be working—just a little more effort, a few more thoughts, another round of experiences and all would be well. The world was my oyster—why wouldn't it open?

Now and then though I found myself thinking about death, thinking that it was still a long way off, thinking that maybe death and the world was all an illusion and that I was the only live actor in a play with mannequins. I'd quickly push these irrational thoughts from my conscious mind and return to the hard physical reality which, so said family, friends and teachers, was all of existence. In the early '80s after my return to graduate school, I remember remarking to one of my professors with regard to our studies, "It's all just a way of passing the time between birth and death." He seemed impressed by my perception.

Earlier, right after college in my first year of graduate school I learned that my closest friend was marrying his girlfriend, whom he dated while we were friends in college, because she was pregnant. I came to the shocking realization that people actually *did* it; they *actually had sex*—and I didn't. And I was attracted to boys.

A few days later I did the hardest thing I've ever done in my life saying "I think I have homosexual tendencies" when I called student health services at the University of Pennsylvania to ask them for an appointment to fix me. Nine years of therapy later, the last five with a well known, kindly but homophobic group therapist, I finally gave up on turning straight as the solution to the end of suffering.

Dr. Haddon reproached me for abandoning my quest, and I riposted, "Dr. Haddon, it's been almost ten years. I can just imagine that someday, when I'm 85 and in a nursing home in my wheelchair, I'll spot this little old lady in her wheelchair at the other end of the corridor and think, 'Wow, that's just what I've wanted all my life.' Even if true I don't think it's worth waiting 'til then to live my life." By that time I'd noted that none of the members of the group were turning straight and, usefully, learned from them most of the more popular cruising spots.

"So many men, so little time" was a popular slogan of the nascent gay movement. By the end of the flower-child '60s, I turned with a vengeance to the pursuit of salvation through bodily friction.

In the early '70s I read *Be Here Now* and tried out mantras and chanting. When the mantras and the chanting didn't solve my problems in an hour or two, never having heard of practice with its hours, months and years of patience, I put them aside and returned to boys. By 1973, I'd found my first lover and moved him in.

This allowed me to fulfill one family mandate, to have a relationship. In my family manual, being attached was more important to being a successful person than even the gender, race or religion of the "attachee." Within months of my first attachment, feeling stirrings of family success, I informed my parents of my gayness. They responded not unkindly with their concerns, the durability of gay relationships and my happiness. More fulfillment of desire seemed better and safer. I continued my pursuit of faster and better salvation through many more men on the side.

At the start of the '80s, browsing in a Marin County bookstore with the same friend whose marriage had impelled my journey while visiting San Francisco, I happened upon Stephen Levine's recently published *A Gradual Awakening*. My spiritual self peeked out. I purchased it and read it quickly. I was impressed but quite incapable—or unwilling—of following the practices suggested. I kept the book.

By the late '80s, I had twenty-five years of the daily discomfort of a sleeping disorder, like that of my mother's forty-five years on once or twice nightly sleeping pills. This and the absence of a spiritual center left me perennially weary and grasping for surcease through drinking before bed and through the momentary forgettings of self through sex, reading and eating. Twenty years of momentary flashes of joy from sex with many, many partners still left me often weary, often joyless. Thousands of novels left me distracted momentarily while rounds of eating and dieting found me ever a few pounds over the weight I thought would attract the playmate and partner of my salvation.

By 1989 I wrote in my Journal:

> *I grew up in a family that seemed to me normal and OK; I discovered my at-traction to other men; I got an education and found a job. Then came a lover who decided he'd be better off alone, another who traveled down the road to active alcoholism and a third, now dead of* AIDS. *A couple of more tries with other men who couldn't handle intimacy and many, many "tricks" (a word I hated but have now come to use) along the way left me in a great deal of emo-tional pain.*

My second relationship, starting in 1975 and lasting seven and a half years, began with a wonderful man. Two years later, I began to realize, as did he, his alcoholism was becoming increasingly active, a behavior as unfamiliar to my insulated Jewish upbringing as gayness had been years earlier. We went to a gay couple's counselor in Philadelphia, the late David Keller, who said, "Your relationship will never work until you, Rich, give up your alcoholism and you, Lee, give up your sex addiction." *I* thought he was right about Rich! Still, I did decide to practice monogamy a bit to prove *I* wasn't addicted; selecting the moment with care, I made it success-fully through an entire month—for obvious reasons I did choose a Febru-ary in a non-leap year.

Four years later, my suffering led me, desperate, to my first experience with a 12 Step Fellowship, Al-Anon (for families and friends of alcoholics). In the latter half of the '70s and the earlier half of the '80s, I wended my way through the meetings of various of these Fellowships, Al-Anon, later followed and accompanied by SLAA (Sex & Love Addicts Anonymous). By the late '80s, I joined the 12 Step meetings of ACOA/D (Adult Chil-dren of Alcoholic or Dysfunctional Families).

Each taught me something. In Al-Anon I learned that the roots of my suffering lay not in another but in myself. In SLAA I learned that what I thought only lust, a sex addiction taking too much time and providing too little relationship, was more deeply a love addiction. Love, not in the Buddhist sense of an encompassing unity but rather in sadly transient feelings of closeness and fantasy which frequently accompanied my sexual trystings.

In those very feelings, I thought, if I could just learn to make them permanent, lay the path to the end of suffering. I never fully surrendered to the dictates of SLAA but found the meetings and readings of some help in controlling my pattern of sexual compulsion. This, I hoped, would allow me to find happiness through successful romantic love.

It was in these Fellowships that I first came into regular contact with the concept of practice, there called "meditation and prayer," a beginning recognition of spirituality. I got the concept of "something" beyond my narrow suffering self, but I continued ignorant of how to connect with this something. The Fellowships mention meditation as a worthy and useful practice but say little about how or why or where; it seemed a minor aspect of their "cure."

Then in my Journal of Tuesday, November 15, 1988, I wrote:

> *Interesting day. Last night, after my ACOA meeting, I went to hear Patrick Carnes [one of the founders of SLAA] speak at a special SLAA meeting. It was a much more striking experience than I had anticipated. While some of the technical data was interesting, the part that left me stunned was his spirituality. I realized that I have been seeking a spiritual foundation of life for a long time in many places* and *that it can't be expressed in cognitive, analytical terms.*

Perhaps this was my first clear recognition of the existence of a different path. I believed then—and still believe today—that one path for the healing of the spirit lies in also understanding the tricks and travails of the mind.

Soon after my encounter with Patrick Carnes, while waiting in a gay and lesbian bookstore, to meet my then roommate and half-available boyfriend, I picked up a book on co-dependence—*Co-Dependence Misunderstood, Mistreated* by Anne Schaef. He was late. I devoured Schaef's short book from cover to cover in barely an hour. As a result I decided to stop living with this person I loved who seemed stuck in patterns of addiction—a choice which seemed to me intensely painful. In confusion, seeking a way of handling the pain and healing my life, I began attending ACOA/D meetings.

I soon came to believe that there were remarkable parallels between the family roots of co-dependence with which ACOA/D dealt and the patterns of gay culture. By the late '80s, in the writings of such as Anne Schaef, Janet Woititz and Melody Beattie, a recognition had arisen of certain typical patterns in childhood family messages and the rules and roles learned by the children of these alcoholic and dysfunctional families.

The remainder of my 1989 Journal note read,

> *I learned that I had come to suppress most emotions, that I hadn't cried in years, that I was rarely able to feel anger or express it, that serenity was just a word to me, that my nighttime drinking allowed me to suppress the pain that followed fleeting sexual encounters, that a great deal of what I learned from my parents just wasn't true.*

I began to think that my psychological patterns of belief and behavior stemmed not only from my family but from our gay subculture. This subculture itself may be analogized as "the child" of the larger Western culture from which we have emerged to our fragile maturity. I put together a picture of the parallels between co-dependent families and rules and the patterns then typical of gay culture.

ACOA/D Patterns*	GAY SUBCULTURE Parallels
CHILDHOOD	*Pre-COMING OUT*
Chaotic or repressed family with lots of confusion; child withdraws or becomes an actor	Confusion; learns to disguise/distort/repress recognizing the truth about oneself as gay
Family ROLES:	*Gay ROLES:*
Hero—but imperfect and resented	—Community leader, BB, Stud
Scapegoat—takes attention off our faults	—Nerd, Fatty, Femme,
Lost Child—"he's never *any* trouble"	—"Sweet young thing" (puppy),
Mascot—"so cute," has to always be "up"	—Jester
Family RULES: Don't trust. Don't talk (about anything serious). Don't feel (don't admit any pain).	Talk about trivia. Don't believe anyone whether about love or gay politics or personal details. Appear happy and the life of the party—or no one will like you; B.S. is where it's at.
DOUBLE MESSAGES: We love you—don't bother us; I'll be there—not showing up.	I love *you*, I only *tricked* with him. Don't drink too much; let's meet at the bar.
ACOA's lie—when it would be just as easy to tell the truth	"My phone # is . . ."; "I *love* you." "Meet you at the bar—Weds. at 9."—all lies!

---

*REFERENCES: *Adult Children of Alcoholics*, Janet G. Woititz; *Co-Dependence Misunderstood, Mistreated*, Anne Schaef; *Co-Dependent No More*, Melody Beattie; Presentations by Dr. Ed Ellis, therapist.

ACOA/D Patterns	GAY SUBCULTURE Parallels
ACOA's "Guess at What Normal Is"	Gay & Lesbian culture lacks accepted workable standards and role models
Be Perfect (judge self without mercy)	Have a perfect body, perfect clothes, an ideal apartment, witty conversation —*then* maybe, maybe, *someone* will love you. BUY, BUY, BUY, Try, Try
ACOA's have difficulty with intimate relationships; lack successful family models.	Gay relationships are often ephemeral, end when lust ends, we're afraid to be vulnerable; lack successful relationship models.
Some ACOA's learned from family models to hang in hopeless relationship	Two extremes:—one night stands OR —desperately staying stuck in destructive relationships.
Excessive impulsivity learned from family behaviors	Changing jobs, lovers, cities, bars, hair styles, *chaotic*—all subculturally suggested as "solutions."
ACOA's constantly seek approval	Many paths, one goal: approval —sexual addiction, "mother"-ing, enabling, paying.
ACOA's don't know how to live through & learn from emotional pain.	Drugs, alcohol, partying, travel, etc.—to avoid pain—Result: exhausting repetition, zero learning.

Now, I find these patterns less constant. Role models and our ability to learn from each other face-to-face and through our own and the general media, have expanded. A new gay generation which has grown up with the clearer, more physical threat of suffering of AIDS constantly present, has begun to make changes. Yet when I read and hear of continued hopelessness which leads some to expect either that infection is inevitable, or worse, that physical health doesn't matter in their painful lives, I know that our healing is far from complete, that we still need to strengthen the spiritual center in our own lives and in our community.

One of the statements of the Fellowships which members use to remind each other of the positive side of suffering is "No pain, no gain." The traditions of Buddhism—or at least my own tradition of Vipassana or mindfulness—responds to our pain by reminding us that the greater the hindrances, suffering, anger, grief, the greater the opportunity for healing. In my own life had I not wearied of pain and suffering, never would I have come to the practice of meditation and the perceptions of Buddhism.

In 1990 not long after I came to these first recognitions, I began another relationship with someone loving, insecure and needy. Again our three year tryst did not satisfy, and I continued "tricking" with others. He did not provide the caring that I desired to feel that love was real; I did not provide the appreciation and praise he sought. Again, this relationship led to further steps along the path.

In 1991, after a year together, I encountered my first practice community in a day long yoga sitting at Green Gulch Zen Center near San Francisco. Finding some relief in the practice from my long struggle with the surrender of sleep, I determined to continue the practice.

Returning to Pennsylvania, the college where I taught management offered a yoga course and teacher. Attending my first session I learned the teacher offered a Friday evening course in a practitioner's apartment just around the corner from my home. My lover, initially reluctant, joined my exploration but soon became far more dedicated and skillful than I. Impelled by his interest, I continued the practice.

One after another I find the messages of the Buddha in the years of my life. Rereading my Journals for this article, I find again stories of suffering. My predominant emotion reading these Journals is sadness—not sadness for particular moments or people; sadness that the people and places mentioned are no longer in my life. Sadness and anger at impermanence.

Coming out late in the '60s, I found myself driven by a search for sexual satisfaction, activity much valued and approved not only by the gay subculture but by the larger Western culture in which we are embedded.

Yet I also longed for emotional love and intimacy, for a relationship that would connect me to . . . I knew not what. I only knew I felt disconnected, isolated. Before Buddhism and meditation the only way to alleviate the pain seemed to occupy myself fully with desires and their pursuit.

For me the primary vehicle was boys, endless boys, hot and cold boys, running boys—running towards me and running from me, Black boys, white boys, playful boys who would distract me, sad boys with whom I could occupy myself with caring, young looking boys perhaps reminding me of the younger self I wished so to heal. Gradually, oh ever so gradually with pain, I began to understand my predicament.

First would appear mere simple discomfort, loneliness, boredom, an urge for excitement. If I didn't distract myself, I would soon tense up in body and mind, thus turning discomfort to pain. Choosing clothes, making plans for success, I would slake my thirst for experience, my hope for joy, cruising the streets, the bars, the ads. Finding a partner after hours or days of effort, the pain would leave to be replaced by joy in the moment of forgetting self.

I once calculated that it took approximately twenty hours of doing one thing for the sake of another—first losing weight, then choosing clothes and styles, next going to the cruising grounds, making contact, developing interesting apparently attentive conversation, then suggestive comments and touchings, the "invitation," social conversation and a drink and drug or two, going to the bedroom, getting undressed, having sex—for the minute or so of loss of self in orgasm. After orgasm, discomfort would return, but a few drinks often allowed a night's forgetting in sleep.

Yet in the days which followed, these events repeated hundreds of times, the tension and pain would return. Repeating the mantra which I learned too well, "Woe is me," would complete the movement from discomfort to pain to suffering.

Practice is simply practice, the incessant repetition of any act or pattern which then becomes conditioned, familiar, and soon comes to occupy an incessant place in our lives. My actions which soon became my conditioned practice as well as the repeated actions, patterns, of our gay subculture, now seem to me only a starting point on a path which we have a chance to follow.

Judaism, my birth faith, seemed to bring no answers even though I helped found Beth Ahavah, Philadelphia's gay and lesbian synagogue. As an ethical base, as a source of friends and community, all these it filled. Emotionally and spiritually I continued to find a void.

Still I contributed, a perspective perhaps as present in Judaism as in Buddhism. Over a decade I supported Philadelphia's first and second and third gay community center, serving on the Boards through political clashes, raising funds, running coffeehouse introductory workshops for struggling newcomers. I joined in building and served as a volunteer for Philadelphia's gay and lesbian telephone counseling hotline, brought the message to Harrisburg and started another hotline there, worked in politics to end discrimination, and later spent three years with the Safeguards in HIV prevention—worthwhile work but not work which ended my suffering.

In quick succession in less than a year and a half, in 1992 and 1993, came the loss of my job; the imminent prospect of being forced to move from my apartment of twenty years with the sale of the building; the death in California of my mother; and the move of my former lover, now become closest friend and downstairs neighbor, across the continent. The thirst for suffering unslaked, Rich (no connection to previous "Rich"), my lover of three years decided to end our relationship.

Since my mother's mind filled with dismay at the thought of dying in a hospital, I flew West to join my father attending her during her final illness at their home in California. I brought two of Stephen Levine's books, *Who Dies* and *Healing Into Life and Death*, Vipassana Buddhist and eclectic, in the thought these might help my parents. Though they didn't pursue them, I did.

I began to find the beginnings of practice in my daily readings in the closing weeks of 1992 in my parents' home in Laguna Hills in the apparent spiritual wasteland of southern California. I read Levine's guided meditations on "soft belly" and "loving kindness" to my mother. She didn't comment but seemed comforted. Her practice through her many years focused on criticism of myself and others [and largely unspoken, upon her self] in the belief that this was her duty to impel others upon the path away from suffering. Still, I heard her talk to the visiting nurse, not knowing I was listening saying, "I've had a good life. I have a good son." I felt comforted.

After my mother's death on January 8 of 1993, I returned to Philadelphia. I began reading and practice of Levine's guided meditations, particularly his beginning metta meditations on loving kindness and soft belly. It was months of daily readings and these meditations before I felt ready to try occasionally the mindfulness meditations on watching breath. Soon I attended several practice sessions with three other practitioners in Philadelphia's tiny zendo, a small, austerely attractive room in the home of a woman Zen priest. I joined the only gay and lesbian Buddhist group in the entire region. A half dozen participants met only monthly and soon dissolved.

Nearing the end of my twenty-two years in Philadelphia, I wrote on March 21, 1993:

Spirituality, Love and Recovery

Due to the work I've been doing in this fifty-third year of recovery, catalyzed by early reading in the new guide I've just acquired, Stephen Levine's Guided Meditations, Explorations and Healings, *I came last night to a renewed recognition for lightening my life.*

It is such a paradox. Scott Peck [in The Road Less Traveled*] points out, following the words of Buddha—"[the first great truth: life is suffering—but once we recognize and accept this truth, suffering is lessened.]" Our "failures" become no longer failures. Neither criticism nor change is required; yet, if these are chosen, they too are perfect. In the words of Zen master Suziki Roshi, "[though everything is always perfect, it can always be improved]."*

Bathing my self in feelings of love, allowing my self feelings of kindness and mercy as if I were a loved one, as if I were "my only child," I put aside the roiling temptations of the mind to correct and plan, to circle in upon itself snapping like an angry dog reaching for its prey. Accepting.

Rejecting anything, even suffering, creates more suffering. As death intrudes, as standards are only partially met, as our hearts break, as we blame ourselves— and others—we create spiraling new rounds of suffering. We attempt breaking our chains yet our dearest desires disappear in an instant into death, decay, change and conflict.

Our minds will not disappear while we still live. Yet their wild energies can be harnessed to the path of lightening suffering. Meditation upon loving kindness for self, for those for whom I recognize my love and for all beings prepares the way. Watching sensation links body to mind and allows a deeper awareness, focusing on breath or on the words of guided meditation calms the turmoil and allows deeper recognition.

"And then," questions my mind, "how will I manage 'hewing wood and drawing water'?" When will I do the tasks of daily living while this body/mind exists? I do not yet know the answer but suspect that as practice expands, the apparent separation of daily task and healing will dwindle.

And the hindrances which place themselves in the way of recovery? My eagerness to criticize others, my passion to criticize self which often turns me to anger, to hatred, to the pain of assumed failure? These too require acceptance, these thoughts and feelings too are disarmed and made peaceful loving demons not by rejection but by love, more grist for the mill of examination of what is.

Having learned this much, my new perception remained to be forged more strongly. At last I had the basis for the beginnings of a practice. I had found and experienced the words of Thomas Merton, "True love and prayer are learned in the moment when love has become impossible and the heart has turned to stone."

Surviving my depression and anguish with the bare beginnings of a practice, I was not yet prepared to give up my suffering. In the traditions of the "practice" which I had developed, I sought another lover and many casual sexual contacts to lessen the anguish. These again proved themselves weak reeds and the pain continued.

Within a few months, at last I had had enough; in the words of the Fellowships I had finally "become sick and tired of being sick and tired." In a final ironic signpost to me, even my therapist, about to have her first child, decided to retire for a time from her practice.

It was clear; it was time to leave.

In my early fifties, I left my city and my home and moved across the country to northern California, a move I had wanted to make for some thirty years. Driving across the country just ahead of one of the fiercest storms of the decades, visiting my father in southern California and heading north days before the '93 Los Angeles quake, staying with friends for a month, I soon found a new home with a roommate in Noe Valley of San Francisco and began teaching part-time at a local university.

In San Francisco, center of the nascent gay Buddhist movement, my practice gradually deepened; I found the sangha lacking in my prior city including multiple gay Buddhist groups and places of sitting. I explored several groups whose practice I found impressive but whose sangha seemed cool to the point of coldness. After some months I settled upon a unique group of eclectic Buddhist practitioners, GBF, the Gay Buddhist Fellowship.

Founded four years earlier, it met for two hours on alternate Sundays following a 30-minute silent meditation, many on cushions, others on chairs, with dharma discussion and a more social tea break. A smaller group meets mid-week for a similar practice session followed by tea and discussion. I attended both. Occasional retreats of one and two days with GBF served to deepen my practice. Some Saturdays spent serving meals to the homeless with a GBF group of volunteers began to deepen sangha.

A year later in this uniquely gay and Buddhist-friendly city of San Francisco, I began a short but daily practice of an hour composed of three twenty-minute periods of warmth-and-patience breath as suggested in a text of Stephen Levine. Though this lasted only a few weeks, at the end of the first week, through some happy serendipity, I found that which I had devoutly sought, a partner. In a day, I committed myself to monogamy, something which I had been unable or unwilling to do over the course of more than four prior relationships of living together as lovers. A few months later I found the teaching job I sought. Two more months and my new partner and I found another couple with whom to build community and found a house to rent together.

In our home in a quiet section of the city, my practice continued. I invited the Thursday night gay Buddhist group to meet monthly. A few months later I invited the group to have potlucks before our sittings. Finally six months ago, I changed from my intermittent and casual sitting practice to a commitment to an hour a day of sitting breath meditation. As an apparently direct result, at last, after some thirty-five years of discomfort, my sleeping seems slowly to be healing. And if I stop this practice, the sleeping problem returns, keeping the message clear and present.

The suffering has not fully departed. I continue to listen, and with more empathy, to the pains of my gay friends. Recently one was contemplating suicide in his pain over the imperfectability of the human race and his inability to fix it (and perhaps his recent breakup with his alcoholic lover), another was in a state of depression for unknown reasons, a third, my closest friend and former lover, suffers daily from his own anger and the pain he sees in his work with PWAs.

The roots of our suffering remain while we dwell in this human plane and, more particularly, in many of our families and patterns of our culture I described earlier. And I myself, by any reasonable standards in a state of bliss, began writing this piece out of my own pain and anger and the need to use Levine's guided Forgiveness Meditation over a debt reneged upon by a former roommate I thought a trustable friend.

I still have moments of anger, desires to escape, poor nights of sleeping, occasional aches and pains, fears of death in the imagined ending of my conceptualized self. Yet I find myself returning to the path, finding meaning through my practice and support through my sangha. New work arises; I construct a symposium on Spirituality & Management for my professional association. I take comfort in the bedrock strength of our community with its changes built upon the suffering of AIDS with which so many of us deal with such generous giving compassion.

Having a partner is part of my practice. Noting one morning the purple curtains he constructed for our bed canopy and windows to help my difficult morning sleep hours, I came to conceive this cloth of cotton as embodied love. Out of that realization I have come to think that all the artifacts and people and actions and even natural objects are themselves embodied love. That even the apparently worst of men or the most evil of acts are imperfect strivings towards embodied love, desires to win the esteem of others, to cease suffering apparently real in the moment or to protect the imagined self from imagined future suffering, to care for family or friends, to leave something of ourselves to be remembered in love and a thousand other variations of the theme. When, as frequent, suffering instead arises and continues for self and others, it is only as in Thich Nhat Hanh's poem, "Call Me by My True Name," the unskillful acts of he who "does not yet see."

My partner doesn't practice formal meditation so I need to keep alert to moments for learning. One morning, as we were about to leave for our first long vacation together, we talked in bed about how to stay asleep by retaining focus on our dream object when we wake during the night. Sleeping, as mentioned, has been my central problem in my adult life with visits to three sleep clinics complete with a dozen electrodes and much advice from doctors with little effect. Only practice and the perspectives of Buddhism have been helpful.

With wry self-doubt, I commented to him paraphrasing Descartes, "I suffer therefore I am." He riposted, "I love therefore I am—it's cheaper for the soul;" and continued, "it's funner too." It's moments such as these that I am reminded how central this relationship has been to my healing practice.

Today, in the waning hours of 1996, my partner and I have moved to a home with an amazing view of San Francisco's city and bay. Tonight we'll share the New Year's evening around a fireplace with friends and my father and welcome another year.

I continue to be gay. I continue to suffer and practice. I continue to learn. I continue.

My First Year in Buddhist Practice
September 1995–September 1996

Tom Moon

I. All That Glitters

The majority religion in the United States may be Christianity, but the *dominant* religion in this country is romantic love. Our popular music celebrates romance with a fervor and in a language once reserved for religious devotion: you're my all and everything, our love is perfect and eternal, and so on. Popular films and books teach us to expect sexual love to bring us the sort of transcendental bliss that other cultures associate only with deep spiritual experience.

Muktananda, the Siddha Yoga master, was once asked by an American devotee, "How can I find my soul-mate?" Muktananda didn't speak English, so the question was translated into Hindi. The nearest equivalent for "soul" available to the translator was "atman." But in Hindu theology, there really is only one "atman." That is the point of the saying "Atman is Brahman"—*That art Thou*, the individual soul is the soul of the universe. To ask how it can find a mate, then, is an absurdity, a fact which Muktananda brusquely pointed out to the questioner. His response must have been disconcerting. We in America have confused the spiritual quest with the romantic quest, and we are startled to discover that other cultures don't share our adolescent outlook.

I've long been intellectually skeptical of romanticism, but in my heart I've been a true believer in this religion for most of my adult life. I sometimes suspect that gay men are especially vulnerable to developing an intense form of this religion in response to the isolation and loneliness we so often have to endure growing up. I know that I kept going through my own scared and closeted teenage years by living on the hope that I would some day find Mr. Right, the ideal and loving man who would rescue me from a cold and hateful world. Mr. Right would be the one human being whom God had specially created to meet all my needs. He would have the body of an Adonis and be perfect in bed, of course, but he would also understand me completely, love me unconditionally, forgive all my shortcomings and always know exactly what I felt and wanted without my ever having to tell him. In short, Mr. Right is mother—with a big dick.

TOM MOON MFCC was born in 1948 in San Francisco, where he still resides. He is a psychotherapist in private practice serving a predominantly gay clientele. His column on gay mental health, "The Examined Life," appears monthly in *Frontiers* Magazine (San Francisco edition). He also participates in the Bay Area's Gay Buddhist Fellowship.

In my 47th year I actually seemed to be enjoying the fulfillment of my dream. I was in the fifth year of living with a lover who was passionately devoted to me. Marcello was fourteen years younger than I was, and he had a just-got-out-of-the-army hypermasculinity that drove me wild sexually. He was half Filipino and half Caucasian and the mix made him strikingly handsome. He was a "major leather dude" and a title holder in the leather community. Every leather guy in town was trying to get into his pants, and I privately gloated over the fact that so many men were jealous of my position. Marcello also loved to cook. I remember returning home one evening to find him naked except for a jock strap, standing over the stove and stirring a pot of pasta. Every morning I left the house with a sack containing the lunch he had made for me, on which he'd scribbled little hearts and love notes. He was the most romantic man I ever knew. One winter evening he told me he had a gift for me. He took me outside and pointed into the clear cold sky at the three aligned stars which form Orion's belt. These three stars were the "I love you" stars, he said, and he was giving them to me so that if I was ever away from him I could look up at them and remember that his love for me was deathless. I had truly reached the end of my spiritual quest. I had died and gone to heaven.

On September 8, 1995, Marcello walked away from me in a movie line and never came home again.

He called a few days later and refused to tell me where he was, but I soon discovered that he had moved into the home of his "best friend" Jack, a multi-millionaire who had been trying to buy him for years. Marcello had always denied to me that they were anything but friends, but a week after he left he appeared on a radio talk show in his capacity as leather spokesman, and publicly declared his love for Jack. My father heard the radio show and called to ask me who Jack was. I was not only betrayed, I was humiliated in front of my entire family.

On the same day as the radio show his "friend" Daniel came to my door looking for his boyfriend. He was completely shocked to learn that I had known nothing about their love affair, because Marcello had told him that I knew all about it and didn't care. A little later friends revealed that Marcello had bragged about having three lovers from the podium at leather events in the bars. Soon, with depressing regularity I was hearing from other acquaintances the phrase, "I probably shouldn't tell you this, but . . ."

I was devastated. First he had taken our future away from us, and now he had taken our past as well. What had really been going on between us all these years? Had he ever loved me at all? The day after the radio program I changed the locks to the front door so that he couldn't come in anymore when I wasn't home. The message I was trying to convey was that he had lost any right to my trust, but many of his belongings were still in the apartment, and he interpreted my action as proof that I was trying to steal his possessions. He called and left a message full of malevolence and hate, threatening me.

When I heard his voice on the answering machine, what was left of my world came crashing down around me. The love of my life, who had lived in apparent devotion to me for almost five years, was in fact someone I had never really known at all. I felt nauseated and dizzy. There was no solid ground under my feet. For several days I was numb, but when I began to return to myself I was full of unbearable grief and anguish.

I was also aware of an intense longing for a deeper spiritual life. I was certainly ready to change my religion. This man thing was not delivering the goods.

I had been a practitioner of various forms of yoga and mantra meditation for over twenty-three years, although my practices had never become a daily routine. But the agony of losing Marcello left me with the feeling that all my coping strategies were bankrupt, all my usual diversions useless, and all my ideas about the purpose and direction of my life erroneous. Spiritual life was no longer a luxury item or a hobby to pursue in my spare time. It was an absolute necessity if I was to survive this loss with my sanity intact.

II. The Which Than Which There Is No Whicher

About ten days after Marcello's departure I went up to Spirit Rock Meditation Center for a day of instruction in Buddhism and Vipassana meditation. Spirit Rock is in some beautiful rolling hills in Marin County. The land has a creek and walking trails, but not much has been built there yet. There is not much more than a building for dining and two double wide trailers which serve as a meditation hall, yet it is already one of the most active and vibrant centers of American Buddhism in the country. It is destined to grow as the dharma flowers in the west. One day in the not too distant future there will be buildings for residential retreats and a monastery.

In the hall I sat with my eyes closed and tried to watch my breath. The technique was novel to me. Instead of focusing my attention on a mantra, I was trying simply to be aware of the present moment. I was surprised at how easy and natural this felt. This way of meditating seemed made for me.

Periods of loss and mourning are auspicious times for meditation. The sorrow of loss makes us slow down. We withdraw from superficial busyness and become quiet, indrawn, and pensive. In the pain of my loss I was cornered. I couldn't do anything to escape the intense pain anyway, so I was less resistant to observing it. I surrendered to it, and I watched as wave after wave of anguish and grief and rage arose and disappeared. By the end of the day I was feeling a deep stillness and an unusual clarity. I felt as if I were a detached observer of the movement of tides on the ocean of change. I witnessed the cycles of becoming, and I was calmed and reassured. The pain had not disappeared or even lessened, but it seemed to float in something vast enough to encompass all sorrow. I knew that Vipassana meditation was the tool I needed to survive this period in my life.

Buddhism is really *the* religion about loss and grief, and I didn't have to make any great leap of faith to accept the hard truths which it asks us to face—that suffering is inescapable in this life, and there is no secure refuge in anything in the world because all things are impermanent. I had no argument with the idea that attachment and clinging are futile. It was obvious that they were responsible for all of the suffering I was experiencing. But these truths were also profoundly disorienting. I felt a little like the kid who has just learned that Santa Claus doesn't exist. I had been sold a bill of goods. Everything in this life seemed grey and empty and flat.

During this same period I lived in a constant state of deep pain. I ached for Marcello, and I was always on the verge of tears. Sometimes, late at night, a sound would wake me and I would think it was his key in the front door or I would roll over to his side of the bed and try to put my arm around him. Then I would fully awaken and remember that he was never coming home again. Or I would look out the window and catch a glimpse of the "I love you" stars and feel the full bitterness of broken promises and betrayal. Those moments were some of the blackest of my life. Some part of me wanted to get on the phone and beg him to come back on any terms, no matter how badly he treated me. I was protected from doing this, not by self respect, but by a rage at his abuse and lies and betrayal which was as strong as the longing for him. I hated him when I thought of how he had abused and humiliated me, and I used to rehearse in my private monologues the speech I would make to him when I finally saw him again, the words that would cut him to ribbons. (It wasn't just speeches that I imagined, though. I also thought about dismembering him.) The anger was as painful as the grief. I didn't want to believe that it was possible that I could so thoroughly hate the person who had once been the love of my life.

The only thing that made this time bearable was daily meditation. It didn't lessen the pain, but it made it possible for me to live with it. From the very beginning of my practice I regularly caught glimpses of a deep and abiding peace within me, and I understood that this feeling was what I had been seeking in relationships with men. I began to sense that my own happiness really didn't need to depend in any way on Marcello or on anyone else. Marcello, I began to think, had been a conduit through which God's love had flowed to me: an imperfect and flawed conduit—which only served to remind me to seek the Source directly. In the moments when I deeply felt this I had no fear that when he left, he had taken something essential to my well-being. All that I had been given remained. In those moments I was free of suffering and my attachment to him burned away like fog. Unfortunately, like the fog, it returned again and again.

During this period I also began to think of grief and mourning in a new way. If loss is inevitable, then so is mourning. I had always thought of mourning as a kind of aberration, a period in life when things were out of kilter, and had believed that the goal of the mourning process was to "get over it" and return to "normal." I saw Elizabeth Kübler-Ross's well-known six stages of adapting to loss (denial, isolation, anger, bargaining, numbness and depression, and acceptance) as a kind of road map, and the destination of the trip was acceptance. But as I watched my sorrow in meditation without trying to change it in any way, I understood that grief is not pathology, and is not my enemy. It has a rightful place in my heart, and it has its own dignity which needs to be respected. I began to relax into it. I stopped wondering how long it was going to take for me to get over it, and began to ask, instead, how I could learn to live with it.

I have always advised my psychotherapy clients who are trying to make basic changes in their lives—whether it's quitting smoking, losing weight, learning to exercise, or almost anything else—that it is always easier to do if they don't try to do it alone. Hook up with others who have the same goal, I tell them, and success will come much quicker.

I believe that anyone who wants to take up the practice of regular meditation, especially in our culture, where there is virtually no support for contemplative life, needs to find a *sangha*, a community of practitioners. I began to return to Spirit Rock for more weekend day-longs, and to think of it as my refuge, and my spiritual home. One of the teachers at Spirit Rock, Howie Cohn, held a Tuesday evening sitting group not far from my home in San Francisco, and I became a regular there. I found that meditation is almost always deeper when I do it in a group. It is as if some kind of group energy carries me farther than I can go on my own.

I discovered the Gay Buddhist Fellowship in December. This is a group of gay men who support each other in Buddhist practice. It sponsors weekly sittings in members' homes, biweekly Sunday sittings, retreats, and social gatherings. The GBF newsletter has subscribers all over the world. There are gay Buddhists in prisons and in anti-gay cultures whose only link with a gay-positive spirituality is our newsletter, and an important part of several members' practice is to correspond with these men. The GBF welcomes all traditions—we have Tibetan, Zen, and Vipassana practitioners. We have no recognized teacher or leader, but we do have a number of members who have a kind of elder status because they have done many years of monastic practice.

When I first heard about the GBF it still wasn't possible to think of much except Marcello, and I was constantly looking for his double wherever I went. So I arrived at my first GBF meeting hoping to meet a young, but deeply realized major leather dude. That hope was dashed immediately. Most of the members were as old and stodgy as I am (sorry, gentlemen). I haven't met very many young Americans who are attracted to Buddhism.

Most of them seem to find it too austere and depressing. It takes most of us three or four decades before we begin to catch on to the truths of suffering and impermanence. Even the Buddha was 29 before the significance of these realities dawned on him.

What I found in the GBF was not a new venue for sexual and romantic intrigue, but a genuine spiritual brotherhood of dedicated and intelligent practitioners. I felt honored when they asked me to join the steering committee after I had been a member for only a few months, and more honored still to be entrusted with the responsibility of lining up speakers for the Sunday sittings. In that capacity I was able to explore the richness of the dharma in the Bay Area, and to meet many deeply awakened American Buddhists, both gay and straight. We don't have to go to Asia or India any more in search of enlightenment. The ancient wisdom is flowering in our own culture.

The holidays were a particularly difficult time that year, because I was used to spending them with Marcello, and because I was withdrawn and in no mood for festivities. I had been told when young that the thing you are doing at midnight on New Year's Eve is the thing that you will be doing the most throughout the coming year, so I had always made sure to be in the middle of a sweaty sex scene at the stroke of midnight. That year, however, I spent New Year's Eve alone, contemplating the previous year, resolving to live a spiritual life in the coming year, and meditating. I was doing Vipassana at the stroke of midnight, and as I heard the shouting and firecrackers and horns in the cold night air all around me I felt, by contrast, the warmth within, and I was grateful that this path had opened for me.

Howie and my brothers in the GBF advised me that periods of retreat are an important tool for deepening practice and insight. I attended four residential retreats during that first year of practice. The first was a five-day Vipassana retreat at a Catholic convent in late March of '96 in Santa Rosa. I had some trepidation about it: five days of complete silence doing nothing but meditation from 6:30 in the morning to 9:30 in the evening seemed a little more spiritually butch than I was up for, but I was also drawn to the idea.

I was relieved to discover that my fears were without foundation. After a few hours of restlessness on the first day, my mind quickly settled into the routine of walking and sitting, and I found the schedule restful and easy to follow. By the third day I had, for probably the first time in my life, moved below the surface chatter of the mind. I was more quiet than I had ever been in my life.

That day, while doing a walking meditation, I had an experience which completely changed my life. I was focused on the pressure of each foot as it touched the ground. Thoughts came and went, but less and less frequently: I could see the spaces between thoughts. It was in the middle of one of those spaces that, without intending to, I just let go. And then it was as if the gates of heaven opened to let me in. I seemed to dissolve into a pure awareness that was outside of time altogether. This awareness was not just emptiness: it was light and love and joy and peace. It was fulfillment itself, beyond all suffering and fear. I couldn't walk any more. I stood still with my eyes closed and felt myself lifted out of the confines of my body in That which had always supported me when I couldn't stand on my own two feet. Body consciousness returned after a few moments, but when I opened my eyes everything I saw was glowing with light and love.

It happened that after this walking period I was scheduled to meet in a small group with some of the other retreatants and one of the teachers. I went to the meeting in a state of awe and gratitude. Light seemed to be pouring from the faces of everyone around me, and I assumed they were all experiencing the same thing. I was disconcerted to hear them talk, instead, about knee and back pain, restlessness and negative emotions. When my turn came I opened my mouth to describe what I was feeling and found it impossible to say anything at first. When I tried to put this inexpressible thing into words I choked and burst into tears. Thinking that I was in some sort of emotional crisis, several people reached out to hold me, but I held up my hands to signal to them that I was fine. I was about as fine, in fact, as I had ever felt in my life. When the words came, all I could say at first was, "It's so beautiful, it's so beautiful." Then I added that I felt as if I had seen the face of God, which is not something one usually says at a Buddhist retreat. But all words were inadequate. I once heard Alan Watts describe this Reality as "the which than which there is no whicher," a description which is about as good as any other.

I tried to compose myself, but it was very difficult. I felt too open and exposed and I was afraid that I was making a fool of myself, so I was glad after the retreat was over when several people came up to me to tell me they had at times in their practice experienced the same thing. A few others said they envied me. On the last day of the retreat we began speaking again. We all formed a circle and each person said a little about how they were feeling. When my turn came I said, "I haven't been this happy in three thousand years."

III. Freedom

I felt longing for Marcello to return almost every day until nine months after he left. But as I got more used to living without him the constant state of feeling bereft slowly gave way to a sense of dread. I felt that I was in some kind of nameless danger, and I was disconcerted and helpless because, since I didn't know what the danger was I didn't know how to protect myself from it. Fortunately, because I was meditating every day I had developed some ability just to sit and watch what the mind was doing, even when that was painful.

I saw that, on the surface I was afraid of abandonment. Memories of abandonments in my personal history floated by, and I got a panoramic overview of my "dysfunctional family issues," as we like to say in California. Looking a little more deeply, I saw that all relationships, dysfunctional or not, end in death or divorce—I am going to be separated ultimately from every person I have ever loved or ever will love. It wasn't just abandonment I dreaded. I dreaded all loss, and the knowledge that loss is inevitable. Looking more deeply still, I could see that what I really dreaded and sought to be protected from was the unpredictability and insubstantiality of life itself.

In meditation I watched as dread gave rise to greed, which is a movement of rage and defiance at life. I grab at life and try to compel it to give me security and permanent happiness. I saw that it is greed that makes our relationships with each other so difficult. Other people can't help but fail us when we expect them to give us so much. I witnessed the futility of greed. I saw it hold dread at bay temporarily—mostly through forgetfulness—and then I watched dread overcome any temporary victory I imagined I had over it.

It slowly dawned on me that since I couldn't defeat dread, the only alternative left was to make friends with it and to approach it with compassion. I lived in fear, but for the first time in my life I wasn't ashamed of that fact because I realized that what I had thought of as a shameful little secret and a personal failing was in fact the human condition itself. We're *all* afraid.

The paradox was that when I approached my own terror with loving attention I became unafraid. And when I became unafraid I didn't want to hate other people any more. The rage I was still feeling toward Marcello became increasingly distasteful to me. I realized that this relentless anger at him, which on the surface is such a separating emotion, was actually the tie that still bound me to him. It was clear that I couldn't be free of my suffering over losing him until I stopped hating him.

So every day for three weeks I did metta (loving kindness) meditations and forgiveness meditations for Marcello. Every day I called up his image and told him that I forgave him. I then asked him to forgive me for the suffering I had caused him. I followed that with a prayer for his well-being, and I ended with my own version of the traditional loving-kindness phrases: "May Marcello be happy, may he be peaceful, may he be healthy in mind and body, may he have ease of well-being, and may he find perfect freedom."

This practice evoked a veritable civil war within me. I felt my mind heave and lurch like a bull trying to throw me off. I was tossed back and forth between elation and despair. Moments of inward reconciliation and gentleness toward him were overwhelmed by counterattacks of vengefulness and hatred. To the part of me that observed and noted it, this was all a very instructive and engrossing spectacle. I remember saying to myself, many times, "Wow! Look at that!"

I saw that I resisted forgiving because I was afraid of it. I believed that forgiveness could hurt me. Somehow it would weaken me and leave me vulnerable to more hurt and betrayal. In time I understood that there was a big difference between keeping my heart open and keeping my front door open. Forgiving someone who had abused me did not mean that abuse was acceptable or that I wouldn't protect myself from it in the future. And when I remembered the law of karma it was clear that forgiveness was an act of rational selfishness—whenever I let go of the idea that another being deserved to suffer, a tremendous amount of suffering instantly went out of my own life.

This is partly because at the most basic level, forgiveness *feels* more pleasant than hatred. This easily verifiable fact of everyday experience entails a tremendous truth: that if we are really serious about ending our own suffering, we have to learn to relinquish the dubious pleasures of righteous indignation and wounded innocence.

But if forgiving him was difficult, asking him to forgive me was far more daunting. I was more attached to my identity as the wounded innocent, the wronged and victimized lover, than I had ever been to Marcello. "What do I need him to forgive *me* for?" I indignantly asked myself. Hadn't he deceived, betrayed, abandoned and threatened me? But when I looked honestly at that question, another one immediately came to mind—why had I been so susceptible to deception? In retrospect the evidence of his dishonesty had been overwhelming and obvious for years. My brother and several friends had tried to warn me that they didn't think he was honest, but I had dismissed their "lack of trust." It had taken a lot of deliberate, if unconscious, work to keep myself from seeing the truth. Why had I worked so hard to avoid seeing the truth? Because I was in "love"? But what did that mean? That I had been attached—addicted—to an image of Marcello, and that I had been willing to do almost anything to preserve that image in the face of massive evidence of its unreality. This didn't mean that his deception was acceptable behavior. What it did mean was that I was not an innocent victim of anyone else. I was a "victim" of my own attachments and illusions, of my own mind; that is, of my own karma. To rage forever at Marcello as the cause of my suffering was dangerous to me because it helped me avoid the real causes in my own mind, and because raging at him suggested that the problem was just that I had been with the "wrong" lover and needed to find the "right" one. That kind of thinking would preserve my religion and certainly ensure more suffering in the future.

The religion of romantic love is really a worship of surface appearances. I was attached to Marcello's good looks, his muscles, his masculinity. I was enamored of my image of us as a "cute couple," and to being envied by others. I was addicted to "love"—that is, to sentimental feelings derived from popular music, television, Broadway musicals. All of this was empty of anything real or abiding, and none of it had anything to do with actually knowing Marcello at all. If he had lied to me I had *lived* in a lie. The stark truth was that I had connected with a dishonest lover because I was myself unwilling to live in the truth. I had never been Marcello's victim. I had merely reaped the karmic consequences of the seeds I myself had sown.

And so in my meditations I found myself asking him to forgive me for worshipping him rather than for ever trying to know him, and for participating with him in a romantic *folie a deux* that had been destructive to both of us. At this point the civil war in my mind subsided and I emerged from the mood swings. I discovered that I was free of rage at Marcello, and it was only then that I really began to know him. Freed from the need either to pedestalize or demonize him, and from my own hunger and aversions in relation to him, I felt as if I could see clearly into his heart and recognize the same dread in him that I had befriended in myself. But it wasn't his dread and my dread that I was seeing, it was *the* dread, the autonomous, almost impersonal, terror which no one owns and everyone knows. Compassion for him felt natural because we weren't separate.

And then I was free.

Vipassana meditation was the tool that allowed me to experience something deeper than romantic idolatry. The religion of romanticism is based on a sense of being incomplete, flawed, and alone, and it promises wholeness through the magic of "love." But when I simply watched the painful feelings of loneliness and inadequacy in meditation, without trying to "fix" them or alter them in any way, they invariably gave way to a deeper understanding of who I really am. Then my individual "soul" opened to the world at large, the illusion of fragmentation dissolved, and I directly experienced the wholeness that is my true nature.

Carl Jung used to say that in the latter half of life the center of the personality begins to shift from the ego to the Self. "Self" for him was really a mystical concept: he wrote that the archetype of the Self and the archetype of God were indistinguishable. Jung's Self bears a strong resemblance to the Atman which is Brahman in Hinduism, and to the Clear Light or Buddha nature of Mahayana Buddhism. As my first year of practice drew to a close, and as the mourning for Marcello began to subside, I was aware that there had been a profound shift in the center of gravity in my own being. I actually felt that my true center was not in the world of my experience, but in the timeless awareness in which it occurred. More and more I felt still and quiet inside, and there were times when I could sense that stillness even in the midst of mental agitation. Looking back I saw that I had gone through a rapid process of maturation. I had taken a big step toward outgrowing childlike dependence and adolescent romanticism.

And I had changed my religion. I knew that my refuge and my sure heart's release were not to be found in any being, but only in That which sustains all beings. I still hoped that one day I would find another man to love, but I was aware that it was far more important to have an open heart than to have a lover. When my heart is really open I am not lonely and intimacy is plentiful whatever my outward circumstances, because intimacy is the atmosphere of an open heart.

I had planned to spend the first anniversary of Marcello's departure, which was a Sunday, alone with my feelings for him and saying a final good-bye. I had intended to pore over the picture albums of our life together, and to have a good long cry and an extended suffer. I had to put it all off, though, because I had a date that day.

As my first year in Buddhist practice drew to a close, I was astonished to find that I was grateful to Marcello. Of all my spiritual teachers, he alone succeeded in forcing me to face life's most painful truths, and in so doing he catalyzed a spiritual transformation.

The days grew shorter, Orion's belt appeared again in the night sky, and when I looked up at the "I love you" stars I saw in them a reminder of a love which really is deathless after all. What purpose can we have for taking form in this world if it is not to embody that love ever more completely? In my mind and memory Marcello stands like a sentinel, pointing into that great sky. When he came into my life he opened my heart, and when he left it he opened my spirit.

Wisdom Mind Meets Gay Sexuality

Anthony E. Richardson, M.D.

A growing number of Buddhist gay men wish to have sexuality addressed. This article is not an erudite Buddhist text, but the thoughts of a gay psychotherapist in relationship with his Buddhist teacher.

I met Gyalsay Tulku Rinpoche, the man who became my guru, in Australia. I had already had some empowerments from Buddhist teachers about clearing up bad influences. I knew very little about it, but I was doing the short practice pretty consistently. I went to teach a group in Australia. These people were living together with the shared intention that their community would thrive. However, it wasn't functioning very well because it was being held back by a controlling and crazy woman who had set herself up as the wisdom source, the answerer of all questions. I thought I would be leading a strict psychotherapy group using elements of body and expressive work, but, as a spiritual practitioner, they expected me to teach about spiritual wisdom. I was surprised because I wasn't saying then that I was on a spiritual path nor had I included such concepts in my teaching.

I agreed that I would show them my Buddhist practice, and they would demonstrate some of their ritual and practice. Whilst I was doing my daily practice the group energy changed quickly and dramatically. People left the room, others felt very insulted, and a whole lot of immense and strong feelings came up, including a little anger. I felt the presence of the deity I had been practicing with. This was a strong experience for me, an unusual one, and I noticed that the group was very disjointed at the end. In those days I wanted to end my workshops in some sort of harmony, but this one was unhappy, and it worried me. (Later I heard that within several weeks the whole commune broke apart because they started to confront the woman who had set herself up as wisdom.)

I flew back to Sydney, and on the way, all of a sudden the plane hit a pocket and dropped 2,000 feet and then stabilized again. That morning I went to my friend Julie's house, and she said, "Would you like to come meet a teacher for tea?" I walked in, she explained that I was from San Francisco, and he looked at me and laughed and said "Sky quake." I said, "No, earthquake, earthquake." He said, "No, no, sky quake," and then I remembered about having fallen 2,000 feet. I laughed and told him the story, and he laughed in a way that showed me he had intended the joke. I asked him about what had happened with the group I had just finished

ANTHONY E. RICHARDSON (San Francisco) was born in Australia in 1949 and now practices within the Tibetan Buddhist tradition as a student of Ven. Gyalsay Tulku Rinpoche, a master who departed his body on November 21, 1994. He works as both a Board Certified psychiatrist and a somatically oriented psychotherapist.

working with, and he said, "Good wong," which meant that the deity empowerment was still having strong effects in me. He led me to see that the process going on for this group was a good thing and that the deity practice had stronger effects than my usual psychological style. That's when I recognized that he had knowledge of energetic realities I didn't know about. I was instantly his student.

It was with this strange man that, as a strong relationship developed, sexuality was discussed and played out. Most of the time when we talked about sex, he disparaged the notion of the physical act of two beings rubbing bodies together as spiritual practice. That sort of sex may be done for many different reasons—to exert power over each other, or to express one's love onto another, or to relieve a sense of urgency or fullness, or to dump some sense of despair. It could be to make oneself feel alive, make babies or have fun. There are hundreds of reasons people have sex. But Rinpoche was not interested in and wouldn't allow prolonged discussion about these result-based states. And I find nothing in the reading of Buddhist stuff that suggests there is any interest in talking about these things. On many occasions I have seen the teachers' disinterest in soap opera-making, and that is especially true around sexual drama.

Rinpoche showed slightly less disinterest in sex when it included a coming together with the shared intention of finding some level of communion. He gave me no information about forms of sex that involve things like sadomasochism or ritualized scarification or body piercing or large differentials of power such as between adult males and young boys or any of those things. My thoughts, in terms of sexuality, are in response to my teacher's provocation and the stories of my clients. My private practice is largely gay Buddhist men, but the Buddhist issues around sexuality are not stirred only by gayness; they are stirred by sex in all its frames of reference, including those of straight people I work with.

The Venerable Gyalsay Tulku Rinpoche was Wisdom Mind. Being with him expanded my way of viewing the world. Although the Dharma is proscriptive in its usual forms, with rules about numbers of partners and where to put penises and so on, Rinpoche would not impose nor would he let me use the Dharma to impose restrictions on my sexuality. There were times when I asked for instructions, references to read to tell me how to be correctly sexual. He would say that in my beginning stages they would only confuse me. So there were no rules about monogamy or fidelity, no restrictions on consensual body probing and exploration.

In Tibetan Buddhism what is meant by "wisdom mind" is the embodied enlightened mind, that is, a teacher who has reached enlightenment and has chosen to be reborn into another body in order to be of aid to sentient beings. Such reincarnations, of whom there are many in the Tibetan culture, are known as "Tulku," and, if they undergo sufficient rigorous training, they are given the term "Rinpoche," "precious jewel." Many of them are now coming to the West, some working primarily in the West. Wisdom mind came to me in the form of the speech and actions of my teacher, but now that he is no longer embodied—he died three years ago—I'm aware that the relationship continues. His presence is strong, and that presence I still consider to be wisdom mind.

So back to the issue of sex. It is quite possible to have a very satisfying rubbing together of bodies. There can be sexual exchanges that encourage growth at a psychological and physiological level, that enliven the organism and feel good, but that does not necessarily mean these exchanges move a person along in a spiritual sense. Of course, if they are useful and beneficial to the organism itself, good-o. But that isn't the same as spiritual experience.

And sex has inherent problems. Pleasure, ecstasy, bliss can make people very self-centered, encourage us to think we have the answer and make us feel that everything is all right now. That's a wish used to generate fantasy, and these fantasies prevent our seeing what is true. This is called an "obstacle." So the question is how to use sexual energies—most gay men are bent on using them—in a way which will encourage you to see more of what is true, rather than less. This obscuring of the real is fulfilling in its moment, feels good in its moment, but ultimately doesn't take people along in any way. Tibetan Buddhism seems to suggest that you don't try for enlightenment through sex, yet I am convinced that Rinpoche saw the insistence of my gayness even more than I did and included it in his teachings with me.

Sex is of primary importance to us. Insistence on the importance of sex is one of our differences from most straight folks. It begins with the gay five-year-old; he goes into action, wanting to touch men, wanting to be touched by men, and sex is part of what he's looking for. At this age the child begins to feel sensual, sexual urges towards other folks. With gay kids this normally means towards fathers, uncles and so on. When a straight kid moves toward relatives of the opposite sex there is a response in his environment that emphasizes it (the response may be excitement, fear or jealousy, depending on the family's attitudes). But for gay kids most often the movement is ignored. Ignoring him leads to a problem for the child who has strong and persistent urges inside which no one around reacts to. The gay kid is either driven away from his family by his feeling of sexualness or he must extinguish his sexuality. Since extinguishing sexuality would be the same as learning not to be hungry or thirsty, it is not often accomplished.

Due to the family's profound ignorance about this stage, the kid feels annihilated because he isn't met, and not being met feels like annihilation, but, in fact, it isn't. The unresponded to, unsupported kid still has his sexuality. Sexuality becomes the driving force, the engine of change. That is the difference from annihilation: The engine is still hot, still running, and this force within the child will continue to push him. Now, given that it is so foreign to the rest of the family that it gets ignored, gayness gains great importance for the psychology of the growing child. It is as though the engine is pushing him away from his family because they don't respond to it. He is on the brink of moving out of relationship to the source of everything he knows. When you move out from the family you also move out from its assumptions. Gay kids give up on their families to have their sexuality and deal with the costs of that later.

This starts at age three to five, and it changes what gay kids think about their lives from six to seven and eight and nine and ten. The split is there, and it will grow wider over the next ten or twelve years. For a gay teenager it becomes increasingly more important to attend to his sexuality than to attend to his family. Of course, both straights and gays have all the stuff that goes on at fifteen and sixteen when they rebel against their families and hate them and take drugs and so on. But, for gay people, it reinforces an earlier truth. For straight people it's the first time they experience this split, but for us it's building on what we already know: We are different.

Now let's add Buddhism to this dilemma. From the point of view of a Buddhist, there is only one place to go. There are many paths to follow and many sidelines like getting reborn in hell realms and stuff like that, but, when it's all said and done, it's about getting enlightened, and everything else is on the way to it. So, even somebody who ends up in one of the lower hell realms of disgusting awfulness, when he's finished with that for all those eons, ultimately the stream of karma will re-present him towards enlightenment because that's the way karma moves. That's the way we are all moving.

And, if you do "ordinary" sexuality well and you've experienced the pleasure and the fullness and the richness of it with another person in a meaningful way, why would you want to go on past that satisfaction? Biologically, there is a push from within to start to move toward a larger satisfaction, to interact with a wider community. It feels like you want to take your sense of sexuality—comfort and loving and warmth and whatever else arrives for you, the bliss—and have that bliss in relationship to all sentient beings.

Now, who's going to do that? Once you start this task there is betrayal and humiliation to deal with over and over again due to the strange combination of loving creating vulnerability and people being different from how we wish they were. Not only that, but most people aren't having a good time and they don't like you having a good time. All up, it's easier to keep your pleasure to yourself. It's more comfortable, but that won't get you on past the "ordinary." Most folks will say, "Well, I'll retreat and feel safe," and *that*, in Buddhist practice, is considered to be the genesis of slovenly mind. Slovenly, lazy, diffuse or dull mind leads to the brain having difficulty noticing what's happening. This and over-active mind, when the brain is having too many thoughts, are states of obscuration.

That's why the teachers prefer to work with suffering rather than pleasure. They think pain makes us much more available than pleasure does.

Pain is generated by our attachments and ignorance. To escape the pain we have made, we may generate pleasure so that we don't know we suffer. In Vajrayana Buddhist practice it's absolute that progress on the spiritual path arises from engagement, rather than escape. It's a very strong pushing into the grinding stone. You move into the stone; you don't move away from it. The grinding stone strips away ignorance and attachment and the making of suffering. Withdrawing into manufactured happiness is an attachment, as though it is better to feel one way than another. Having discovered, say, sex—endorphins and feelings, rubbed and touched, hot and sweating, relaxed and friendly, whatever your preferences are—it is difficult not to want that again and again as though it's an end in itself. Perhaps we think that if we could do it right sexually then we would all be all right, relationship would be all right, everything would be fixed. It's one of the places in which we Westerners have put a lot of mystical belief patterns. It's not spoken of very much, but we act as though good sex means everything is good. In the gay culture getting the sex right is supposed to be how everything else falls together.

I think that one of the reasons for feeling that the answer is in getting the sex right is the failure I talked about of a gay five-year-old being acknowledged. That leads to some sense of "I don't know what they were about when I was growing up." They were talking about romantic love, and I wanted to get it on. I wanted to be touched, I wanted someone to get inside me, I wanted to get inside somebody, I wanted to know all about him, how his physiology worked, what he smelled like, what he tasted like, how his hair stuck on. I wanted to play with him. I was interested in him, and I wanted him to be interested in me.

Rinpoche played with me, allowing me to see all of these dynamics. He maintained a sense of playfulness and confidence around the events that took place. It was very clear to me that for him—not necessarily for him personally, but for him in reference to me—sexuality was an embodied reality. It was something which included the organism, and with it charge moved, energy moved. And pleasure came, his organism became more available, my organism became more available, I felt sparkly on the outside, I felt sexual, I felt alive, I felt sensuous. He was straight; I am gay. We didn't fuck.

We didn't read heavy tomes to look at the concept of sexuality; it was much more about embodying it in the relationship, having it be part of the relationship. I still have in my lounge room a bronze corkscrew in the shape of a young man; the corkscrew part is the penis. It's hanging from the lamp in my living room, and Rinpoche put it there playfully and joyously. He referred to it, and looked at it often with me in the room, clearly letting me know that sexuality was a part of our relationship. Many times I would try to make sex go away. Sex wasn't working with him my way, and, because he wouldn't let me use the tricks I used in similar circumstances, sex stayed up, making me ask the questions, feel the feelings, have to work through the issues. My relationship with Rinpoche made me be the gay man I was already.

My favorite trick with an attractive straight man was to make myself less gay around him. But Rinpoche would not allow me to hide myself. He would wear very tight shorts, he would lie around languidly in a sarong, and he would make sure that there was a lot of sexual charge. He even asked me to measure his inner thighs for pant length. (He dressed left.) I would comment on all this, and he would just laugh and laugh and laugh.

One of the practices he asked me to do was picturing him sitting in ecstatic union on my head in the form of a deity. As I was driving two hours a day doing this visualization, I had the spontaneous sense of his penis hanging down off the end of my nose and just hitting the tip of my mouth —delicious and disturbing, as well as pleasurable. I mean, this is my teacher and a straight man and I'm visualizing his penis running down my nose. When I told him about it (under duress from my friends), he laughed, told me he had a donkey dick, and that my practice was going very well and I should continue it. His okay-ness with this spontaneous vision was so strong that I didn't think that it was in any way a bad thing, and so I continued the meditation with seemingly good effects. He was very consistently supportive of my being a sexual being and not taking that out of the relationship. He was entirely playful and relaxed; there was no contraction. There was no sense of manipulation of me or that he had a suppressed need he was trying to act out with me or any of the things you might ordinarily expect.

I had all the fantasies and feelings, you know. I had the bizarre rich sexual fantasies, the incredible fantasies of converting him to being gay, of feeling totally inadequate and incapable of giving, of having sex with him or being sexual with him, of being controlled by him, of wanting to control him, the huge amount of anger and fire around the fact that it wasn't happening between us sexually and wanting it so bad, fearing it so much. Thinking I required it in order to have him or happiness, riding the cycles of all those fantasies.

Having a relationship in which the fantasies are contained in a nondestructive way has been very useful in working with myself and my clients about what gay sexuality is: what is it that constitutes being gay and being sexual, and what sorts of issues you're going to bump into as a gay man. I became aware that most of my straight friends, some of whom love me dearly and whom I love dearly, treat me as though I am a straight man who has sex with other men. They don't treat me as though I'm a gay man; what they have done is to put my sexuality some place else, and then we are just mates or friends, getting on with having fun with each other. It became pretty clear to me that, if I was not going to be allowed to put away my sexuality in order to be in relationship with Rinpoche, I was certainly not going to put away my sexuality in order to be in relationship with my straight male friends.

This has created waves of disturbance because I've gone crashing against them saying, "You guys have bodies and your bodies are male and I like male bodies, and I like your shapes and your smells and the feel of you and I like brushing against you and I like smelling you, and just as you like being around women and you feel that response inside yourself, it's happening to me all the time and I won't have either one of us say it's not happening." You can imagine the tension and difficulty this has created for me and the men I work with. I must say to their credit that, over several years of being confronted by this, their availability to me has become greater and greater. This ability to come play with me and be with me in this sexual field does not require us actually to have sex, but we have quite a field to play in, and I feel clearly included as a gay man in a group of straight men. I'm not needing to be straight in order to be part of maleness. In some cases, the difficulty is extreme, but most of my friends are dealing with it pretty well. However, it started off as hard work for me, too, so I see why gay men feel forced back into groups of other gay men; it's easier.

The results have been very interesting. I don't feel so routinely deadened, and I don't carry so much of the sense that they don't like me or that I'm not liked inside myself. It's not something I suggest everybody do; I'm just saying that with Rinpoche it became clear that this was an appropriate thing for me to do, and, of course, it has also become a more appropriate thing to do in my therapeutic relationships. I hadn't realized how much my gay clients and I didn't talk about sex. We might talk about issues around how to find a partner or we might talk about what it's like to be without a partner, we might talk about relationship issues, but we didn't talk about sex. We didn't talk about what it's like to be a sexual gay male walking around moment to moment. There's been a change in that.

Since we are very defensive about our right to be sexual because of the price we have paid for it, I would never have stood for it if my teacher had said, "You are wrong to live your sexuality," and he never said it. That's where wisdom mind came in: He didn't let me create a dichotomy between Buddhism and being sexual. With him I gradually dropped aside stuff that wasn't useful any more, and I moved in the direction that was useful and sustaining for my relationship with my teacher. That had to happen. My own need to be a certain way sexually—to see people as sexual objects, to see men as potential sexual objects, to have sex be about getting my rocks off—had to dissolve, it had to go. Now I can see it, but if he had said that to me when we first met I would have walked out of the room and said, "I don't want to spend any time with this guy."

For a Vajrayana Buddhist, there's only one useful thing to do with sexual energy. Nobody's criticizing you if you don't do sex this way, but, if you have an intention of taking your sexuality into Buddhist practice, then there's only one way to do it, and it's the same with all practice. The intention is to hold spaciousness, wisdom and compassion.

But sexual styles are very strong in gay men, and so you can't go to them and say, "Well, you know, if you continue to do that you're not going to move on in a Buddhist way." Often gay men have particular preferences about the sorts of people they find attractive. If you go into that directly, it is rarely beneficial for the client and only ends up in an argument. For example, someone could have a pattern of finding young, annihilated men who are very depressed and incapable of caring for themselves. He has chosen such a partner hoping to find transformation in the sex, but the young man can't contribute enough power to the experience to allow any transformation.

You have seen plenty of patterns like this in yourself and your friends, and if you criticize directly, it won't help. I learned from what Rinpoche did with me (I had plenty of these sorts of preferences), and what he did was absolutely demand that I remain with the sexual charge whenever I was with him. He never judged it, but he also didn't move it toward him. He didn't say, "Let's get sexual together," so there was always a very charged atmosphere, and, at the same time, it wasn't seemingly going anywhere. That turned out to be a very, very ripe and fruitful experience—still is, actually. It also led to transformation of those feelings, the hallmark of Mahayana Buddhism.

He was expanding my definition of who I was. Nothing got taken away without something coming in its place. I don't feel a loss. I feel a sense of competence and a stronger sense of my sexuality in a way that is not so driven. I don't have the sense of "have to, have to, have to," and that has been very nice for me. It's an enormous relief. I've also seen with my clients and with some of my friends that it's very helpful because one of the things that gay men both hate and love about themselves is their sense of being forced and pushed by this urgency. It's one of the ways we define ourselves: Because we have this need to be sexual with other men, we *are* this need to be sexual with other men.

We hope that the culture will develop a recognition of what it's like to be gay. Perhaps one day educated people and parents might even understand the world as it is, be happy their children sexualize in whatever ways they sexualize, and accept their children even though the children may be different from themselves. There is some suggestion that the gay teenager who has been recognized earlier does have more connection with his family of origin. In that case, being gay would be culturally inclusive rather than exclusive. Without the sense of inclusion, the gay culture has had to develop separate from the straight culture, and, because of that, some of our assumptions are different. By having different assumptions than the rest of the culture, we serve a function.

For example, when a culture starts to become decadent there's an increased number of homosexuals and homosexual acts. When the mouse population in a laboratory grows larger there's an increased number of homosexuals as well. This has been talked about as a sign of decadence, and what is implied is that we are part of the cause. But, you know, Rinpoche told me about this and said, "Yes, this is an exactly normal thing," without negative judgment. I began to notice that we are one of the balancing factors for this time of degeneration.

This increase is an appropriate thing to happen. There should be more gay people in the times of decay. We are part of the antidote. We are a response to what is going on. I think about that in terms of the fact that most gay people don't have children, and the world has far too many people. And gay people have different thought patterns. We're willing to have relationships which are not simply bifocal and monogamous. We're willing to work with all sorts of variations in how things may be.

My teachers say we are in a time of great decline. I'm not expert in this area, but it does occur to me that, with the increased number of publicly gay people, we have something to say that may be useful at a sociological level. I see the sorts of responses that have arisen out of our community because of AIDS, the degree to which our community has been placed in difficult places, the degree to which institutions had to be looked at and changed, and how we didn't go quietly but were loud, obstreperous and difficult, and I see that all the world now benefits. Sometime someone is going to sit down and write. "The gay revolution did this to the whole world, something happened out of this."

Gay culture is evolving. Our family becomes primarily other gay people plus those straight people for whom it is truly okay for people they love to be gay. Our need, our perceived need, to be sexual as a way of showing that we are alive and that we exist has changed to more of a social phenomenon. Our need to be with each other and have a movement, our need to be respected for being gay, our need to have our relationships ratified, our need to be recognized as more than just sexual beings, has overtaken the need to be sexual. It's not that we have given up being sexual, although a number of us did do that in order to save our lives, but we don't have the same absolute fervor we had. We can easily get back into that fervor. It's very easy for us to take that position any time against a straight environment that says we shouldn't be doing this sex act, or that sex act, or this particular form of sex, or sex in this particular way. Then we jump into their rigid system and say, "Well, it's our right to have sex however we want to have sex," but even that is less common than it used to be. We're becoming more tolerant; there's a lot more room and space for people to have sex in many different ways. We include drags, transies, leather queens, slaves, and even Buddhists.

And so I come back to the issue of sex in relationships. This was a difficult area with Rinpoche. My friends and I would go to him pretty consistently with an idea that something would happen in the sexual coming together of two folks, two committed loving folks, which was of such meaning that it would change and move the psyches and organisms of the two people on towards enlightenment. And, every time we presented a scenario like that, all the teachers, including Rinpoche, would look at it as though it were just clear bunkum. He would refuse to talk about sexuality. He would refuse to talk about tantra in terms of sexuality, would come back with quips—"Sex is just sex, tantra is tantra, they're not the same thing, they don't mix, they are not mixed, there is no tantric sexuality, mother-father tantra is not sexual"—yet at the same time we could feel what was apparently sexual charge as part of the tantric process with him.

And, when we would take that to one of the teachers, their denial of it was very strange to us, and for a long time their denial was absolute, like it wasn't happening. There was even one stage at which Rinpoche was using the metaphor that the place in which we live is all a movie, that everything we see and everything we're in is part of the movie, that Buddhism may be the best movie around, but a movie it is. I came to him in my naiveté and my fervent wish that there be something more constant and more meaningful in the world and asked him about the experience of being a lover or being loved. He quickly and expertly sliced that to pieces by telling me love is also a movie. That has stayed with me, and I notice the effects and benefits of those sorts of statements, leaving me with the following view.

Sex is a strong and fast-moving force that can open up new creative places or reinforce limitation. It depends on the levels of development of the individuals. You might create or limit a bit fancier, prettier, more fun, or more all at once, but you do in sex what you otherwise do with people, and that's dependent on the qualities and growth and patterns of the two human beings involved. Sex is not more meaningful than anything else you do with other people. You can't do anything in sex that you can't do in relationship. And you can't stabilize the force of the sexual experience if you don't have the ground of caring and affection. The degree to which we forget that the people coming to the sexual act shape the experience, the degree to which we forget who we are and who the person we are having sex with is, is the degree to which we make a fantasy. This is not useful in the spiritual sense.

From the Dalai Lama to Rinpoche, it's clear that in this gay sex is not different than straight sex. The place at which sex is intimacy, the place at which sex is loving combined intimacy with the generation of the new, is just as difficult for all folks. The ground rules are that both people already care for themselves and love makes them care for each other, honest and equal in intention; they both want to open ecstatic bliss, a state of union; and they take with them a continued relationship with all other beings, feeling compassion for the suffering in the world, not using sexual ecstasy as an escape. Not using pleasure to forget their connection to all beings.

It's an extraordinarily difficult thing to do.

How do you know if you're staying honest and connected in sexual embrace when self-delusion arises so easily with pleasure? You can't at first because ecstasy is very attention-consuming. It is hard to notice anything else. It takes continued inquisitiveness in the face of bliss and satisfaction to take attention elsewhere. Buddhist practice requires a loving and caring and precious holding of oneself; then being with another in passionate closeness; and then, according to Rinpoche, an equal compassion and respect for all life whilst holding all suffering. That is the only down-to-earth sexual advice that he was willing to give me.

I find it very difficult to have sex and not be self-involved. Combine that with all the technical difficulties of "tops" and "bottoms," leather or feathers, to cum together or not—holding the self and the other and making space for a third thing is downright difficult. When the space comes, we need to not freak at its unexpectedness. It will always be different than we expect because it confronts the fantasy we have made about the sexual encounter. In Buddhist practice the fantasies get confronted by the realization that there are others and they are different from us, another experience of the grinding stone.

Moreover, the teachers are part of Tibetan culture, and the Tibetan culture isn't very good at this sexual practice. I haven't found a lot of support for it. I haven't found the teachers willing to talk very much about it, and I have found the monks and the nuns and the everyday Tibetans homophobic. They're very nice and wish very much to care about everybody the best they can, but they are profoundly ignorant about what homosexuality is and they don't want to know more about it. They say it does not portend to them. It's not of interest to them, it doesn't have a meaning for them, it doesn't have a place for them. Recognizable bullshit to most of us.

The other issue is that we come to them with such a sense of urgency, such a need of recognition and of having our questions answered. I was very pleased when finally not only His Holiness, the Dalai Lama, but also two of my teachers—two of my younger teachers—said unequivocally that there is no difference whether you're gay or you're straight. It is not different. They wouldn't go so far as to make me feel all right about being gay, but they wouldn't let me flagellate myself about being gay, either, and that gave me the ground to find out that it was okay to be gay. It was really okay to be gay, but they weren't going to let me use them to make myself feel okay about it.

The gay culture is saying, "We need to have gay role models. We need to have us ratified." I think the recognition of gayness by Tibetan teachers is beginning to happen, but I don't think it's happening publicly. I don't think there's going to be a big show of "yes, yes, gays, fine, fine, fine," but I think it's happening much more at an individual level. Some of the teachers are slowly softening, and even teachers I have known who present themselves as homophobic and say things which I feel are very homophobic are very generous and heart-open and loving to me and my lover and a group of gay men doing practice. Very supportive of us and a little bit dismissive of their own countrymen when they demonstrate homophobia around me. So I see a change, but it's taking quite a number of years.

When we say to them, "Tell us about sex," we're going in a particular direction, and what they're saying is, "What about before sex, what about the actual making of sexuality, what is that?" I ask my teacher to tell me about the place where sexuality is meaningful, and he goes back to "Where does sexuality come from?" when I'm only interested in "What can it do for me?" I miss out on a whole lot because of my point of view.

You go to a teacher and say, "I have this problem. If you tell me the answer to the problem, I'll be okay." Very rarely will the teacher buy into that. From the point of view of the teacher, the making of the problem is the issue, not the solving of it. If you make the problem in a sexual arena, the teacher will not respond. Once I was driving with Rinpoche and two lesbians who were testing him to see if he would be a good teacher for them. They said, "What about lesbians?" And he said, "Well, there are some gay men in Tibet, but there have never been any lesbians." And it was the most outrageous statement I had ever heard. I had a lot of trouble staying on the road. He was living in a gay household at the time, and there were lesbians coming in and out, he had been very pleasant and comfortable in that environment, and he says, "No, there have never been lesbians in Tibet."

The women were shocked and outraged and stayed outraged for a long time, and, you know, they were profoundly affected by his death. Profoundly. I expected them to disappear him or write him off and give him no entrance whatsoever, yet both these women often spontaneously start talking about him. I would have thought that, given the way the question was asked and what they were asking, his response was really a slap in the face. I don't know what was engaged between them with that answer, but the women stayed and are staying in relationship with him. Perhaps the guiding principle was that Guru Yoga is more important than ratifying sexual preference; it will have longer and greater effects.

This is not to suggest there is no homophobia in the Dharma or that individual teachers are not homophobic. But my teacher was so incredibly brave that he let himself be seen as homophobic in order to connect with these women. He didn't need you to like him or stay in a relationship with him. You can spend the rest of your life hating a teacher and saying what an incredible asshole he is, but, if doing that brings issues to the fore and insists on you dealing with them, then he has done you a service. And, if you decide he was just being a provocative asshole and you never want to have anything to do with him again, then that's tolerable for the teacher because he knows the deeper connection between you. Gay folks' issues around sex are a vehicle the teachers use to provoke change.

Finally, I want to talk about one of the experiences which taught me that having a particular point of view is just having a particular point of view. A very high teacher came to teach about death and dying to a group sponsored by an AIDS foundation, and he did a really beautiful annunciation, showed us all the stages of the bardos, took us exquisitely through the death process. He created a sense of what it was like to die, what the stages of death were like, and what the stages of transforming from death to rebirth would be like for us. It was a very moving experience for me and a really, really high teaching.

The following week in a local gay paper I saw an article written with rage that this teacher had never discussed AIDS, never mentioned the word ''AIDS,'' never mentioned HIV, never mentioned gay. He was sponsored by a gay organization, but he never said anything public about any of it although there were a number of people in the audience who were in the process of dying of AIDS. And the man who had written the article was absolutely right: At the sociological and political level, nothing had occurred.

And he let that annihilate what had happened which was so astounding, so beautiful and so deep. Of great benefit, I thought, to everybody there.

This fury in the gay press about the teacher's not dealing with the political aspect of AIDS is a metaphor for what we're doing right now. We all want to read, ''Gay is special, different, as good as everyone else.'' Gay is absolutely okay, and that doesn't make it any easier or harder to take sexuality into Buddhist practice. But I can't help it if people are reading this to be told that being gay is okay. The practice is based on the assumption that being gay is okay. Now you get to mess with everything else.

Photo of Maitreyabandhu

Coming Out into Dharma Bliss

Maitreyabandhu

I was brought up in a small town in Warwickshire, England. I sang in the church choir, went to the local school, did a paper round and generally tried to fit into groups: my rather large family, the local church and school. However, I had a secret: I was having sex with other boys on a regular basis in one of the many secret dens and hide-outs I'd built in our sprawling and junkyard-like garden. My parents ran a small coach firm. Whilst my father was a keen gardener, he was also fond of hoarding various items of junk which, with the odd dilapidated coach body, made excellent hide-outs for my furtive amorous encounters. I was terrified of being found out. I remember I used to pray every night that I wasn't gay, and yet I knew I was, and that meant that I didn't fit in. I didn't fit in with the assumptions and mores of a parochial English town. I was bullied at school for being a sissy and I felt only too keenly that I was in fact no angelic choirboy! Looking back on it, I feared rejection most: that I would be rejected and reviled by my family and my schoolfellows. I had so wanted to fit in and yet I knew, or felt I knew, that being gay meant that I didn't. I intuitively realised that the Group of the Family, the Firm, the Union, the Church or the State is at base a more or less blatant power structure. Conform or else!

I find it interesting if I compare my own experience of coming-out and the consequences of that with my heterosexual brother. Until very recently he has remained much more unthinkingly bound up with the Group and its expectations. He went to work in the family firm, got married, had a family and went on holidays by the sea just like our parents used to. It is only now that his marriage has broken down that he is waking up to the limitations, expectations and assumptions of the Group. Like me when I came out he is having self-awareness thrust upon him. After all, with its Group values, Group norms and Group-think, the Group is not only a power structure, but a soporific; if "Religion is the opium of the people" then the Group is the Valium.

My first experience of the gay scene was a very drunken visit to a club in Coventry. Unbeknown to me I'd arrived on drag night. The evening was

DHARMACHARI MAITREYABANDHU (London) was born in Warwickshire, England in 1961. He was ordained in the "Western Buddhist Order" in 1990. Since then he has lived and worked at the London Buddhist Centre in the East End, one of the many worldwide centres of the "Friends of the Western Buddhist Order" (FWBO). He has initiated various courses and retreats for Gay men to introduce them to meditation and Buddhism. The present article first appeared in somewhat different form in *Rouge* (London).

spent propping up the bar, getting depressed and watching a bunch of men dressed in saris camping it up on the dance floor. It was not a good start.

Then I came to London, managed the difficult process of coming out, went to art school and tried to figure out what I really wanted from life. My first priority became finding a man. I went to The Bell at King's Cross where everyone acted as though they had just popped in to buy a packet of cigarettes and were far too good looking to actually talk to anyone. I felt a mere mortal in a world of unattainable gods. At the LA (London Apprentice) I wandered around trying to look tough—among a lot of other men trying to look tough. I went home wishing I bore even a passing resemblance to a Tom of Finland drawing. I went to my local gay pub, got anaesthetised by inane music, bored by bitchy conversation and bemused by cheap innuendos. I decided that something was wrong with the gay scene. I had seen it as the light at the end of the tunnel, now I saw it as simply another tunnel (albeit better lit).

The gay scene seemed to me to be increasingly characterised by sexual competitiveness, vapid small talk and endless wanting. Its obsession with the body beautiful, with the pursuit of pleasure as an end in itself, with youth and style seemed to trap gay men like myself in either painful superficiality or isolation. The alternative, however, seemed to be an increasingly domesticated "straight-acting" conventionality.

Despite all this, I know that coming out for me would have been so much more difficult without the gay scene. I needed places where I could meet gay men and feel a sense of identity with them. It allowed me to explore my sexuality and to experiment with ways of being which departed from the assumptions and expectations of my family and the narrow-mindedness of the small town I grew up in.

Now, years later, I have been ordained into the Western Buddhist Order.* I live with a community of men in a converted fire station in London's Bethnal Green, I meditate, teach Buddhism and go on retreat. I was attracted to Buddhism because of its commonsensical approach to becoming a happier, healthier human being. It taught me ways to develop emotional positivity and concentration, it encouraged me to think for myself and take responsibility for my actions. It gave me a context in which to practice a spiritual life without having to deny my sexuality, either publicly or privately.

Until then, I had assumed that any sort of spiritual life inevitably meant God and therefore the concept of sin and guilt. In Buddhism there is no

---

*The Friends of the Western Buddhist Order (FWBO), is a movement founded in 1967 by Sangharakshita, an English Buddhist monk, who had spent twenty years in India. On returning to the West he decided to found a movement (and the following year an order, the Western Buddhist Order) to transmit the essentials of Buddhism in a manner relevant to the modern West. This movement now runs centres throughout the world and is the largest Buddhist group in the U.K.

God, no notion of sin and no unchanging soul. Buddhism offers a practical path of spiritual development for all, irrespective of race, gender or sexual preference. It shows the individual how to grow, shows him or her, by means of actual methods, how to develop awareness, how to develop emotional positivity, how to live creatively and spontaneously, and how to take responsibility for oneself and others. In other words, it shows the person how to become a true individual.

A true individual is committed to developing self-awareness. Usually we are not very self-aware. We may think that we are individuals, that we think and feel for ourselves, but in fact we are very much determined by the expectations and assumptions of those around us. To the extent we have not fully differentiated our thoughts and feelings from societies and not taken full responsibility for our actions, we will be group members. We will be characterised by the unthinking prejudices and "moral" assumptions of the group rather than by our own individual awareness.

We can see this very clearly in our experience of coming out. When we come out we realise that we do not fit in to the expectations of the group, whether it be the group of our immediate family, the church, our peers or our work colleagues. Our lives take place with a vast interlocking network of groups from the nation state to the family unit. Whether big or small, however, the principle of the group remains unchanged, that it is a collectivity organised for its own survival in which the needs of the individual are subordinated to that of the collective. We need the group to survive. As children, we literally need the family group to survive into adulthood. However, we pay a price, the price of conformity. Often this isn't a perceived problem, it may never occur to us that we are conforming, that we think and feel just as the group does. However, when we come out we have that awareness thrust upon us. In coming out we have to define ourselves as distinct from the group. For me this was a very frightening and isolating experience. I so wanted to fit in. I so wanted to conform to the group. But I couldn't. I was gay. Coming out is a *special feat* of self-awareness and as such can be the beginning of a truly spiritual life, a life devoted to developing our individual self-awareness.

The emergence of the gay scene and the gay community, with all its groups and sub-groups, has vastly improved the lives of millions of gay men, as well as radically changing our understanding of human sexuality. It has provided new models for sexual relationships and given gay men a chance to live a whole life—so unlike the damaging secrecy and pretence that goes with being in the closet. We need to rejoice in all this and feel gratitude to all those unknown people who have made it possible.

We must also be aware of its limitations. In other words, we need to be aware that it is a group, that the gay scene is a collection of groups, all with their accepted ways of behaving, of talking and of acting. If we are not careful, we will move from one set of constricting assumptions to another, our gay liberation will become a gay limitation. The self-awareness we started to develop in coming out will be borne down in a torrent of recreational drugs, deadening music and sexual compulsion. Either that or smothered with the pink duvet of banal consumerism and hetero aping.

We shouldn't confuse the true individual with the individualist who is really the group writ small. The true individual moves away from the group in terms of developing greater awareness. The individualist alienates himself from the group by rebelling and reacting to it. The individualist simply wants more of what the group offers—more money, more status, more fame, more lycra outfits.

My experience of the gay scene has been mainly in the context of a long-term sexual relationship with a New Zealand communist I met before I became a Buddhist. It is an open relationship and I don't see any particular problems with the fact that he is not a practising Buddhist. In the early days of my involvement I still went on the scene occasionally but still tended to find it an unsatisfactory, if not unpleasant, experience. I spent the evening yelling over the music or standing around getting bored.

I was talking this over with another gay friend who was ordained at the same time as me and we hit upon the idea of running gay men's meditation and Buddhism classes. These proved very popular and we soon started running retreats. The experience of meditating together with a group of gay men was a very significant one.

Many of the gay men who came along were tired of the superficiality of the gay scene or felt isolated within it. They were looking for a lifestyle which included being gay but which wasn't limited by it. They were looking for a way of developing as individuals. Over the past four years of gay men's activities I have seen more and more gay men get involved in the movement. Following our example, other centres of the Friends of the Western Buddhist Order have started running similar events and this past summer we organised our first national gay men's retreat in Norfolk.

Gay men have so much to offer the world—we challenge so many assumptions. The lack of family responsibilities means we can commit ourselves wholeheartedly to what is most important in life—the development of universal lovingkindness and true individuality. If this is to happen we need to rediscover our radical roots and reconnect with the urge to change ourselves and our world. We will need to appreciate what the gay scene has done for us, while admitting its limitations. If we are able to capitalise on the self-awareness we gained in coming out, if we can develop and refine that, then we have the basis for the development of our *true* individuality.

Gay Zen Nature

James Soshin Thornton

It took me much of a lifetime to get to Taizan Maezumi Roshi. He was a small and graceful man whose name meant Big Mountain.

Maezumi spoke of Zen this way. "Our practice," he said, "is a practice of bliss and repose." Bliss and repose. He gave me a gentle way of going beyond the edge of the mind and returning. A way of experience, beyond theory and dogma.

It was desperation that took me to him. I was living in New York's Tribeca, renovating a loft with my lover, while we played at being young, gay and chic in New York in the early eighties. And then the relationship was over. I found myself living in the East Village, waking up in the middle of the night reciting my name, age and profession. Over and over again, a prisoner of despair.

"Well this must be what a breakdown feels like," I told myself. Something had to be done. Where could I find help?

I had been Catholic as a boy, and devout. But being a little Jesuit at heart, I researched the theology, and found that the Catholics reserved a special place in hell for homosexuals. Being devout threw me into a double bind: I had been made by a loving God and this same God, I now discovered, condemned me to hell for what He had made me. For there was no doubt it was He who made me gay. How else could I have liked boys from the time I was five years old?

There were two exits from the bind: I could repress my gayness, or I could reject the Church. In rejecting the Church, I made the right move, but paid a price. All sense of the sacred was put off limits. Any communion with a Source of Being bigger than my ego was ruled out. When I tried to connect, I would find a black, thick, high wall inside, cordoning me off, turning me back on my ego self.

I tried for an exit in relationships with men. But after my breakup, in my breakdown, I knew this wasn't working.

I remembered Zen. I recalled the claim that there was an unbroken chain of masters stretching back to the Buddha. This gave me something to hold onto. I reasoned, "Their enlightenment is something I can test. If they are really enlightened, they can help. And I can test their claim for myself."

Looking for a Zen master to meet and test, I found Maezumi in Peter Matthiessen's book *Nine Headed Dragon River*. Maezumi sounded like the

JAMES SOSHIN THORNTON (Santa Fe, N.M.) was born in 1954 and has practiced in the Sōtō Zen tradition for some time. He has recently completed a book on spiritual practice and the Earth: *A Field Guide to the Soul*.

premier Zen master in America. To be near him, I moved to California, without ever having met him. And without ever having sat Zen. That is how desperate I was.

Getting to Big Mountain

Maezumi ran the Los Angeles Zen Center. I called from San Francisco, where I got a job as a lawyer with the environmental organization in whose New York office I had worked.

I asked when their next intensive retreat was being held. It was in a few weeks. I asked to be included.

"Have you ever sat Zen before?" the woman on the phone asked.

"I've experimented with it a few times at home," I said.

"Can you sit all day for seven days?" she asked.

"I have to," I said. She laughed and agreed. I asked her how to prepare for it.

"There's no way to prepare," she said, with another laugh.

A few weeks later, I arrived at the Mountain Center, then run by the Los Angeles Zen Center. The retreat center faces West near the top of Apple Canyon on the easternmost ridge of the Southern California Coastal Range. Three hours drive east of Los Angeles, the center is a mile up. If you walk a few hundred feet up to the top of the ridge you look down on Palm Springs in the desert a mile below.

This last ridge of mountains catches whatever rain remains in the air moving in from the ocean. It falls in the mountains, leaving the desert in the mountains' rainshadow. This rain makes the canyon moist for that part of the world. Huge ancient cedars and pines mix in the canyon with younger pine and scrub oak. Some of the ancient trees seem as big as middle aged redwoods.

Spotted owls, cougar, and rattlesnakes are seen. A profusion of fern and wildflowers grow in the meadows. Groups of acorn woodpeckers fly around together, their calls loud tooting laughs. A welcoming natural setting.

The retreat started. I meditated for two days, in a state of excited discovery. It was a completely new thing for me to meditate for such extended periods of time, and it made me agreeably high. I felt like a duck who has walked across the desert most of his life, and finally come to a lake. If this was swimming, I wanted more. I found myself thinking, "This is so good, how can they let you do it in public?"

On the third morning, I met Maezumi Roshi for the first time. He was giving interviews in a tiny cabin on a hillside. It was before dawn when we were called to the interviews. We waited outside in the mountain chill of an August morning. The stars were clear as I took my place kneeling in line. As I waited, the sky flushed rose. A Western fence lizard, tan and brown, took his place on a rock in front of me. We both sat unmoving. Much to appreciate.

As I walked up the hillside to my interview, I remembered my plan. I was taking the claim of enlightenment seriously, and was here to test it. That meant testing the master. This man was supposed to be enlightened. Enlightenment was supposed to translate into compassion. My gayness provided a test.

I would test the master. I would tell Maezumi I was gay. If he was compassionate, I would become his student. If not, I would spit in his face and walk away, having proved in my own terms that Zen had no purchase on enlightenment.

I entered the tiny cabin. Maezumi was sitting on the floor cross legged, in an elegant moss-green silk robe, only a candle illuminating the room. In the formal manner that had been explained to me, I bowed, stated my name, and knelt on the floor with my face not two feet from his.

"Please come closer!" was the first thing he said. I did, inching my way forward on my knees. We were then knee to knee, our faces perhaps a foot apart. I stated my practice.

I had assigned myself the classic question "Who am I?" I chose this question because it had been the central question of my life for a long time already.

"Who assigned you this practice?" he asked.

"I assigned it to myself," I said.

"Hmm," he said, using the masculine Japanese particle of flexible meaning. He seemed pleased, though.

"Tell me about yourself," he said. I mumbled something.

"Tell me about your family," he said. I said something about my parents.

"But you have no family of your own?" he asked.

"Well, I thought, "here we are one minute into the interview and he's asked the question." So I said, "I have no family of my own, because I am gay."

"*Hmmm!*" he said, the inflection rising and falling, expressing a strong reaction, one I could not read. "Means you have no family of your own?"

"No," I said. I thought, "Well, he's a middle aged Japanese man, comes from a homophobic culture, this doesn't look good."

"Please to be very careful about AIDS!" he said. This was soon after the virus had been identified.

Unsure what tack he was taking, I said, "Thanks, I am. I am very conservative in that regard, too much so for my own satisfaction."

"*No!*" he said, "I mean *very careful!*"

The intensity of it was reassuring. He was prepared to speak loud enough to get through my emotional deafness. Still suspicious of anything that seemed religious, however, I was not completely convinced of the compassion.

He continued, "What are you doing after your week up here in the mountains with us?" I said something about a solo hike in the Sierras that I was planning.

"Why don't you go back to L.A., and check out our city center? There is a man there that I think might enjoy meeting you very much. He is about your own age. May I ask how old you are?"

I laughed, and rejoiced. Here was a Jewish grandmother Zen master. For him, my being gay called forth a direct and practical response. Compassion had been demonstrated unfailingly. And in the only way I could then perceive it.

I told him at that moment that I wanted to be his student for the rest of my life. He accepted me.

I then asked him whether I could become enlightened. "Why not?" he said. "Thousands have done so throughout history. If you choose the Way and follow the practice, why not you too?"

Just Sitting

After I became Maezumi's student, I'd travel down to Los Angeles to sit with him. I was working as a lawyer in the San Francisco office of the environmental group NRDC. I covered issues from off-shore oil and gas drilling to forestry, pesticides, and so on. Getting to know California, taking walks on weekends.

There were five weeks a year of vacation, and I spent them doing week-long retreats with Maezumi. I'd usually show up so tired that I slept upright sitting on my cushion for the first few days.

I felt guilty about this for years, and one day asked Maezumi about it. "If you need to sleep, then sleep," he said.

I asked him if he ever slept while meditating. "All the time!" he said. We laughed, and I learned to take care of myself a little bit better.

During the first three years of studying Zen, I kept working on my question, "Who am I?" I worked on it while at the office and in meetings, and while on hikes around the Bay Area. I tied it to the awareness of every breath I took. I tried to answer it in every way I could. I sat on my cushion for long hours, faced the wall and worked hard.

One morning while we were doing walking meditation outside in downtown L.A. before dawn, I realized just how barricaded inside my mind I was. In seeing this, I also admitted to myself how afraid I was to give up hiding in the rational mind that constrained me. The rational mind I'd taken refuge in when deprived of the spiritual solace Catholicism had given me as a boy.

The time had come: all my ideas, which I'd labored so hard on, had to go. I thereupon resolved to drop them, and find out who I was without them. Yet my identification with my thoughts was complete. I wept, in grief at the incipient loss, until my hands were wet with tears.

I had an interview with Maezumi moments later. "These tears are my thoughts," I said, "which I thought so important."

"How nice," he said, "that you have tears."

After three years of intense effort, my mind relaxed a little one day. I became content to just sit for the first time. I went in to see Maezumi, and said, "I no longer know why I sit, I just do it, and I'm going to keep doing it." He said, "That's enough on your question 'Who am I?' I want you now to just sit."

Maezumi and Martin

It was Maezumi who showed me that Nature is my teacher. I heard the message through another. Martin, my partner, came to pick me up at the Mountain Center after a week's intensive retreat.

It was ten years by this time since I had first met Maezumi. During those years, I would mention problems with boyfriends, and Maezumi would always laugh at me in a good natured way. From the first moment he heard about Martin, though, he was serious about him.

"You must have our picture taken together!" he said straightaway. I thought it sounded like a wedding. It turned out to be the only time they were to meet before Maezumi died.

When Martin met Maezumi for the first time, he said to him, "Thank you for your teachings, which have been so important in James's life."

"I am not James's teacher," Maezumi said. "Nature. Nature is his teacher."

It was a stunning piece of news to me. In all our years together, I had never discussed Nature with Maezumi. I suppose I never needed to. Perhaps I had never noticed the truth of what he told Martin because it was so obvious. But also perhaps because I needed a human teacher to let me into Nature's ways as an adult.

Maezumi told this to Martin at their only meeting, several months before Maezumi died. As I look back, it feels as if my soul father chose that conversation with my lover to pass me on to Nature to complete my studies.

Nature is a willing teacher for us all if we train our eyes to see, our ears to hear, our heart and mind to open. Children do this easily. As a small boy I loved everything that crawled, and wanted to study spiders as my career.

I chose spiders because they seemed under-appreciated. In grammar school I attended meetings of the Arachnology Section of the august New York Entomological Society. Years of collecting, studying, learning to think like a spider, an insect, a bat, a snake, a fern, an aspen, bacteria in the soil. Breeding black widows and tarantulas.

Gay Zen Nature

Being gay is the most natural thing in the world. Birds build nests; orcas swim in the ocean; people are gay. For a long time I didn't know this. Whenever I was struggling with the judgments of others, and the judgments I made about myself for being gay, I turned to Nature as a teacher.

I'd tell myself stories of animals that were gay. One of my favorites is the greylag goose, which lives in Europe. These geese mate for life, and are faithful partners. It so happens that in some flocks, there are gay geese. They form male-male partnerships, which also last for life.

Because the gay geese don't have to devote any energy to raising young, they become the leaders of the flock. They watch over the whole flock, and take up the hardest job when the flock is migrating: flying at the tip of the V-shaped wedge of flying geese, where the air resistance is strongest. I've always wondered if flocks that have gay leaders also have more stylish nests, and better conversation as they fly.

Connecting with the natural world puts things in proper perspective. Whatever anxieties we have melt away when we feel part of the web of life, all natural, all one. We can then see clearly, know ignorance for what it is, and accept our gay selves as part of Nature's glory.

Nature is as close as our lover's heartbeat. When I need to reset my rhythms, I listen to my partner Martin's heart. It's a lovely practice. My ear to his chest, feeling the beat of his heart. Knowing as I hear it the absolute acceptance of my being, my gay being, in this body, in this world. Let me share a poem about listening to Martin's heartbeat:

> Your heart beats out
> the rhythm of my days,
>
> and I lay listening, my ear
> to your chest, hours at a time:
>
> like the first man to discover ice
> like the first man to discover roses
>
> like the first man to discover fire
> like the first man to find solace.
>
> Your heartbeat teaches me to breathe
> your heartbeat teaches me to see
>
> your heartbeat shows me how to be
> this medium-sized mammal I am.

There are love stories hidden throughout the living world, countless numbers of them. The more we know them, the more we know our gay selves as part of the natural order of things, as part of the necessary rhythms of life. Here is just one more of these love stories: thin threads of the euphoniously named mycorrhizal fungus entwine intimately around the roots of trees.

Far from harming them, the fungus helps the trees thrive. It dissolves minerals from the soil for the tree to use, and receives nutrients in return. Most plants around the world live in intimate partnership with this sort of fungus.

We have only been learning about it recently. Here is one of the central stories of why plants grow, and we are just beginning to learn its details. Details that encode a wisdom of cooperation among beings that we thought of as separate.

The natural world is full of a wisdom that makes all of human accomplishment appear as the first steps of a child. Billions of years of learning to live intimately together. This is the reason to protect biodiversity: that we may learn wisdom from it.

Nature was never remote from our Buddhist ancestors. It inspired them into self-acceptance. This self-acceptance is the key to our practice. We are already perfect. This can be difficult to feel. Most of us who are gay have taken in so many poisons from our culture about being gay.

Yet we are already perfect. Our way of being is perfect. Our way of loving is perfect. We are already perfect. How can we know this for ourselves?

One time I brought Issan Dorsey down to the L.A. Zen Center to meet Maezumi Roshi. Issan was a fabulous transvestite in his earlier years, and when I knew him he still boasted of being the highest paid bar girl in Alaska at the time when thousands of workmen were laboring on the Trans-Alaska Pipeline. When I knew him, Issan was a Zen priest running the Hartford Street Zen Center for gay people in the Castro.

Visiting L.A., Issan stayed in the room Maezumi used for an office. I was eager to find out how Issan felt about meeting Roshi, and asked him.

Issan said, "Maezumi came in and saw that I'd been sleeping with my feet toward the Buddha. He corrected me. He was very tough with me!" With a squeal of delight he added, as he adjusted the hem of his priestly robes, "And I just loved it!"

I asked Roshi if he had any problem with Issan's flamboyance. He was surprised, and said, "How could I? There are many different styles, but the Dharma is all one thing!"

How can we use our practice to go so deep we find the pool inside ourselves that holds the poisons our culture feeds us about gayness? And when we find this pool, how can we drain it off? How can we let our natural perfection out?

Nature can help us. The Buddha awakened while practicing outdoors.

He awakened under a tree, and when he looked at the morning star. These were no accidents.

Dogen, the Japanese master, went to China to find his awakening. He walked all over the country through the great forests that then existed throughout much of China. How much of his enlightenment came from sitting, and how much came from long walks, carrying his open heart through the forests from master to master as he sought the meaning of his life? What did the forests teach him?

As we go through the stories of the ancient masters, we see their practice happened and their stories unfolded in the natural world. Their intimacy with nature is revealed everywhere in their stories.

This intimacy between the ancient masters and Nature is generally now overlooked, because we are so urban. We need to welcome the Earth into our practice again. The Earth welcomes our practice, supports our practice, aids our practice.

When we are in Nature, our city cares grow dim. In a healthy woods, it becomes hard to remember what it was that so upset us. Climbing the flank of a mountain, we can pour out all the anger we feel at our difficult boyfriend or boss, and feel the mountain absorb it. The Earth aids our practice.

The Earth also needs our practice. Our actions as global humans have begun to unravel the web of life that the Earth has been weaving in her wisdom for billions of years. When we welcome the Earth into our practice, and invite the Earth to teach us, she will. She will help us awaken. She will begin to give us the strength and insight we need to awaken and so live more harmoniously with each other, and all the living beings of the Earth.

Our culture will flourish or fail depending on whether we can enter into this harmony with the Earth. Our practice can bring each of us into it, so that we experience it for ourselves. When we experience this harmony within ourselves, it begins to spread quite naturally to those around us. This is the practical value of interconnection: that by changing our own mind we can change the world, one mind at a time.

One Square Foot of Earth

We can begin to open to the wisdom of the Earth very simply. We can do it by letting ourselves connect with the organic beings that live in one square foot of Earth. Try it. Go out to a place where things grow. It can be in the wilderness, or in a city park.

Find a spot that draws you to it. Let the Earth call you, and let yourself feel the call. Find a square foot of Earth, one that is alive. Mark it out at the corners with rock or twigs. Sit comfortably near it, in a posture you can maintain for about an hour.

Now relax, and follow your breath into your body. Feel your breath, and feel your body. Let yourself become fully present.

When you are fully present, give your awareness to what lives within that one square foot of Earth. Hold your gaze there, relaxing, attentive. What is alive there? What plants, what insects, what else?

It will take about twenty minutes for you to slow down to the rhythms of what is living within your one square foot.

Let yourself slow down to the rhythms of the real. Awareness is love. Let your love flow out to all that is alive within your one square foot.

Things you did not notice were alive will begin to startle you with their subtlety. There is a universe at every level of scale. Let yourself open to what is before you.

If a question arises in your heart, ask it. It can be anything at all. Let your heart open and ask. When you do this, an answer will come. You will find yourself understood, and intimately answered.

When we ask to awaken we are heard. When we ask with all our heart the Way is open to us. Of this there is no doubt. Let yourself try it, with absolute sincerity.

Let yourself enter into dialogue with the Earth. Whenever you are lonely, whenever you are afraid, enter into dialogue with the Earth.

Offer the Earth your problems, and you will feel them run to ground. Ask the Earth for help, and you will feel comforted. Try this for yourself.

The Earth never forgets a single one of us. When we know this with our whole body, there is no being lonely ever again.

*   *   *

When we attend to what lives within our one square foot of Earth, we are cultivating in the outer landscape the keen, kind awareness we need to bring to our meditation. When we open to the Earth in this simple way, we are penetrated by the wisdom of the Earth, and receive its many benefits.

Let us practice with the Earth. Let us feel the Earth as our body, and open our minds to her wisdom. Let us also open our hearts. Let us open them to the needs of the Earth so completely that we cannot act except in harmony with the Earth. Let us merge with the Earth in this way, and then we will awaken, for the sake of all that lives.

Photo of Jon Bernie, © 1997 Steve Savage.

Monk in Drag

Jon Bernie

Suzuki-roshi talked about our "innermost request"—that most profound desire to be free of suffering, to be liberated, to be one with all being. The purpose of Zen Buddhist monastic practice is to put the seed of that innermost request in the hothouse of intense meditative and mindfulness practice. In that environment, the seed will have an opportunity to germinate and grow. The whole idea of right livelihood is to find work that encourages and supports the seedling's continued growth. My reason for choosing the healing arts as a profession was that I believed it would provide fertile ground for continued spiritual growth. Now, after 15 years of private practice, I can say that my choice was the right one.

I would like to begin by traveling back in time to 1969. I was 16 years old, an achievement-oriented, nonreligious (Jewish background) concert violinist and straight-A student in the top 1% of my class. I thought I was on my way to Stanford and medical school. But "Sweet 16" was not that sweet! I was painfully in love (unrequited, of course) with George, a pretty blonde straight friend, and the fast pace of my young life had begun to engender a profound questioning of the meaning of all that intensity—and about the meaning of my life.

I came out that year in San Francisco. I told my parents and brother that I was gay. I carefully selected friends and relatives to share this "news" with—people I felt would still love me and be sympathetic. It wasn't easy, but I couldn't hold it in.

I attended Gay Liberation marches and Gay "Rap" groups. I answered gay personal ads in the *Berkeley Barb*, an "underground" newspaper of the times. I looked older and could get into bars. I went looking for love in the gay bars of upper Grant Street (North Beach), Polk Street and of course the original Stud on Folsom and 11th. In 1969 it was a gay hippie bar. I loved it!

One of the Gay Liberation marches I attended had about 100 people in it; it eventually became the Gay Freedom Day Parade. This all happened around the time of Stonewall. That whole period was a very difficult time for me emotionally. I certainly wasn't happily dating the "boy next door"! My emotional needs were not really being met, and I was sexually frus-

JON BERNIE (San Francisco) was born in 1953 and has been practicing meditation for twenty-seven years. His primary practices have been in the Sōtō Zen and Vipassana traditions. He is a faculty member of the Harvey Milk Institute where he teaches meditation. Jon is in private practice as a transformational therapist where he assists individuals in spiritual expansion, emotional clearing and structural balancing.

trated. I poured my heart out through my violin! I definitely wasn't happy.

I observed the "successful" adults I knew and I didn't see anyone who looked happy. They appeared to be struggling, not really satisfied with their lives or at peace in themselves. The seeker of truth in me (the inner monk) began to drive my life. I felt that I had to discover the meaning of life— otherwise I did not see the point of continuing it.

An intense period of inquiry and revelation followed (this was a completely personal process that was revealed to no one and lasted over four months). This is how it all got started: At 11 years old I argued wth my Sunday school teacher about the existence of God. I wasn't buying it. I came home and told my mother I wasn't going to Sunday school any more, I was too busy practicing the violin. "OK, Honey!" she said. I decided then that when I saw "God," I'd believe it. At 16 I had to know what the meaning of life was about. My first insight came when I realized that there indeed was some "creative force" in the universe; after all, there was all this stuff around! I was beginning to experience the awe of the mystery of life. Looking at flowers and how my hand could open and close fascinated me. I *knew* there was a creative force. *Now*, I *had* to discover what it was.

The next insight that came was that of course I could discover what the creative force was—I was part of it! I was incredibly excited by this discovery and immediately came up with a plan. When my parents went to bed I would sit naked and cross-legged in my large furry bean bag chair, stare at the wall and not move until I discovered it. (Ann Armstrong, a well-respected psychic, 4 years later told me I had many lifetimes as a monk and I knew from that past-life knowledge what to do in this life to engender the experience that was about to unfold.)

Well, my parents had gone to bed—it was 11:30 p.m. and there I was in the bean bag, staring at the wall, determined to not move until I discovered it. I can honestly say that the level of importance this had for me was such that I was willing to die if I had to. My arm started to itch—I didn't scratch it. I felt like moving—I didn't move. My mind started to wander—I didn't let it. (All those intensive years of concentrated violin practice and discipline were paying off.) Something very interesting started happening: I observed a wave-like motion in the walls, and there was a light emanating from this wave motion. *And* I could *feel* it!! Amazing! Far Out! I intuitively knew how to allow this experience to develop. The experience gradually became more and more intense. The waves got bigger, the light got brighter and the feelings got stronger. It kept increasing in intensity. It got so strong and powerful that I was struck with terror. It was as if I were stuck in a car that was accelerating faster and faster and would very soon crash through a barrier and go over a cliff into an infinite abyss—and it couldn't be stopped! In the middle of the terror a voice came to me and said, "Just stay with your breathing." OK! Anything to get me through this one! There was an explosion into infinite light. There was no more "me," there was no room where I had been—there was just vast intense light—like the sun—everywhere. The feeling I described at the time was like a millionfold orgasm. It was as if every atom in my body had exploded. When consciousness returned to the body the whole room was being imploded into me, and then exploded out of me—in synch with my breathing—it was as if I were being ripped apart. I started crying and shaking. I got up and covered myself with a blanket. I'd been there 3 hours. I felt that if I died right then my life had been worth it. What was present for me after the experience and remains to this day is a profound and deep sense of meaning in life, an intuitive sense of being guided through life, and seeing and feeling "the light." After the experience I told my mother I was going to become a monk. "OK, Honey!" So 1969 was a landmark year: I came out sexually and I came out spiritually!

The twenty-seven years between 1969 and 1996 have included a wide range of spiritual and therapeutic practices and training. I began with 3 years of studying yogic meditation, breathing and asanas. The next 11 years were mostly Zen meditation, including Tai Chi and Chi-Kung practices. Then came 7 years of Vipassana meditation. For the past 6 years I have worked closely with teachers from the lineages of Advaita Vedanta—a non-dualistic teaching that originated out of the Hindu yogic tradition. In this tradition the non-verbal transmission of the truth of our essential nature is conveyed directly from teacher to student. The Advaita path most closely resembles the Dzogchen teachings of Tibetan Buddhism as well as the quintessential Zen experience. Professionally I am certified in the Alexander Technique (1981), Neuro-Linguistic Programming (1983), and Amanae™ (1995). The Alexander Technique is a gentle hands-on technique that re-educates one's movements so that one becomes relatively free of habit patterns which create unnecessary stress and strain. Neuro-Linguistic Programming is a set of communication tools which enables one to be free of limiting belief patterns. Amanae™ is transformational body work in which deep breathing and deep tissue work are used to release issues held at a cellular level—and this results in clearly accelerating spiritual unfoldment. I have also been deeply influenced by training in cranial-sacral therapy and Zero Balancing: both of these systems originated out of the Osteopathic tradition and work with the structure of the bones and energy system simultaneously.

Being drawn to helping others was at the root of the Bodhisattva ideal of "assisting others in being free of their suffering." In the Eight-Fold path that the Buddha taught, Right Livelihood was work that supported one's own and other's spiritual evolution. My work is not about feathering my own nest, it is not about building up my own self or enriching myself. It is about serving others. Naturally, by giving to others and supporting others, I support myself in the deepest way by opening to "big mind," where we are all interconnected and one.

When I first started training in the Alexander Technique I was fresh out of the monastery and wanted to help people with their meditation posture. A lot of people had problems sitting in Zen meditation cross-legged on cushions. Back problems, knee problems and neck problems were common. I knew many people who gave up meditating Zen style because physically it was too difficult for them. I had a lot of difficulty sitting because of past back injuries and knee problems, and the Alexander Technique made all the difference in the world for me. I really felt that the meditation posture should be easy and effortless—that it shouldn't create unnecessary physical suffering. Meditation practice, after all, was about letting go! When I left the monastery I knew I had the gift of healing with my hands, which I had since I was a child—and I wanted to help others. Since the Alexander Technique had been so beneficial to me, I decided to train and become a practitioner so I could help others as I had been helped. One of the reasons I was drawn to the Alexander Technique is that its underlying principles are very similar to Buddhist understanding. The work is very subtle, yet quite deep and profound—very similar to meditation practices, which can engender deep healing processes. The work emphasizes non-interfering awareness and focus, identical to mindfulness and concentration practices. Alexander work emphasizes balance, ease, and effortless physical functioning: Buddhist teachings emphasize freedom from the struggle with "what is." I realized that the Alexander Technique was a wonderful way to present the insights of 2500 years of Buddhist realization as a practical set of tools for learning how to function more effectively in ordinary daily activities while indirectly supporting the natural spiritual unfoldment of the individual. As the years have progressed I have continued my education, so to speak, and have learned from many healers and spiritual teachers, and that has not only enriched me personally, but has enriched my private practice as well. My clients love it when I go off for more training, or spiritual retreat, because they know that not only am I going to benefit from it, they will too. So my work in the healing arts and my spiritual practice are quite interconnected. The therapeutic context has become another kind of "spiritual hot-house."

My spiritual practice and my professional work are both growing and evolving; and they are interconnected—each affects the other. As I learn more in the therapeutic context it automatically gets integrated into my work. As I open more spiritually my work becomes informed from a more expansive awareness.

The primary goal in my work is not to have a career, be successful, or to make money—even though those things have happened, they have been secondary. The purpose of my work is to continually unfold the mystery of life—or to continually enter the mystery of life—*experientially*!! The life of inner discovery, transformation and healing is in the realm of experience. Ideas, concepts and beliefs are natural byproducts of experience. My mother taught me to trust my feelings. When my feelings told me I was gay, my experience was clear and direct. I trusted it and acted upon it. When I had a spiritual experience, even though I was opposed to organized belief systems whch could not be questioned or challenged, there was no way I could deny it! I trusted it and acted upon it. I never bought anybody's dogma, and I never sold anybody's dogma. Never did, never will! The only true spiritual path is personal unfoldment; that is why I emphasize experience and not beliefs.

The work I currently do with people not only supports their spiritual process but can actually catalyze it. By directly supporting people in developing mindfulness, awareness of body sensations, emotions and energies in the body, I find that a deeper awareness often emerges into consciousness. This awareness is our fundamental nature—the seed that germinates through spiritual practices. It is often experienced as an openness, as a vastness, an unlocatable interconnected sense of oneness. Clients describe a range of experiences from radiant light and feelings of great joy to peace, bliss, and vast openness. This is our natural state—our natural being. Suzuki-roshi called it "big mind." It's also referred to as Buddha mind. It's interesting that the word Buddha means awake—awakening to one's true nature.

In a way I'm coming out in my work by writing this article because I don't normally bring up the subject of spiritual experience until it's in the client's direct experience. I may say that my fundamental focus is an energetic or spiritual focus, but not from an idea or a conceptual point of view. If that is real for them, then that will emerge in their experience. Usually I don't even approach the subject. But as the person has the experience of a much bigger sense of themselves, which may be very new for them or very profound for them, it can be very cathartic, and it can be liberating. Once you've had the experience, it's appropriate to discuss my understanding of it, or others' understanding of it. A famous Zen saying comes to mind: "If you have it, we'll give it to you. If you don't have it, we'll take it away." In the words of the Bible: "For those that know, no explanation is necessary. For those that don't know, no explanation is possible."

In truth, the primary focus of my work is to support people's spiritual unfoldment, so in a way, I never left the monastery. I've continued to teach the essence of Buddhist practice through my work. Even though I assist people in therapeutic modalities through structural balancing and integration, movement awareness development, emotional and mental clearing work; all of that fundamentally is informed by a deep spiritual mirroring of the other person's essential nature. When working with someone, I don't experience my awareness as separate from theirs in the deepest sense. The oneness is present and because I'm conscious of it, the resonance is very available to them. It's like hanging out with somebody in a really bad mood—you may start to feel their bad mood. And if you hang out with someone in a great mood you might start feeling great too—sort of a "contact high." This is why meditating in a group is usually easier for beginners than meditating alone. There is a combined energy that lifts people's practice up. So I would go so far as to say that my work is not separate from my spiritual practice. It is an extension of my spiritual practice into the world. There have been times when, being a "monk in the world" I have felt isolated and lacking support. It's not like wearing robes and being "out" as part of a religious community. Being gay, I have felt an added isolation. Until recently there hasn't been the kind of gay spiritual networking that exists today. I am glad to contribute to this book because I feel it can help the process of building a gay spiritual network. Meeting other gay men whose spiritual unfoldment has been as foreground in their life as it has been in mine fills my heart with gratitude. I felt very isolated as a young person, particularly after the awakening I had. When I met other young men that I was interested in and they found out I had a serious meditation practice, they didn't understand it and made fun of me. This was very difficult. When I was involved in monastic practice I did have gay friends who were also serious practitioners, but today most of those people have passed away.

Over the years, my clients have asked me to teach in groups and lead retreats, which I have started doing more and more. I teach meditation classes at the Harvey Milk Institute in San Francisco, which has the largest gay curriculum studies program in the world. I'm helping people in their meditation practice not specifically from a Buddhist perspective, even though I draw upon the Buddhist practices I have worked with personally for many years. I am not teaching Buddhism, even though my life has been deeply informed by Buddhist practice. I take a more generic approach in teaching people—and fundamentally it doesn't matter what they believe, because it's their experience that guides them along the way. That's what's important. Even so, I often recommend Buddhist teachings for help in understanding the meditative process, because there are so many great teachers in the area of Buddhist practice. You don't need to be a Buddhist in order to meditate and get the value of meditation. Ultimately, Buddhism is not even about being a Buddhist! It's about living life fully and becoming fully human. As the Dalai Lama pointed out, the purpose of life is to be happy. I sensed this simple truth at age 16. I wasn't happy, and the successful people I saw around me weren't happy. I saw that the purpose of life wasn't to accumulate more stuff, to find the perfect lover, to achieve fame, fortune, status, or power—to find creative fulfillment or even to save the world from suffering. None of these would guarantee happiness—because real happiness does not rely on circumstances. Circumstances are impermanent and unreliable. Real happiness is our fundamental nature—it's totally reliable and never changes! Direct experience of our one true nature is the key to understanding these radical statements.

Gay culture has often looked for happiness in the superficial and materialistic—in "all the wrong places." Having a perfect body, perfect clothes, and a fantasy lover are all well and good—but don't expect them to bring you *real* happiness. *Real* happiness does not come through acquisition or attainment. It doesn't come through circumstances. It is our natural beingness that is in itself happy. The purpose of Buddhist practice is to allow that essential seed not just to germinate, but to sprout and to grow—to flower and bear fruit. At the highest level of spiritual understanding and opening is the fruit of happiness and realization of our true nature: We are one with all being.

Steve Lowell, a self-portrait in his San Francisco studio, 1972.

Gurus and Lovers

Donn Tatum

The relationship between Steve Lowell and myself (we were gay lovers) was not all that unusual. We lived together, worked together, tricked out, fought, lived separately, got back together. We became prominent on San Francisco's Castro Street scene. But through it all we practiced Buddhist meditation. That's because we were fortunate enough to have met the most extraordinary meditation master ever to have come to America. We went from Gay liberation to Buddhist liberation. As our relationship became intertwined with our relationship to our teachers, the whole thing became an extraordinary experience, particularly as we began to grapple with the core issue of living-dying.

Here are some notes from my journals.

When Steve Lowell goes away on meditation practice retreats, the beginning is marked with a lot of vacuum cleaning. A purifying cleansing is his way of arrival, whether it's a new home, or a rural practice hut.

We're at Rancho El Pomar in the spring of 1992. It's an old barley and almond farm in the rolling hills of northern San Luis Obispo County with some shacks and a garden gone wild. Early on Steve began using the ranch for solitary meditation retreats which he would insert into a busy schedule running our San Francisco bookstores. Going off on retreat has been an integral part of Buddhist practice for 2500 years; extensive solitary retreats have traditionally been considered the heart of attaining realization.

I had first met Steve in 1971 in the back of the Midnight Sun bar on Castro Street. He was tall and slender, with a long nose, great deep-blue eyes and luxuriant hair that cascaded over his shoulders. Gay hippies were liberating the territory and an outrageous, revolutionary culture of gay brotherhood spontaneously erupted on the streets and in the communes. The vibes of love would sweep away a repressive society, psychedelics would open the doors of perception. The world would change drastically—but not the way we had envisioned. Underneath the hippie trappings, Steve and I formed a bond that I suppose could be called spiritual because it transcended some sharp-edged personality clashes, but we had a similar way of looking at things that probably had to do with both being thirty-something California boys.

Steve and I opened Paperback Traffic bookstore on Castro Street which

DONN TATUM (Ojai, CA) is a Tibetan Buddhist Kagyu practitioner. He is currently writing a book on the mythology of the Pacific Coast, as well as doing free-lance projects. With Steve Lowell, he co-founded Paperback Traffic Bookstore on San Francisco's gay Castro Street.

quickly became a literary center for the exploding gay culture. We fixed up a couple of Victorian buildings, watched as gay refugees from all over the country flooded into the Castro. Boys camped on our doorstep, a finger-snap away. There were about five good years of the flowering of gay liberation culture. Then spontaneity became transformed into ritualization, with serious attitude, power drugs, and maxed-out sex. AIDS, the ultimate seriousness, followed. By then Steve and I had moved on to new careers, and in the early eighties when Steve was diagnosed HIV-positive, we were in Los Angeles.

The thirtyish man is encased in shiny black leathers—motorcycle jacket, skin-tight pants. He greets new arrivals with a breathy reek of liquor redolent of an all-night revel not yet slept off. It is not the gateway to further excess, however, this early morning in the mid-seventies, but San Francisco Dharmadhatu, and Steve is on duty to give meditation instruction. Fledgling Buddhists straggle in for sitting practice.

The Sunday *nyinthun*—all-day sitting practice—was always a challenge to make if you had been out Saturday night partying, the activity of choice, straight or gay, in those heady times. To sit still amidst the swift currents of emotional upheavals was arduous, sometimes agonizing. Yet the ability to practice mindfulness, to continually let go of whatever train of thought might be chugging—or hurtling—past, was frequently exhilarating. It left one walking out the door refreshed, able to feel the tangled skein of one's life was workable. That result (no guarantees) was frequent enough to inspire coming back to the simplicity of sitting practice.

The early students of the Tibetan Buddhist meditation master Chögyam Trungpa Rinpoche were a wild and crazy bunch, a match for the unorthodox, sometimes controversial methods he employed in teaching the Buddha-dharma. Many younger Americans disaffected by the wrenching social and political tumults of the Sixties embarked on a spiritual quest beyond the sham values of Western materialism. The search was abetted by the counter-culture's psychedelic experimentation which at least pointed to the possibility of a consciousness expanded beyond conventional pieties. But naïveté opened the floodgates for all manner of charlatans, imported as well as home grown, a phenomenon which continues unabated. People shopped from one teacher to another in the great spiritual supermarket. Beneath all these quests, the frantic pursuit of pleasure was short-circuiting, the personal pain of existence lay rawly exposed.

For a Buddhist teacher, this was workable ground—people were open to hearing the teachings.

The Vidyadhara the Venerable Chögyam Trungpa, Rinpoche, was the real thing: the Eleventh Trungpa Tulku, an authentic Tibetan reincarnate lama strictly trained since early childhood to master the extraordinarily rich, vivid, and powerful teachings of Vajrayana Buddhism. Exiled from his Surmang Monasteries by the Chinese invasion in 1959, he was the first to present these teachings in America systematically and in English. A quick study, he combined the conventions and lingo of Western culture with sometimes outrageous methods—magnetic displays underlain by an extraordinary kindness—in order to capture the hearts of students raised in the aggressive, speed-driven American cultural milieu. In this way he presented pure Buddha-dharma, teaching the essential Buddhist sitting practice of meditation, the path of non-aggression. He wrote *Cutting through Spiritual Materialism*, a masterpiece which clarified—then as now—the pervasive muck of smarmy spiritualism, presenting meditation practice as doable for ordinary Americans.

Credentials aside, those of us who became his American students did so because he could describe the pain we were in with unerring accuracy. He taught the dharma in terms of the everyday lives of his listeners. Students quickly opened dharma centers as he began to travel and teach, flocking to hear this groovy guru who discoursed with brilliance, gentleness, and dead-on humor. Buddhist meditation practice was the key to understanding the nature of their own minds, that viscous gray matter from which the world manifests.

Many gays became students. Trungpa Rinpoche was devoid of the kind of judgmental, hypocritical censure that passes for a moral philosophy in much of contemporary America. He invited his students to come as they were, without preparation, credentials, false fronts. In Vajrayana Buddhism neurosis and sanity are indivisible aspects of the energy of mental projections. Belief in the separation of the two, in a dualistic world of good and bad, of self and other, creates craving for external salvation, for pleasurable experiences. With meditation practice you could relax your mind, ventilate the root cause of suffering: grasping at, and fixation on, solidified beliefs.

Trungpa Rinpoche taught in the Bay Area frequently in the Seventies, and Steve would drag me to see him. Initially I did not know what to make of him, surrounded as he was by such a bizarre chaotic scene, but he was so real and genuine. People crammed into VW busses to go off to teaching and practice retreats all around the country. Steve became an authorized meditation instructor, among the first Westerners to teach basic Buddhist practice. It was an enormous responsibility, to work authentically with fledgling meditators.

A constant flow of prospective meditators came through the doors of the Dharmadhatu. But many didn't stay around, because the practice of meditation requires perseverance, and our culture celebrates the quick fix. Working with your mind can be boring and terrifying by turns. If you stuck it out, the joke was that you could still be bored or terrified, but you could relax with yourself as you are, with the world as it is.

Direct transmission of instruction from teacher to student is at the heart of the Kagyü school of Tibetan Buddhism. Devotion to your teacher harnesses the human emotion of love to the chariot of liberation. He reflects the basic sanity of the student's own mind, with all its neurosis, fear, wisdom. Once embarked on the journey, it is best to follow his instructions in order to avoid the many pitfalls laid out along the path by ego's deceptions.

There is currently a trend toward guru-bashing in some areas, particularly directed toward those most powerful in working with students. In my personal experience it is a fear of mind's projections, which is what meditation practice works with. But the truth is powerful, and can provoke ego's fear.

Steve—true queen—from the first became Decorator to the Kagyü Lineage. In order to celebrate our connection to the brilliance of the Kagyü teachings it became a challenge to see what elegant housing we students could produce when teachers visited. Steve and I hosted several visits. On short notice and shorter budgets we scrounged the best of the meager possessions of sangha members, borrowed from furniture stores, scored yards of satin and brocades. The most extravagant environments were for the visits of His Holiness Karmapa, the head of the Kagyü lineage altogether, whose mere presence manifested the splendor of the Vajrayana Buddhist teachings. Elaborate household staffing arrangements provided students access to the teacher and the opportunity to practice generosity by serving others. The service and the implied hierarchy proved excellent, frequently comical, practice in working with ego's resentment.

Meanwhile, back at the ranch—retreats are work. Emotions intensify, like a sauce being reduced. To experience the raw, unsugared energy of mental projections is considered auspicious. You get to look at them and see them for what they are—transparent, passing, workable.

Steve and I are doing simultaneous retreats. He's in two weeks solitary lock-up, not leaving the cabin; I'm in the main house. I can hear his *ghanta* and *damaru*—the hand-bell and hand-drum, the Vajrayanist's accoutrement—resound across the farm as the cabin lights burn late. A view out the back over the barley field slopes aesthetically up to the whirling vanes of the wind-pump on the ridge; migratory birds fluttered about the almond tree branches. We develop a kind of telepathy, play at not relating to each other, though he might glimpse me going to the garage. How extraordinary for us two queer mahasiddhas-in-training to be so ordinary in practicing this ancient spiritual discipline that is always *au courant*, the living authentic ear-whispered tradition, whispered indeed into my ear by my lover Stephen F. Lowell of Fresno, CA. Or bitched at me, to the same effect. We practice like those eccentric yogins of ancient India and mediaeval Tibet, impelled by a hunger for liberation from the cycle of samsara—the maddening, insatiable anxieties of living and of dying.

The tantric method is to discover the truth of one's innate wakefulness. Our confusion is induced by clinging to a fixed view of reality—who we think we are and what we think we're doing. The hard work with ourselves is to dissolve the encrustations of ego, which grasps at transient pleasure, so that we can glimpse the vividness and spaciousness of our basic nature. But trying to explain meditation practice is like trying to explain a love affair, or a storm at sea. You need to have been there.

When Trungpa Rinpoche fled his monastery in 1959, the full Vajrayana teachings had never before been given outside of Tibet. They had most certainly never before been practiced by a gay native Californian, a member of which tribe was, as I began this discursion, stripped to a jock strap attacking with a vacuum cleaner the cabin where he was about to seal himself into solitary confinement. I know that meeting his own mind on a practice retreat is the best possible medicine. It is so precious, so very rare a thing to do in this world, the best possible preparation for inevitable death. For him, there is that urgency, for he's been living ten years with HIV, and time is running out.

It is March 1993; Steve and I have moved to Ojai, a picturesque town nestled in a valley of orange groves an hour-and-a-half north of Los Angeles. They shot the movie *Lost Horizon* here.

We can no longer gloss over his fevers and exhaustion as the flu.

Being up close and personal to the decay of a lover's body is a visceral reminder of the wisdom of practicing of non-attachment. For the Buddhist meditator, the question is: can there be a clear expression of sanity while in the dying stages, and at death? There are bardo instructions and such, but the simplest is for a practitioner to recall the face of his or her guru.

A community of old dharma friends had moved here to support the Vajra Regent in his final retreat. Steve could spend his last days practicing with sangha friends here; they would help care for him.

That's pretty much what we did: practiced with him for six weeks until he died, and a bit after. To be able to help maintain the continuity of awareness of his mind up to that point through practice was extraordinary, outrageous.

For Steve, working with his illness means cultivating a wakefulness, an evenness, not being swayed by hope and fear.

Steve and I move into a small condo while we house-hunt. I have a feeling it will be the last stop. It's central and pleasant, a seasonal creek gurgles alongside; Steve suns himself by it in the deck chair. His second-storey bedroom has a view to the south over the low town to oak-clad Sulphur Mountain, framed by traceries of nearby pines and eucalyptus. I sweat pulling out furniture from our storage locker crammed with the accumulation of twenty years' life together. I move stuff around the living room until he's satisfied, directing me with a stick. I'm exhausted already from the strain. I go out for liquor for a stream of drop-in friends.

We go up to Shantigar, the Regent's former retreat house where a friend will go through the final care and instructions for the dying with us. It sounds so mundane, which is probably the way it should be, but I've got the heebie jeebies. Steve doesn't seem to flinch, but then he's got the bigger problem.

We talk about the Vajra Regent's death as a template for dying as a practitioner. He cultivated awakened mind as the sole way and style of working with dying. Whatever arises, recognize it as simply the play of the mind, and let it go. With this view, true compassion arises, not only toward others, but toward oneself. It's important to not be embarrassed by one's sickness, disabilities, and dependence. The Regent was able to let go of sexuality, money, parents, the whole thing, dissolve clinging to this lifetime. The idea is to celebrate not the tragedy of death, but the ultimate opportunity to practice.

The whole point: relax your mind whatever is going on.

Lunch follows on the porch overlooking the lush gardens. A visiting young Tibetan lama joins us. We tell him stories of lamas at Disneyland. His Holiness Karmapa said the Space Mountain ride was like experiencing the Bardo; Trungpa Rinpoche was enamored of the ghost realm of the Haunted House, and the Pirates of the Caribbean he likened to evading the bandits of hope and fear on the Buddhist path.

We then watch a video: the young lama sits on a couch, his legs drawn up under him. We all laugh hysterically at *Night of the Living Dead*. A Buddhist joke—the movie is more accurate than its makers could have imagined.

Steve's lack of emotional upheavals is remarkable. It seems the mark of a practitioner. It is as if he has resolved his mind to the inevitability of his death. I don't know that he thinks about it particularly. His mind seems to work pretty much as it always has, though with a kind of aerated, drifting thought train. He takes things as they come, which is not the same as a giving up in despair. He is invariably cheerful, and greets everyone with concern, wants to hear all the gossip.

We hold a Vajrayogini feast practice with about ten people downstairs and a few more up in the cramped bedroom with Steve. The abhiseka icon cards are taken up so that he can see them, each one carefully elucidated. During the feast section, everyone gathers around his raised-up bed, Steve grinning broadly under his moustache. A toast is raised to love and devotion, the very lifeblood of the Kagyü lineage. All sing the Shambhala anthem. Steve joins in on both. He begins a question, but loses the train.

Later, I sit on the meditation cushion at the foot of the bed facing the shrine and quietly prepare to practice. With a sudden jerk, I raise my arm toward him, shout pointing-out instructions. The shock tactic gets his attention, his eyes open wide lock on mine. It becomes the look of lovers who know their time together is drawing to a close.

I enunciate the sadhana so that he can hear it; his voice merges in and out, reciting the mantra along with me. From memory he says the closing chants along with me. It is as vivid and awake a practice session as I can recall. How rare, how extraordinary in this world is our fortune as lovers that we can communicate with such sanity as the hour of death approaches. In helping him along to the closure of this lifetime, I witness how he handles it, with grace, equanimity, fearlessness—the warrior's way. There is no struggle. That is not to say that he particularly likes the idea of dying.

At the end of the session, I am drenched with sweat.

A phone call comes from Pema Chödron. She is the directress of the Gampo Abbey retreat center in Nova Scotia. She's an old dharma friend from San Francisco, former society matron, now the first American Kagyü nun. I hold the receiver to Steve's ear as he lies on the pillow, speaking in a whisper at length. Then I have to interrupt this final time together in this dearest of friendships. His last words to her: "au revoir." I cried. Later, a friend laughs: "What a character!"

As I write this journal entry, the high noon of a warm, clear spring day approaches. I have bicycled over to Soule Park where I sit on the greensward under a canopy of large shade trees, looking northward toward Wheeler Gap in the mountains opposite. A sea breeze has just now sprung up. I recall a line of Trungpa Rinpoche's: "the only problem with death is that it's so fucking painful." I think how fortunate I am to have somehow got a karmic connection to Trungpa Rinpoche, to sense that it is possible not only to die sanely, but to not be paralyzed in life by the fear of death. My life might well have been otherwise.

Gone blind now, Steve lies emaciated, attended 24 hours. He's still there, though, with amazing alertness, gentleness, lack of complaint. He whispers to ask visitors how *they* are, then soon wanders off. Being told he's about to get some morphine; he croaks: "Are you sure you know what you're doing?" A friend observes: "It's like the bardo state. You see flashes of habitual patterns, but they don't particularly lead anywhere, they're just remnants, disembodied traces."

I read from the *Rain of Wisdom*, the songs of realization of the Kagyü gurus. I again give him the pointing-out instructions, ask him to remember. "Yes, sir," he sasses faintly. It's our last interchange.

Steve is dying! The news reaches me as I am pinioned with acupuncture needles for a flaming sciatica.

Under a weepy overcast sky I rush down the valley, stomach bubbling, guilt rising at having left Steve when death was imminent. But he had been in good hands, and a friend had been able to give him the essential instructions at the time of death. His end had been peaceful.

I sit dazed at the bedside, pick up the practice mantra. Friends come over, food and liquor appear, practice shifts are set up to provide continuity for him. His body is washed. What should he wear? The silk brocade Japanese robe? We opt for his tuxedo, the armor of the warrior of Shambhala, with his Shambhala service pins. In his hands crossed on his chest we place bone mala and dorje, the familiar ritual objects of the Chakrasamvara practitioner.

Practice shifts continue for three days until the Ceremony of Sukhavati is performed with him in an open casket in the shrine room. It is a liturgy for helping friends and loved ones let go, to enable the deceased to continue his journey.

Afterwards, over a stiff Scotch, the Regent's last New Year's gala is recalled, when Steve had helped transform Shantigar into a crystal palace, a fitting environment for the warriors of Shambhala. Having studied Japanese flower arranging, he had made the stunning, elegant table arrangements. Out of the tripartite elements of heaven, earth, and man would emerge the simple beauty of form and space. He would stand back to look critically, his right hand hanging limp at the wrist.

The Ventura crematory is set up like they never expected visitors. The van backs up, attendants roll the coffin into the oven, and, at my nod, they light it off. We chant a guru yoga. I choke up on it, the utter finality. I look back at the thin smoke rising cleanly from the stack, a vision of melancholy.

Bloody Marys follow at the wood-shingled Pierpont Inn. I lead off the toasts. Once he had met his teacher, Steve never hesitated, applied himself wholeheartedly to dharma practice. The elegant households he created for visiting teachers helped draw me in. He never let up on me, encouraging me, bitching at me to practice. He was sometimes temperamental, petulant, but he really applied the slogan: "humbleness is the dwelling place of the forefathers."

Younger students recall Steve's generosity in allowing them into the space of his dying, his ability to maintain confidence, equanimity, amidst bodily decay. They had danced in dialogue as he spun back and forth across the boundaries of reality: "I have just been prostrating with Pema Chödron; practice is about your ordinary life." It hadn't seemed to matter whether he was in the past, the present, or the future: eyes unseeing, barely audible—but fully awake.

He's recollected at the last Fire Offering performed in Ojai. He's somewhat disheveled, can't find his glasses, the AZT pillbox keeps beeping, he's so skinny that when he stands up his shorts slide down, revealing all in the face of his seatmate. But there he is, joyfully practicing in the group intensive. Yeah, this is it, the tantrikas practice in the charnel-ground. Of his manifold qualities, that is what I'll remember most.

Furthermore, there's this, the flute-like utterance: it's up to you.

Homophobia and Spiritual Teachers:
A Coming Out "Affair"

Robert K. Hall

I was forty and a divorced father of three teen-aged children when I came out in 1974. Before that, I was trying to find some meaning in a busy and rewarding life as a physician, psychiatrist, and co-founder of a school for New Age seekers. I was masquerading at the time as a straight man in the strange giddy world of LSD, gestalt therapy, meditation and yoga, rock music and encounter groups and San Francisco. In fact, I was even a teacher of the New Age spiritual life that horrified "religious" middle-America. They called it "secular humanism." The work of the devil.

It's never easy to lead a double life. A lot of us gay folk know about that. I was trying to live in the closet, but publicly. That closet felt like a cramped dark room where I stood, body pressed against the closed door, entangled in hanging clothes that had served well in some past identity, costumes from past productions, draped over my eyes and mouth. I was calling to a world I knew was outside. But, of course, that world couldn't hear my muffled voice. I was begging for full membership, to be connected. Inside that closet the sound was deafening.

I decided about six times a day to open the door and step out into whatever was to be there. I would stand in front of the bathroom mirror, look deeply into those eyes and say to that face, "I am a gay man, I am a gay man." Sometimes, a voice would answer casually from way back in my psyche, "yes you are—no big deal, go for it—be who you are." Then I'd realize once more that I was just like all the clients I had ever worked with, just another someone trying to accept himself, someone wanting to relax into the truth. That gave me courage, and I'd vow, one more time, that I would openly acknowledge to everyone what I had known to be true since childhood. I was one of them. Those strange ones who loved their own sex.

The hardest part was being honest with my children. A well-known psychic lady I had heard about, who had become a sort of guide to many of the "human potential" types, warned me that my son needed to "see my feet of clay," as she put it, before he could seek his own path in life. I knew what that meant.

I went right home and confessed to my children. I tried to let them know

ROBERT K. HALL (Tomales, CA) was born in 1934 and is a psychiatrist as well as a meditation teacher in the Vipassana (Theravada) tradition. His most recent publication is *Groundworks: Stories of Embodiment* (Northpoint Press, 1997).

how happy I was to be discovering myself finally, so late in life, thinking that of course they'd rejoice with me.

I was so nervous that, instead of happy, I sounded like a penitent and guilty child-molester when I told them that their father was a gay man. My daughters were silently horrified, but tried to put on a good face. "We love you, Dad." They were confused and took their distance. My son wept uncontrollably. Then in an attempt to reassure me, he said, "It's alright, Dad, I'm just crying." He was thirteen.

And that began a long time of broken connection between my son and me. We didn't find each other again until he was well into his twenties, when he said one day, "You know, Dad, I'm glad you're gay. It has taught me to accept differences in people. I'm a better person."

My oldest daughter struggles between her suspicion that homosexuality is an abomination in the face of God, versus a deep and undeniable love for her father. We struggle together, have gone into therapy together, struggle some more, take distance and then come back at it for another try. Sometimes we find peace in our love for each other.

My youngest daughter has accepted me and my partner into the family. She and I always had the most contentiously passionate respectful love for each other, but it took her a long time to accept me. Finally, she has. Their mother, my childhood sweetheart, was the one who told me it was time to come out of the closet, in the first place, and she never stopped her support. If that isn't love, I don't know what is.

We had been married almost twenty years. We met when we were both ten years old, children together. She simply decided to divorce me and set us both free from an outdated marriage vow we had made in 1954 in order to do the right thing and lead a conventional life. In those days, you got married if you wanted a real life. After the divorce, which I didn't want, but agreed to anyway, we went about the business of building a life-long friendship based on being parents, grandparents and fellow travellers, together, in this dark world. Thus, by sheer determination and a deep abiding love for each other, she and I transformed a long and failed marriage into a living family of siblings who became friends, grandchildren, and cousins. All of them are guided, in their sense of belonging to each other, by the friendship between their homosexual father and their steadfast mother.

Shortly after my confession to the children, romantic love for another man came tumbling into my life and I tumbled along with it. The magic was so powerful that I didn't care what any of them thought anymore. It was time. And he was it.

He was ten years younger than me and had just re-entered the Western World after many years of Buddhist practice in the Far East. He was out of robes, but had been celibate for all those years. He was still a monk at heart, and just beginning to navigate through the complexities of sexual freedom and "let it all hang out" values. He was wide open. So open, that the first thing he did in California was to strain his back. All that tension in his body from massive culture shock!

That's how we met. I had a reputation for fixing back pains, and his friends brought him to my house so I could examine his back. I suppose the whole thing was unethical since I am a doctor, but the moment we looked at each other, not to mention the way his body responded to my touch, it was obvious, even to his friends standing there, that we were going to be something together. We enchanted each other. Love at first sight. His back got better.

He asked if we could have some time together, and we met a few afternoons and evenings at my house. Our first time, he asked me if I was capable of having a relationship without attachment.

That was my introduction to Buddhism.

I said I was pretty sure I could, because I had been attracted to men for years without having full-on relationships. He had never had a relationship with anyone, male or female, other than his close connection with his meditation teacher in India. We were both starved sexually so the sex happened on the first visit and it was passionate, hot. After all his years of meditation practice, his body exploded with the first kiss, the first sensual touch. So did mine. We could hardly stop touching each other long enough to eat and sleep.

He talked about his calling to teach Buddhism in the West. We were not going to be together for long periods of time because he would have to travel in order to teach. There was a deep well of mendicant monk in him, and I saw it early on.

About a week into our love affair, he had to travel to a distant city and begin teaching the wisdom he had brought from his years of practice in the East. I was scheduled to be in New York at that same time, so there was no problem in arranging a five-day rendezvous on my way back to California. We met at an airport, drove to a motel and spent the next five days in bed. We left our room for meals and took a walk or two, but the rest of our time was spent in a wonderful cocoon of intimate touch and heart talk.

I saw that he was an extraordinary man, and I wanted to be near him as much as possible. After I returned home, and for the next several years, he wrote incredibly passionate love letters. I remember one letter that was nothing but my name written over and over many times, and then, "I miss you."

Buddhism and our relationship became synonymous to me. I was his student. I attended a number of his silent meditation retreats, some of them thirty days long. There was no problem in my being his student as well as his lover, because our love had little to do with boundaries. I soaked up his essence and his innocence as well as the teachings that came through him during his brilliant and lucid dharma talks. Between teaching engagements, he returned always to my house to rest, and our relationship grew into a deep ocean of trust. There was always laughing. Our lovemaking was often just an excuse to surrender. We became enchanted children together. How can I describe the freedom and absurdity of our play?

"I want to pat your head, your little headie. My hand and your head" (strange vocal cooing sounds).

"I like it when you put your tongue in my ear, better."

"First we play head and then the ear" (great bursts of laughter).

"You look like a giraffe, I'm going to bite your neck."

We would move from that kind of ridiculous dialogue to a room full of students in my school where he would deliver an astonishingly clear lecture on Buddhist philosophy. I saw that he was a truly great teacher. Sometimes we traveled to distant towns where we would teach workshops together. I taught body awareness and a kind of psychophysical therapy. He taught meditation. Once we taught a group of Catholic monks. During the breaks we resumed our silly intimate play. We even taught the monks to make blithering sounds to each other as a way of communicating outside the confines of linear thought, to find that place where the heart speaks. Those cloistered monks blithered and patted each other's heads like children, and we laughed with delight. The world was a playground when he and I were together. When we were separate, we both immersed ourselves in careers and teaching duties. He became very well-known, and the demands on his time more and more insistent.

He had a book to finish, a publication that made him more of a visible figure in the historical force of Buddhist thought moving rapidly over the landscape of post-psychedelic America. There was the ever-lengthening schedule of retreats to lead, the demand for more instructions in meditation practice from more and more people. He was always traveling. We met for a few days in those intervals when he stopped to rest briefly, to catch his breath and then move on to the next retreat location in Montana, in New Mexico, in Hawaii, wherever the next call was heard.

Our close friends knew of our relationship and accepted it without difficulty. Both his friends and mine often came together during those short vacations. We shared rooms at ski resorts, motels at beaches, and often my home was full of itinerant Buddhist wanderers; their sleeping bags littered the living room floor, the kitchen was full of their laughter and intelligent wit while vegetarian meals appeared out of communal chaos.

My children mostly stayed away. They would tell each other, "The Buddhists are in town," meaning that their ordinarily disappearing father was going to be out of sight totally for a while. They would venture in and out of the house with their friends, stepping carefully, like pedestrians making their way around the street homeless. Polite, but anxious to avoid contact. They were used to their home being overtaken by gestalt people, bodywork students, meditation groups, and general self-improvement junkies. The Buddhists were just a little more exotic. Which didn't make Buddhism more attractive to teenagers trying to fit into the conventional crowd. They just wished for a more normal home. Sometimes, though, they reflected on the observation that many of their friends' families seemed dysfunctional and unhappy, while good humor and laughter happened regularly at our home, weird as it was.

Then my lover began to occasionally reflect on his growing discomfort with our relationship. It didn't fit well with the rapidly materializing vision of himself in the role of spiritual teacher. A homosexual relationship was discordant with his obvious destiny. He was to be teacher and guide for many people. That much was obvious. And so his personal life was bound to be scrutinized more and more as he entered into that life calling. Besides, he had never been deeply accepting of himself as a gay man. His public life demanded that he come to terms, somehow, with his own homosexuality. He began to have catastrophic dreams of himself rejected, poor and homeless, an outcast on the streets, unloved and reviled.

Our relationship began to lose its glow. Our conversations became more serious and a grey cloud of worry began to condense around us. No matter how loving our relationship was, homosexuality did not fit into the picture of his life that was becoming more vivid each day. For him, the sexuality started to become an embarrassment. He wasn't comfortable with our relationship and he was sure that his spiritual calling was more important. Even more paramount was his conviction that the general public would never respect nor allow an openly homosexual man to teach Buddhist meditation. I reluctantly and privately thought he was right about that, and felt only disappointment. It was time to face reality: the reality of homophobia, both within us and in the societal mind. Our way of being together had to change, and I didn't really want that change to happen. But, if everything in this world is impermanent, why think anything else could be true of our relationship? We were Buddhists, after all.

The final break happened when he decided to get advice from his mentor and spiritual teacher. He sent a letter to India in which he told of our relationship and, particularly, that we were sexual partners. He asked for his teacher's opinion about what we had found together. His teacher, who had empowered him to return to the States to teach, quickly answered in unequivocal terms: homosexuality is just another form of greed, and therefore our relationship was founded on greed, also. That was the final word.

I thought there was much more involved than greed, but I would never have dared to object to the teacher's appraisal. So we both gave it up. But I felt rejected, discarded. My anger festered and grew. I expressed it openly and emotionally to him. My anger became a pain between us that lasted a long time. He didn't have any anger, so he said.

I quickly rebounded into a series of relationships with men much younger than myself. They all evolved into mentor, older man—young man archetypical situations that were rich and valuable for both of us, but destined to end when it was time for the younger man to leave the nest. My task was always learning to let go, and I practiced diligently. Whether with a partner or alone, I understood, letting-go is the business for all of us.

About four years passed. Then one April, while I was teaching a class in body therapy to a group of psychologists in Hamburg, Germany, I heard through the spiritual grapevine that my first spiritual teacher (not my former teacher-lover) was travelling through Europe from India and would be speaking to the public at the Kurhaus in Wiesbaden a week hence. I hadn't seen him in eight years. This was the spiritual master who introduced me to meditation and who had initiated me onto the spiritual path many years previous, and to whom I granted devotion without question. He was, to me, the embodiment of love and all goodness. I was very excited about getting his darshan one more time. Particularly excited, because I was scheduled to return to America in several weeks and had finally committed myself to live in partnership with a man, to share a home together.

My lover and I had been carrying on an international romance for several years, seeing each other for a week here and there, meeting in airports around the world for a few days together, then returning to separate lives until the next opportunity to grab a few days of intimacy. We had gradually fallen truly in love, and he was at my home in California, waiting for me to return from Europe. We had decided to put our lives and bodies together under one roof, and to see what living together would bring us. It was a major move for me. Finally, I was going to live openly with a male partner, and I was feeling a whole new life waiting for me in California. That was the mood I was in when I got on an overnight train from Hamburg to Wiesbaden; excited, joyful, expectant, and wanting some kind of blessing for my decision to finally open my heart and life to another human being. I was "in love," wanting to see the one who taught me about real love, the kind of love that has no expectation, no agenda. My teacher was the embodiment of unconditional love.

When I reached Wiesbaden, I found a room in a very luxurious hotel across the park from the ancient and magnificent Kurhaus. This was to be a celebration, no expense spared. My hotel window looked out on the splendid gardens around the huge granite and marble edifice, a monument to pre-World War I days, when the hot mineral baths were used by Europe's wealthy for relief from their gout and arthritis. The Kurhaus, itself, was an architectural wonder, with its long circular drive curving in front of a great portico, huge stone pillars standing at its entrance like guardians of propriety. I was impressed. My teacher would appear there the next day when so much of his work was done in the world without such public visibility. The occasion seemed momentous.

The next day, I took my seat inside the great hall, and that was the first disappointment. I sat in a balcony far above the stage. Far below me, he was seated center stage on a large throne; he looked tiny down there. My memories of past meetings were of intimate gatherings, where I could see the individual hairs in his long white beard, hear his melodious voice without microphones. Now it was different. From his throne, center stage, he took questions from those seekers who had the courage to approach the stage and speak from far below him into another microphone. The whole scene was cold and impersonal. I was shocked to see several thousand people in that huge meeting room. The marble floors and stone walls with their tall crystal glass windows created echoes as though voices were being heard within great halls of state. In turn, his amplified voice exploded into the vast space like the voice of Jehovah passing sentence on us wretched humans. I sat there in the balcony shivering, my mood a mixture of excitement and outrage at the staged authoritarian atmosphere of the place.

About twenty people took their places in line, waiting to speak their questions to this regal figure in his traditional white garments, his glistening white turban, his white beard and his presence which could best be described as that of an Emperor. There was no way I could have spoken to him, then. I decided to listen carefully, in hope that what he spoke would be heard as a personal message.

All went smoothly. Each person in line asked his or her question about diet, or the meditation practice, or what was proper behavior for someone just beginning the spiritual journey. The questions were routine. I had heard them all before. His answers, as always, referred the questioner back to the commitment to meditation, to see all of life as a journey of return to the Divine Father. A journey we all must take, regardless of color or nationality or station in life.

Then, a startling event occurred. Having waited in line for a long time, a young Dutch woman stepped up to the microphone and spoke in a clear sweet voice. "Master," she said, "some of us are wondering about homosexuality . . . "

He interrupted her abruptly, his voice harsh and ungentle, "Sister, I have said it before, there is nothing to discuss. I condemn it! Do your meditation."

She reeled a moment, then tried again: "But Master, some of us are concerned about homosexuality in our lives . . ."

Again, he interrupted her. More loudly than before. "I've told you, I condemn it. There is nothing to discuss. Do your meditation."

The great hall was silent. Aghast. The whole scene suspended outside of time and space. No one moved. He signaled for the next person to step forward.

I sat there stunned and unable to comprehend what had just occurred. I who had just committed myself to an honest love with another man. The young Dutch woman turned without looking around and proceeded to walk slowly and purposefully out of the hall. The sound of her heels striking the marble floor marked every step of her way through the vast silent space.

I could hardly breathe. My mind stopped. Whatever else happened between him and the other seekers made no impression at all. When it was over, I walked back to my hotel room like a zombie. I spent the rest of the day and that night weeping. I didn't leave the room. As though someone close had suddenly died, I struggled to understand what had happened to me.

The next morning, I returned to the Kurhaus, exhausted and emotionally numb. There was to be a reception with refreshing drinks and food. It was said that the master would be there to speak with anyone who wanted to have a personal conversation. I vaguely thought about approaching him. Maybe he would explain his position, maybe he would exempt me from this decree, because the new love I had surrendered to was such a pure and good thing in my life, just what I needed now, not some horrible transgression. He arrived in a black Mercedes, and walked into the reception room. Everyone seemed in awe and awkwardly self-conscious. Very few people ventured near him to speak. It was as though people were frightened of getting too near. I have a vivid memory of him standing alone in the center of the room, all of the disciples standing around the outskirts of the room just looking at him, but not engaging in any way. It was a strange sight. He looked suddenly so small. So alone. I didn't dare approach him. I felt wooden and mute. I left quickly, and went back to my hotel room. More weeping.

And then, finally, in the early morning hours of the next day, the second night without sleep, a realization came that has remained in my memory as a defining moment in this lifetime.

I was recalling his words, "I condemn it." They seemed so cruel, so rigid. Suddenly, something let go, some deep surrender happened somewhere in my psyche, and I said aloud. "Of course I'm condemned. I've always been condemned. So what?" And I started to laugh and laugh, rolling around on that hotel room floor, laughing in great joy, knowing that in being condemned, I was also set free. The next day, I boarded the train back to Hamburg. It was midmorning, one of those days when the birds sing and the sun shines and the newness of everything ordinary sparkles; even the old train station with its sooty windows and scuffed floors looked glorious.

Zen in Black Leather

Vajra Karuna

The following article does not claim to speak for all Buddhist or Zen practitioners. It is solely the musings of one man who has been a Zenist and a power exchange person (S&Mer) for many years.

Since this article is an attempt to relate my religious, sexual and S&M practices into a whole, let me start with some definitions.

Religion for me is 1) the universal recognition that human beings individually and collectively experience a profoundly disturbing sense of separation or alienation from a greater beingness, or a wholeness which is the inherent right of all. Jews, Christians and Muslims call this God; Hindus, the World Soul; Taoists, the Tao or Nature; Zen, Interdependent Beingness. 2) A series of practices that try to overcome this alienation: prayer, meditation, rites and rituals.

Zen I define as a school of Buddhist thought which believes in looking into one's own mind or nature for the truth of who or what we are. Not depending on what others have said, through dogma or Scripture, but on one's own experience. While past or even present teachers can help point the way, ultimately everyone's mind is unique and thus each must find his or her own way to wholeness.

The term Sadomasochism originally came from the medical profession and means the desire to harm or be harmed physically or psychologically. This, however, is not the definition employed by this writer. S&M is the use of pleasure and pain, dominance and submission, not for the detriment of anyone, but to get in touch with one's deepest, often repressed, needs and wants; and to harmonize and integrate these into a stronger, more content, healthier, and more whole personality.

Here we see that Zen and health S&M have something in common: each helps us to understand ourselves far more deeply than we do at the ordinary level and to use this understanding to enhance our wholeness.

The history of Mankind has more often than not misused or corrupted what should be used to enhance people's lives. Religion in general, Zen and S&M in particular, have not been immune to this. Each has been used for power trips rather than for empowerment. Power is the ego-centric desire to control others and is based on fear. Empowerment seeks to make both

VAJRA KARUNA (Norman McClelland, Los Angeles) was born in New York City in 1944. He took his lay and priestly ordination at The International Buddhist Meditation Center in Los Angeles (Vietnamese Zen tradition). His own practice is in the Red Thread tradition of Zen: the integrating of one's spirituality with one's sexuality. He has been the teacher of L.A.'s gay Buddhist group for the past twelve years.

oneself and others strong. It is the understanding that only by both giving and receiving power, by a power exchange, is real or permanent power to be had. Empowerment is based on compassion and love, and this is what my Zen and my S&M practice are about.

But has not Buddhism traditionally rejected S&M, especially its sexual aspect? In fact, has it not been anti-sexual throughout most of its history?

Buddhism teaches that every Buddhist should follow a five point moral code. This is 1) Not to harm sentient beings; 2) Not to speak falsely; 3) Not to take what is not given; 4) Not to indulge in improper sexual acts; 5) Not to become intoxicated.

For our purposes we need to look closely at numbers 1 and 4. #1. Harming means subjugating oneself or another to physical or mental damage. As stated earlier, what distinguishes a healthy or self/other-enhancing S&M activity from the psychopathic and criminal type is specifically not harming or damaging anything. I, as an S&Mer, have never sought to harm or damage myself or another. Neither pain nor pleasure are synonymous with damage or health. Both are very relative concepts, and pain as well as pleasure can be used as much to enhance as to harm. The two inviolable rules of a power exchange are (a) everything must be consensual and (b) everyone's limits must be respected.

An outside observer witnessing me being flogged (when I bottom) or me flogging (when I top) might assume that extensive physical and mental harm is occurring. The very opposite is true, but more of this later.

#4. Improper sexual behavior is defined as having sex with another person's mate, minors, and persons institutionalized (under the care of others). The rule says nothing about specific sexual practices or the gender of one's own partner (heterosexual or homosexual). The purpose of the rule is to prevent sex from being exploitative or demeaning. Sex should always enhance a person's worth. It should, indeed, help relieve one's sense of isolation or alienation.

But what about Buddhism's long tradition of a celibate monkhood? Also, to the degree that S&M practices could be equated with extreme forms of asceticism, should not Buddhism be opposed to these?

Unlike some religions (i.e., Christian and Shiite flagellants, and Hindu self-torturing ascetics) Buddhism, with a few rare exceptions, has been opposed to extreme religious masochistic practices. The Middle Way of the Buddha was to find a path between the self-indulging lifestyle of the laity and the self-torturing activities of Indian asceticism. The key word here is extreme. So, let us look more closely at celibacy.

Few have ever claimed that celibacy was an easy, unstressful or a non-downright painful practice. To suppress the natural, physical and psychological sexual urges, especially if it is uncompromised by avoiding even masturbation, is questionable non-masochism; moreover, is celibacy really the renouncing of sex or is it the redirecting of its energies inwardly?

Celibacy may not be the extreme asceticism of starving oneself to death (a popular religious activity of the Buddha's time) but nonetheless, it is asceticism. In fact, my own experience of a year and a half of totally uncompromised celibacy gave me more pain than any later short-term whipping of my back.

Why then did I enter into it? I had several reasons.

First, while my lover at that time and I were still very much in love with one another, sex had ceased between us; and choosing not to have sex outside of the relationship, celibacy seemed a noble escape.

Secondly, I felt a deep dissatisfaction at the belittling way I desired others and wanted them to desire me: as impersonal sexual objects.

Finally, there was the promise of generations of "holy men" that spoke of having to abandon lust to obtain a higher, indeed the highest, level of consciousness. So, I took the plunge.

Why then did I eventually give it up? Because it worked and it did not. I came to realize through the celibacy itself that my value as a human being did not depend on getting laid; that I and others were much more than just meat; and while I had told myself this was true before, it was the celibacy that enabled me to experience it as true. I also realized that I was not, in fact, giving up sex so much as I was trying to redirect it inwardly, into some hoped for psycho-cosmic orgasmic experience. Lastly, it was a self-defeating way of trying to get rid of my sexual frustration; but being honest with my lover and myself and going outside the relationship worked. I saw that as long as I could treat myself and others as having value far beyond just the sexual, I could trust my sexual needs. The result of all of this was a gradual reorientation from alienation to integration, which meant wholeness, perhaps even a moderate amount of holiness. This I believe was the start of my awakening to the core teaching of Zen; the unconditional worth or Buddha Nature of myself and others.

Shortly after this my lover was diagnosed with AIDS and my life, including the sexual part, was put on hold for the next year or so. But even this brought me to a deeper and more constructive view of sex, pleasure and especially, pain. It allowed me to trust my own power (worth) in all of these.

The greatest change, however, came with my lover's death. For 16 years there had been no I, but only a we, and so I suddenly found that I had lost myself along with him. He was dead, but where was I? I had to be reborn.

My lover had had no interest in S&M and therefore I had not pursued it. The fantasies had been in my head, but even that was a problem. Since an interest in leather, uniforms, handcuffs, sensory deprivation, etc., were things which I could not explore, the fantasies themselves further alienated me from whom I thought I should be. But just as formerly I was able to see that my worth ultimately transcended sex, so it did with all of these. Now, partly through the very power of the pain of grieving, I found the empowerment to safely descend into them. I was them and yet I was greater than any of them. I was my little sexual, S&Mer ego, and yet a part of that ego or self beyond all selves; or the closest thing that Zen can call God.

Frustration, grief, a dying to myself, these and Zen are what awakened me to the next level of truth.

Zen teaches that everything is a part of a universal interconnected/ interdependent beingness. This beingness is complete and perfect just as it is. Furthermore, we all share in this perfection right here, right now. My final acceptance of this made me realize that I already had complete unconditional worth (empowerment).

Unconditional meant not accepting any "ifs" (conditions). It was no longer that I was worthy only if my mommy said so, or if people were attracted to me, or if I never got angry, or if I did not have sexual desires, much less unconventional sexual practices.

It was that I was worthy no matter what I thought or even did. Regardless of everything else, my fundamental beingness was already Buddha (The Enlightened One). My practice was from then on to cultivate this awareness. To grow in the faith of my present wholeness (Buddha Nature) and to become free from all self and other alienation.

I realized that to practice constructively I had to do so with my whole being. If I were alienated from (felt negative about) my S&M orientation I could not give my entire self to my practice, much less accept my conditional worth. It was not that I wanted to make love through a whip that was important, but that I must always acknowledge my partner's unconditional worth as much as my own. This was perfect love and morality.

Further, I realized that only by being true to my S&M could I go back to my inner child, to my hunger for a Daddy, could I escape from the always in charge, painfully over-controlling adult that I was. I needed the form of power that was the hand, the belt, the whip of the Daddy/Master. This was the power, this was the pain that would further liberate me, that would dissolve me in the greater beingness of the Master, and through him to an awareness of being beyond both of us; perhaps even a prelude to, a small taste of, the mystical surrender to the inevitableness of death.

Thus over several years to find the absolute I went from one intense method of entering into my own body and mind to another. From absolute renunciation to absolute indulgence the wheel turned, and in turning I discovered not only a new me, but a new awareness of others. I might even call this a new asceticism.

As time went by and I became progressively more comfortable with the self-indulgent me I found I had to accept non-judgmentally the self indulgence of others. Yet even more, I began asking my self what right do I have to be unaccepting of, or judgmental, towards anyone?

There are plenty of people in this world that would gladly suggest that a homosexual Buddhist monk into sexual sadomasochism is in the same category as your average heterosexual thief or murderer, and maybe even worse.

I had spent too much of my life labeling myself and others in terms of bad and good, when as a Buddhist I should have been thinking of everyone in terms of sufferers.

Returning to the Zen teachings of unconditioned worth or the Buddha Nature in all of us, was there anyone who did not have something redeeming in him or her?

My head said "people do evil things," but something deeper inside responded with "but does this make them evil?" I guess it was my own recently discovered sense of unconditional goodness that answered "*no.*" Again my head (intellect) kept saying, "Norman, you're going too far, you're on dangerous ground." But my heart countered with, "Don't listen to your head; it is in the dual world of self righteous judgment; listen to your Buddha Nature and go with faith."

What do I mean by faith? I mean unconditional forgiveness and compassion. For those who know Buddhism this may sound a lot more like Pure-Land than Zen, but the Vietnamese tradition, that I was soon to ordain in, is of this mixed tradition.

I said earlier that I might call this a new found asceticism (one of the ego vs. the body). What did I mean by this? I mean the daily painful struggle my head and heart go through in trying to let go of my self righteous ego and its hatred, and to allow myself to feel compassion and forgiveness towards those very people who are a threat to me. This is sometimes even more stressful than was celibacy. My logic says to hate my loud obnoxious neighbor, or my boss, or the homophobe trying to take away my civil rights, or the man who just murdered a bunch of people in a mall, or a foreign government persecuting my fellow Buddhists; but my faith, seeing them as fellow sufferers, says to show loving kindness towards.

This does not mean to accept their action, but to separate these from their beingness. It means that although I must accept them as Buddhas, some Buddhas belong in jail.

As bizarre or even crazy as all this may sound, this has become my practice: to try to assume as much as possible a Bodhisattva mind set. After all, I did take Bodhisattva vows and I have the burn scar on the top of my head to prove it.

How do I switch back and forth from whip and chain, paddle and pain to faith in self sacrificing love? That is a koan.

Summary

I have tried to explain some of my personal reasons for believing that there is a cross-over between my spiritual and sexual practices. I have discovered over the years that for me the concepts found in the highest forms of spirituality are also to be found in the best of S&M practices. These are:

1. Faith: Knowing intuitively the goodness and truth of feelings and not needing to justify or defend them to others (non-S&Mers).
2. Tolerance: Accepting the extraordinary diversity of others' needs and wants (their kinkiness) even though it may not be my own particular scene.
3. Compassion: Feeling the intense need of another and being willing to help satisfy it; however, staying within the limits of myself and my partner and refusing to go beyond what is safe.
4. Self-worth: Understanding that my aggressive, even violent fantasies are a part of my conditional goodness, especially in that I have a positive, creative and even artistic way of channeling them.
5. Courage: As a top, knowing that I can take my partner into certain risks without being afraid of losing control, or, as a bottom, my willingness to enter into a new, unknown and sometimes risky experience.
6. Belonging: Being part of the S&M community; that can be close-knit and supportive.
7. Liberation: The personal, physical and psychological catharsis I experience through a scene; as well as the freedom from the external authority or mores of conformist society. The finding of authority from within and using it to expand my cognitive, emotional and bodily needs to their most constructive limits.
8. Joy: The shared feelings of satisfaction and happiness between a partner and myself after a well-played scene or ritual.
9. Power: As a top, the physical and psychological control over another. As a bottom, the right to give or withhold permission to be controlled.
10. Peaking: The often ecstatic altered states of consciousness that concentrative pain, bondage or sensory deprivation can bring about.

Who's Lonelier Than a Gay Teenager?

Daniel Boutemy Fernandez

In July of 1992 I attended the BPF Summer Institute on Engaged Buddhism, and participated in the gay men's group. Eight of us met together every afternoon for a week. For most of us in this group, it was our first experience of being visible as gay men in a larger and very supportive, predominantly heterosexual context. It was a welcome opportunity to explore the relationship between our homosexuality and our spiritual lives, and between ourselves and the sangha as a whole. Along with our social visibility, new aspects of our identities were able to emerge. I myself discovered a sense of wholeness and personal integration that continues to be empowering.

Much of the unfolding story was of pain, as we brought to light a common pattern of abuse we had experienced growing up. Our woundedness bound us together with increasing intimacy as we shared our stories and discovered how our particular pain made us accessible to the message of the dharma. We found in ourselves a wealth of spiritual resources that makes this connection natural for us. We came to feel that out of our understanding as gay men we can make an important contribution to the larger sangha. In this article I'd like to share some of the thoughts and insights that came out of that small group.

With surprise and increasing anger one of the painful conclusions we came to was that the homosexual child in our culture is almost always an abused child.

Our society does not normally think of children as being gay. Parents, teachers and pastors routinely treat all children as budding heterosexuals and create socialization programs for children on that assumption. Yet most gays and lesbians are aware of their sexuality by the time they are teenagers, and many (like myself) have memories of homosexual affect going back to infancy. Rare is the adult who recognizes the signs; rarer still is the adult who can offer a benign response. Most parents react with pressure for gender-conforming behavior; some go as far as physical abuse. A few, like my own mother, take a hands-off approach—"leave the kid alone, don't put any trips on him." This is a fairly enlightened attitude, but it does nothing to protect the child from the massive psychosocial damage he is about to experience in school and society.

Is there anyone who has any ideas about how to raise such a child? Or if we are hesitant to make determinations about the direction of a child's

DANIEL BOUTEMY FERNANDEZ (Santa Cruz, CA) was born in 1955 and has been practicing in the Theravada tradition for twenty years. This article first appeared in *Turning Wheel* (Fall 1992).

psychosexual development, is there a way to protect the child's freedom to develop naturally, free of pressure and the fear of abuse?

One member of the group recalled being fourteen years old and wandering through New York's Central Park, desperately hoping some older man would pick him up. He did so not just to take care of his sexual needs, but so that he could spend time with someone who would understand him and love him as he really was, who would give him the fathering he couldn't get at home, who would be the model he could not find in his teachers.

For all of us in the group, the lack of social acceptance was at least as painful as the unavailability of sexual experience. As for myself, from the age of 13 to 18 I was deeply depressed and often suicidal. This constant sadness did not lift until I was free to leave home at 18 and find gay society.

It is not surprising then that a gay youth will often take up with an older man who fills the role of friend, father, and often lover as well. Many people, both straight and queer, feel uncomfortable with this blending of parenting roles and sexuality, and it is in fact a contested issue these days in the gay/lesbian/bi community. But until our society changes its attitudes toward teen sexuality in general and homosexuality in particular, this pattern will remain one of the principal solutions to the grief and loneliness most gay teenagers live with.

We need to beware of a dangerous heterosexist assumption: that developmental needs are the same for homosexual as for heterosexual children. I am unaware of any serious research that addresses the question of what is normative for a child who is developing as a gay person.

Adolescence is a time when young people are struggling to find their social and sexual identity, seeking their reflections in the eyes of their peers. Unless a gay teenager has a circle of accepting friends (which is unlikely, and at best very small), he must purchase friendship with the coin of dishonesty, all the while believing that if his friends knew the truth he would be hated. Many of us therefore grow up with a double self-hatred, consisting of the terrible things we were taught to believe about ourselves (what choice is there? where are the queer-positive models in history books, pop songs, television and movies?), and the self-loathing that comes from living a lie. The social isolation is profound. The person hidden behind the constructed persona is invisible to peers, family and teachers. And when we are really successful, we are invisible even to ourselves.

The fatigue of chronic depression during our youthful years is enough to make anyone feel old before his time, and so much internalized hateful imagery leaves many of us feeling ugly and awkward as adults, even when we clearly are not.

How does a boy know he has "become a man"? The phrase itself seems saturated with straight men's sexuality. The message that we gay men get from our fathers and male society as a whole is that we have failed to become true men.

Having suffered from a lack of good parenting ourselves (and I am referring to the collective adult responsibility for parenting), we in the queer community are becoming increasingly aware of our role as parents. We do have children, all of us. Who else is going to take care of all the queer kids who arrive daily in all our major urban centers? Many are runaways, whose parents have rejected them. Many end up on the streets, selling their ass to survive. And even those who don't are AIDS bait, even the ones from "nice" middle-class homes. They may have learned about the value of higher education, but they probably didn't learn about sex-positive STD prevention, because our society refuses to acknowledge teenagers' sexuality. It seems we love our ideologies more than our kids—but that's nothing new, we've been sending them to die in wars since forever.

Our group had a vision of a kind of lesbian/gay big sisters and brothers organization. We also talked about group homes for gay kids, gay foster parenting for gay kids, and more funding for queer youth social centers. More spaces need to be provided where these kids can meet caring role models, listening elders, and their own peers. We are a minority born outside our own community, isolated from birth, raised by the "enemy," among whom we must survive by our own wits, often believing we are alone. We need the clinical and therapeutic advocates from our own community to counsel kids in the school system and help them enter into their own peer community.

So far I have dwelt only on the cost of our difference, but lesbian and gay young people need to be made aware of the peculiar gifts that life has entrusted to them. At a young age most queer kids develop an unusual degree of psychological insight. The person and the persona are distinguished precociously. The lack of social "mirrors" often leaves a gay person without a clear sense of identity. The gay teenager learns to change like a chameleon in changing circumstances. This was recognized at once in the gay men's group as a link between our gayness and our Buddhism. I have never met a gay Buddhist who did not feel naturally comfortable with the teaching of no-self. We also agreed that it is far easier to deconstruct an intentionally architected self-concept than one you internalized on faith from society. This has made us skillful actors—we've been doing it all our lives. The combination of fluid persona and sense of no-self also leaves us very open to religious experience and the language of altered states.

We learned at an early age to develop our communication skills for self-defense. (Was it a coincidence that every man in our group spoke at least two languages, and some three or four?) Our fear of being ugly has made us sensitive to beauty; as a community, we have always been known for our concern for aesthetics. Our experience of isolation has made friendship of primary importance to us, and that is how we build our families. And we do have family values of our own to teach: What else lies behind our extraordinary support, organizing and solidarity around the AIDS crisis?

Acting, precocious social and self-awareness, communications skills, fascination with religious experience, aesthetic sensitivity and community orientation: Is it any wonder we have been so disproportionately represented in music, literature and art? Or that we have packed the ranks of priests and priestesses, monks and nuns, shamans and bards for so many centuries and in so many cultures?

We must work for the day when queer kids will not only have the parenting and social resources they desperately need, but will also learn pride in their heritage and awareness of their creative and spiritual resources. The current waste of human potential is tragic, not only in young lives and in suffering, but in creative resources lost to society as a whole, as our energy is sapped by the struggle for survival and healing.

The gay and lesbian community has a unique contribution to make to the emerging discourse on social difference—we, who are so unacceptably different from you and yet found amongst all of you, despite race or nation.

Surviving High School
A Gay Buddhist Graduates in the Heartland

Christopher Osborne

I can hardly believe I'm finally graduating. As I think back over the past four years, I can vividly remember my experiences of being a young gay Buddhist in a homophobic Christian community. There is wisdom one can gain through being a practicing gay Buddhist in a closed Christian community.

The most memorable aspect of my life was the loneliness. The only contact I had with other Buddhists was through the mail, and the only contact I had with other homosexuals was slim also. I knew one "open" homosexual whom I dated for awhile; however, since being gay is strictly prohibited here, he felt forced to stay in the closet. I came out as a Buddhist before I came out as gay. A few of my close friends told me a major advantage of my being Buddhist was that I was totally trustworthy.

So before I was criticized for being gay, I was constantly criticized for being Buddhist. I was often attacked verbally and once physically. On one occasion, as I sat in class, someone asked who I prayed to; but before I could respond the teacher jumped in and said, "Those Buddhists worship wooden statues! We Americans should go overseas where they come from and teach them who the real GOD is!!!" Suddenly the whole class burst out in laughter and were yelling, "You're going to Hell, stupid! If you don't believe in God you're crazy! You had better never come around me, or I'll knock your teeth down your neck! You Buddha boy!!!"

As the teacher sat back and watched, what was I to do or say to defend myself against the ignorance of 20–30 students and a teacher? As time passed, I found myself in more and more situations like that so with all that pressure I sure wasn't going to come out about being gay which I finally did in my junior year. During one of these situations, I couldn't say anything so I got up and walked out. I went to talk to the principal who said, "Son, this country was founded by Christians, for Christians, and it will always be run by Christians. So all I can say is live with the ridicule." Then I decided to propose a multi-cultural class to inform students of the different religions they will encounter throughout life, and his response was, "The parents just wouldn't allow it. We just couldn't teach about anything other than Christianity. This is a Christian town and it's gonna stay that way!"

CHRISTOPHER RYAN OSBORNE (Hyden, KY) was born in 1979 and is a practicing Buddhist—but not within any particular tradition. The present article appeared originally in the *Gay Buddhist Fellowship Newsletter*, San Francisco, June 1997.

My first year of high school was also my first year of practice as a Buddhist, and I quickly learned it wasn't going to be easy to practice. I found myself being attacked by people constantly asking questions like, "Do you believe in God? Do you stick pins in dolls to put spells on people?" Here in my town people know so little about Buddhism that my fellow classmates and family thought I practiced "Voodoo." Why else would I light so many candles and incense and meditate? When I would try to explain, my classmates, teachers and often family would twist my words to make it sound as though I was some type of psycho. You see here it is a deadly sin to be gay or Buddhist, and I was made aware of that daily by different people who would protest, "It just ain't right fer ya ta be a voodooist!"

Somewhere in this process of practicing in high school I realized that Buddha's dharma of impermanence which is usually thought of as pain causing actually worked both ways. Not only did all comfortable states soon pass away, but so did all the uncomfortable ones. Armed with this inexhaustible truth, I found a certain peace in all my future experiences.

It was not until my junior year that I decided to come out to the small group of friends that I had gained in hope that if one of them were gay knowing that they were not alone would comfort them. To my amazement, this seemingly anti-gay group of friends took it really well. However, soon the word got out and more and more people found out that I was gay. Now I was faced with a new criticism and I was teased with fag jokes which for some reason didn't bother me as much as Buddha jokes.

Soon a few people came to me and let me know that they were gay, and that it helped to know that they weren't alone. I soon discovered that homosexuality was so forbidden in Christianity that these people were afraid to even think about being gay and wouldn't come out to other gays for two main reasons. First, their parents would kick them out of the house if they ever found out. The actual quote often heard is, "If I ever found out that ya was a gay, I would kick yer ass, kick ya out of da house and disown ya as my child."

Secondly, they would definitely go to Hell if they even thought about this "deadly sin." Nevertheless, knowing that I had brought some comfort to these friends brought a change to my painful state of existence and brought me happiness. As I have read more, I realize that we see our experiences "locally" and feel the ridicule of all homosexuals as our own. However, if we imagine that we were on the moon and could see everything on the Earth all at once we would be able to see all experiences of everyone not just ours alone. Understanding this need for universal compassion also helped me to deal with life in high school.

Despite the dangers of coming out to your family, I decided to come out to my mother just a few months ago. She says she always suspected it even though I had dated girls in the past. But soon she started to deny it by saying things like, "You really do like girls don't you?" Now that stage is over and she can accept it. On occasions she tells me she knew she should have stopped me from being Buddhist and "this wouldn't have happened." Similarly at school the rumor spread that all Buddhists were gay. In a way I believe it is a reassurance to her that she didn't do anything wrong in parenting. Now most of my family knows, but don't comment on it a lot. I think they are still trying to figure out why lighting incense and being kind are so important.

Throughout these past four years of pain and criticism, I have been able to use all of these negative experiences to nourish my practice like the lotus and the mud it grows in. I thought I hadn't gained any attachment to high school, and I wished every day to hurry and end so that I would be closer and closer to graduation. But now that it is here I suddenly realize how much I'll miss all the people who have been kind and showed understanding to me.

Throughout it all, my practice has become very strong. As I'm standing here ready to graduate, I feel impermanence settling in. College is just around the corner and I am sure it will provide a more positive environment for me as a homosexual and as a Buddhist. I know I will meet new people who will actually have some things in common with me. As for my loneliness, I have met a beautiful man who, along with the Dharma, is my greatest blessing.

As hard as it has been, all the pain has served as an excellent teacher, and I am sure the pain I am feeling now will soon pass like all other things. May all beings attain peace, happiness and long life! Om Mani Padme Hum!!!

Mahakala: In Search of the Great Black *OM*

Larry L. Saxxon

During the early '80s, after working in direct services for the San Francisco AIDS Foundation for about three years I decided that I could make a more powerful impact on slowing the AIDS epidemic within the African American community by working independently. This would afford more direct contact with the black Community Based Organizations (CBOs), which had historically been resistant to contacting agencies like the Foundation. I noted that the few black CBOs who had voiced any concern with combating this epidemic suffered from the same predictable maladies, with homophobia being on top of the list. They also appeared to know very little about program and fund development or the art of grant writing. As a result, I developed an openly gay and bisexual consulting firm, Saxxon Quinn Associates, in the latter part of 1985 which was aimed at assisting minority organizations develop their own AIDS programs, tighten their infrastructure, promote greater organization solvency. I decided that addressing their homophobia would have to take a back burner in the face of responding to the immediate needs of combating AIDS. Additionally, I figured that they'd have to make some initial covert decisions regarding their organizational positions on sexual minority politics if they hired my firm. In the end, the consulting firm was a smashing success.

It was in my capacity as a consultant with Saxxon Quinn Associates that the Northern California Grantmakers' AIDS Task Force (NCG), contracted me to assist a small AIDS hospice in Richmond, California. They informed me that I'd be working with the Metta Vihara Hospice which was run by the Venerable Banti Suhita Dharma. Little did I know that this man with the unpronounceable name would ultimately lead me down a whole new path.

I arrived at what appeared to be a rather unassuming little home in the Richmond area of California. The name of the program was carved on a small wooden hanging sign that looked like ones we made in a junior high school shop class. There were lots of very odd flowers growing everywhere. I saw cactuses, roses, lemon trees, and an assortment of other growing things that I couldn't begin to recognize, yet it all seemed so very peaceful and appeared to just belong—without question.

LARRY L. SAXXON (San Francisco) was born in 1952 and practices within the Vietnamese Zen tradition. He co-authored a chapter (with Dr. Calue Lester) "AIDS in the Black Community: The Plague, the Politics, the People" in the book *AIDS Principles, Practices and Politics* (1989); also "AIDS in the African-American Communities of America" in the Conference "Homosexuality: Which Homosexuality?" (Free University, Amsterdam, Holland, 1987).

I was greeted at the door by what I thought was an Asian gentleman wearing a brown robe with saffron yellow undergarments. His head was shaved and he appeared exceedingly happy to see me. I was a little circumspect by his lack of ego, his childlike effect. He said, in a voice slightly tinged with what I thought was a suggestion of the black vernacular, "You must be Mr. Saxxon. Oh, we've been waiting for you. Please come in." Actually, I really couldn't tell what race he was because he has a sort of light caramel colored skin. I simply chalked the accent off to living in a predominantly black community and defaulted back to my original assumption of his being Asian.

Mr. Suhita invited me in and asked me to make myself comfortable while he got his papers for my review. He bounded out of the room, almost skipping, leaving me alone to take in the surroundings. I guess it was the robes and all that made his walking style so out of place. It all appeared like a mixture of what Alice must have felt in *Through the Looking Glass* melded with a chapter out of *Arabian Nights*. It was so exotic and so beautiful. The moment I set foot in the house I was bombarded by some of the sweetest, most soothing incense that I'd ever smelled. It was literally everywhere from the kitchen to the bathroom and it was wonderful. There, in the middle of the living room, was a lifelike golden figure of some person sitting in what must have been a very uncomfortable posture with lots of little strips of paper placed very carefully around it, and with small dishes containing colorful things in them that were unknown to me. I wanted to ask a thousand questions but I was embarrassed and didn't want to intrude. I kept telling myself that I was here to complete a job—and not to pry. There was something about this strange house and the very kind little man that both excited and scared me. It was that strange mixture of excitement and fear that I had felt many years earlier when I began to realize that I was not quite like the other boys on the block. I vividly recall when I finally saw another guy that psychically clicked with me. Without words, we just simply knew; it was both scary and elating. It still is.

Mr. Suhita brought out arms full of paperwork which appeared to have no order at all and plopped them down on the kitchen table. He stood there for a few seconds with a very confused expression on his face, mumbled something and then announced that we needed tea. Without waiting for an answer from me, he then went off to make a pot. The assignment briefing hadn't prepared me for any of this and I must have looked like a very bewildered child watching an old much-loved adventure film.

"They keep telling us that we need to report this, report that, and I must admit I just don't understand what they want. We're doing a very good job of caring for all of our clients and they don't seem to understand it. I wish they'd come out and visit us. They'd see then, they'd understand it all, but oh . . . all these reports." It was difficult concentrating on the job because I found Mr. Suhita, this very odd man, strangely riveting to the extent that programmatic review was a bit of a strain. I didn't understand anything about Buddhism at the time and frankly, wouldn't have given a second thought to this beautiful way of life had I not been thrown into this caring monk's path. I remember thinking, "I don't understand what it is that this guy has, but whatever it is, he seems to be at peace with the world. *It must be nice.*"

After a couple of weeks work, we finally started setting some bureaucratic order to his program configuration. During this time I had observed his every move and doted on his every word. I would interject a little consultant's pomposity here and there to maintain my role as the alleged expert, but we both knew who was *really* in control. I must have appeared awfully funny during those initial meetings.

Banti Suhita, I'm sure, could feel my attraction to the path. Throughout all this extensive time of consulting, he waited for me to ask any and all questions about his religion. He never volunteered anything unless asked beforehand. With my ego and affect-blaring overtures heralding programmatic expertise, I'm sure he could tell that this one was a stubborn one. I'm sure he could also feel my fear of the unknown, which by this time had become a permanent partner sitting on my right shoulder. He seemed to know instinctively that I was only asking one out of every 20 questions that were flying through my mind. Ego and fear kept my curiosity restrained. But underneath the surface I burned with marvel and fascination.

After the job was over he offered me what he termed a gift. Immediately, *I refused, assuming that this would be monetary. You see, I had already been paid for my work by the original contractor, NCG. The Metta Vihara Hospice owed me nothing. I was a professional and I had ethical standards! Taking anything from the client would have been in violation of our agreement; it would have been what is termed "double dipping" and I'd have nothing to do with it.* He looked so oddly at me while I was spouting this pomposity. He had a smile on his face. And, when I finally came up for air, he said, "I just wanted to give you these few things. Please take them. They are from me to you. I made one of them myself." I looked in his hands and he was holding several small pamphlets on Buddhism and a large sheet of rice paper on which he had drawn a beautiful picture of the Buddha holding a dana bowl. I wanted to cry because they seemed to be the most beautiful gifts that anyone had ever given to me. They were ingenuous, but I didn't know how to *receive.* I took them, very formally shook his hand, and wished him luck with his agency's endeavors in the future. And, finally mustering all the diplomacy that I could command asked, "Mr. Suhita, . . . are you black?" He smiled warmly and broadly and said, "Why . . . of course." Nothing else needed to be said.

I was sweating when I got into the car and it wasn't warm outside. It was heat coming from within. It was the burning that occurs when one sees truth and hasn't the courage to embrace it. I remember thinking during the drive home, "What a wonderful, frightening, and powerful man. I'll have to look him up again some time in the future when I've got this stuff figured out a little more." He gave me a gift—and I felt like a child again!

Well, as they say, *reality bites*. After the initial glow of this almost surreal experience, I finally put both the drawing and the brochures on top of the bookshelf in my bedroom where they were to sit for six months. I don't think there was a day that passed by that I didn't think of Mr. Suhita, the experience at his hospice, his gifts and my fear of what all the aforementioned meant. I desperately wanted to reach out, but my conditioned flight response was just too damned strong. I have since come to appreciate how difficult it is to overcome our conditioned delusional behavior. Even though we know it doesn't work for us, we become used to it. It's like *a familiar* which follows us everywhere we go. It may annoy us but we know this character. And, a familiar presence sometimes is better than the unknown and the associated loss of control which accompanies the unknown.

I knew that I wouldn't last much longer. I simply had to know what the hell this guy was running on. Whatever it was—I wanted some, but—how do I ask, and—will he share it with me? I remembered that I had the brochures on top of the bookshelf and I started reading like a maniac. The story of the Buddha's life, the disillusionment with the established religious hegemony, the study under other Masters, and again, the disappointment. Finally, the journey alone towards truth. This was to shake up everything that I had held as fact until then. It was amazing. This was the real truth and I felt it in my bones.

There was no longer a need to question. I just knew that this was finally truth. This was spiritual nourishment that didn't require a pound of flesh, nor an analogous guilt/punishment syndrome which I had come to associate with other religious doctrine. I allowed myself to receive his wonderful gift—and there began the rest of my life of becoming.

A Path Alone

As with any great gift, an even greater pleasure is giving it away to others. I immediately called one of my friends and told him about "my conversion." He was decidedly not impressed. In fact, he likened my embracing Buddhism to a frog's need for a bicycle. He said it was another fad; "Honey, don't worry, it'll pass." I had miscalculated; it never dawned on me that there was anything unusual about being an African American Buddhist. What an odd reaction on his part. He made it sound as if I were passing a gallstone or something. I called Suhita to get a reading from him around this reaction from my other friend. I remember hearing a slight sadness in his voice when he told me very diplomatically that I might find that not all African Americans are ready to deal with Buddhism and especially Buddhists that were black. He too said something like, "Don't worry, it'll pass." It became abundantly clear to me that this particular path would have to be walked alone by and for me. And, who knows, perhaps I'd discover something that I could give to the world ultimately. I knew, or hoped, that there were others out there like me. I just had to start looking for them. There was so much that I simply didn't understand about this new way of life and I felt that I needed guidance badly. So, I set off to find a Sangha that would adopt me.

The Search for an Inclusive Sangha (the Perfect Sangha)

Months later while I was walking back from the barber shop one Saturday afternoon I spotted a bright yellow sign plastered on a telephone pole on the corner of Steiner and Page Streets. It announced that there were openings in a Beginning Buddhist Meditation Class. The class was apparently being offered by the San Francisco Buddhist Center and their site was way the hell out on Cabrillo. I took the number down and called as soon as I got home. My palms were sweaty when I made the call and I prayed that this attempt at finding a Sangha would hit paydirt. When the phone was answered, it was a machine, so I left a message for a Mr. Parmabodi [another unpronounceable name] to call me back regarding the upcoming meditation classes. I waited anxiously for a few days until I got a return call and after a brief period of negotiations addressing logistics I signed up. Here was the beginning of a most wonderful journey for me. During the first night of the class, which was taught by two incredible women named Karnadavie and Karen, I was initially the only attendee so they placed me into another class that was being attended by other practitioners that had more experience. I simply couldn't believe these people. They were actually for real. Again, I was, typically, the *only black* but it didn't seem to matter to either them or me at the time.

I stayed under the tutelage of the San Francisco Buddhist Center for quite a while until I gained my sea legs. They offered retreats at the Jocoji Buddhist Retreat Center in the Santa Cruz mountains, special meditation classes, and most importantly, a men's meditation setting every month! I actually attended my first men's Buddhist retreat with members of this Sangha! I was in heaven and had found a spiritual home.

My great initial thirst had been nourished. It appeared that there really were people out there that actually lived their practice. There was truth in the path. I made and still have a large number of loving spiritual friends from the experiences at the San Francisco Buddhist Center. They were additionally a comfortable fit with me *because all the great traditions are sources of study and practice within this school of Buddhism.* The San

Francisco Buddhist Center is one of a world-wide network of Buddhist Centers through the Friends of the Western Buddhist Order which was founded by the great western Buddhist scholar Sangarishita. Although I regard them as my first and primary Sangha I needed to find other gay and bisexual males and more blacks that were also practicing. So eventually, I took my leave and resumed my search with both their understanding and blessings. In fact, it was one of my teachers at the San Francisco Buddhist Center that turned me on to the Gay Buddhist Fellowship. Paramananda came across a brochure announcing an event sponsored by the Gay Buddhist Fellowship and called me to see if I was interested in attending it.

My first meditation session with the Fellowship was a warm, calm, energizing experience. It was the first time I ever recall being in the presence of a large number of gay/bisexual men and not have everyone be led around by their genitals. Of course, there were a number of attractive men there, but that didn't seem to be the draw. They/we were there for something else and we found it in the practice of meditation. There were lots of people that actually said welcome during the tea break and I felt that they actually meant it. Here I was not invisible, I was another fellow human looking for the same thing that they were looking for.

I was allowed to simply be, which is all I've ever asked for; nothing more, nothing less. One thing led to another and I eventually became involved with an ongoing Buddhist study/meditation class that the Fellowship offered. Here again I was to meet wonderful people that were loving, kind and giving. We spent a great deal of time laughing at ourselves when we'd get into discussions about different schools of Buddhism. It was a pretty diverse group with respect to Buddhist schools of orientations. Everything from traditional Tibetan practice, traditional Japanese Zen, to Nichiren-shoshu were represented. Despite our outward differences, we managed to create a safe place where differences were to be a source of strength instead of leverage for divisiveness. They were and are great guys. I love them all. After a while there still seemed to be something more that I found myself searching for, so I continued to search.

Louis, a very dear friend of mine, was the only other African American Buddhist lay practitioner that I knew. He and I often would talk about the need to form a black Sangha. We had lots of fantasies about how it would feel, so finally we co-founded what we called the *Mahakala Sangha*, which at its height was a total of 13 African American men meditating en masse. I remember thinking once when I opened my eyes while the guys were meditating, "This will save our people. This path will give them heretofore unimagined power because truth is the ultimate vessel of self control. This will give them choice." It all seemed too good to be true. There were even a number of gay and bisexual dudes among the gang, but sadly, this Sangha was not to last. There were no dramatic dynamics that caused the breakup of the Mahakala Sangha, it just wasn't the right time. The guys wandered off, one by one, until there were only a few of us left to continue. I took the dissolution of the group very hard. I think in retrospect that one of the dynamics which contributed to the group's lack of cohesion was the fact that the primary motives of many of the guys attending the sittings was their powerful need for friendship with other African American men in a non-threatening setting. One observation of note was that many of the guys that were Christian-identified felt odd practicing meditation and engaging in Buddhist ritual. They reported feeling that they were being made to choose between Christianity and Buddhism. Although I could understand their posture, I clearly did not agree with it. However, not being a Christian myself, it was one of those issues which I felt compelled to keep silent on. There is a strong possibility that my friend and I as co-founders were pushing the group too hard and too fast. We had both been victimized by mainstream Buddhist practitioners and both wanted so badly to have an ongoing Buddhist experience with a black face. Somehow, my ego had gotten involved and I felt responsible for the *failure* of the group. Despite it all, however, I still made a number of loving spiritual friends. Now I no longer search for the ultimate Sangha, because it's everywhere. I have learned that Mahakala comes from within. I've also learned that it is just as important to know when to leave something as it is to know when to stay. I am much of the time also *fully here now*. I am exceedingly grateful for the moment. I am still Buddhist—no, it wasn't something that was to pass. Most importantly, I am so grateful that the Buddha chose to, as my grandmother would say, ''tarry a while'' to share his wonderful gift. The circle is clearly complete and has always been, and the ego is ever more amusing by the day!

III

INTERVIEW

MANTRA OF PADMASAMBHAVA

OM AH HUM VAJRA GURU PADMA SIDDHI HUM (*Sanskrit*)

Pronounced: Om Ah Hung Benza Guru Péma Siddhi Hung

"I invoke you, the Vajra Guru, Padmasambhava, by your blessing may you grant us ordinary and supreme *siddhis*." [siddhis = spiritual accomplishments]

Tibetan Buddhism teaches that this mantra carries the entire blessing of the twelve types of teaching taught by Buddha, which are of the essence of his 84,000 Dharmas. Through reciting this mantra, we receive the blessing of the wisdom mind, the noble qualities and the compassion of Padmasambhava and all the buddhas. Padmasambhava (8th century C.E.) is a founder of Tibetan Buddhism and to practitioners of the Nyingma School he is considered a "second buddha."

(See complete description of this mantra on pp. 386–389 of Sogyal Rinpoche's *Tibetan Book of Living and Dying*.)

H.H. Dudjom Rinpoche and John Giorno, Kalingpong, Darjeeling, September, 1973.

Winston Leyland, Petchaburi, Thailand, 1995.

John Giorno

interviewed by Winston Leyland

JOHN GIORNO was born in New York in 1936. He is one of the most influential figures in the world of contemporary performance and poetry. He is founder of Giorno Poetry Systems which sponsored the Dial-a-Poem series (Museum of Modern Art, New York City, 1970, etc.). He has published over forty LPs and CDs of writers reading from their own work: William Burroughs, Allen Ginsberg, John Cage, Charles Bukowski, Sylvia Plath, Anne Waldman, Frank O'Hara, etc. In 1984 he started the AIDS Treatment Project, helping people with AIDS by giving cash grants for food, rent, medicine, nursing, emergencies. Giorno was the star of Andy Warhol's first film, *Sleep* (1963). He also directed the film *September on Jessore Road*, starring Allen Ginsberg (1971). The John Giorno Band performed throughout the country 1984–88. He acted in Samuel Beckett's play *Eh Joe* in New York and Rome (1995), and (playing Mark Twain) in the E.T.C. Theatre production Mark Twain, *Keelboat Talk and Manners* (NYC 1996).

John Giorno's own books of poetry include *American Book of the Dead* (1964), *Balling Buddha* (1970), *Cum* (1971), *Cancer in My Left Ball* (1973), *Shit, Piss, Blood, Pus & Brains* (1977), *Grasping at Emptiness* (1985). His most recent book, *You Got to Burn to Shine* (Serpent's Tail, 1994), collects his intensely rhythmic, sexual and political poetry and memoirs.

John Giorno is a Buddhist in the Nyingma Tradition of Tibetan Buddhism, practicing for over thirty years. His teacher is H.H. Dudjom Rinpoche (see below), whom Giorno invited to America in 1975.

The present interview was conducted in New York City, September 1996, by Gay Sunshine Press publisher WINSTON LEYLAND and transcribed by Trebor. An earlier 1974 indepth John Giorno interview (also by Winston Leyland) was published in *Gay Sunshine Journal #24* and later included in the book anthology *Gay Sunshine Interviews vol. 1* (San Francisco: Gay Sunshine Press, 1978); that interview (still in print) also deals in part with Giorno's Buddhism and gayness.

WINSTON LEYLAND was born in Lancashire, England in 1940 and has lived in the U.S. since childhood. For the past 28 years he has been publisher of Gay Sunshine Press in San Francisco which (together with the second imprint Leyland Publications) is responsible for the publication of some 120 books covering a wide range of gay sexuality and culture—from anthologies (*Out of the Blue: Russia's Hidden Gay Literature*; *Partings at Dawn: Anthology of Japanese Gay Literature*; *Angels of the Lyre: A Gay Poetry Anthology*) to novels and short story collections (Pai Hsien Yung's *Crystal Boys*; Gore Vidal's *A Thirsty Evil*), to poetry collections (Allen Ginsberg's *Straight Hearts' Delight*; Jean Genet's *Treasures of the Night*). An in-depth autobiographical interview on his life is printed in *Gay Roots: An Anthology of Gay History, Sex, Politics & Culture, Vol. 1* (1991). His own translations, essays and poetry were also gathered in this same volume, along with work by 100-plus authors, artists. He practices within the Tibetan Nyingma tradition.

H.H. DUDJOM RINPOCHE is mentioned many times in this interview, and a bio. note is pertinent (based on biographical data in *A Handbook of Tibetan Culture*, ed. by Graham Coleman, Shambhala, 1994):
Born 1904 into a noble Tibetan family, the late His Holiness Dudjom Rinpoche,

Jigdral Yeshe Dorje was recognized as the incarnation of Dudjom Lingpa (1835–1904), a famous discoverer of many concealed teachings (terma). Dudjom Rinpoche studied with many of the most famous lamas of his time. At the age of eight, he began to study with Orgyen Chogyur Gyatso, a personal disciple of the great Patrul Rinpoche. He returned to the central Tibetan monastery of Mindroling to perfect his studies. Unique in having received the transmissions of all the existing teachings of the Nyingma tradition, Dudjom Rinpoche was famous as a great terton, whose Termas are now widely taught and practiced, and as a leading exponent of Dzogchen. A master of masters, he was acknowledged by the leading Tibetan lamas as possessing the greatest power in communicating the nature of mind. He was also famous as a very prolific author and a brilliant scholar. His writings are celebrated for the encyclopedic knowledge they display of all the traditional branches of Buddhist learning: poetics, history, medicine, philosophy, astrology. A writer of poetry of compelling beauty, he had a special genius for expressing the meaning and realization of Dzogchen with crystal-like lucidity. His *Collected Works* were published in India in forty volumes. Upon leaving Tibet he established Nyingma communities and monasteries in India/Nepal, and, beginning in the 1970s, major centers in the West. He died in France on 17 January 1987.

His disciples include his sons, the Nyingma teachers Thinley Norbu Rinpoche (author of such books as *White Sail: Crossing the Waves of Ocean Mind to the Serene Continent of the Triple Gems*), and H.E. Shenphen Dawa Rinpoche, head of the Nyingma meditation center Urgyen Samye Choling in France. Also Sogyal Rinpoche, founder of the Rigpa Fellowship teaching centers; and Lama Tharchin Rinpoche, founder of the Vajrayana Foundation/ Pema Ösel Ling center, near Santa Cruz, California.

WINSTON LEYLAND: Let's start by a follow-up on some of the things we discussed in our 1974 interview. At that time you'd just returned from India where you met H.H. Dudjom Rinpoche. Why did you go to India in the first place?

JOHN GIORNO: The reason I went to India in 1970 was to try to escape my suffering. I knew from books and intuitively that Buddhist meditation and teachings were a path from suffering, and to realize the absolute nature of mind. The 1960s were fabulous, but we also really suffered a lot. One was working with one's mind and didn't know what one was doing. That also can be good as it is very pure. I took LSD, and if it was a good trip, it was totally great. But if I had a bad trip, because of my grasping, my mind was on a roller-coaster in hell. I went to India to find a way out of my suffering, and it seemed to me intuitively that the Tibetan Buddhist lamas in northern India were the key. It was sink or swim.

Somehow, even as a child, I thought of myself as a Buddhist. I don't know why. I grew up in a modern Italian catholic family, who were not religious, in Roslyn Heights on the north shore of Long Island. But I had a nanny, Veronica, who was Irish catholic and who made me pray every morning (this was the early 1940s) until I was six, when I said, "I refuse to do this any more!" And it was ok with my mother and father. I think I escaped the catholic thing without too much damage.

LEYLAND: Like yourself I had a catholic upbringing, perhaps more intense since I was a priest for several years as you know. When a teenager I read one day about Buddhism and remember feeling an intuitive (though inchoate) shock of recognition. Only now, forty years later, looking back, and after taking refuge, can I understand and appreciate that instinctive karmic recognition of the reality of the Dharma.

You studied at Columbia in the 1950s I understand, John.

GIORNO: Yes, I studied Buddhist philosophy at Columbia College here in New York in the middle 1950s—seminar courses in the Oriental philosophies. They were created or innovated by Walter LaBarry, with a young Alan Watts. A handful of students sitting around a board table in Low Memorial Library. It was a great teaching. We learned all the concepts, all the theory of Buddhism, as well as those of the other Asian religions: early Hinduism, the Vedas, from Lao to Confucianism and Zen. This was before Tibetan Buddhism reached the West, because it was before the 1959 invasion of Tibet. When I look back, I think that Tibetan Buddhism was hinted at. I went every other day at 2 p.m. to the seminar room, always with a terrible hangover. And it was nice and comforting to learn all that stuff. Form is emptiness and emptiness is form. I understood all the concepts. But it didn't change my life. My mind remained the same: a mess!

I read endlessly. Being a poet, and a literature major, I had to read everything. But after studying all this philosophy, my mind was still my fucked-up mind. Because there was no meditation practice. I did not have access. Meditation practice is what works. Zen practice was not my preference, and I had to wait until Tibetan practice became available to me. I didn't know it at the time.

In the 1960s, I drank a lot of Jack Daniels and took drugs. All drugs, the clarity of working on speed, and in particular, LSD and the psychedelics. Drugs sometimes numb the nerve ends, and allow the natural clarity of the mind to flow free. So drugs can be totally great, because they get you to first base, or at least show you the possibilities. But drugs do not get you there. Meditation practice does.

I had many extraordinarily wonderful trips. Fabulous sex, and great bliss and the union of wisdom and emptiness. Great clarity resting in great equanimity. Relaxing in the heaven worlds for one hundred thousand years, many times. But I also realized that my mind was like a wild drunk elephant, that ancient Buddhist metaphor. Elephants that raided Indian villages, breaking into the clay, thatched storehouses, and eating the grain, which would ferment in their bellies, getting them drunk. I'm sure they felt totally great. When they got hangovers, they would come back to the village for more, knocking over the thatched houses and thrashing around. I realized that my mind was like a drunk elephant, thrashing around having a good time, and causing suffering, and suffering myself.

I realized through experience that meditation practice could possibly end suffering. I didn't know what to do, but I knew that to meditate was the only possible way out, of suicide among other things. And since I didn't know how to meditate, I had to invent it, through trial and error, as I went along. I knew what somebody looked like when they meditated: a sitting Buddha statue or a photograph in *Life* magazine of a Ceylonese monk sitting cross-legged.

I sat in full lotus posture with a straight back, sitting with the rear-end raised a couple of inches was more comfortable. I closed my eyes. And let my mind rest. That's how I learned to meditate. On LSD, a person becomes very aware of the mind, perhaps short-circuited into realizing the empty nature of all phenomena. Becoming aware of the empty nature of thoughts, as they arise. I figured out that if I followed my thoughts, it made it worse. Following a thought of pleasure or grasping or anger, was like falling down the stairs, it hurt. But if I saw the thought as it arose, and its empty nature, and just let it rest, let go of it, then the thought disappeared, popped like a water soap bubble rainbow into emptiness, resting in great equanimity, the vast space of primordially pure mind. I had, through necessity, to save my life, sort of invented it as I sat. For me the 1960s were often very spiritually desolate. I picked up scraps as I went along. From Zen practice, watching the breath, and counting the inhale and exhale from one to ten. But also Hatha yogi to calm and soothe the nerve ends twisted from drugs.

LEYLAND: Did you have any contact with Zen at this time?

GIORNO: Japanese Zen is very important to Buddhism in America. Zen had made it here very early, and more strongly in California. If you were a Zen practitioner in the 1960s and living in San Francisco, you had one of the greatest teachers of all time: Suzuki Roshi. Many friends of mine had the good fortune to have him as their teacher. Around him was a mini golden era of Buddhism. There was a Zen Center in New York, but I didn't go to it. And a big one in Rochester.

The point is that I have a propensity for Tibetan Buddhism. But in the middle 1950s, it did not exist yet in America. In 1959, Tibetan lamas were in refugee camps in the Himalayas, and it took time for us in the West to find out that they were there and what were the treasures they had to offer. And first people had to learn to translate the Tibetan into English. And I didn't even know the first thing. That's what's so amazing; we went looking for something, and got given whatever it was, and something a million times more precious.

In 1957, LaBarry mentioned in class that tantric Buddhism was in Tibet. That sounded very attractive, but I didn't exactly know what it was. I didn't know anything. I had read Tucci and *Secret Tibet* by Fosco Maraini, and was utterly fascinated by every travelogue detail. And I knew I couldn't get a handle on the nature of my mind. Then in 1959, with the Chinese invasion, the fall of Tibet, and the fleeing of Dalai Lama into exile, and the destruction of the monasteries and the smashing of the Buddha statues and all that, I was inexplicably utterly devastated. I internalized the catastrophe, and had a small nervous breakdown. This also coincided with one of the worst times in my life. I mention all this to show what is a propensity. I have been a strong Tibetan Buddhist practitioner for thirty years now; but maybe the roots are elsewhere and traces come to the surface.

In 1970, I realized that I had to do something more than this sort of made up meditation of a few mantras I had been given by odd friends. I went to northern India to find out. My karma took me to various places and I met many great Tibetan lamas, including the Dalai Lama. After three months, I met my teacher, His Holiness Dudjom Rinpoche. Then I started doing formal practice, and became a beginner.

I met my teacher, His Holiness Dudjom Rinpoche (1904–1987), in Darjeeling on the opposite end of the Himalayas, near Sikkim and Bhutan. He was a totally amazing Enlightened being, head of the Nyingma tradition or early translation school or red hats. He was infinitely simple and infinitely illustrious. I took refuge, and received teachings, and did retreats, and he guided me. I went back to India to visit him in 1971, '73, '75, '77, for six or nine months each time, getting teachings and doing practice. I invited him to America in 1976, for six months, requesting that he give teachings and start a center in America. I had the very good fortune of becoming very close with Dudjom Rinpoche, and I lived in his house as a member of his family, as a sort of son. This was very rare good fortune. And I did a lot of meditation practice. The whole point is to realize the nature of mind. The only way you do it is through practice.

My teacher, H.H. Dudjom Rinpoche, who was a genius, a great scholar and famous writer (acknowledged in this world as one of the great writers of the 20th century), said: "You've never known anyone becoming enlightened reading a book! Ever! In the history of the world! You have to study, of course. You have to learn, but you don't become enlightened reading. Study must be in a balance with practice. It's through meditation and devotion to your teacher, that you attain a degree of realization, that grows. As you do more practice, your realization gets more firm and more vast."

LEYLAND: Lama Tharchin said the same thing at the retreat that I took at his monastery Pema Ösel Ling near Santa Cruz, California. That one shouldn't depend too much on books. You've got to practice the teachings under the guidance of a sensitive, experienced teacher.

GIORNO: Lama Tharchin is a disciple of Dudjom Rinpoche, who is my teacher. Of course, he thinks that way. That's the path.

LEYLAND: Was Dudjom Rinpoche at a monastery in India at this time?

GIORNO: Dudjom Rinpoche was married, so he lived in private houses in Darjeeling and Kathmandu, among other places. And he had many monasteries. He was the incarnation of Padma Sambhava in this world. And as head of the Nyingma tradition and because of his extraordinary qualities of enlightened mind, all the Nyingmapas, millions of people venerated and worshipped him. The monastic tradition (monks and nuns), the yogis (male and female tantric practitioners), and the lay people. He was very simple and very brilliant.

Dudjom Rinpoche died in 1987, at age 84, or he attained parinirvana, dissolving his mind into great equanimity. But Dudjom Rinpoche is as alive to me today, as he was when he was alive and I was very close to him. My practice is strong these days, so sometimes he is even more alive to me.

LEYLAND: Why don't we give here, since it may not be elsewhere in the book, a brief comment about the history of the different Tibetan Buddhist traditions and their differences. Nyingma, in which I also practice, is the oldest tradition, of course.

GIORNO: The Nyingma tradition is the oldest in Tibet, comprising the Buddha's teachings that came to Tibet from India in the 8th century A.D. The teachings were brought by a great teacher Padma Sambhava and include the vajrayana or tantric practices. Padma Sambhava first incarnated about 20 years after the Shakyamuni Buddha (2500 B.C.). He had many, many incarnations, and in the 8th century A.D., brought the teachings to Tibet, where they flourished. And from Tibet, they're being brought to America, now, by the present incarnations of Guru Padma Sambhava. It's been an unbroken lineage.

In Tibetan Buddhism there are four main schools that arose over centuries: Nyingma, Kagyu, Sakya, and Gelug. Basically from political differences, every several hundred years, a new Buddhist school arose, also ruled the country of Tibet. Of course, there are philosophical differences; each went to India, re-translated and re-interpreted the teachings, and different views arose; sometimes shockingly uncompromising.

Dudjom Rinpoche, in the 13th century, reincarnated as a great lama called Namgyal Phagpa, who converted Kubla Khan to Buddhism, which gave rise to the Sakya tradition. Dudjom Rinpoche was a great Nyingmapa in this life, but was a great Sakya lama in the 13th century. Kubla Khan was converted and a new tradition, the Sakya, came into power. None of the politics matter, because each tradition has these totally great lamas, miraculous masters, absolutely enlightened beings. And that's what it is all about.

The Nyingma are both a monastic tradition and a yogi tradition. There are monks and nuns; and men and women tantric practitioners who marry, or who make love; and lay practitioners. There are monastic vows, and ngagpa or yogi vows. The meditation practices are the same. In the monastic one, in the higher tantras where a consort is required, the monk visualizes the consort and achieves the same results as a yogi who's doing it with a partner, both are using sexual energy internalized. Two ways of doing it, one's not higher than the other, depending on one's personal propensity. They're both equal and have the same great results.

In Tibetan Buddhism, when you see a wisdom deity or Buddha yab yum, that is, with consort, it doesn't mean sex and sexual orgasm. It means the absolute nature of mind, which is the union of wisdom and emptiness. All concepts dissolved in the vast expanse of primordially pure mind. Subject and object dissolved in one taste, duality dissolved, the union of the male and female energy, the union of bliss and emptiness, the union of whatever it is you're doing. Absolute wisdom is symbolized in a sexual position, but it is not sexual intercourse and desire worlds.

The yogi tradition and the western worldly preferences are quite different, where lovemaking is gross appetite. Because we're very limited in our understanding. Of course, at the moment of orgasm, sometimes concepts are completely dissolved, allowing a glimpse of something else. That is why cumming is so pleasurable, a hint of bliss.

LEYLAND: Where have you chosen to focus your own creative spiritual/sexual energies?

GIORNO: I have chosen in this life to focus my attention and energy on the suffering of gay men and lesbian women. They suffer more. Everyone suffers, but sometimes some people suffer in more special ways. Compassion for gay men and gay women has been the object of my life's work. Even before I knew what I was doing, I was doing it. Before I knew that what was arising in my heart was called compassion. Those early 1960s poems that were pornographic in your face, were intended to break all concepts. I wanted to liberate myself and the poem, so that everyone would be free.

LEYLAND: Foci for the two of us are remarkably similar. I, too, have chosen to direct my energies to the intellectual/spiritual/sexual needs of gay men for almost thirty years—in my case with the publication of some 120 books expressing a wide range of gay consciousness. I have tried to make compassion in the Buddhist sense central to my life—both personal and creative. Nor is the ''bottom line'' my main criterion in accepting a book for publication as it is with most commercial publishers. I foresee *Queer Dharma* as being an immensely catalytic volume; but, at over 400 pages of gay Buddhist insights, it ain't gonna sell like *Peyton Place*, and is heavily subsidized by Gay Sunshine Press itself way beyond its normal book budget.

Most of the people I approached for written contributions to *Queer Dharma* were startlingly open and enthusiastic. But at times during the preparation of the book I've been more than a little hurt by certain gay Buddhists acting dismissively, or puritanically. (One prominent gay Buddhist scholar refused to permit his writing to be used in *Queer Dharma* unless he saw everyone else's work first to make sure it was "Dharmically wholesome"! And he didn't get the chance! Censorship sticks in my craw.)

Perhaps you'd expand further, John, on gay people and Buddhism.

GIORNO: Gay men and lesbian women and *Buddhism*. The Shakyamuni Buddha is gay friendly, and I'm sure he was gay in some of his countless lives. Each of us contain male and female energy, and some of us need more of one than the other, and some have more of one than the other and need less. All love between people is to be enjoyed and appreciated, and it doesn't matter how it configurates itself. As long as one is mindful and loving. The point is to allow a relationship to improve one's practice. And if, while you're making love, fucking, you can manage to generate more compassion to all sentient beings, this is a good thing. The nature of mind is empty and pristinely pure.

This is a very complicated subject because Buddhism has evolved over the last 2500 years, and has absorbed a lot of cultural influences from the very beginning and along the way. When the Buddha gave teachings, he didn't do it in a vacuum, and he didn't do it to Enlightened beings. He gave teachings to a very primitive culture, in which homosexuality was a taboo. That early Vedic culture, the predecessors of the Hindus, was very patriarchal, very demeaning to women, and very homophobic. And the Buddha seemed to reflect their views, by allowing it, so that he would be taken seriously. If he had said that it is ok to be lesbian and gay, these straight men would have rejected him. And so some of these views of sex and gender became the basis for the first level and the vinaya: to include the morality of the day. As the Buddha worked up, teaching the higher vehicles, all these concepts fell away.

The Shakyamuni Buddha had infinite compassion for gay men or lesbian women. There was no discrimination in his mind. I think it is time now for Buddhism to purify any homophobia that has attached itself from small minded local culture, from the early Brahmins to the present day.

I often pray to all the Buddhas, for teachings that are made especially for gay men and lesbian women, using the propensities and abilities that are special to them, for teachings to enter this world to help them more quickly attain Enlightenment.

LEYLAND: Of course in those early centuries there wasn't a structured gay life anyway. Was perhaps homosexual practice in early India more similar to what we have today in Islamic countries, where there's a natural bisexuality, and men freely have intercourse with other men when they're married to women?

GIORNO: No, because the religion of 2,600 years ago in India, was Vedic, or pre-Hindu, and the basis of Brahmanism is purifying themselves, and also structures of social control, like the caste system, so they can stay clean. Brahmanism is about abstaining, about not doing. And the Islamic world can be very gay, when they're not being fundamentalists; as we know, Morocco and Egypt are two very gay countries, very gay-bisexual; and there is minimal discrimination. Every man is just bisexual, and if he wants can make love to other men and boys. And I think in the Buddha's time, the Brahmins were primitive fundamentalists, purifying, not doing that or anything, abstaining. Whether heterosexual or homosexual, abstain from the nasty activity, certainly not be a fag, purify yourself of desire and attachment.

Whereas in Buddhism, you purify yourself, of course; but you also use all your phenomena; you work with it, rather than get rid of it. You use your propensities, first transforming them, and then the poisons themselves are compassionate activity. Anyway, you become enlightened with your own phenomena.

In Buddhism, you purify your negative karma, the results of actions, accumulated over countless centuries in thousands of consecutive lifetimes. You purify all your karma with practice and devotion and when that is accomplished, you just are a completely enlightened being, seeing all phenomena as wisdom, absolute wisdom. And compassion arising in that wisdom. And you live radiating infinite compassion which benefits every single person who comes in contact with you and beyond.

But the point is, back to Buddha's time, he was operating in a not very ideal situation. His meditators were on the New York subway. That was his given. So, he taught what he had realized: the four noble truths, and the long full path, gradually the Mahayana and Vajrayana teachings, and then Dzog Chen. And in those early teachings he couldn't say it's ok to be lesbian and gay, because he would have lost his audience.

Now the second point is that the Buddha gave many many many teachings. The general figure is 84,000 teachings. This is a real and symbolic number. 84,000 symbolizing that there are at least 84,000 different kinds of people, with 84,000 different needs and personalities; and each teaching being a person's path to realization.

LEYLAND: Not all of these teachings have been handed down, or some have been handed down in changed form.

GIORNO: Teachings change to meet the needs of a people at a particular time. Teachings arise from compassion. The sutra teachings are the words of the Buddha. First the Buddha's teachings were an oral tradition, being perfectly remembered and spoken from one generation to another. The Buddha's words were first written down about 400 years after he spoke them. I question if they were remembered so perfectly; more likely they were slightly elaborated upon during those 400 years. And that's where the occasional homophobic and demeaning-to-women views entered. I wonder what it would be like for us to try to remember something that somebody said in 1596 and get it right. Of course the great monk scholars and realized beings had amazing qualities, and so I'm sure they got it basically right. The sutras are the Buddha's teachings.

And then in the Nyingma tradition of Tibetan Buddhism, there are teachings called terma, hidden away a thousand years ago to be revealed when the time was right. Terma are secret teachings that are put away or hidden in an object or rock, or in another non-physical realm, to be brought out when they are needed, and particularly to help sentient beings in a certain time. The terma teachings are revealed by someone called a terton, a completely enlightened being, who has these skills in his meditation practice.

LEYLAND: And Dudjom Rinpoche was one of these.

GIORNO: One of the great tertons.

Padma Sambhava brought the Buddha's teachings to Tibet around 750 A.D.; and he taught many disciples, who became wonderful enlightened beings, and then they taught. This is the lineage of the Nyingma, the old or ancient ones, that had come down to today, having been transmitted from one generation to another, and the teachings are being practiced today here in America, and quite strongly.

The teachings of the Nyingma are vast. At the time of Padma Sambhava, some were not yet needed. Padma Sambhava and his consort, a great woman meditator named Yeshe Tsogyal, hid these teachings in many various places, in rocks, in the sky, in objects, to be brought out when the time was appropriate. Many of these terma teachings have been brought out over the years, discovered in the 12th century, or 18th and 19th centuries, and now. Terma teachings were revealed here in New York by H.H. Dudjom Rinpoche. And more teachings will slowly arise in the West, as they are needed, to help a master guide people to realizing the nature of mind. The needs of men and women today in the 1990s, is slightly different from those of a 19th century monk, or a 12th century yogi. The subtle guidance changes. I think some teachings that are appropriate to us now, might have seemed incomprehensible in the 14th century.

From the bottom of my heart, I have made one big wish-fulling wish: I have requested of Guru Rinpoche and the Buddhas, that teachings be revealed now that are particularly appropriate to gay men and lesbian women. Using being gay, through skillful means, to even quicken the results on the path to enlightenment for gay and lesbian meditation practitioners.

LEYLAND: And the Buddha's mind?

GIORNO: The Buddha's mind is vast and empty, primordially pure wisdom. He gave many teachings. In the Nyingma tradition they are divided into nine yanas, nine levels of teachings. The lower yanas are the Theravada, as seen with the monks of Thailand and Sri Lanka. The next three yanas are Mahayana levels, having more to do with the great expression of compassion. The examples being Japanese Zen Buddhism or Chinese Pure Land. Then there are the three last vehicles, the tantric or Vajrayana paths.

The reason to have so many different categories is because there are at least that many different capabilities. One is not better than another. There is no discrimination. Just people with different capabilities. You can become completely enlightened on the Theravada road. Some people work best with the monastic tradition. Others in the Mahayana, which is also monastic, but develops compassion. And some people work best with the Vajrayana or tantric vehicles. All this gets to the same place, the individual practitioners getting Enlightenment.

Beyond the nine yanas is Dzog Chen, the great perfection, the highest teachings. Where the poisons are transformed, and then the poisons are themselves wisdom.

H.H. Dudjom Rinpoche gave this little story. There was a tree growing big and beautiful, gorgeous flowers and leaves, but it was poisonous. It poisoned the air, killed people who smelled of the flowers or touched the trunk. The Hinayana tradition cuts down the tree, but it grows; then digs out the roots, but they grow back; and the poison tree is gorgeous again. The poisons are attachment, anger, ignorance, jealousy and pride. The Mahayana is slightly more complicated. They cut down the tree and burn the roots. They pour gasoline, and let it seep down, and burn and burn the roots, but the beautiful poison tree grows back. On the tantric level, it gets even more complicated, chemicals, radiation and technology, destroy and eliminate. But it grows back stronger and ever more beautiful and deadly. On the very highest level, Ati yoga, Dzog Chen, the great perfection, the practitioner is likened to a peacock, who eats the poison flowers and leaves, and becomes more beautiful, gorging the poison leaves only to have more gorgeous feathers. The poisons are wisdom and compassion used for the benefit of all sentient beings.

On the higher levels of Mahayana and the lower levels of the Vajrayana, you eat the poison and transform it. But on the highest level of Dzog Chen, you don't do anything. The poison is absolute wisdom and infinite compassion.

The lower vehicles of Buddhism, unfortunately, are like all other religions: it is a sin to be gay, or negative karma, it's bad. Being homosexual is what they call "sexual misconduct." They say that you cannot become enlightened being gay, it actually retards your progress. This is the view of many Theravada practitioners and is included in all levels of Buddhism.

I believe the Buddha had infinite compassion for all gay men and lesbian women. He started monasteries as a simple first step to work with the problems of practitioners. Straight lay people in almost every country in the world are homophobic, in every period of time from pre-Vedic India to China to Rochester, New York. Buddhism arose in many homophobic worlds, and the negativity in the teachings comes from the culture. Anyway, for a monk to have sex with another monk, that's desire; and if he thinks that's ok, because he's not doing it with a defiled woman, that is worse. If you choose to be a monk, you abstain from sexual activity. This is a wonderful path, but there are others.

My point is that you do not have to abstain from sexual activity to become a realized Enlightened being, and especially if you're gay and lesbian.

Gay and lesbian practitioners should just use their phenomena to further their practice, and use it in the display of compassionate activity. Straight or gay, it doesn't matter; the job is realizing the nature of mind.

On the highest levels of the Vajrayana, and I've heard this from many great Nyingma lamas; it's just personal preference. Straight or gay, monk or yogi. Everyone, man and woman, has masculine and feminine energies. Some people have more of one than another, or need more of one than another. The balance is slightly always different. Those needs create desire for gay and lesbian, and heterosexual men and women. Each person is a complicated play of male and female energies.

A person can become enlightened doing meditation in a monastic tradition, where the sexual energy or tiglei is internalized in practice; or a person can practice in a yogi tradition, with a consort, and exchange juices. One is not better than another, just which works best for you. It is the same wisdom mind in both cases.

Besides loving relations, you should try not to cause suffering. This being an impossible task, at least try to cause less suffering. Misconduct is causing suffering, not being gay.

There is a new brilliant generation of young high Tibetan tulkus, on the "His Holiness" level, who are taking a sharp look at the teachings, and clarifying them. One of them is His Holiness Druk Chen, the 12th Gyalwang Drukchen Rinpoche, 32 years old; I've known him since he was six years old. He is a great master, head of the Drukpa Kagyu lineage, and because he is a completely enlightened being, he can say what he damn pleases. He is gay friendly and he said to me:

"John, the Buddha, the Shakyamuni Buddha, had only love and compassion for people who are gay. Reflecting the customs of his time is how homophobia crept into the teachings. The Buddha Dharma is like a great big tree with many branches, but some of the branches have grafted on to it from the cultures, the many cultures in which it has been taught. It has become a bit overgrown. It is time for the tree of the Dharma to be pruned. For irrelevant appendages to be cut away, as you would any tree to keep it healthy."

LEYLAND: It is a great joy to hear such words of insight from a spiritual teacher. Over centuries many non-essential accretions have attached themselves, like barnacles, to the Dharma. Buddhism needs practitioners of great wisdom who can indicate what needs to be pruned or cut away and what are core teachings to be preserved and nurtured. And the outmoded theology which refers to gayness as "sexual misconduct" is certainly one of these barnacles. Within all Buddhist traditions, including Tibetan, there are now many gay practitioners despite a homophobia which can be virulent at times. Even though high lamas, such as H.H. Dudjom Rinpoche, have been very gay-friendly, homophobia has not been eradicated.

GIORNO: Tibet tends to be a less homophobic country. I have a theory: everyone who has a gay propensity there, becomes a monk. When you're young and you realize that you have homosexual feelings, you take refuge in a monastery or nunnery, with other people of the same persuasion. This is a joy, like coming out; and a monastery is often a way to earn a living or stay alive in this world. As a result, you find few gay people in Tibetan society; they're all in a monastery.

Homosexuality in Tibetan monasteries is rampant. Almost every one of all the monasteries of all the four traditions, Gelug, Kagyu, Sakya, and Nyingma are totally gay, in heart, if not sexually active. "It is condoned," said H.H. Druk Chen, smiling pointedly. I thought, this is wonderful, being a gay man. But I also think if you take monastic vows, you should abstain from sexual activity. Desire, straight or gay, is desire.

The monasteries are very very gay, but they don't think of themselves as gay. In 1971, when I was first being introduced to it all, I remember staying in a monastery in Sarnath, India. There were these beautiful young men, nineteen years old looking like they were fourteen, and with the emotional worldliness of a twelve-year-old, sleeping in each other's arms, in a rapturous embrace. They tried to keep it hidden, but often I'd come upon them. There were three monks and three beds in every room. They may not call it gay, but they were lovers. They loved each other, their hearts were open and their bodies were open. I really liked this vibe, a great deal of love from the heart center in a completely male world, so I really liked being with them all, as I studied and did practice.

Of course, then, there is the funny and sweet way they have sex, when they do. According to the monastic rules or vinya: it is really bad for there to be penetration and ejaculation. No tongue in the mouth, no rimming, no asshole fucking, no deep throat blow jobs and cumming in the mouth. Monks have these sex routines, like putting their dicks between each other's legs, and cumming. And it is done very secretly.

This is a far cry from the great accomplishments of our Western sexuality: great bliss and clarity, fist fucking on LSD and crystal meth in the summer Olympics, going for the gold with full ignition, open and vast as the sky.

Monks, as they get older, get less interested in the physical aspect of being gay. As they become great meditators, they are not attached to anything; and because of the hassles of a homophobic world. Others go straight, give up their vows, and have girlfriends and wives, working with their sexual energy that way. This often happens when monks go west. Whatever they do, it doesn't matter, as the primary activity is to fully realize the nature of Buddha mind, and compassion.

Homosexuality in monasteries in Thailand and Sri Lanka is even more rampant. A substantial number of those orange-robed monks everywhere, the young ones and the old ones are gay. But slightly different from Tibetan monks, more out and gay in your face, and relaxed about it.

To get back to your question: Buddhism is homophobic, as all religions are homophobic, whether they call it a sin or sexual misconduct, even though Buddhism liberates that cultural appendage early on. The wisdom of the Shakyamuni Buddha somehow was also made into a religion, with all the tyrannies of religious dogma. For instance, in the lower vehicles of Buddhism, there is the belief that you can only become enlightened, you can only achieve realization if you're a fully ordained monk. Now that's a lot of hogwash. Or it's true for some people. But often it becomes about control and political power. It's a way for the monastery to gather and keep their power; they hold the key to heaven, just like in Christianity, Judaism, and Islam.

Buddhist fundamentalists, and even the Gelug tradition, say that you can only become enlightened if you're a male monk. If you're an ordinary lay person, forget about it; it is not possible to realize your Buddha nature. If you're a female, also impossible. If you're a woman, you can become a nun, then in your next life, if you're lucky, you can be born a man and become a monk and can become enlightened. That's all a bunch of hogwash. All men and women can become great meditation masters, fully enlightened beings, by simply doing the practice.

The Dalai Lama said in an interview in 1994, that it is ok to be gay, as long as you're not a monk, and don't cause suffering. I thought that it was totally wonderful of him to say that, a giant step forward, a breakthrough for the Buddhist, "It's ok to be gay!" The Dalai Lama is a totally heroic being. But now in 1997, the Dalai Lama has recently formally and publicly said (in his visit to San Francisco): "We have to make distinctions between believers and unbelievers. From a Buddhist point of view, men-to-men and women-to-women is generally considered sexual misconduct." (See article "The Dalai Lama and Gay Love" on pp. 351 of the present book.)

This is unfortunate. The Dalai Lama is totally great, but he is also a Gelug; and it is impossible for him to go against the teachings of these strict fundamentalist lamas. Unfortunate that he had to retreat to a small minded view. Gelugpas have a great understanding of great clarity, but they have no understanding of great bliss. Both heterosexual and homosexual great bliss frightens them.

LEYLAND: You said that if someone is within a monastery, they should be celibate. Are you saying if they are practitioners of Dzog Chen . . .

GIORNO: Simply that if you choose the monastic tradition, you should do it thoroughly, abstain from sex, and you will get amazing results; or if you choose the yogi path, you'll get equally amazing results. But I request of the Buddhas that there be a third path, *gay yogi*. I mean that humbly and respectfully. Teachings and practice specifically for lesbian women and gay men, for their needs and working with their suffering, which might be ever so slightly subtly different from the monastic and heterosexual yogi traditions.

A heterosexual yogi can sometimes think not so well of lesbian and gay. He might think it is an obstacle. He's an old fashioned straight guy. I propose that there be a third path that works directly with the specific needs of lesbian women and gay men, using their phenomena to more quickly become Enlightened; with teachings and practices adapted or the wisdom of fully realized beings.

I'm happy that some monks make it with each other, I'm happy they do it. And if they want to keep it secret, that's ok. It is the *secret consort*. That's what the wife or girlfriend of a heterosexual yogi is called *sang yum* or *secret female consort*. I hope it is not blasphemous to say *sang yab* for a gay male partner. Just to say the words *lesbian yogini* must be terrifyingly horrible to ordinary straight Buddhists, a sacrilege! For Dzog Chen practitioners, there's no discrimination, no bad and no good; everything is the display of wisdom and compassion.

I have never thought for a second about becoming a monk, even though I'm a gay man. Not once. Because I always have been interested in working with sexual energy, to become enlightened for the benefit of all sentient beings. Why take a vow against it? Anyway, meditation has nothing to do with sexual activity. Meditation is watching your mind, seeing clearly the thoughts as they arise and their empty nature, and resting in great equanimity.

LEYLAND: You're saying that in these monasteries, there are many monks who are gay, or gay sexual relations are going on. Do these include two monks who are almost like lovers together?

GIORNO: Yes, indeed! Two teenage boys in love with each other, or an older and a younger one, it's human nature. A tulku, or a khenpo, or a geshe, often has many attendants, serving food, doing secretarial work and sometimes one of the younger monks is the lover, attendant, always helping him do things.

LEYLAND: But there are also, for instance, within the Nyingma tradition, lay teachers such as Lama Tharchin Rinpoche at Pema Ösel Ling near Santa Cruz. He's a man of late middle age and maintains heterosexual relationships. Are there equivalents—say someone who is gay who is in his fifties or sixties, who might still have a relationship like that, a similar relationship with a younger man within the monasteries?

GIORNO: Yes, yes, there are many! Some are really close friends. One in particular, a Khenpo who is a great scholar in a monastery in south India, in his forties, has had a wonderful Bhutanese monk attendant/secretary for years and years, living together for at least ten years in a relationship. They sleep in a room in separate single beds. I don't know how often they make it anymore. They are the great example of a wonderful bonded love relationship between two men, although they would never call it gay.

LEYLAND: Could you talk a little about how you started to help people with AIDS, especially those in the Arts. Five years ago when my lover Manuel was ill, we were able to draw on this resource.

GIORNO: I run the AIDS Treatment Project, which helps people with AIDS by giving them cash grants for emergency situations: back-rent, the telephone bill, utilities, medicine not covered by Medicaid, nursing, taxis, food, whatever is needed. Money given right away, with almost no questions asked, and with love and affection.

My intention is to treat a complete stranger as a lover or close friend, in the same spirit as in the golden age of promiscuity when we made fabulous love with beautiful strangers, and celebrated life with glorious substances. Now that life is ravaged by AIDS, I want to offer love from the same root, in the form of boundless compassion.

I began the AIDS Treatment Project in 1984, in Giorno Poetry Systems, my foundation, as a response to the overwhelming catastrophe of the AIDS epidemic, and it's taken many shapes over the years. We've given away over a million dollars, with much care. We run the Poets and Artists With AIDS Fund, and sponsor the Tibetan medicine AIDS program of Dr. Trogawa Rinpoche, among other things.

We give money with strong emotional support. I do it personally and directly. I go to the hospital or the person's apartment, or they come to my house, whatever is appropriate. Compassion without partiality, directed at each individual person with AIDS. I hug them as good friends, as they are, or as 15 years ago I might have had fabulous sex with absolute abandon with the same stranger. Now that beautiful stranger is a walking corpse.

I keep doing it and keep talking about it to encourage other people to help a person with AIDS. I know everyone is convinced, knows the facts, and does; but I keep saying it and doing it over again, because as the AIDS epidemic gets only worse, we must help, and inspire and re-inspire people to help someone or help someone you're helping some more.

THE WORLD IS GETTING EMPTY OF
EVERYONE I KNOW
ONE BY ONE
IN EVERY DIRECTION
THEY ARE LEAVING
THIS WORLD
FOR SOME PEOPLE
EVERYONE THEY KNOW HAS DIED

John Giorno 1990

TREAT A COMPLETE STRANGER
AS A LOVER, HUG THEM
AS GOOD FRIENDS, AS THEY ARE
OR AS 10 YEARS AGO YOU MIGHT HAVE HAD
FABULOUS SEX
WITH ABSOLUTE ABANDON
WITH THE SAME STRANGER.
NOW LIFE IS RAVAGED
AND WE OFFER LOVE FROM THE SAME ROOT OF BOUNDLESS
COMPASSION

John Giorno 1989

In 1984, it became very clear that the AIDS disaster was beyond comprehension. Many friends died. Countless poets and artists died, and all my lovers died; and enormous numbers of people I didn't know died. It was such a heartbreak, the failure of everything that had been accomplished. Some of the worst years of my life were '82, '83, '84. I saw everybody dying and I didn't know how to deal with it, or what to do. I was at a complete loss. So in '84, I started the AIDS Treatment Project. It occurred to me that what a person with AIDS needed most was money, and loving. Needed most, most difficult to do, and what must be done.

Often, when a person got sick, after being in and out of hospitals, all their money was gone; they would lose their job, and on leaving the hospital, find themselves evicted from their apartments. We give grants to help with the time before disability and Medicaid start.

I spend one or two hours a day, seven days a week, every week, every month, every year; and I'm happy to do it, because the loss and suffering is so enormous. And I am HIV negative, through some miracle, since I am certain I came in contact with the virus many times, and somehow I'm negative.

In 1984, coming after two decades of fundraising for all the worthy causes, the last thing I wanted to do was to start fundraising for people with AIDS; but I bit the bullet, and did. I started with the royalties from the Giorno Poetry Systems LP records. Husker Du and William Burroughs and Laurie Anderson, Patti Smith, and all the poets gave their royalties, unless I thought they needed the money more. That was how it started, with the LP money. And then we gave benefits. Now thirteen years later, it still goes on.

I never wanted to make the AIDS Treatment Project into another big AIDS organization with a big budget, staff and payroll. There are no salaries, no administration expenses, and no fundraising fees. All the work is given free and all the money goes directly to help people with AIDS. Any miscellaneous expenses are absorbed by Giorno Poetry Systems. It doesn't cost anything to be generous. There are always just enough resources to help everyone.

LEYLAND: What would you say to a person with AIDS, who is close to death and has not taken refuge as a Buddhist, but is attracted and aware of the teachings? How would you speak to someone like that about going through the bardos of dying and death?

GIORNO: Just relax. Let go. . . . . I would encourage them to seek a Buddhist teacher in any of the traditions. And if they wanted, immediately try to connect them to any Nyingma teacher who happened to be in town. A Buddhist teacher to explain to them how to calm the mind, and what practice seemed appropriate. But most important is to make the person's mind feel good, and relax. Often I just sit in the hospital room, and just do my personal practice, and send it to them. It is too late for a sick person to become a great meditator. Their life force is very diminished. If they haven't started before they get sick, then it's difficult. It is hard enough to do meditation practice when you have the full force of excellent health. But friends of mine, accomplished meditators, having done long strict retreats, had totally wonderful deaths, radiating great blessings you could feel, some even with miraculous signs.

Then when the moment of death comes, when the breathing stops, and dissolution process begins, it is very important to leave the dead person alone, quietly, let the consciousness rest in the corpse.

LEYLAND: Some Buddhist teachers say that for many people it's like a three-day blackout.

GIORNO: After the subtle breathing stops, and the white and red elements come together, there is the black state, that for most people lasts for three days. A black state in which nothing happens. After this time, there is great clarity, when there is a chance for Enlightenment. Everyone who dies goes through this black state, which has correlations in other religions. For realized beings like His Holiness Dudjom Rinpoche, the black state lasts for an eighth of a second, and their mind rests in the great equanimity, dissolved into primordial wisdom.

When a person stops breathing, he or she is not dead yet. The subtle breathing can go on for hours and hours; it can go on for days in some cases. When somebody is officially dead, and white as chalk, they're not dead yet. Their subtle breathing is still taking place. And the way you can test it, is to place a small hand mirror just under the nostrils, and you'll see it cloud up. And their consciousness can still see and hear. Their consciousness is still in their bodies. The person is beginning to recognize, "I'm dead!" Like you're asleep, and you wake up and you're dead, and you keep trying to go back to sleep, because it is terrible to be dead. Then the dying process continues. Being dead, is a little like being a homeless person. The worst has happened, you've lost everything. "I'm dead!" This has happened to almost every person who ever died in the world, and who will.

LEYLAND: So death is not absolute at this point; there's still consciousness of some kind within the body. But what about if a mortician takes away the body in two hours and burns it?

GIORNO: Then the consciousness gets really jolted. The worst is our culture here. In France, they have this thing called lying in state. Even an ordinary or poor person. They leave you in your bed for a day or two. And that's the best. To leave the person alone and to permit them to exit in his or her own time. Like one friend of mine, who didn't die of AIDS—he had melanoma. It wasn't five minutes before he was in a body bag going down the elevator. That's the worst. But I know someone who died of AIDS in a hospice in western Massachusetts, and the hospice allowed the body to rest in the bed for three days after the death. With friends doing meditation practice. That's the best.

LEYLAND: It is within the Buddhist beliefs then that consciousness can stay there anywhere from a few hours to a day . . .

GIORNO: It's all up to the individual person. Generally it's only a few hours. What happens is that after the person has stopped breathing, the subtle breathing goes on for awhile. Maybe one hour. Maybe 3 hours. Maybe 6 hours. And then they go on to whatever is their natural karma.

When H.H. Dudjom Rinpoche died in 1987, he attained rainbow body. His consciousness remained in his body for three weeks, in absolute meditation, resting in great equanimity. One sign was that even though he had long ago stopped breathing, there was a slight warmth in the chest area. But nobody touched him, and there was no rot and no decay. He smelled like perfume—radiating the great blessings of Enlightened mind, a force field of purification if you were lucky enough to be there. Then after three weeks, his head tilted forward, his body collapsed slightly, and he was gone. Or all pervasive, radiating equally powerful blessings to everyone, but particularly to those who were resting in meditation with him. And he didn't go anywhere; he's more alive for me today in 1997, or just as alive as he ever was. It is a great joy.

LEYLAND: Could you talk about the Buddhist concept of harm, vis-à-vis different types of gay sexuality? For instance, you mentioned where harm comes in, and where it's not relevant, in regard to various types of gay sexuality, including intergenerational sex.

GIORNO: The point is not to discriminate, because it's not a certain way; but to allow all possibilities to arise, as a vehicle for wisdom and compassion. If two guys want to fist fuck, if that's what they feel most at home doing, that's great! I use fist fucking as an example because it is highly skillful sex. The only problem with S/M sexuality is being attached and becoming addicted to the great pleasures and bliss, always wanting more; it can become a big obscuration. On the other hand, free of attachment, with mindfulness and skillful means, the nerve ends are numbed and the natural clarity of the mind flows free.

LEYLAND: What about the question that has been brought up by some Buddhist practitioners with regard to S/M sexuality, where they say it's impossible to distinguish the harm from the actual act? Which of course I don't believe myself.

GIORNO: When you're talking about suffering, you mean real suffering; and you're not talking about extreme pleasure. An extreme view of pleasure, which might even have some spiritually beneficial aspects. When you're dealing with S/M sexuality, first of all, you're not dealing with people who are Enlightened beings. So it depends on the people who are doing it. If the pain is actual cruelty, then there is no redeeming value, as a person being angry and causing hate. But there is nothing wrong with S/M sexuality that appears to cause suffering, but actually, with love causes great bliss. It's all in the intention and the practice. Most often S/M sexuality is mutual and agreeable, and even though it appears to cause pain, it is extremely desirable pleasure. The point is it leaves the choice to the individual person, and doesn't make any rules that anything is bad.

When an ordinary person has sex, they experience the mirror image of a mirror image of ignorance. They experience bliss filtered through their obscured mind, through clouds of delusion. When an Enlightened being has sex, it is the display of wisdom and compassion, emptiness and great bliss, and is of great benefit to sentient beings.

I have great sympathy for those gay men and lesbians in conservative Buddhist traditions, where all homosexual activity is sexual misconduct plain and simple. They have a real problem and must suffer more. There is no way around it philosophically, and to go against your teacher is to break samaya. It is really difficult for them and I deeply sympathize with them. There is no way out. My point is that monastic rules are for monks and nuns, but monks try to make them the rules for all Buddhists. On the highest level of Tantric Buddhism or Vajrayana Buddhism, there's no such thing as discrimination against lesbian women and gay men.

Anyway, it's a big problem and I have great compassion for those monks, particularly western men and women who have difficulty being monks. And you can never make spiritual progress or attain realization if you go against your teacher; your teacher's mind and your mind must be one. I fortunately found a tradition (Nyingma) which is able to liberate your mind if you're gay and lesbian, straight and promiscuous, or an ordinary man and woman, monk and nun too, married man and married woman; you can become Enlightened by just doing it. It's hard work, needless to say. To become the Buddha yourself is a difficult job. So I have great sympathy for anyone trying.

Being here for the last thirty years, seeing Tibetan Buddhism, first in India, then come to America, and take root and grow, and begin to mature; and be transformed by Western culture (as Buddhism has always been transformed in the culture), is really wonderful. And I want to work with a tradition that starts out right from the beginning, helping liberate lesbian women and gay men to fully realize their Buddha nature.

LEYLAND: Surely one way out for gay Buddhist practitioners trapped in a conservative environment is to change to another gay-friendly tradition such as Nyingma. Isn't it true, say, even within the Theravadan tradition, maybe on the theoretical, on the official level of teaching, that they discourage gayness and consider it wrong?

GIORNO: That is true. They consider it sexual misconduct. If you're a Theravadan practitioner, the only source of teachings are the Buddhist Sutras that have been passed down historically from the Buddha's time to this time. In those teachings, it says that all homosexual activity is sexual misconduct. There's a big "S" like a big sin. There's no way around it.

On the higher levels of the Vajrayana, where the disciple is working in other ways with the nature of mind, those concepts of the lower vehicles fall away. Compassion and wisdom dissolving any contradictions. A number of Nyingma teachers: His Holiness Dudjom Rinpoche, H.H. Druk Chen, Lama Tharchin, and many more, have said to me personally on many occasions that the "gay is misconduct" theology got into the Dharma in the first place, not as the Buddha's words, but as cultural influences. In other words, he was teaching in a homophobic society, and they thought he agreed with them, and it got into the Sutras. The Sutras are the teachings of the Buddha. The Buddha made monks and nuns from men and women who had problems, and then the Buddha had even more problems. The usual, rampant desire, jealousy, and fighting, which gave rise to the many vows of the vinaya, governing the conduct of monks and nuns. For example, one of the rules forbids orgasm or ejaculation, coming and cum. But in the higher vehicles of the Vajrayana, in *tab lam*, a meditation practice using sexual energies: before, during, and after coming, the sexual juices are manipulated through yoga practices.

LEYLAND: Don't you think also then maybe some of the high lamas within the Nyingma or Sakya traditions shouldn't speak out a little more than they are doing?

GIORNO: The married lamas (yogis) in the Nyingma tradition, like Dudjom Rinpoche, or Lama Tharchin Rinpoche—these are men who are heterosexual and that's why they're married lamas. So, even though they infinitely support gay men and women, they're straight guys, they're into women, so they don't come at it the same way as a gay person would. My words to them, actually to all of the great ones, is that gay men and lesbian women suffer more than ordinary heterosexual men and women because they've got a double dose of suffering. Not only do they have to deal with attachment to desire and their mind and the suffering that's just inherent in relationships, they have to endure the suffering that what they do is a sin, it's sexual misconduct, it's wrong, it's bad, and if you practice this you go to hell. In Buddhism as well as Christianity. So gay and lesbian—I say it often to Lama Tharchin; he's sitting here in that chair listening to me—deserve more help because their suffering is more extreme.

LEYLAND: Don't you think there's not going to be a real breakthrough until two lay lamas (yogi), who have a high spiritual attainment, who are gay and accepting themselves as gay, and who are not monastic, make that breakthrough, come out and live together in a relationship that is open and above-board like Nyingma lay lamas do from a straight perspective? Why shouldn't then two lamas who are gay live together in a gay relationship?

GIORNO: Well they do. Actually I joked with one of the high lamas: "I can't wait until the first His Holiness comes out!" You know that's what you're saying. And he laughed and laughed and laughed, you know, and because it's only on that level, it's only on His Holiness level or the head of a lineage, where they're such great Tulkus, they're so high and their realization is so vast that they're able to see all in perspective. Most often the young lamas grow up in India in the monastic tradition because that's their university system. It's in a monastery and if they're gay then they're satisfied. Because on the inside, it's like a world unto itself. They're happy if they're lovers with somebody inside. They're not like us, trying to change. They're trying to attain realization themselves, they're studying and doing practice and it's all inside the context of the monastery.

It's a little complicated. When I was joking with H.H. Druk Chen about "the first great His Holiness coming out," my second thought was the suffering it would cause the lama who did it. Unending criticism and problems. It would take a really noble effort. I'm sure all the tulkus think it's easier to show infinite compassion to gays and lesbians than to come out. But I look forward to the day when the first His Holiness comes out, from infinite compassion for gays and lesbians. It would take the level of a great terton or His Holiness, because the power of their realization, the power of their wisdom mind, can actually liberate.

One time in 1975, I went to see His Holiness Dudjom Rinpoche—it was the year that your long *Gay Sunshine Journal* interview with me came out, so I brought a copy of it to show him. In *Gay Sunshine* there were all these naked young guys, guys with big dicks, pornographic as you could have been in the early or middle 1970s as well as lots of literary material, of course. And I gave it to him and he just laughed. He didn't read English. And I showed him where I had talked about him. He looked at the art, and my interview was many pages so he looked at that. And then I had brought some extra copies. I went up there with a dozen copies and—it was a little infiltration thing—I gave them to the monks. Just to let them see that this was a possibility in the West. And then, by chance, I had it where I was staying and I gave it to the host who was this cool married guy. We were all in our 30s. I walked into his living room one day and there were five women looking at *Gay Sunshine*, including a couple of old Tibetan ladies. And they were all shrieking with laughter. There was a picture of a couple of guys with big dicks fucking and sucking and they had it open to all

H.H. Dudjom Rinpoche (1904–1987), head of the Tibetan Buddhist Nyingma lineage, and one of the greatest yogins, scholars and meditation masters of this century. Considered to be the living representative of Padma Sambhava, he was a prolific author and revealer of the "treasures" concealed many centuries ago by that great teacher. Photo by Arnaud Desjardins.

"He was small, with a beautiful and gentle face, exquisite hands, and a delicate, almost feminine presence. He wore his hair long and tied up like a yogin in a knot; his eyes always glittered with secret amusement. His voice seemed the voice of compassion itself, soft and a little hoarse."
—Dudjom Rinpoche, as described by his disciple, Sogyal Rinpoche.

these pages. And they were shrieking, hysterically laughing, never ever having seen such a thing. I mean they had heard that maybe something like this happened. But Tibetan sexuality is Asian, it's very primitive, and all that they probably ever did was fuck with their clothes on, nothing complicated. But there was no feeling anything was bad. I couldn't wait to leave the room, but they were really having a gas. That's more or less like where it's at.

LEYLAND: You were telling me you wished that when you were a teenager, you'd had sex, been able to express sexual feelings.

GIORNO: I'm one of those people who was born into the laxed Catholic Right of the 1950s; but I was very protected. I was brought up by a nanny. I realized when I was 12 years old that I had these feelings of attraction for other boys. My heart beat faster attracted to men, and masculine energy. Or gorgeous guys of 30 years old who came to dinner parties at my parents. I might have a crush on any one of them. I longed to be sexually "abused"; but no such luck. Some of their friends were gay. And it occurred to me that these feelings of love for men is what is called a "fag." Or being gay, or queer, or other derogatory words. I was watching my mind. "I'm queer!" What a shock. What does that mean? I believed these feelings of love and attraction to men were pure. These emotions were absolutely pure. And if they would have been physical, they would be equally pure. There was nothing wrong. And if this is what a fag is, then I'm a fag. I will not be deterred from following my heart. I was determined as a knight going to battle for a high cause. This was the straight homophobic 1950s; and there was no support and nobody talked about it. I was all by myself, discovering it and figuring out what to do.

I viewed being gay as a heroic activity and noble effort. And that has actually been my work for all these years. That unconscious thought has governed my entire life. That was when I was 14, and now I'm 59. That's why I wrote those pornographic poems in the late 1950s and '60s, when nobody wrote sexually explicitly, chanting the cause of I'm gay and it's ok. And there's nothing wrong. I wanted to create the possibilities for everyone who wants to be gay, to come out, with whomever they want.

When I was a boy I jerked off, but I never had any sex with anybody. I had never made it with anybody. And finally, when I was 17 years old, I decided if I'm gonna be gay, if I'm gonna be a queer, then I wanna make it with a guy. I went down to MacDougal Street here in New York, to a gay bar called the San Remo, and I picked up somebody, and we went to his apartment, and we made it. Finally I made love with somebody, and it was great. This was in the dawn of the golden age of promiscuity. I was young and beautiful, smart, rich (my mother gave me an allowance for endless years), and a poet; so I could have anybody I wanted, and often I did.

In answer to your question about intergenerational sex. There is a line in one of my poems, LIFE IS A KILLER: *When I was fifteen years old, I knew everything there was to know, and now, that I'm old, it was true.* And nowadays, kids mature even quicker; they learn from life and television, in the best sense, from the enlightened programs; in addition, there are drag queens, gays and lesbians, transvestites and transexuals, daily in every American home via satellite dish and cable. It does my heart good that in every small town, the sons of hardware store men, or red neck families, or those in prisons of small-mindedness everywhere, can watch any sexual preference. You only find what you want by knowing what everything is. The point is to allow people to love each other. It is criminal and a tragedy to have a law saying that making love to someone under 18 years old is statutory rape

When you have sex, sometimes it's good, and sometimes it's not so good, and sometimes it's bad; depending on the person, and the circumstance, and how your energies are flowing that night or day, and karma. You made it with someone and it wasn't that good, and maybe you shouldn't have, but you did. Or you came and it was over, or the chemistry wasn't right, or it didn't work out at all. I think that sometimes things that are called sexual abuse are simply not understanding one of the basic laws of samsara: that everything sometimes is unsatisfactory. You can't have it every time. And the anger of the person accusing sexual abuse can be the *real* sexual abuse. I know there are numberless horrible cases of sexual abuse, and the addiction of a certain kind of sexuality does damage a child. But anyone who rapes anyone should be taught how to make love.

Then there are those cases in the media, like the guy who is 38 years old, remembering through therapy that when he was 12 years old, he was sexually abused by a Catholic priest, and that this has crippled his life. I know there *is* real sexual abuse. But is it possibly that the kid had a really good time on occasion, but he doesn't remember that? I'm sure at times, like everything else, it was horrible. The conservative right, fundamentalists, Christian or Catholic are the sexual abusers of the worst, terrifying kind.

I think people should be encouraged to love each other, at any ages (including below age 18), as long as it's done mindfully, in whatever form it takes. Young people, particularly, should be encouraged to learn these skills. And often, totally fabulous sex is a deep love affair for endless hours with a stranger, or a friend, opening your heart to the sky. Transcendent sex, even though you don't know who he is (and try to be safe); and it works. This is a great accomplishment.

Becoming a fag was a little like becoming a Buddhist. I didn't know what I was doing or getting myself into, but I trusted my intuition. When I first went to India looking for a Tibetan Buddhist teacher, before the Dharma came to America, I didn't know exactly what I was looking for; there was no reference point, it hadn't yet been defined. I trusted my intuition and my inexplicable devotion to the Buddha, and it led me to H.H. Dudjom

Rinpoche.

LEYLAND: Could you talk about your own daily practice? You've been practicing 25 years or more . . .

GIORNO: I do practice everyday. I love doing practice! Specific meditation practices I received from H.H. Dudjom Rinpoche, who died in 1987, or attained parinirvana; but he is as strong for me today, as he was when he was alive. And when His Holiness was alive, I lived with him for many years. He had many disciples, who are now great lamas; and when I have any questions, or need something clarified, I ask one of them. It's like getting the answer from Dudjom Rinpoche.

LEYLAND: How much practice do you do each day?

GIORNO: I love doing practice! In New York, I do two hours a day, first thing in the morning, but I have a very busy schedule, and I'm swept away by the many things I'm working on. I live with somebody, who has a country place on the eastern shore of Maryland, where we spend a lot of time. There I do two hour sittings, three and four times a day. It's quite natural to do practice.

LEYLAND: So you've had a relationship with a man for about 15 years?

GIORNO: Yes, we've been lovers for 17 years now. He's a classical pianist.

LEYLAND: Is he a practitioner?

GIORNO: Yes, he's a practitioner, a disciple of Dudjom Rinpoche and Dilgo Khyentse Rinpoche. And it has really simplified my life. Because, strangely enough, I've been a Buddhist for all these many decades, but I've had very few Buddhist lovers. This can make for obstacles. Living with someone who does the same meditation practices, is a very strong support, invaluable. I consider it a blessing from Dudjom Rinpoche.

LEYLAND: Would you like to conclude by a final comment about Dudjom Rinpoche, your root lama, your root teacher? He has been a vital presence in my own practice, too.

GIORNO: His mind was vast as the sky, and being with him was like eating the sky.

LEYLAND: And the way he viewed sexuality?

GIORNO: A great spaciousness with sex. And you should just be who you are, just relax and be gay.

IV

ESSAYS ON CONTEMPORARY BUDDHISM AND HOMOSEXUALITY

THE ESSENTIAL NATURE OF MIND

No words can describe it
No example can point to it
Samsara does not make it worse
Nirvana does not make it better
It has never been born
It has never ceased
It has never been liberated
It has never been deluded
It has never existed
It has never been nonexistent
It has no limits at all
It does not fall into any kind of category.

DUDJOM RINPOCHE

Buddha with condom.
Concept/artist: Stuart Sherman. Photo: Don Felton.

Applying Buddhist Dharma to Casual Sex

Clint Seiter

Sex between partners may be a personal act of self-to-self acknowledgment, a means of expressing close feelings between two people who already have achieved at least some degree of intimacy. In this case, the sex act is used as a means of expressing and enhancing this emotional bond. This type of sex could be referred to as Intimate Sex. It can develop into an intensely personal physical connection that only grows stronger as two individuals reveal their selves to each other.

There is a second type of sexual motivation, however, that operates on quite a different plane. This sex draws strength primarily from fantasy, where the partner is actually a vessel for something bigger, the ideal of The Male (in gay sex). In this situation, the partner is fulfilling the role of an archetype, whether it is The Beautiful Youth, The Daddy, The Rough Trade, The Androgyne, The Masculine Man or any number of other generic types. The pleasure derived from this type of sex is directly proportional to the degree of success that the partner has in assuming the archetype. Archetypes by definition are limited: the more an individual reveals his own distinct personality, the more difficult it is for the partner to maintain whatever fantasy is being invoked. Personal disclosure is lethal to Archetypal Sex.

The Western Judeo-Christian culture has for centuries extolled the virtues of Intimate Sex while roundly condemning Archetypal Sex. In this cultural perspective, only Intimate Sex can lay any claims to "the Spirit"; Archetypal Sex is dismissed as an urge of our animal bodies (or in Fundamentalist churches, the temptation of Satan) that must be transcended for the sake of our spiritual development. This results in expressions of Archetypal Sex invariably linked to feelings of shame, remorse, and a need for penance. Most schools of Western psychology have picked up on this theme and enhanced it. Intimate Sex is the manifestation of a well-adjusted, actualized personality; Archetypal Sex is the sign of arrested development, an immature personality stuck in adolescent fantasies. Within this context, it has proven extremely difficult to examine Archetypal Sex nonjudgmentally. Attempts to understand its nature are colored by pejorative

CLINT SEITER (San Francisco) was born in 1951. He is an active member of the Gay Buddhist Fellowship and heads its "Feed the Homeless Project," as well as being involved (as baker) for the Green Gulch Zen Farm in Northern California. He makes his living as an environmentalist and practices within the Zen Buddhist tradition. This article is a revision of one which appeared originally in the *G.B.F. Newsletter*.

assumptions and terminologies (witness all of the baggage the word "promiscuous" carries with it). In the culture we live in today, the options regarding Archetypal Sex include repressing the urge, sublimating it, or acting it out in secretive, furtive ways that carry a stiff penalty if the perpetrator is caught (just call to mind the image of Jimmy Swaggart confessing his trysts with prostitutes before the camera, tears of remorse streaming down his face).

And yet there are characteristics of Archetypal Sex that can take on the aspect of a "religious experience." Archetypal Sex seeks to *transcend*, to connect and identify with a concept greater than our personal selves. The partner loses his own personality and identity and becomes an ideal of The Male. In successful Archetypal Sex, the egos of both partners can dissolve into the act of sex itself. Archetypal Sex is a form of worship to a principle of beauty momentarily incorporated within the body of the partner.

Despised as it is, Archetypal Sex *does* happen. And in the already marginalized gay subculture, it happens a lot. But because this subculture in many ways has incorporated and institutionalized the values of the main culture that despises it, the arenas where Archetypal Sex is most frequently played out are full of contradictions. The same guilts and condemnations that accompany Archetypal Sex in the mainstream, can manifest themselves in the gay world in a number of different ways (a lack of respect towards one's partners, contempt, rudeness, emotional coldness, to name a few). More often than not, Archetypal Sex is split off from the day-to-day experiences and identities of gay men and relegated a separate role. It's not *incorporated* into the rest of our personality, or imbued with our humanity and compassion. What results is a type of schizophrenia.

Problems also arise when partners fail to recognize the differences between the two sex drives. A partner seeking Intimate Sex may view a partner seeking Archetypal Sex as shallow and objectifying. A partner seeking Archetypal Sex may see a partner seeking Intimate Sex as clinging and smothering. Since Archetypal Sex is more associated with male energy and Intimate Sex with female, this is a particular issue in the heterosexual world. But because both genders carry both Archetypal and Intimate sexual needs within, albeit in different proportions from individual to individual, this is an issue in the gay and lesbian subculture as well. The homosexual subculture does have one distinct and powerful advantage over the heterosexual main culture: a much greater opportunity to experiment with different types of sexual roles and relationships (our "outlaw status" at least has *some* compensations). About the only relational model that the straight world offers up as acceptable is one-on-one monogamy. This model goes a long way in validating Intimate Sex, but it discredits and suppresses Archetypal Sex almost entirely (except in fantasy role playing between monogamous partners, and even that is usually a grudging concession).

There is no room for *balance* in this scenario. Insomuch as Archetypal Sexual needs are even acknowledged, partners are expected to meet these needs as well as the needs for Intimate Sex. They must not only be each other's friend and lover, but also the embodiment of whatever fantasy fuels the other's imagination. When the partner is unable to meet these conflicting expectations (and few can), suffering can happen, whether in the form of frustration, disappointment, resentment, or just a diminished sense of joy.

An interesting challenge would be to look at Archetypal Sex in a non-judgmental manner and speculate how it could be integrated into our lives in a way that could conform with Buddhist dharma. If this were possible, then what form would Archetypal Sex take? Could an individual openly and honestly balance an Intimate relationship with one person successfully with Archetypal sexual experiences outside of the relationship? Are Archetypal Sex and Buddhist dharma innately contradictory, or can common ground be found between them?

Criteria set by Buddhist dharma include a movement away from greater suffering and towards greater inter-connectedness. If the Archetypal Sex drive is acknowledged and understood, if partners enter into an Archetypal Sexual experience openly and honestly, if care is taken to treat each other lovingly and with joy, could this form of sex, even if between strangers, be consistent with Buddhist dharma?

To better examine this, it might prove useful to examine criticisms levied against Archetypal Sex and try to respond to them.

Archetypal Sex treats the partner like an object.

Actually, it treats the partner like an ideal. The partner isn't just a body, but an avatar of The Male, in whatever particular image is being currently evoked.

Archetypal Sex lacks intimacy.

This depends on how "intimacy" is defined. Archetypal Sex does little to acknowledge the day-to-day identity with which a partner usually associates himself. But Archetypal Sexual experiences can bring two (or more) people together sometimes in some powerfully transcendental ways. If they walk away afterwards and never see each other again, this doesn't mean that intimacy did not occur for the moment.

Archetypal Sex can become addictive.

So can Intimate Sex. The challenge is to remain aware and conscious and strive to act in the moment.

Archetypal Sex leaves a person feeling empty afterwards.

If a person is seeking Intimate Sex and engages in Archetypal Sex instead, this can be true. The challenge here is to attempt to be clear in one's motives and desires. Engaging in Archetypal Sex needn't preclude having intimacy needs met in other relationships, sexual or otherwise.

Archetypal Sex discriminates in favor of the young and physically attractive. Those who are neither are treated as second-class citizens.

Archetypal Sex "discriminates" in favor of whoever most successfully embodies the archetype in question. The American culture does tend to fixate on youth and sets up specific standards of beauty. But there are archetypes that define beauty in ways different than the norm (e.g., the "Daddy" archetype finds older men more desirable). However, whatever the given archetype is, it's true that there will be people who fall outside of it. But condemning this will not make the dynamic stop, it will just push it underground. There are ways for someone who falls outside the archetype to still honor it and participate with it in some capacity. If participants of Archetypal Sex also honor the dharma, then the challenge is how to deal with potential players with kindness and respect, even in the act of rejection (this same challenge exists for those seeking Intimate Sex). An even greater challenge, however, would be in finding creative ways of including would-be participants who might normally be excluded.

In closing, it should be stressed that Archetypal Sex cannot respond to and satisfy all basic human needs for intimacy and love. A steady diet of nothing but Archetypal Sex would lead to tremendous imbalance, which in turn would most likely eventually result in dissatisfaction and suffering. However, as mentioned above, exclusively Intimate Sex creates its own imbalance with its own potential for suffering. Arguably there is a potential in every human being for creating multiple relationships that allow both Archetypal and Intimate Sex into their lives. Those who choose to explore this can at least consider whether this can be done in ways that do not violate the basic Buddhist dharma. Experiencing enlightened Archetypal Sex is a difficult challenge in a culture that condemns and despises it. We occupy a unique position as gay Buddhists in this dialogue. Gay sensibilities can offer as valuable a perspective on Buddhist views on sexuality as Buddhist dharma can on gay views. It's up to us to at least open up a dialogue where new types of relationships, embodying both the Intimate and the Archetypal, can be examined.

Queer at Heart:
Dharma Practice and the "Gay Self"

Myo Denis Lahey

It is fundamental to an understanding of Buddhism that no one has yet been able to locate a self. The traditional view is that the search for a self as the locus of suffering propelled Shakyamuni Buddha out of his comfortable life as a member of the ruling class and into the forest, or, if you will, the desert, which refers metaphorically to that vast region where confrontation with Being occurs, no matter what the geography. In all his six years of harrowing effort, he was unable to find that which his contemporaries might have called the "atman," the putatively unchanging and irreducible kernel of individual existence. Instead, Shakyamuni found an exquisitely synchronized flux of experience, which he conceived of under five aspects: "form," the "stuff" our bodies encounter as we move through space and time; "sensation," the agreeable, disagreeable or neutral quality associated with the content of any given moment of experience; "conception," the mental recognition and labeling of a datum of experience; "impulse," i.e. momentum, or the mental tendency to cling to what is pleasant or to try to escape from what is unpleasant; and "consciousness," the field of awareness in which the entire perceptual process occurs. Apart from this, there was no presiding entity, no ultimate "watcher," to be found. Additionally, since Shakyamuni's time, no one has been able to produce incontrovertible evidence in support of a distinct, ultimately existent self.

For this reason, it is peculiar indeed to speak of a "gay self" in the context of dharma practice. What could be the useful focus of such a topic? I think it can only be the question of whether or not our experience as members of a sexual minority might have an influence on us as Dharma practitioners. I believe that it does; the reader is free to agree or not, as seems fit.

If we reflect for a moment on what befalls those whom society has marginalized, we might be moved to speculate that, because they do not stand at the center of the herd, but rather have been pushed to its periphery, they are presented both with a privation and an opportunity. While they are denied the protection and warmth which a surrounding herd can provide, they also have possibilities of movement, of enterprise, which those squarely in among their fellows cannot manage. The resources of the herd are meted out to them in smaller portions, but so is the herd's ability to police and

Myo Denis Lahey (San Francisco) was born in 1951. He is an ordained priest in the Sōtō Zen lineage of Shunryu Suzuki-roshi.

restrict. It will not tax our imaginations to think that those reared in the throbbing, fecund heart of the herd may come to adulthood with an ingested identity more solid, and hence less yielding, than those who knew themselves to be numbered among the outlaws, even if they didn't understand at first how they came to be so classified.

Granting that the coherence of our experience of the world is language based, and also that language, broadly conceived, is the medium for the inculcation of cultural values, consider the following scenario: Young Billy and Teddy are playing quietly together in the sandbox, in close proximity to an admiring group of adults. Without warning, Billy leans over and gives Teddy a big kiss. Teddy is unruffled by this display, but the onlooking adults are visited by a sudden, embarrassed silence, broken only when someone addresses Billy's father, saying, "Oh, well . . . there's always interior decorating!" or some other such witticism. Uneasy laughter ensues. It would be a mistake to think that any of this is lost on the children. Billy and Teddy are both extremely sensitive beings, the uncertain properties of whose world obliges them to attend to what transpires around them, particularly among their caregivers. The scent of discomfort that laced the air in the wake of Billy's gesture is almost certainly dissonant with his interior feelings of affection and safety. In this brief encounter, Billy has been subjected to shaping behaviors on the part of the adults in his life which contradict his self-expression.

Now, let us assume that another young family arrives on the scene, bringing their daughter Sally, a rough contemporary of the other two children. In due course, she is introduced into the sandbox as well. The toddlers pursue their "parallel play," as children that age do, but they are not unaware of each other. This is demonstrated when Teddy leans over and gives Sally a big kiss. At once there are choruses of "Aw, isn't that sweet," and other appreciative noises. The bounds of what is considered gender-appropriate conduct by the dominant social group have, in the space of a few moments, been clearly limned, for the supposed benefit of the children and the reassurance of the adults.

Now let us turn for a moment to our young friend Billy. His insouciant display of affection for his friend met with no reinforcement whatever, save perhaps the negative reinforcement of the discomfort that ensued, something that is all but certainly palpable even to very young children. And what might be the effect of such a response on Billy, should a sexual orientation towards his own gender already be in place, as some theorists suggest? Bearing in mind that, throughout this essay, I am using the term "self" only in its conventional sense, that is, as a provisional construct or "shorthand" reference to the phenomenological aspects of being, and that the status of the self as an independent *ens* remains unproved, we may say that the child would have been initiated into what might be called the Absent Self, a phenomenon likely familiar to all gays and lesbians who must grow up in a homophobic culture: As we look upon the world, we are seeking our own reflection as a source of knowledge of where our place is, of how we are to live, how to understand ourselves in relation to our fellow beings. But an enormous piece is missing: Where our sexual and affectional selves should be in the pictures reflected back to us from the world we live in, there are only blanks. We cannot see ourselves as beings valued by the members of the herd for our ability to love and to express that love sexually, because, by the herd's narrow, survivalist standards, our self-expression is not merely faulty but detrimental.

Consequent upon numerous repetitions of such scenes, and reinforced a thousandfold by film, advertising, and ordinary literature, in all of which venues the member of a sexual minority cannot see his/her own heart accurately reflected, one whose sexual/affectional self has been purloined in this fashion must overcome significant challenges in addition to those which confront each person who wishes to move toward maturity. And if, as is still the case for so many in this society, there is no access to resources such as gay-positive literature, support groups, or the like, to attenuate the initial insult, then the young gay man or lesbian may, for a period of years, simply not develop at all as a being who knows him/herself to be loved, and who can love in return. That this is extremely painful scarcely bears comment. Such a person may come to adulthood presenting what we might call the Inchoate Self, that is, one in which the capabilities of the heart have remained rudimentary. This is rather like remaining a child in some respects. Much work will have to be done, first to exorcise the nagging sense of unworthiness frequently felt by those victimized by homophobia, and then to grow into a person who can meet other beings fully, love them, and rejoice in being loved in return.

Another course of development followed by some who must find a way to deal with the Absent Self leads them to acquire an unusually *ersatz* version of the ego. A man or woman can construct a usable *persona* or face to present to the world out of fragments gleaned from what is cast off or denied by society at large, or from an arbitrarily confined subset of the identity elements permitted to those who have a seal of approval from the majority. Thus, a gay man may hear the message, "Your mannerisms mark you as outcast. Therefore, you may have a profession, but only one suitable to your ilk. You may be a hairdresser, an interior decorator, or the like, and whether any of these express who you really are is irrelevant." For many gay men, such professions are, indeed, perfectly expressive of themselves. But for many others, they only represent corners of society where they can make a living while escaping some of the torment which may have pursued them from childhood, when others first perceived that there was something "queer" about them. Thus, the "clothes" they wear never seem quite to fit properly, and a feeling of dissonance may dog them constantly.

There are other patterns of selfhood which, for some, may offer an avenue of relief from the subtle imprisonment that follows upon their trying to live as members of this society. People have turned to sadomasochism, bondage, transvestism, aggressive promiscuity, and other socially disapproved styles, seeking room for their hearts to grow and mature. It can reasonably be argued that many, through their own talents and good fortune, have been successful in this. It is also clear, however, that others have made for themselves only a more ghastly confinement, in building what we might call a Distorted Self, a pastiche of ill-fitting elements that is nonetheless functional, and serves to occupy the internal void created by meditating on the image in society's warped mirror. Over time, the Distorted Self may come to feel like an ache that has been present so long as to seem natural; yet unless this interim solution is abandoned, the wider horizons of human growth may remain beyond reach.

It will already have occurred to some of those accustomed to thinking along Buddhist lines that any "self" is, to an extent, constructed over and against a more-or-less hostile world, and that a "self" is likewise based upon a primal distortion, i.e. the fabricated status of the individual as possessing ultimate, separate existence, from its own side, as the Tibetans might say. To this degree, gay men, lesbians, and members of the social mainstream all face a similar daunting task: How to extirpate once and for all this deep and divisive illusion? Shakyamuni Buddha taught that endemic to the human situation is the experience of *duhkha*, or "unease," and at the very heart of this unease is a subtle but pernicious ignorance of the true nature of our existence, namely, that our existential milieu contains no fixed referents. There is no ontological island on which any entity may take refuge as a self-existent being, from which to confront and manipulate the universe to its own satisfaction. That we nonetheless invest tremendous energy in unconscious mental acts which fly in the face of this truth is the cause of untold suffering. Because of the illusion of separate selfhood, we dig in our heels when shocked by the relentless ebb and flow of existence, which we inevitably are, moment after moment. A body is born, then there are sensations, then either hunger for or aversion to those sensations, and the rotational force of karma feeds into the maelstrom, propelling the whole system, age after age, birth after birth.

What, then, is different for those of us who have found that our lives fall outside the pale? An element of great importance is the experience of oppression. For many of us, oppression has meant growing up with a subtle habit of alienation from the cultural matrix which supplies our ordinary identity. This alienation reveals itself as we become aware of the base hypocrisy, fear and ignorance which we encounter in the course of trying to establish our own integrity amidst a society that excludes us. And with that awareness comes anger. It is sometimes presented as a truism that all people are oppressed, that the wounds of the human situation spare no one.

Such a stance whitewashes the fact that not all oppressions are identical. There are political, economic, and public health consequences of membership in a sexual minority which are not paralleled by difficulties experienced by the vast majority of heterosexual white males in the course of their lives in the dominant social group. Gay men and lesbians who cannot, or do not choose, to "pass" as heterosexual are likely to find themselves on the receiving end of the kind of treatment meted out to people of color in this country for many decades: discrimination, disrespect, and even violence. And as anyone who has experienced it can tell you, when it is the sexual/affectional persona that bears the brunt of the oppression, it cuts right to the bone. The very heart you present to the world is received with spite and derision. Anyone who doubts that some of us do not recover from the assault need only consult statistics on suicide in sexual minority groups, particularly among gay youth.

Now it may happen that some of those bearing the onslaught of social opprobrium come to hear Buddha's teaching. In paraphrase, Buddha says, "Do you wonder about your life, about suffering? Come sit still with me awhile, and I will tell you what I've learned." As a gay man, I myself heard this invitation with my wounded heart, and something told me that I needed to know what Buddha had discovered. I knew that I suffered, and later I found that I and many of my gay brothers and sisters suffered in the especially poignant fashion of those whose offering of themselves has been spurned. I believe that what I sensed in Buddha's words was the possibility of healing, and it is of the kind of healing effected by the medicine of Dharma that I would like to speak next.

Dharma practice is, in a fundamental sense, about healing. It is about healing the ancient rift between "self" and other, between the sphere of the putative perceiver and the universe putatively perceived. At the basis of this healing is the experience of what has been called the Undivided Self, or the Primordial Self, or even the True Self. Various code names have been used in Buddhist history. In the Zen school, one hears of the Original Face, or perhaps the True Person of No Rank. To experience oneself in this way is to embody the dynamism of existence, as encoded by Shakyamuni Buddha in his formula of the five aspects, noted above. Sometimes, the ancestral teachers pointed the way with a question: "What sound is made by a single hand clapping?" In the unrepeatable, universal world of the True Self, a single hand sounds like thunder, the whole body claps, the whole universe chimes. Compare the biblical Psalms: "Rivers, clap your hands!" It is towards this deep reorientation that Buddha's teaching is directed. And from this springs a unique healing: It is the balm that finally soothes the ache at the heart of life, that inescapable unease or *duhkha*, born of the primal misunderstanding that "I" and the universe are ultimately separate. I would suggest that this illusion of separateness has especial poignancy for those of us reared in a society prepared to exclude us the instant we are caught being who we are. And ironically, being who we are is at the root of healing.

In fact, being just who you are is the supreme and most demanding of all the dharma gates. In the Zen halls, we say it is the practice of Shakyamuni Buddha himself. It is simple, disarming, and inexorable, it is the artless abandonment of body and mind. It is so artless that we have to submit ourselves to the discipline of art in order not to hinder its accomplishment; we must master the serene and refined art of being exactly who we are.

Of how to go about this there will be more to say later. First of all, we must address a paradox: In order to heal, we must have a certain level of health. It is known that some potently curative medicines can further injure someone who is too weak to sustain their effects. This is also true of the medicine of Dharma. It is sometimes necessary to begin with a minute dose of reality, of things as they are, lest a being take fright and do him- or herself some mischief. This is particularly true when a person lacks a fully functioning "self," that entirely contingent but necessary pseudo-entity who appears in the world as one separate being in an army of others. It is this contingent self, the "small self," whose nature must be accurately perceived in order to break the spell of *samsara*, the endlessly revolving phenomenal world where beings coalesce, endure for a time, and dissolve, over and over again. If the illusion itself is improperly formed, then liberation is likely to remain elusive, because the very ground from which understanding must arise is defective. Therefore, we must first care for and treat with respect that which is later to be unmasked. For many gay men and lesbians, this will mean enduring, to one degree or another, the painful process of coming out, of emerging in the world as one capable of profound love of his or her own sex. It may be prudence will dictate that this process will have to be carried on in secret, such that only the woman or man engaged in the endeavor can bear witness thereto. But more often, family and friends will be involved, and will have to learn how to relate to these new aspects of personhood, perhaps heretofore suspected, perhaps not, which their loved one is revealing to them.

The process of coming out can have a distinctly Buddhist flavor for gay men and lesbians who are Dharma practitioners, particularly for those who have adopted the practice of the Bodhisattva Precepts. These are sixteen public promises which make concrete our commitment to embrace fully the great matter of birth and death for the sake of all beings. The first three are the Three Refuges. In saying them, we vow constantly to return home to, to base our lives on, the Awakened Mind (Buddha), the pure Teaching (Dharma) which flows therefrom, and the vast Community of beings (Sangha), visible and invisible, who have likewise sought refuge. Taking refuge effectively calibrates our spiritual compass, so that, again and again, the needle can be turned to point away from egocentric concerns and into the numberless universes inhabited by suffering beings.

Next are the Three Pure Precepts, three great vows which align the whole universe with our intention to live as Bodhisattvas: We vow to avoid all that is evil, we vow to undertake all that is good, and we vow to save all beings without exception. Now, what do we mean by "evil"? It is a word loaded with obfuscating and unhelpful associations here in the West, yet it has a certain numinous quality that deserves respect. Most simply, the germ of evil is alienation, from the deepest human truth, which is the truth of how things are, instant after instant. And the blossoming of evil is just the cultivation of alienation, the deliberate pursuit of ignorance, with all its ghastly sequellae. What of "good," then? Bearing in mind the danger of establishing such polarities other than as part of a temporary heurisis, we may say that the good we vow to undertake is that of being relentlessly steered by the heart's truth, at once splendid and ordinary, which expresses itself in all our lives every moment. So, with the utterance of the Pure Precepts we vow always to turn away from the kinds of erroneous thoughts, words and actions which encumber our spirit, whatever their gimcrack, numbing satisfactions, and always to turn towards the unimpeachable integrity of the real, even when we can't say what that is, even when to do so terrifies us. And we vow to do this with the spacious, unshakable mind that, just as it is, includes every being, leaving nothing behind.

A useful specificity and accountability emerges with the avowal of the Ten Grave Precepts: Having declared ourselves Buddha's disciples, we then acknowledge that such disciples do not take life, do not take what is not given, do not misuse sexuality, do not speak falsely, do not intoxicate mind or body of self or others, do not proclaim others' misdeeds, do not praise themselves at others' expense, are not possessive even of the teaching, do not harbor ill will, and are not abusive of Buddha, Dharma, or Sangha. Though these are but ten in number, they will touch our lives at every possible juncture if we allow them to do so, as all who sincerely have attempted this practice can attest.

The observance of these precepts is based on integrity we already possess, and which we must determine how to actualize in our lives. And it is important that our vow include from the outset the understanding that we may not indulge ourselves in thinking either that we are successfully keeping the precepts, or that we are miserably failing. Rather, we vow to remain open and accountable to the voice of our own conscience and the voices of our fellow beings as we ask "How am I doing?" without ever expecting a final answer.

Calling one's Dharma brothers and sisters, and by extension all beings, to witness these intense commitments, is a crucial step on the path for all Buddhists, though the form of these precepts may differ substantially from lineage to lineage. And for me as a gay man, there is a special beauty in seeing my gay brothers and sisters stand up in community and take these precepts as fully fledged Dharma practitioners, without a trace of apology or diffidence, as is our right.

There are two ways in which this relates to coming out: First, appropriate conduct as exemplified in the practice of the Precepts rests on the peculiarly Buddhist observation that one cannot become the kind of rigorous witness of things as they are who sees through the subterfuges of the provisional self, if one's mind is not reasonably at rest. And the great problem with "unwholesome" conduct is not that it constitutes a cosmic offense against a supposedly objective morality, but that it disturbs our minds, inasmuch as it is rooted in an imperfect understanding of the nature of things. Similarly, if there should exist in my mind a schism between an adventitious, shallow heterosexual self-concept on the one hand, and my heart's clear call for love of my own sex on the other hand, then I am in essence speaking falsely, both to myself and to the world around me. Then I shall not be able to enjoy the peace of authenticity and integrity, but rather I shall know only the exhausting tension which springs from maintaining an incongruent and dissimulating self, over and against my heart's wish for truth and freedom. Under such circumstances, the practice of mindfulness and meditation becomes excruciatingly difficult.

Second, there is the matter of uprightness. Once, the great teacher Tung-shan was about to take leave of his master, Yün-yen. Realizing that they might never meet again in this life, Tung-shan asked, "If in later years people ask me what you were like, how shall I represent you to them?" Yün-yen was silent for a long while, and then he said, "Just this person." Indeed, it was shortly thereafter that Tung-shan departed, never to return. However, later on, when Tung-shan experienced great enlightenment while fording a stream, he turned back in the direction in which his teacher's monastery lay, and bowed deeply. "Just this person" is the essence of Yün-yen's lifetime of Dharma practice, his practice of entirely being himself, the meaning of which was finally understood by his student Tung-shan. It is living water flowing under the ice, teeming with life. It is also a charred stump, a naked skeleton, an incomparable gift. It is the fist and the banner, an echoing valley at dawn. Its complete integrity defies flaccid intellectual categorizations. And it epitomizes uprightness, the practice of being resolutely still in the face of what is. The inescapable truth of our lives is ever-present, leaking from our eyes, like a brilliant light in a basket. Who are you, actually? Can you say? Are you a man, a mollusk, a cloud, a sunset? Are you a queer? Please display your heart, your understanding of "just this person." To sit down and fold the limbs, to form the body into a silent pyramid, is a radical act of witness, a testament to our unequivocal, uncompromised nature. This is "coming out" in its true sense, namely, confronting each moment in your entirety, beyond rote explanations or convenient categories. It is the instantaneous practice of the Sixteen Bodhisattva Precepts, and it is fierce as fire.

Sometimes, people will hear of this kind of practice and immediately think, "Oh, that's too much for me, I can't manage it!" For those of us who are gay, there is a certain danger that we will believe this readily, because of the degree to which we may have internalized society's message of our unworthiness. To do this is to cave in to ignorance and oppression, and flies in the face of an important fact about being gay or lesbian: We tend to be survivors. Recalling the words of psychoanalyst Viktor Frankl, we should recognize that that which hasn't killed us has made us stronger. And for the sake of our brothers and sisters, born or yet-to-be-born, we must carry forward our legacy of survivorship indefinitely. But even more importantly, we need to realize that this practice doesn't depend on "I" in the conventional sense, except that, as alluded to above, we must be able to function fully in the ordinary world. Rather, when we enter the Buddha Way, we do so with all beings as one being, as one life, which is revealed to us as we come to know the identity of the True Person of No Rank. The practice of the Bodhisattva Precepts is the essential expression of that person, of that life, and we can rely on all beings, tangible or intangible, awake or slumbering, to bear us up.

You may now wish to sit down somewhere out of the way and be silent and still. Sit cross-legged, or perhaps in a chair with your feet flat on the floor, with your back straight and your hands carefully in your lap. This stillness is like diamond, and though considerable refinement of posture is both possible and helpful, in your simple stillness you are bearing celebratory witness to things as they are. You are acknowledging your full stature. You can do this because your human life makes it possible. And if you are gay, the taste of freedom may be all the sweeter in contrast to the taste of oppression that you may have known. Because you stand aside from the great herd, you can that much more easily slip the bonds of conventional time and sense rhythms longer than a single life, a single universe. This is a great treasure.

You will need patience, however. In the Perfection of Wisdom literature, and in the Platform Scripture of the Sixth Ancestor, it is suggested that nothing at all actually arises. The truth of this is subtle but devastating. Because of its subtlety, you may need to be still a long while before obscuring habits of body and mind yield to the pressure of reality. And because of its power, you will need to cultivate a great nonattachment, an heroic courage in the face of vast, fruitful, trackless emptiness, the churning yet bottomless sea of appearances. But you have the heart of a hero already, do you see? It is your queer heart, which has kept you alive, which kept beating defiantly in the face of those who would try to tell you how to love. It is your warrior's heart that I now invoke.

"Being Different": Zen and Gay Love

Rev. Chas. Koren Baker

This article is for the gay youth (of all ages) out there who might appreciate a little encouragement. After all, growing up is no piece of cake, and growing up gay can be a nightmare. It's not a sane world and it's a very unforgiving one if you don't fit the professed social standard. For me it was extremely painful from earliest adolescence on. I was overwhelmed with the complications of who I might be sexually, socially, and psychologically. Since I was feverish with horniness, I was constant crisis—like a starving person feeling guilty over being hungry. Just nuts!

One thing was very clear to me early on—I was different and it was not a good difference. That famous "love that dare not speak its name" was mine, and so bad that society wouldn't even talk about it. I remember when *Look* (maybe *Life*?) ran an article on homosexuality in the late '50s or early '60s. The great progress was that burning at the stake was no longer a proper way to deal with this "psychiatric condition"—professionals were instead experimenting with aversion therapy. What a world for an adolescent! What great elements to incorporate into your identity.

And yet, how bizarre it seems to me now. During those years of adolescence my sense of alienation and frustration was nearly unbearable. I sure the hell wished for an "uncle" to talk with in those days—someone to reassure me, inform and encourage me. So, if any of this rings a bell with you—buckle up, and keep reading. This Zen uncle remembers very well being young and gay in an unaccepting world, and would like to ease your way as best he can.

I assume that the readers of this article have some personal interest in how Zen, homosexuality, and life all fit together, and if they fit together. Perhaps you're shopping for a spiritual home that is compatible with the reality of who you are. Maybe your son, brother or father is gay and you're shopping together. Maybe you and your lover are searching. Maybe you're just drawn to Zen and would read anything about it. Whatever the case, the subject of love and sex, homosexuality in particular, is a very effective tool for revealing essential elements of any religious model. Homosexuality is such a loaded issue, it makes a good acid test, burning through the crap right away. Here we go.

At a retreat for gays and lesbians we held a few years ago, a participant asked what our abbot, a Japanese-born Roshi (Zen Master) had to say

---

CHARLES E. (KOREN) BAKER was born in Phoenix, Arizona in 1950. He currently lives and practices as a Zen priest at the Zen Center of Los Angeles, where he is Head of Training and assists in publications.

about being gay. My lesbian co-leader and I both were silent for a moment as we searched our memories for some tidbit. Finally we looked at each other and laughed: Roshi never had much of anything to say about being gay. Everything is practice and there's nothing in your life to exclude from practice and nothing that you actually *can* exclude. When I first arrived at the Zen Center and was in my first face-to-face interview with Roshi, I thought, "well let's get this out right away." He responded with concern about being careful out there—the AIDS wave was just beginning to crash all around us. There had been several gay members at the Center over the years and some were dying with AIDS. He didn't seem to care about the sex part at all. He did care about staying well.

So, does Zen accept or reject gay relations? The answer is a resounding "neither-nor." It's simply not about sexual preference at all. It's about revealing who we are beyond conceptual dualities such as me/you, gay/straight, and right/wrong, etc. It's about ceasing from harm and doing good for self and others. It's about manifesting clarity and kindness in what we do and say, and about bringing harmony and well-being into the world. It's about being whole. In sex it might mean letting go of practices that cause harm, not because they're "sinful," but because they cause unhappiness. In other words, it means cultivating sexuality that brings about positive experiences, like closeness, well-being and exuberant abandon. It means cultivating sexuality that is an occasion to be truly, 100% there with another person, completely and utterly naked—open and vulnerable, directly sensing that other person as another manifestation of that very same One Body that is you. This is the kind of intimacy that really appreciates whose lips you're actually kissing. The point is that Zen is about life itself and our attitude as life unfolds as us.

Really beautiful, huh? But life lives us in many ways. You're in the locker-room—land of earthly delights and abject terror—and all those "fag" cracks start flying around. Some call them jokes, but they're the sounds of ridicule and humiliation and they *are* meant to be taken seriously. Oh God, no! don't let me turn red! If you're growing (grew) up gay in America, then you know the fear, shame, and frustration. You know what it is to be on guard all the time. If you haven't been victimized, then you know someone who has or you know someone who has promised to do the job for (to) you. You know what it is to wonder deeply, with just cause, what's going to become of you. You surely know depression and a sense of hopelessness. It's the roughest when you're young, before you've established a strong network of gay friends and found positive role models. And now there's the threat of AIDS on top of it all. Caught between horrendous hormonal urges and castigating social pressures, life can be hellish. It was brutish for me and I thought there would be no end to it. No matter what I did, I was somehow out of sync with the world and lived feeling alone and wanting. Sometimes, these experiences are so intense and last so long that we can't stand it any more and things end in tragedy. The world of mental and physical ill-health is well represented by gays that have crashed and burned in one manner or another.

We can't help but wonder why we're attracted to other men, and why so much of society hates us for being different in this way—what's the big deal? How can life be filled with the good things in this state of affairs? These are difficult questions and what's most difficult is that they are questions that arise in the head because of the pain in our hearts. If you're reading this article, I bet you've already checked out what the social sciences suggest about many aspects of homosexuality—such as its biological and social determinants; how well (or poorly) gays integrate in society at large; political oppression and power brokering; and, how healthy gays are psychologically, etc. There's a lot of good information out there, and you *do* need to be familiar with it. And coming from a generation when this sort of information was not there, I beg you to also please be thankful for it! But if we try to answer our really deep questions with "head stuff," it won't work very well. The head will just be busier than ever.

One thing is quite clear: being gay brings with it some distinctive and remarkably potent elements of suffering. Some are unique to us, others we share with all disenfranchised groups, and some we share with everyone. Whatever the flavors, suffering itself is something that is common to everyone. We all must put up with what we don't like, and lose what we do like. Then we die. No exceptions. No exemptions. About 2500 years ago in India, the young Buddha sneaked out of his palace to see the world. And what an eyeful he got! . . . sickness . . . old age . . . death. Guaranteed misery that even he, a prince, couldn't avoid. It changed everything for him. In fact, it was his need to resolve this matter of suffering that propelled him on his spiritual journey. He had to find a way to get free.

It may not be nice, but we simply must face up to this rotten aspect of our situation—acknowledge and appreciate it, just as it is, without any exaggerating or minimizing. It's this pure acknowledgment, with no judgment, that can break our spiraling involvement in an unresolvable predicament. This involvement itself is really a trance in which we unwittingly cause our own misery. It is not only chronically painful, but shrinks our awareness of life, *the life*, thus propelling us further on the downward spiral. This involvement is like grabbing a high voltage line—the shock is so strong you can't let go; or being caught in flypaper—the more you wrestle with it, the more you're stuck! This is suffering in the Buddhist sense, Dukkha—the "setup" is inherently unsatisfactory and you just can't win no matter what you do or how hard you do it. No amount of drugs, sex, rock 'n' roll, money, fame or love ever gives lasting satisfaction. It's all temporary. The game *is* rigged and nobody even asked if you wanted to play.

There is, however, some good news—not necessarily easy to handle, but good just the same. All that suffering has been in our heads the whole time; all that negativity is just a way of thinking and feeling ("just" he says). And we don't have to think and feel that way. Why? Because things aren't fixed and we're not obligated to act as if they were. This is, of course, obvious, but we don't pay attention to it. We're too engrossed in all the goings on, like getting a grade, getting laid, getting even, etc.—all these things centered on "I, me and mine." All of us have been very thoroughly trained in this self-centeredness. It's a basic rule of the social game and all those psycho-socio-politico-economico-religio-etc. models give us various descriptions of and justifications for it, thus further supporting the notion that the "I" is really there. And it is this "ego" that's both the bait and trap. An acute bout of suffering is often the only thing potent enough to break down this tunnel vision so that we can see *anything* else—even if it's just that something's going on that really doesn't work. At these times, if we're fortunate, we see things without the elaborate and deeply ingrained filters of what we *think* things are or how they *should* be. And sometimes we might even get a glimpse of things with a full presence of mind that takes you beyond yourself and into a direct contact with "what is." There's a good chance that you have had this sort of openness at one time or another. Most likely it quickly faded away in all the hub-bub of your life and went unappreciated—these glimpses are not an approved part of the game . . . don't ya know. If you're interested in Zen, you probably have some sort of intuitive sense of this other perspective, no matter how vaguely defined.

A cornerstone of Buddhism is this quiet little fact that *things are not fixed*. Everything is always changing and nothing is permanent. Nothing/everything is meant to be all-inclusive. It means that we, too, are just temporary arrangements of components that come together and are collectively in motion, much like waves crashing onto the shore. Each wave is made up of elements that come together, appear as a form and change. The wave rolls in according to its particular causes and conditions, plays itself out, and the water returns. There was never a wave separate from the ocean and nothing separate was born or died. Nothing went anywhere. A lot of water changed shape. And we're like that too. "Wave" is just a way of talking and thinking about the fact of water changing shape.

Our difficulties arise because we, unlike the wave, are deeply attached to the notion that we're separate beings. Once you're that far, then the other fantasies of good/bad, gay/straight, etc. just flow on out automatically. It's like "fries" on a menu—neither the print nor the picture is the food. We get so bedazzled by the menu of our thoughts, we forget the real thing—the actuality of being. We suffer from ignorance that is further confounded by our imaginings of an identity. In this blend we develop a rather grand and deeply rooted myth of who we are, and this becomes the world in which we live—a dream world. The social alienation we feel as gay people in an unwelcoming society is a dramatic, but really superficial parallel to the greater human circumstance of profound alienation from the "true nature of things" ("ground of being"; "God"; whatever). Social prejudice *is* awful and it *is* painful, but it's barely a drop in the ocean of the big picture. The more profound alienation is what prevents all of us from enjoying a lasting sense of peace and completeness. Delusion is what makes us so sick at heart.

It's foolish to believe that all this talk is going to help much. The momentum of our thoughts, feelings and actions is so incredibly strong, it keeps the old ways cropping up. The delirium of delusion does not lift easily and even when you do see something clearly, the power of habit is absolutely astonishing—ask any smoker. A key component in Zen practice, then, is to persevere. Just keep up the effort—seven times down, eight times up. People often come to Zen for a brief time, but disappear when no magic bullet is found. There isn't one; this isn't a beer commercial. It's your life, *the* life, and so we keep working at it. The great flow of things keeps unfolding and we stay in the moment as best we can, staying clear, open and kind as best we can. Here's where Zen can get tough and there's no way to cheat. It's in the practice of the moment—washing dishes, driving to work, making love, burying our friends. All our activities are the activities of Zen; nowhere need we be separate.

But we lose it from time to time and again make ourselves (and others) miserable. You get derailed when a locker-room jerk shoots his mouth off and there's a confrontation. Or you feel bad because you didn't have a confrontation and stand up for "yourself." "But . . . but," we all stammer, clutching that high voltage line of delusion, myth, and unhappiness. Then we take our attention back to the practice—coming back to the moment and coming back to our breath. We make some space for ourselves, all of us. Remembering that we all suffer from the same illness, we cultivate a little tolerance. We practice letting go of it. Letting it be, we open up again to where we are.

Here is the heart of your uncle's message: don't be fooled by the dramatic myth of who you are or the deluded blather of others. Just don't take any of it too seriously. It will only distract you from the business that only you can do for yourself—revealing who you *truly* are. So, I encourage you to make good use of what practitioners over the centuries have found to work well in this endeavor—very important things like meditation, group energy, and coaching from those farther along the path. I encourage you to be scrupulously (but not brutally) honest with yourself, not hiding from your experience—neither the shit nor the joy. I encourage you to remember that this body, like everything else, is impermanent. So do not waste time. I encourage you to have faith that the delirium does lift, and that peace and deep satisfaction are there for you. I encourage you to just keep going, always unfolding.

On Meeting a Spiritual Friend

Ven. Khenpo Karthar Rinpoche

The following article is a revised version of the transcript of the talk "Meeting a Spiritual Friend" given at the Albany, N.Y. Karma Thegsum Choling (KTC) on November 9, 1987. The talk was translated orally by Ngodup Burkhar and revised by Laura M. Roth. It is reprinted here by permission of the Albany KTC. It appeared in a slightly different version in the *Gay Buddhist Fellowship Newsletter*, September 1995.

This talk is in the tradition of those spiritual teachers of depth who have dealt with this topic through the centuries: "On Spiritual Friendship" by the 12th century northern English mystic (and probable gay), St. Aelred of Rievaulx, comes first to mind. Although the present talk was obviously not aimed directly at gay people, the gay Buddhist can find much of relevance to his/her own specific needs. We ought to open ourselves up in spiritual intimacy when we find someone simpatico with whom we have a "meeting of minds"—a different kind of intimacy from that we have with our partner/lover. This is perhaps difficult for gay people because of our tendency to sexualize people who approach us with an open heart. This article, however, should help us to cut through the obfuscations so that we can respond in turn with an open heart when we are approached by another.

—*W.L.*

I would like to extend warm greetings to everyone here. In talking about meeting a spiritual friend, we might begin by asking, what is a spiritual friend? What does it mean to meet a spiritual friend, and having met a spiritual friend, what should one's approach be to the relationship? What should be the outcome of having met a spiritual friend? I would like to share some thoughts with you about these points.

The Meaning of "Spiritual Friend"

To explain what is meant by "spiritual friend," in Sanskrit the word is *Kalyanamitra*, and in Tibetan *gewa chenyen*. *Gewa* means literally "of vir-

VEN. KHENPO KARTHAR RINPOCHE (b. 1925) was born in Tibet and received full ordination there from Situ Rinpoche. He left Tibet for India in 1958 and in 1975 was given the title of Choje Lama by H. H. the Karmapa (of the Tibetan Kagyu lineage). A year later he was appointed abbot of Karma Triyana Dharmachakra Center in Albany where he continues to teach. He is author of the book *Dharma Paths* (Snow Lion Press, 1992).

tue" or "of goodness," something that is wholesome. The word we are using here, "spiritual," may not exactly express it, but *Kalyanamitra* has to do with wholesomeness, something that is in the correct direction.

The second word "*che nyen*," is generally referred to as friend, but really means more than a friend. Of the two syllables "che" has the meaning of friendship, and "nyen" means kinship, which is a family or blood relationship.

Someone who generously shares with you whatever proper understanding, whatever wholesome knowledge and experience he or she has, is expressing friendship. The knowledge and insight this person has can become your knowledge and your realization.

Through this sharing of knowledge and realization, you develop a precious and special relationship, like a kinship, with such a spiritual friend. In the case of a family, we are related to each other through the bloodline. An equally intimate relationship takes place through the means of the teachings, with the possibility of common understanding.

A spiritual friend is also able to extend one's understanding about what is unwholesome and destructive in one's life, what things one should be aware of and avoid getting caught up in.

Meeting a Spiritual Friend

How does one meet such a person? This can happen in two ways. One is a ripening of previous good connections, a previous history of having worked and studied with the help of a spiritual friend. In this case, because of the continuous ripening of wholesome karma, a good relationship that one has started in the past, in some former lifetime for example, is able to continue, and so it is a matter of making a reconnection.

This is actually the best way, and the experience is also very special, in that when you meet such a spiritual friend there is a sense of coming home. It is like a good friend whom you have not seen for a long time. When you see that friend again, there is a mutual recognition, a good, relaxed feeling free of uncertainty or hesitation. As for the guidance of such a spiritual friend, and the inspiration that one can receive from such a spiritual friend, one does not have any question. There is a genuine, effortless confidence.

But such a meeting is rare, because one who meets a spiritual friend in this way must be very fortunate in having made a good connection, and must have a good history of cultivation of what is wholesome and virtuous, as far as mental development is concerned.

The other way one meets a spiritual friend is because of auspicious coincidence, because certain circumstances brought one to the situation. Auspicious coincidence does not mean simply by chance. While the meeting with a particular spiritual friend is not because of previous connections, and it is not the same spiritual friend whom you have worked with in the past, the fact that you can have this experience at all is because of some degree of previous connection with wholesome Dharmic activities. When you come into contact with such an auspicious circumstance, which can lead toward the experience of awakening the mind, this happens mainly because of two things.

First, one has some history of conducting one's life in wholesome and virtuous ways, coupled with an aspiration that in all future times until complete awakened mind is experienced, one may always be able to continue cultivating such qualities of mind, and one may find the necessary conditions to do so. That is the reason on the part of the student.

Then on the part of the spiritual friend, the fact that particular teachers of the Dharma are able to effect benefit in the lives of others is not only because they have cultivated some realization and accumulated some knowledge, but also because of the strength of their aspiration. That is, whatever knowledge and insight and realization they have, they aspire that they may continuously be able to extend them toward the benefit of others. Because of these two situations meeting together, the auspicious circumstance arises.

Recognizing a Spiritual Friend

With regard to meeting a spiritual friend, how does one know that one has met a true spiritual friend, not just in name or appearance, but in reality? That is not very easy to know, because whether someone you have met is a true spiritual friend or not is not immediately apparent from looking at the outward appearance of the person. The depth of knowledge and realization, the level of commitment to helping others that a spiritual friend has, are qualities of the mind that are hidden from being immediately visible.

Nevertheless, it is not impossible to know whether one has met a proper spiritual friend, if one has some degree of intelligence and common sense, based on what this person, known as a spiritual friend, is saying. Are the words and the knowledge that are being shared intelligible and reasonable? Are they sane and beneficial? Then, more importantly, does his or her action go along with the words? What is said may be very sensible, intelligent and beneficial, but are the actions reasonable and wholesome?

And so, if not immediately, at least given time one would have the ability to know. With regard to this, Shakyamuni Buddha said that it is difficult for ordinary people to have insight into other people's minds. Nevertheless, it is not impossible to know about them without having exact knowledge of their minds. Where you see smoke, there you see the possibility of fire. Where you see swans, there you see the possibility of water. Where you see actions that are like the actions of a Bodhisattva, there is the possibility of the Bodhisattva mind. Where there is sane action there is the possibility of sane mind.

There are a few characteristics or marks of a true spiritual friend that I would like to share with you. One is that in regard to helping and guiding others, from the side of the spiritual friend there is no discrimination between old and young, weak and strong, poor and rich, man and woman. He or she is simply and purely concerned with benefiting whoever needs help, whoever could be reached by what he or she can do.

Another is being able to maintain these qualities month after month, year after year. Anyone can be impressive once or twice, without any discrimination or favoritism—that should not be difficult. But being able to remain the same way, to have an even mind all of the time, is not so easy.

Another mark of a true spiritual friend is that he or she is consistently responsible for a relationship that has been made. It is not a case of being initially excited and concerned and then later withdrawing, when whatever personal interest is involved is no longer being fulfilled. If a spiritual friend is interested in the well-being of others, the experience of awakened mind of others, he or she should remain interested until the others have experienced the awakened state of mind.

Then again, when sharing knowledge and understanding, the true spiritual friend does so with the intention to help others, not with arrogance or pride or a superior attitude, not bullying others' ignorance, but rather being patient with others' ignorance, being sympathetic with others' not knowing. A true spiritual friend knows that he or she started that way also, that his or her own understanding and realization were not there to begin with.

Another virtue is not becoming inflated by praises and compliments, and not becoming deflated and shrinking because of criticisms. These are some of the characteristics of one who might be regarded as a proper or true spiritual friend.

In this way you can actually examine and recognize a proper spiritual friend, even though you do not have insight into the mind of the person. A simple example is that if an object with a terrible odor is wrapped in silk or brocade, it is immediately very impressive, but slowly the odor comes through and it smells more and more, so you have an idea of what is inside the package.

On the other hand if an object that is full of fragrance and freshness is wrapped in rags or any simple piece of cloth, at immediate glance, it may not seem even worth keeping. However the longer you are around such an object, the more the fragrance comes through, and the more you value it. So, based on common sense and a discerning mind, it is not difficult to have a sense of whether someone is a proper spiritual friend or not.

Nurturing the Relationship

In our times it is absolutely rare to meet a proper spiritual friend, some-one having the marks and qualities I have talked about. Given that real-ity, if one has met such a true spiritual friend, then it is extremely important that one make the connection and maintain that connection. First of all, such a true spiritual friend is very rare to find, and second, being able to come across another is almost impossible.

There is a Tibetan saying that finding a true spiritual friend is like see-ing stars in the daytime, or seeing flowers in the winter. In the cold and rugged climate of Tibet, it is almost impossible to see flowers in the winter. If that ever happens, it must be a sign of something special and auspicious. It is known that once in a while, at the passing or rebirth of some great teacher, a flower is seen growing in the snow or in some rugged place. So it is not impossible, but it is certainly rare.

If you come into contact with a true spiritual friend and you recognize that, there is a good possibility that you will be able to appreciate and recognize the wisdom and insight that flows from your relationship with such a person. Now you are entering a true relationship, and when you be-gin to receive such knowledge, there is friendship and kinship happening.

In the relationship between parents and children, there is the passing down of genes or inheritance, which is very special and which we should respect and acknowledge by all means. But nothing is more special than be-ing able to inherit the knowledge and wisdom of someone else, and to have that become integrated into one's life.

So when you have a proper relationship, this can be extremely benefi-cial to you because the conditions for things to happen in a wholesome and proper way are there. If, let us say, there is a piece of scented wood that is very fragrant, and if another piece of wood with no scent at all is put in contact with the scented wood, given time, that second piece of wood be-comes as fragrant as the first. When good things meet, good things happen.

Once again, such a meeting with the proper spiritual friend is rare. But once such a relationship takes place, that could be the most beneficial thing and the most important occurrence in one's life. Because whether we be-lieve it or not, the reality is that from beginningless time, for eons and eons, we have experienced birth in cyclic existence. The completely involuntary way of the mind has been in accordance with the dictates of confused conditioning.

When the mind is experiencing confusion, that causes suffering and pain, and pain and suffering cause more confusion. This has gone on choice-lessly, from birth to death, again and again. Also, the present experience of our lives is quite temporary. We should know that this life is very fragile; we will not have it all the time. While we do have it, when we have the op-portunity to make the best use of it, clearly we must take advantage of that.

Taking Responsibility When Working with a Teacher

There is a very serious form of ignorance that people like to hold on to, a very strong wishful thinking, and that is the idea of natural evolution. This is the notion that from lifetime to lifetime, we naturally become more and more refined, better and better, and then at some point, we reach some culmination, and we are there.

If that is really true, should it not have happened a long time ago? This idea denies the truth of cause and effect, which is not simply an individual opinion or a possibility. From a material point of view and from the point of view of mental activities, the truth of cause and effect is obvious. We know that when we do certain things we experience certain results. If our actions have been wholesome, we experience some happiness, even if it's temporary, and if our actions have been unwholesome and very destructive, we experience the result as pain and suffering. That is the truth of cause and effect.

On the other hand, we would like to have a natural evolution taking place that is not of our doing, but comes from somewhere else. However, if there is such a thing as natural evolution, there is no point in telling anyone to do wholesome and beneficial things. You could be doing the most heinous of crimes, but natural evolution will take care of you. You could be doing the most incredibly wholesome things, but it does not matter because you are subject to natural evolution. So the notion that things are going to work out by themselves, and obviously for the better, is an illusion and wishful thinking.

We are responsible for our actions, and we are responsible for our thoughts. We are responsible for the influence that we have on others. We have the ability to have a wholesome influence, and we have the ability to have very unwholesome influence. We are responsible for the harm that we do to ourselves, and we are responsible for the harm that we do to others.

So it is more realistic to take care of one's own work, whatever one has to do, rather than to count on natural evolution. Given that understanding, when there is an opportunity to form a relationship with a true and proper spiritual friend and to foster that relationship, one cannot afford to miss it.

As for the experience of the ultimate happiness of one's mind—the experience of freedom from suffering and confusion—absolutely nothing that one does will bring that about, other than working with one's mind through the help of the instructions and the guidance of a spiritual friend who has true knowledge and realization.

We have the potential to become free of suffering, to become as totally enlightened as anyone else who has experienced the awakened state of mind and has become endowed with absolute wisdom. We have incredible potentials; we are profoundly resourceful. But if we imprison ourselves and let our potentials remain completely obscured, our potentials by themselves are not going to evolve, without our facilitating the development of those potentials by receiving guidance and then integrating it into practice.

We are doing so many things in our lives. We will try to move any obstacles, do anything, to be able to experience some degree of stability of mind, some freedom from dissatisfaction. But if our actions are limited to things that are not directly related to confronting the problems and potentials of our minds, they are all wasted efforts.

Finally, how did fully awakened Buddhas and Bodhisattvas, endowed with true wisdom and free from confusion and suffering, reach that state? It is through making a connection with the proper spiritual friend, recognizing the importance of that relationship, and developing the knowledge and the wisdom needed to unravel the defilement and obscurations of their minds and to develop the potentials of their minds. That is what led to their experience of awakened mind. Our situation and potentials and journey are the same.

Obstacles to Intimacy in Gay Male Relationships:
A Buddhist Perspective

Tom Moon

This article and the one following were presented originally as talks at a
"Relationship Forum" sponsored by the Gay Buddhist Fellowship in San
Francisco, Nov. 9, 1996. They have been transcribed, edited and revised
for this anthology. Bio notes on the writers (Mark Marion, Tom Moon)
can be found elsewhere in this book—see pp. 163, 184.

Homosexuality is a very deep hunger on all levels—animal, physical,
emotional, spiritual—for a closeness with other men. It's an ancient
hunger; it seems to speak through us, it's older than we are by eons. It's
a force to be reckoned with—a force of nature. That is a better way of
looking at it than "sexual orientation" or those other tepid phrases we use
to describe this "thing" we come into life to deal with. We become aware
of it, I think, very early. Let me tell a story from my own life about just
how early and how powerful this all is, which will give me a lead-in to the
first obstacle to intimacy I want to talk about.

I'm four years old, and I'm sitting on the landing of my apartment in
San Francisco's Mission District, when Sal, the fireman who lives next
door, comes home from his shift. Bounding up the steps is this gigantic,
sweaty Italian "god"! And I look at him. I'm four years old and it's this
"oh, oh, oh, yeah" kind of feeling. Next to me is sitting Davy, his three-
year-old son, who's waiting for his daddy to come home from work—a
daily ritual. Sal runs up the stairs, picks Davy up and throws him in the air
and then hugs him. The kid's squealing with delight. Then he puts him
down, turns to me and now, I think, it's my turn! He looks at me, our eyes
make contact, and he pulls back. If asked, he certainly couldn't say why
he pulled back; it's unconscious, instantaneous. He pats me on my head
and says, "Hello, Tom." My immediate reaction, probably not even conscious, is: "What's wrong with me?"

To be gay means that we are men who have an intense longing for intimacy with other men. What we begin to find, before we ever have words
for gay, is that the very intensity of this longing is the thing that drives the
object of our longing away from us. That's the fundamental contradiction
of being gay for so many of us: the intensity of our wanting makes men
anxious, fearful, threatened, disgusted, angry; makes them assault us at
times. There's a very interesting book by Richard Isay titled *Being Homosexual* about the whole subject of gay men and their fathers, how this whole

dynamic plays out unconsciously when we're growing up. I'll read one paragraph from the book:

> Very crucial for homosexual children is the fact that "fathers often become detached or hostile during the child's early years, as a result of the child's homosexuality. Fathers usually perceive such a child as being 'different' from other boys in the family, from themselves, or from their son's peers. These boys may be more sensitive, have more aesthetic interests, may not be involved in competitive activities, and may be more seclusive than heterosexually inclined boys. This may lead both to the father's withdrawal and to his favoring an older or younger male sibling who appears to be more sociable, more conventional, more 'masculine.' Some of the fathers of homosexual boys either consciously or unconsciously recognize that their sons have a special need for closeness and an erotic attachment to them. These fathers may withdraw because of an anxiety occasioned by their own homoerotic desires which are usually unknown to them." [p. 34]

I think that who we are as gay people begins to show up very early in life, and right away it begins to get us in trouble with the people we want to love us most. Most of this is unconscious: we don't even know it's going on. It becomes conscious, I think, in adolescence when conflicts with other guys become more obvious. We remember these traumas more easily: being teased in locker rooms, being called a sissy, hiding out in right field and hoping they don't hit a fly-ball to us, being beaten up. . . . Most of us have been in some ways oppressed by other men. It's very difficult for gay men not to come into adult life with, on the one hand, this longing for love from men, and, on the other hand, wariness, mistrust, often anger, bitterness and withdrawal from men. I've never really met a gay man who didn't have some of this; some more than others, but I think most of us have it to some degree.

The second major obstacle to intimacy is that as a result of what I've just described, we are *different*; we see ourselves as outsiders very early on. In a fundamental sense all minorities *are* different; but gay people are the one minority who usually don't come from their own kind. If I were Jewish and beginning as a child to discover what all that means, I'd go to my parents and say: what are we as Jews, what does it mean? There's a whole tradition behind it. Again, to speak personally, I discovered I was gay when I was 14. I didn't go to mom or dad and ask, "What's that?" Instead I sneaked to the local library and looked myself up in the card catalogue: "Homosexuality: see also perversion, psychopathic deviance." That was 1962 and bad news! (Incidentally, stripped of its meaning, the word "perversion" is a very beautiful word; it sounds like it should be the name of a perfume: "Want him? Try perversion!")

Don Clark has really described very well some of the difficulties that all of this entails for us in his book *Loving Someone Gay*. He has several psycho-dynamic generalizations. In part:

—The gay person has learned to feel different. In a society which values conformity, the person who is different feels devalued or worthless, even though he may be outwardly successful.
—The gay person has learned to distrust his or her own feelings. We begin to withdraw from our emotional life as a protective device.
—We may have decreased awareness of feelings; we may feel alone, wrong; we may be the victims of depression which includes some degree of immobility, and we're tempted to dull the pain, which surfaces, through misuse of drugs and alcohol, or even to get rid of pain altogether through suicide.

None of these things I'm describing are in themselves obstacles to intimacy: they are just experiences, painful though they may be. But the way they become obstacles is that our hearts close up in response to these kinds of traumas. We become less aware of our own feelings; we become wary and defensive towards other people. That's how these things become obstacles. It's inevitable that this begins to happen. It's important to remember that it is not the experiences themselves, but how we learn to deal with them that causes our suffering; and this gives us some hope that we can undo it.

We come into adulthood with some of these wounds of the thing with men, of feeling different. Then we flock to places like San Francisco and other urban centers to try to be a community for each other. San Francisco's gay community *is* a community of social refuge. In a sense we're a community of outsiders, a community of people who don't "belong." We come here to San Francisco to try and belong and be a community for each other. What a challenge! It's important to remember, however, that the idea of a gay community is only about thirty years old. I recall a time in my own life when gay communities would have been illegal. There were private gay circles and a gay underground but not a community of men who loved and supported each other. That was illegal! We bring our hunger and longing with us, but we also bring our fear and mistrust. We bring high expectations and a lot of our own "stuff." Is it any wonder that we often let each other down?

Two years ago I did a lot of thinking about all of this when I had an experience along these lines. I went to a national summit on HIV prevention in Dallas. Prevention workers and gay people from all over the country were there to see what we could do about the second wave of HIV infections. It soon became a free-for-all. We fought with each other, were at each others' throats for three days! The most common word was "invisible": I am invisible! Nobody is seeing me! Nobody is valuing me! The young people there felt they were invisible because they were being "patronized" by older guys. The older guys were invisible because they *were* older. The women were invisible to the men. West Coast people felt patronized by East Coast people, who, in turn, felt patronized by West Coast people. The people from the Midwest felt they were caught in the middle of a bi-coastal war and that they were being ignored. Older white guys like myself felt like we were being blamed for everything. Everybody felt invisible! Where was the "in" group? Many of us have an interesting fantasy that there's an "in group" somewhere: gays who really have it good; and the rest of us are on the outside trying to get in or wishing or resenting the fact that we aren't "in."

To feel outside is a very common gay experience. Of course, it's very natural to project this outside. You see this every day on Castro Street in San Francisco: the effect of what happens when we're trying to be "in." How gay men armor themselves, get these gym-toned bodies and strut up and down the street giving each other "attitude" and then begin to recreate the very traumatic conditions from which they fled in the first place. The sad irony of it! How we do to each other what has been done to all of us. Quite unconscious and quite inevitable. The other side, of course, is that there's a lot that's good going on, too. There is a lot of love and affection and support that goes on within our community. We're in ferment, trying to create something that has never existed before.

America is an extroverted society which believes the solutions to all problems are "out there." I think that in this country the majority religion is romantic love and not Christianity. I know that I created "Mr. Right" out of my own loneliness and the rejection that I felt. He was the man who would save me from all this. "Mr. Right" is an Adonis, of course, and always great in bed. Emotionally he'll always understand me because he was specially created by God to meet all my needs. He is "the lover," the person whose job it is to love me. He will always understand, always forgive. He will know what I want and need without my ever having to say a word. "Mr. Right" is mother with a big dick!

We place such incredibly unrealistic expectations on people. I don't intend to demean romantic love. It is one of the great joys of life. I've been in love myself several times and I hope to do it again. That isn't the problem. The reason obstacles to intimacy exist is because our hearts get closed. The issue of intimacy for all of us is how to keep an open heart, how to open a heart that's closed. Both psychology and spirituality aim at this goal.

When the heart is open, the quality of life changes dramatically. Loneliness and separation are the consequences of a constricted heart, and when that condition ends so do loneliness and separation. *Intimacy is the atmosphere of an open heart*, and to such a heart the question of how to find a lover isn't particularly urgent. When intimacy is the air we breathe we become free of the obsession with finding one person whose job is to love us. As long as love is "out there" and someone else possesses it, then we live in anxiety, because others can give it or take it away from us. But when we begin to understand that the "problem" of love has to do with the state of our own hearts, we naturally turn within to the solution of our loneliness and separation, and we become less dependent on other people.

All forms of psychology seek to open the heart by encouraging us to tell our stories. When we can tell others what we have suffered, and when they can witness it with sympathetic understanding, our emotional wounds begin to heal. We become less defensive, less caught by the past, and more able to respond to life in the present. Psychotherapy is one setting in which this kind of story-telling can take place, but it is only one venue. One of the functions of the gay community is to provide safe places where we can come together as gay people and help each other heal the wounds that we have suffered in the larger world. Community is essential if we want to have open hearts. We cannot do it in isolation.

Spiritual practices, especially meditation, also have the effect of opening the heart. We in the West are just beginning to learn how powerful and healing simple attention is. When we cultivate present awareness through the practice of daily meditation, the whole personality is gradually transformed. It is only in the present moment that we can love, and when our minds are all caught up with resentments and regrets from the past or hopes and anticipation of the future, the opportunity for love in the present is wasted.

Meditation also makes us deeply intimate with ourselves, which is a precondition for achieving intimacy with anyone else. When we practice the discipline of carefully watching whatever arises in the mind, without trying to alter it, and without trying either to run away from it or run with it, we gradually achieve many of the same goals that psychotherapy aims at. Our defenses against experiencing the full range of our emotional lives gradually melt away. The "unconscious" becomes conscious. We become more honest with ourselves. I am always amazed at how easy it is to feel deeply connected with other people after a five or ten day meditation retreat. When I am fully attending to the present moment the sense of being a self completely separated from all other "selves" dissolves, and then even an interaction with a check-out clerk in the grocery store becomes an intimate experience!

So the way to overcome our "obstacles to intimacy" is inside ourselves, not in finding a man to love us. The question isn't "How do I find a lover?" but "How do I open my heart?" When we find the answer to that question, the world becomes our lover. People with open hearts also are more likely to attract partners than people with closed hearts, of course, and so our chances of finding the partner we seek are greatly increased. But when our hearts are open we don't experience the state of being single as one of being half alive. We are alive all the time.

Gay Male Intimacy and the Dharma

Mark Marion

There is a Buddhist fable that some people say was written or spoken by Buddha himself some 2500 years ago. It's about a beautiful young elephant who lived in the forest near Benares.

As the legend goes, he was as white as crane's down and his size and strength were so great that the men who captured him gave him as a present to the king. And the king entrusted him to his elephant trainers to be taught to stand firm and to follow commands. But the trainers were harsh with him and beat him with their elephant goads.

One day, maddened by pain, the elephant broke free of them and escaped. He ran as fast as he could for many days, traveling as far into the Himalayas as was possible until he outdistanced the king's men who were chasing him. In time they all gave up, went home, and he was free. But still he raced on and on, and though time passed he did not reduce his pace or forget for a moment that once he had been a captive. Every time a twig snapped or a breath of wind rustled the trees he dashed off at full speed thrashing his trunk wildly from side to side.

Finally, the Bodhisattva of compassion could stand his pain no longer and appeared to him one day, whispering into his elephant ear: "Do you fear the wind? It only moves the clouds and dries the dew. Look into your own mind. It's fear that has captured you." The minute the Bodhisattva had spoken the beautiful elephant realized that he had nothing to fear but the habit of being afraid, and he began to enjoy life again, having finally found true freedom.

I love this story because it really speaks to our experience as gay men. Our experiences growing up are so much of learning to be afraid of who we are, learning to be afraid of other people, learning how to hide ourselves in order to survive. This runs counter to the experience of intimacy and relationship which is all about telling the truth about who you are and opening up. We've got a very deep survival imprint that says we have to be cautious and wary. We have to mistrust ourselves and others. And yet, just like anyone else, we have a longing to be loved.

I was recently thinking about my experiences in a long term relationship of ten years and also as a therapist working with gay couples and facilitating a group, helping gay men develop their capacity for emotional intimacy. In the group the questions that come up most often are: how do I find a lover, and then, once I've found a lover, how do I make that love last, how do I keep it vital and passionate?

My biggest challenge in any kind of relationship is communication, that is, finding a way to tell the truth about who we are, what we're feeling in such a way that a partner can hear us and understand it; and secondly, being able to hear the truth that he is offering to us. Healthy communication naturally develops and maintains intimacy. The major challenge in gay relationships comes from the fact that, for most men, there is no experience or modeling of healthy male-to-male intimacy. Relationships between men are going to be very different from relationships between men and women. For most of us, our frame of reference (for better or worse) is our parents' relationship. When you have two men together, there is a whole different set of dynamics operating. As a result of these obstacles, many men actually despair and somewhere in their heart of hearts don't really believe that a gay man can have a lifetime intimate relationship, a committed domestic partnership that is emotionally vital and fulfilling.

In my therapy work I'm not so much interested in whether people are sexually monogamous. I'm really more interested in whether they have an emotional fidelity. Emotional fidelity means that they really put each other first in terms of time, energy, respect and sharing affection and intimacy. The key to being able to meet the challenge or overcoming the obstacles to healthy gay intimate relationships ultimately lies in the individual psychology of each individual member of a relationship. Self worth questions and doubts corrode the capacity for intimacy. One of the effects of growing up in a homophobic world is that deep down many of us fear that we are just not lovable. As adolescents most of us have experienced a mixture of sexual desire and longing for affection and acceptance towards another man or another boy and feeling his rejection. As a result, we develop a core belief: "If you really knew who I am, you'll go away." There is a very deep fear of really revealing our true selves; and yet that's the very thing we need to do to create this joyful experience of connection.

The willingness to be vulnerable is a special challenge for us as men. Straight or gay, we are socialized to avoid showing vulnerability, especially to other men. Emotional expressiveness, tenderness, admitting fear or failure, are shamed and stigmatized as "unmasculine." Most of the men in our lives when we were growing up (fathers, brothers, uncles, teachers) did not reveal themselves, did not become vulnerable. That's not a classically male characteristic in our society. Yet the capacity for vulnerability and the capacity to honor the vulnerability in our partner is essential for intimacy to grow.

The last component is the *readiness* to engage in intimacy. Many people with whom I work like the *idea* of having a lover; they *want* to want a lover. But again and again they make the choice of choosing freedom, independence, autonomy, instead of vulnerability and commitment. Liking the idea of having a lover is not the same thing as being willing to accept the tradeoffs necessary to create and sustain a healthy relationship. It's not that these men don't genuinely long for true intimacy. It's the same fears: "I'm unworthy of love" or "the odds are just too bad" or "it's too scary to risk opening up to a man given what I've suffered already.''

To put it most simply, the single barrier to creating and expanding the capacity to love and be loved is fear. The central intimacy fears are abandonment, violation and engulfment: abandonment is the idea that if I love you, you will go away; violation, if I let you close to me, you will hurt me in some way, you will betray my trust, abuse me in some way; and engulfment, if I let you close to me, you will so absorb me that I will close myself, become so subsumed into you that I won't have a ''me'' anymore. These fears generally come from our family of origin, from the original relationships in our lives, for better or worse. They are often relationships with our fathers, although they can be relationships with our mothers, too.

When I think of the fear and longing that intimacy engenders, it reminds me of the Buddhist concept of hungry ghosts. There are six realms of existence in Buddhist theology. One of them is called the Realm of the Hungry Ghosts—a search for fulfillment that can't be quenched. There is a description of the Realm of the Hungry Ghosts in a wonderful book by Mark Epstein, *Thoughts without a Thinker*, which is about psychotherapy and Buddhism. He describes all these realms from the perspective of the fact that it doesn't matter whether they exist externally; they are really about different emotional states inside us. He says about the hungry ghosts: ''These beings, while impossibly hungry and thirsty, cannot drink or eat without causing themselves terrible pain or indigestion. The very attempts to satisfy themselves cause more pain. Their long thin throats are so narrow and raw that swallowing produces unbearable burning and irritation. Their bloated bellies are in turn unable to digest nourishment. Attempts at gratification only yield a more intense hunger and craving. . . .The hungry ghost in many ways represents a fusion of rage and desire tormented by unfulfilled craving, and insatiably demanding impossible satisfactions that can never be satisfied.''

We can see how we all have a hungry ghost part of us, representing unresolved issues from our past. These wounded parts of ourselves lead to self-defeating behaviors in relationships that in fact block us from receiving the truly healing experience of being loved. In trying to protect ourselves from re-experiencing the trauma abandonment or engulfment or violation, we are, in fact, setting up a re-traumatization of ourselves and denying ourselves that for which we hunger: healthy intimacy.

From my experiences working with couples in the past and some experiences in my own relationships, I will discuss some good examples of how this re-traumatization plays itself out. In order to protect the confidentiality of clients, I have put together different bits and pieces from different couples with whom I've worked.

One couple with whom I worked not too long ago had been together for four years and were having a very hard time communicating with each other. Though they loved each other very deeply, they were feeling more and more distant from each other. One member of the couple was getting very restless and starting to go out and meet other people; not really having dates with other guys, but going out and doing a lot of things that made his partner very afraid and insecure. As we explored the source of the growing distance between them, it became clear there was an early trauma each had that impacted their ability to trust and communicate. There was a hungry ghost part of each of them that was operating in their relationship.

I had them both talk about their families of origin. The partner who was restless (even though he loved his partner) found himself doing a lot of exploring and testing the boundaries of the relationship. He talked about a family where his dad and mom divorced very early and where he had a lot of responsibility to take care of his mother's and sister's emotional needs. He really became a "parentified child." Throughout most of his childhood and young adulthood, he learned to defer his own needs and feelings and, as part of his survival, to focus on what other people needed. The way he really felt loved and acknowledged in his family was by taking care of other people and avoiding his own needs and feelings. His fear with his partner was a fear of *engulfment*, that there really wasn't room in the relationship for him to be both himself and also love and be loved. Ironically, the more self aware and confident he became, the more he pushed away the love that his partner was giving. Emotionally, he really didn't think it was possible to have both intimacy and also a separate identity from the person with whom he was intimate.

His partner had an opposite problem. In his early years his dad had abandoned the family and that was the pivotal experience in his emotional history. For him the core intimacy fear was abandonment so that the more his lover distanced himself and rebelled, the more he got possessive and clamped down. They had gotten into a vicious circle where the one partner who wanted more freedom would test the boundaries, frightening the other partner. The latter became more rigid and more demanding, terrified that the restless partner was going to abandon him; this, in turn, made the restless partner feel more engulfed and he would pull himself away from the relationship. They went around and around like this. Here were two people who loved each other deeply with a long term, satisfying relationship. But they were, in fact, pushing each other away. Emotionally, both were running with fear—like the white elephant—not realizing the threat was past. Like hungry ghosts they could not take in the nourishment of healing love that each offered the other. As they came to recognize the longing for love accompanied by terror of engulfment in one partner, and the terror of abandonment and resultant clinging, controlling behavior in the other partner, it just brought the level of reactivity and fear way down, enabling them to begin to talk about what was happening *as* it was happening. And they could accept each other's love again, without fear.

Another client (disguised here) had a pattern of being sexually attracted to emotionally distant men on whom he projected a quality of strength. He pursued relationships with such men and then was unsatisfied because, in fact, he found out when he got close to them that they were often unable to open up emotionally, intimacy avoidant, and often a little bit self-absorbed. Through working with him, what became clear was that he was really playing out his relationship with the original men in his life. There was a longing to somehow reconnect with a distant father and other distant men in his childhood in the sense of: if I could get that man over there, the one withholding love from me, to love, then I'll really be healed, then I'll really be whole. But, in fact, he was choosing the very person who couldn't give him the love he longed for.

Like hungry ghosts such people cannot get the nourishment they want. Becoming aware of this really allows them to look at what is happening and to explore what they need to do. We all have a hungry ghost part of ourselves that comes up and limits our capacity to love and be loved. But the question to ask now is: since we have really explored the problem, what is the solution? How to heal the fears that cause us to keep running long after the threat has passed? How to get real nourishment to the hungry ghost who is so blinded by fear, rage and desire that he cannot accept or absorb any nourishment?

What do you do once you recognize this part of you that sets up a self-defeating pattern based on your own personal pain? How do you discover true healing? The answer comes again in an image from Buddhism. In each realm of existence—like the realm of the hungry ghosts—the Bodhisattva of compassion appears carrying or holding something that represents healing or liberation from the suffering of that realm. In the realm of the hungry ghosts the Bodhisattva of compassion appears with a bowl of fruit or nourishment representing the nourishment of the Dharma. This is a true, healing nourishment which provides a kind of food that really can penetrate the part of us which can't really accept that very love we want most.

This involves recognizing the part of us that is the hungry ghost, or an even better image—the image of the white elephant. These parts of ourselves about which we're so terrified are not ghoulish, but in fact are very beautiful. We have only been programmed to look at them as ghoulish and terrifying. Healing is really getting to know the hungry ghost part of us and not being afraid. Through this we can recover our capacity to be vulnerable, open ourselves up to loving, being loved and finding a way to tell our truth to ourselves and to each other. When this happens the very pain that seems to be our enemy can become an ally. This hungry ghost quality, this frightened white elephant can actually help us create intimacy with other people we love. In other words, the very things that seem to rob us as gay men of the opportunity for love—our traumas of abandonment, violation or engulfment—can become the way we genuinely open up, become authentic and allow ourselves to experience real intimacy and connection. I see that happening again and again when people who love each other, whether partners or friends, recognize that frightened part of themselves, accept it with compassion and understand the way it blocks communication, trust and intimacy. And then, slowly, the fear loses its power to control us—and our essential good and open loving heart is revealed.

Buddhism is a teaching on true intimacy. In it is a very practical and wonderful method for becoming more free to love and be loved. The Dharma offers a psychology for liberating ourselves from the traumas of our past and the resultant habitual feelings that only compound the trauma while robbing us of the capacity for intimacy with each other. As a psychotherapist, I know that counseling can help to elucidate the issues and assist an individual or couple to face these issues with acceptance and understanding. But therapy is ultimately only like a good friend pointing the way—each person, alone, finds or doesn't find his path.

For anyone who wants to love and be loved, Buddha is offering to you the nourishment of the Dharma. Meditation practice brings us intimacy with ourselves—and in that expanding compassion and non-aggression we find intimacy with others. In the teachings of Buddhism we discover impermanence. As that discovery penetrates, the hardness of fear and control soften and melt—opening our heart and allowing us to live in the vulnerability of the moment. For it is only in the vulnerability of the moment that the intimacy we seek resides. In taking refuge in Buddha, Dharma and Sangha we slowly become released from the preoccupation with the individuality of our own trauma, whether it be abandonment, engulfment, violation or all of the above. What we find is the courage to love openly (even when it is painful), less worried about what we are or are not getting from our lover, friend, family or the human race in general and more concerned about what we are giving.

A traditional Buddhist folk tale from Vietnam provides a simple illustration, metaphor for the difference between heaven and hell. In hell everyone is given an abundance of food and then given chopsticks a yard long. Each person has all the food they need. But because the chopsticks are too long, the food never reaches their mouths. In heaven the image is exactly the same: everyone is given an abundance of food, and chopsticks are also a yard long. But in heaven people use the chopsticks to feed each other.

The Compatibility of Reason and Orgasm in Tibetan Buddhism:

Reflections on Sexual Violence and Homophobia

Jeffrey Hopkins

INTRODUCTION

Much of world culture views reason and sexual pleasure to be antithetical and relegates the pleasure of orgasm to a baser level of the personality incompatible with the true and the good. This has lent intellectual justification to exaggerated attempts by some males to assert control over the "baser" self (1) by identifying women and, by extension, male homosexuals with these "base" passions and (2) by committing violent acts (including sex) against these lowly creatures. They do this to foster the self-delusion that sexual impulses are under the control of their "higher" self. In Tibetan Buddhist systems, however, there are hints of a compatible relationship between reason and orgasmic bliss in that developed practitioners seek to utilize the blissful and powerful mind of orgasm to realize the truth and the all-good ground of consciousness. The practice is based on an experientially founded tenet that the most profound, subtle, and powerful level of consciousness, the mind of clear light, manifests in intense orgasm and that it can be used to realize the truth in an unusually powerful and effective way. The suggestion is that the sense of bifurcation between reason and orgasmic bliss is the result of not appreciating the basic nature of mind.

Tibetan teachings that present a series of related levels of consciousness in which conceptual reasoning and orgasmic bliss are viewed as parts of a continuum contrast with the sense of radical separation that is present in some situations of sexual violence. Many strands of modern society, especially in the United States, are almost pathologically concerned with controlling others' private lives. Why is this? It seems to me that a single, complex person is being divided into radically separate higher and lower selves such that the so-called higher self is exalted in status even to the point of becoming disembodied. This radical division lays the groundwork for projection of the lower self onto others, especially women and male homosexuals, and consequent even brutal attempts at control. The brutality

JEFFREY HOPKINS (Dyke, VA) has practiced Tibetan Buddhism since 1962. He is Professor of Tibetan Studies at the University of Virginia where he has taught since 1973. He has published twenty-two books, the most prominent being *Meditation on Emptiness* and *Emptiness Yoga* and the most recent being *Tibetan Arts of Love*. His next book publication will be *Emptiness in "Mind-Only" Buddhism*.

ranges from outright physical violence to suppression of information about sex and sexual orientation such that our federal government even refuses to make information on sexual orientation available to teenagers who suffer a high rate of suicide due to conflicts related with sexual identity.

It is indeed an estranged society that fears knowledge of the actual practices of its members; the ludicrous perspective that is suggested by this situation is that of the "sodomy delusion," that is to say, if seemingly "straight" men tasted only once the joys of homosexual sex, they would be so enthralled that the halls of heterosexuality would be emptied, rather than a mere ten-percent defection. One gets the sense that the only way that the advocates of silence feel that heterosexual mores can be sustained is through the maintenance of ignorance, a state not of bliss but of pained projection of temptation onto others. Women and male homosexuals are viewed as tempting otherwise decent persons into their lower selves. Consider the fears that many have of gay teachers, who are seen as ready not only to convert but to misuse their students; the fears, however, are ridiculous in the face of the statistics on sexual abuse by teachers, the overwhelming majority being by heterosexual men. It does not take much profundity to surmise that those who favor ignorance about sexual matters have separated themselves from aspects of their own sexual impulses and, like the paranoiac, are pursued by images of libidinous attackers who are actually manifestations of their own minds.

Our acculturation is often so much at odds with our inner selves that we seek somehow to separate from our own inner being. Also, the external demands to identify with the current presentation of what is socially acceptable are so great that the tendency toward separation becomes institutionalized through peer-group fortification such that the attempt to separate oneself from one's own inner being becomes even more encrusted and difficult to penetrate. It is helpful in such situations to be confronted with systems of therapy that undermine the sense of separation from one's own inner self by uncovering the mechanisms of projection. It is also helpful to reflect on systems of structural psychology that place seemingly unassociated and radically other states of mind in a coherent continuum of mind such that the intellectual justifications for projection are undermined. I find one such system in various teachings found in Tibetan Buddhism, which, although by no means a panacea, offers stimulating food for thought.

BACKGROUND

Buddhism began gradually to be introduced to Tibet in the seventh century C.E., more than a thousand years after Shākyamuni Buddha's passing away (*circa* 483 B.C.). The form Buddhism took in Tibet was greatly influenced by the highly developed systemization of the religion that was present in

India through the twelfth century (and even later). The geographic proximity and relatively undeveloped culture of Tibet provided conditions for
extensive transfer of scholastic commentaries and systems of practice,
which came to have great influence throughout a vast region stretching
from Kalmuck Mongolian areas in Europe where the Volga River empties
into the Caspian Sea, Outer and Inner Mongolia, the Buriat Republic of
Siberia, Bhutan, Sikkim, Nepal, and Ladakh. My sources are drawn
primarily, but not exclusively, from one of the most scholastic orders of
Tibetan Buddhism, the Ge-luk-ba[1] sect, founded by the polymath and yogi
Dzong-ka-ba[2] (1357–1419) who was born in the northeastern province of
Tibet called Am-do,[3] included by the occupying Chinese not in the Tibetan
Autonomous Region but in the Ch'ing-hai Province. Dzong-ka-ba and his
followers established a system of education centered in large universities,
eventually in three areas of Tibet but primarily in Lhasa, the capital, which
in some ways was as Rome is for the Catholic Church. For five centuries,
young men (yes, women were, for the most part, excluded from the scholastic culture) came from all of the above-mentioned regions to these large
Tibetan universities to study; until the Communist takeovers, they usually
returned to their own countries after completing their degrees. My presentation will be largely from standard Ge-luk-ba perspectives[4] on the Tantra Vehicle, also called the Vajra Vehicle,[5] one of two basic forms of what
Tibetan tradition accepts as Shākyamuni Buddha's teaching.

THE FUNDAMENTAL INNATE MIND OF CLEAR LIGHT
IN HIGHEST YOGA TANTRA

In this Indo-Tibetan system it is said that during orgasm the mind of clear
light—the basis of all consciousness and the most subtle and powerful form
of consciousness—manifests, albeit only unconsciously, even to the untrained.[6] The *Guhyasamāja Tantra*, a Highest Yoga Tantra that is parallel
in importance to the *Kālachakra Tantra*, divides consciousnesses into the

---

[1] *dge lugs pa.*

[2] *tsong kha pa blo bzang grags pa.*

[3] *a mdo.*

[4] Given the emphasis within the Ge-luk-ba sect not just on separate monastic
universities but even more so on individual colleges and given the general provin-
cialism of the culture, it might seem impossible to speak of "standard" postures
of the sect, but my meaning here points to generally recognizable, or at least representative, explanations.

[5] *rdo rje theg pa, vajrayāna.*

[6] The section on the fundamental innate mind of clear light is adapted from my
"A Tibetan Perspective on the Nature of Spiritual Experience," in *Paths to Liberation*, edited by Robert Buswell and Robert Gimello (Honolulu: U. of Hawaii Press,
1992).

gross, the subtle, and the very subtle.[7] We are all familiar with the grosser levels of mind—the eye consciousness that apprehends colors and shapes, the ear consciousness that apprehends sounds, the nose consciousness that apprehends odors, the tongue consciousness that apprehends tastes, and the body consciousness that apprehends tactile objects. To understand the perspective of this school of Buddhist thought, it is important that these five be considered not just as sensations known by another, separate consciousness, but as five individual consciousnesses that have specific spheres of activity—colors and shapes, sounds, odors, tastes, and tactile objects. These five sense consciousnesses are the grossest level of mind.

More subtle than the five sense consciousnesses but still within the gross level of mind is the usual, conceptual, mental consciousness. In Highest Yoga Tantra, these conceptions are details as of eighty types, divided into three classes. The first group of thirty-three is composed of emotions, feelings, and drives that involve a strong movement of energy[8] to their objects. Included in this group are fear, attachment, hunger, thirst, shame, compassion, acquisitiveness, and jealousy. The second group of forty conceptions involve a medium movement of energy to their objects; among them are joy, amazement, excitement, desiring to embrace, generosity, desiring to kiss, desiring to suck, pride, enthusiasm, vehemence, flirtation, wishing to donate, heroism, deceit, tightness, viciousness, non-gentleness, and crookedness. The third group of seven conceptions involve a weak movement of energy to their objects—forgetfulness, error as in apprehending water in a mirage, catatonia, depression, laziness, doubt, and equal desire and hatred. Although the difference between the first two groups is not obvious (at least to me), it is clear that in the third group the mind is strongly withdrawn; the three represent, on the ordinary level of consciousness, increasingly less dualistic perception.

Either through meditative focusing on sensitive parts of the body or through undergoing uncontrolled processes as in orgasm or in dying,[9] the currents of energy that drive the various levels of gross consciousness are gradually withdrawn, resulting in a series of altered states. First, one has a visual experience of seeing an appearance like a mirage; then, as the withdrawal continues, one successively "sees" an appearance like billowing smoke, followed by an appearance like fireflies within smoke, then an appearance like a sputtering candle[10] when little wax is left, and then an

---

[7]The material on the levels of consciousness is drawn from Lati Rinbochay's and my translation of a text by A-ḡya-yong-dzin (*a kya yongs 'dzin*, alias Yang-jen-ga-way-lo-drö (*dbyangs can dga' ba'i blo gros*); see our *Death, Intermediate State, and Rebirth in Tibetan Buddhism* (London: Rider and Co., 1979; rpt. Ithaca: Snow Lion Publications, 1980).

[8]Literally, wind or air (*rlung, prāṇa*).

[9]The similarity between orgasm and death in terms of seeming self-extinction is frequently noticed in "Western" literature, Shakespeare being the most prominent.

[10]Literally, a butter-lamp.

appearance of a steady candle flame. This series of visions sets the stage for the withdrawal of all conceptual consciousnesses,[11] whereupon a more dramatic phase begins the manifestation of profound levels of consciousness that are at the core of all experience.

The first subtle level of consciousness to manifest is the mind of vivid white appearance. All of the eighty conceptions have ceased, and nothing appears except this slightly dualistic vivid white appearance; one's consciousness itself turns into an omnipresent, huge, vivid white vastness. It is described as like a clear sky filled with moonlight, not the moon shining in empty space but space filled with white light. All conceptuality has ceased, and nothing appears except this slightly dualistic vivid white appearance, which is one's consciousness itself.

When, through further withdrawal of the energy that supports this level of consciousness, it no longer can manifest, a more subtle mind of vivid red or orange appearance (called increase) dawns. One's consciousness itself has turned into this even less dualistic vivid red or orange appearance; nothing else appears. It is compared to a clear sky filled with sunlight, again not the sun shining in the sky but space filled with red or orange light.

One's consciousness remains in this state for a period, and then when this mind loses its support through further withdrawal of the energy that is its foundation, a still more subtle mind of vivid black appearance dawns; it is called "near-attainment" because one is close to manifesting the mind of clear light. One's consciousness itself has turned into this still less dualistic, vivid black appearance; nothing else appears. The mind of black vastness is compared to a moonless, very dark sky just after dusk when no stars are seen. During the first part of this phase of utter blackness, one remains conscious but then, in a second phase, becomes unconscious in thick darkness.

Then, when the mind of black appearance ceases, the three "pollutants"[12] of the white, red/orange, and black appearances have been entirely cleared away, and the mind of clear light dawns. Called the fundamental innate mind of clear light,[13] it is the most subtle, profound, and powerful level of consciousness. It is compared to the sky's own natural cast—without the "pollutions" of moonlight, sunlight, or darkness—which can be seen at dawn before sunrise.

Because the more subtle levels of consciousness are considered to be more powerful and thus more effective in realizing the truth, the systems of Highest Yoga Tantra seek to manifest the mind of clear light by way of

---

[11] The three sets of conceptions correspond to the three subtle minds that appear serially after conceptions cease, but it is not that the three sets of conceptions cease serially; rather, they disappear together, resulting in the gradual dawning of the three subtler levels of mind.

[12] *bslod byed.*

[13] *gnyug ma lhan cig skyes pa'i 'od gsal gyi sems.*

various techniques. One of these methods is blissful orgasm because, according to the psychology of Highest Yoga Tantra, orgasm involves the ceasing of the grosser levels of consciousness and manifestation of the more subtle, as do dying, going to sleep, ending a dream, sneezing, and fainting. The intent in using a blissful, orgasmic mind in the spiritual path is to manifest the most subtle level of consciousness, the mind of clear light, and use its greater power and hence effectiveness to realize the truth of the emptiness of inherent existence. The theory is that the apprehension that phenomena exist inherently or from their own side is the root of suffering because it induces the plethora of counter-productive emotions that produce suffering. In orgasm, phenomena that are over-concretized such that they seem to have their own independent existence melt into the expanse of the reality behind appearances. The pleasure of orgasm is so intense that the mind becomes totally withdrawn and fascinated such that both the usual conceptual mind and the appearances that accompany it melt away, leaving basic reality.

Through consciously experiencing this process, one can realize that ordinary conceptions and appearances are over-concretized. Sex, therefore, can become a practice through which this exaggeration of the status of appearance and mind is identified and subsumed in the source state. The fundamental state—which dawns in conscious orgasm—is not a dimming of the mind into an emotional state that is opposed to the truth, although it is often experienced as such because all of the usual conceptual minds are withdrawn during it. Rather, it is the basis of phenomena—that into which all appearances dissolve and thus the foundation of appearance. It is the reality behind appearances. Our unfamiliarity with it causes its implications to be missed in unconsciousness. Through developing realization of the emptiness of inherent existence by recognizing the inter-relatedness of persons and phenomena and through developing great compassion by recognizing relatedness over the continuum of lifetimes, one can become closer to this state and thereby more capable of appreciating its significance.

By utilizing this subtle level of mind, the power of the wisdom-consciousness realizing the truth is enhanced such that it is more effective in overcoming what prevents liberation from the round of rebirth and all its suffering. Such a wisdom consciousness is also more effective in overcoming what prevents knowledge of others' dispositions and of the techniques that can benefit them and thus serves to further the altruistic goals that are behind the quest for wisdom.

Sexual expression, therefore, can be used as an avenue for exploring the profound nature of consciousness which eventually brings release from craving from the root. Using an ancient example, the process is compared to a worm's being born from moist wood and then eating the wood. In this example (formed at a time when it was assumed that a worm or bug was generated only from wood and heat), the wood is desire; the worm is the blissful consciousness; and the consumption of the wood is the blissful consciousness's destruction of desire through realizing emptiness. As the First Paṇ-chen Lama, Ĺo-sang-chö-ḡyi-gyel-tsen,[14] says:[15]

> A wood-engendered insect is born from wood but consumes it completely. In the same way, a great bliss is generated in dependence on a causal motivation that is the desire of gazing, smiling, holding hands or embracing, or union of the two organs. The wisdom of undifferentiable bliss and emptiness, which is this great bliss generated undifferentiably with a mind cognizing emptiness at the same time, consumes completely the afflictive emotions—desire, ignorance, and so forth.

Through desirous activities such as gazing at a loved one, or smiling, holding hands, embracing, or engaging in sexual union, a pleasurable consciousness is produced; it is used to realize the truth of the emptiness of inherent existence, whereby desire itself is undermined. The pleasurable consciousness is generated simultaneously with a wisdom consciousness, and thus the two are indivisibly fused. Without desire, the involvement in the bliss consciousness would be minimal, and thus Highest Yoga Tantra makes use of the arts of lovemaking to enhance the process.

In Ge-luk-ba texts, the undifferentiability of bliss and realization of emptiness is explained conceptually in terms of subject and object even though it is beyond all dualism. The bliss consciousness is the subject that realizes emptiness as its object. The reason for making this distinction is to emphasize that the bliss consciousness is used to realize the profound nature of reality, the emptiness of inherent existence—the emptiness of over-concretization—and thus is not a mere unconscious mind of orgasm. The aim of the sexual yoga is, therefore, not mere repetition of an attractive state but revelation of the basic reality underlying appearances. Nevertheless, to experience the union of bliss and emptiness, sexual pleasure has to be developed in fullness, and to do this it is necessary to implement techniques for avoiding premature ejaculation and extending the experience of pleasure; otherwise, a valuable opportunity is lost in the ephemerality of orgasm. The twentieth century Tibetan intellectual, Gedün Chöpel,[16] who traveled to India and wrote his own *Treatise on Passion*[17] based on the *Kāma Sūtra*, advocates the usage of sexual pleasure to open oneself to the profound, fundamental state at the core of all consciousness. As he says:

---

[14]*blo bzang chos kyi rgyal mtshan.*

[15]*Presentation of the General Teaching and the Four Tantra Sets*, Collected Works, vol. IV, 17b.5–18a.1.

[16]*dge 'dun chos 'phel*; 1905–1951.

[17]See Gedün Chöpel, *Tibetan Arts of Passion*, translated and introduced by Jeffrey Hopkins (Ithaca: Snow Lion Publications, 1992), from which I have drawn some of the material in this article.

The small child of intelligence swoons in the deep sphere of passion.
The busy mind falls into the hole of a worm.
By drawing the imaginations of attachment downwards
Beings should observe the suchness of pleasure.

Wishing to mix in the ocean of the bliss of the peaceful expanse
This wave of magician's illusions separated off
By perceiving the non-dual as dual, subject and object,
Does one not feel the movement and igniting of the coalesced!

Phenomena that are over-concretized such that they seem to have their own independent existence are burnt away in the expanse of the reality behind appearances:

If one really considers the fact that the one billion worlds of this world system
Are suddenly swallowed into a gigantic asteroid devoid of perception or feeling,
One understands that the realm of great bliss
Is that in which all appearances dissolve.

Gedün Chöpel also speaks of deities that are present in the body during sex:

> At the time of pleasure the god and goddess giving rise to bliss actually dwell in the bodies of the male and the female. Therefore, it is said that what would be obstacles to one's life if done [under usual circumstances] are conquered, and power, brilliance, and youth blaze forth. The perception of ugliness and dirtiness is stopped, and one is freed from conceptions of fear and shame. The deeds of body, speech, and mind become pure, and it is said that one arrives in a place of extreme pleasure.

The question is *how* to sustain sexual pleasure so that its spiritual value is not lost and the experience turns into an unconscious dimming of mind. He proposes forgoing cultural prohibitions so that sexual pleasure can be deepened and extended such that it penetrates the entire physical structure. With lyric beauty he advises that inhibitions be cast aside:

> Smear honey on each other and taste.
> Or taste the natural fluids.
> Suck the slender and bulbous tube.
> Intoxicated and confusing the memory, do everything.

As a technique to lengthen the experience of sexual pleasure, he suggests pausing in the midst of intense feeling and letting the feeling of bliss pervade the body:

> If one does not know the techniques of holding and spreading the bliss that has arrived at the tip of the jewel [i.e., the head of the phallus], immediately upon seeing it for a moment it fades and disappears, like picking up a snowflake in the hand. Therefore when, upon churning about, bliss is generated, cease movement, and again and again spread [the sense of bliss throughout the body]. Then, by again doing it with the former methods, bliss will be sustained for a long time.

Through techniques of strengthening and lengthening sexual pleasure, both mind and body become bathed in bliss, opening the possibility of realizing the nature of the fundamental state.

The practice of sexual yoga is, to my knowledge, always explained in terms of heterosexual sex, in which a consort of the opposite sex[18] is used. The reason given concerns the structure of channels or nerves in the respective sexual organs, and thus insertion refers not just to insertion in the vagina but to contact with special nerve centers in the vagina that are lacking in the anus. Thus, colorful drawings of male and female deities in sexual union decorate the walls of temples—not those of same-sex couples. However, the type of sexual yoga that Gedün Chöpel describes has its foundations in the doctrine—found in the Old Translation School of Ñyingma[19]—that the blissful mind of clear light pervades all experience and is accessible within any state. This is the theoretical underpinning of his advice to extend the intense state of sexual bliss in order to explore the fundamental state of bliss. It seems to me that this *can* be done with same-sex or other-sex partners and *should* be done with whatever type is more evocative of intense feeling on all levels.

The ultimate goal is not just to experience this basal state into which phenomena have dissolved but also to perceive all the various phenomena of the world *within* the mind of clear light, without exaggerating their status into being independent. One is seeking to perceive interdependence without an overlay of divisive concretization. Emptiness does not negate phenomena; it negates only the exaggerated status of inherent existence and hence is compatible with love and compassion, which are enhanced through recognizing the connectedness of persons and of other phenomena. It is said that, with such a perspective, truly effective altruism is possible since the faculty of judgment is not clouded by afflictive emotions such as anger. The final state is not abstracted away from phenomena but is an appreciation of connectedness and embodiment. All phenomena are seen as manifestations of the mind of clear light, still having individuality but not exaggerated into being autonomous. Viewed in this perspective, the mind of orgasm as experienced in this type of sexual yoga is a means of linking

---

[18]The female is called "mother" (*yum*), and the male is called "father" (*yab*). The terms are rich with suggestions (never made explicit in the tradition) of copulating with one's parent; it would seem that for heterosexuals this would be the parent of the opposite sex, and for homosexuals, with the parent of the same sex.

[19]*rnying ma.*

to others, promoting intimacy and relationality, and is not an abstraction of oneself away from others into an auto-hypnotic withdrawal although it might seem so at first.

To summarize: The innermost level of consciousness is the fundamental innate mind of clear light, which is identified as the eighth in a series of increasingly subtle experiences that occur frequently but unconsciously in ordinary life. These deeper levels of mind manifest during the process of dying, going to sleep, ending a dream, fainting, sneezing, and orgasm in forward order:

1 mirage
2 smoke
3 fireflies
4 flame of a lamp
5 vivid white mind-sky
6 vivid red or orange mind-sky
7 vivid black mind-sky
8 clear light.

These eight also manifest in reverse order when taking rebirth, waking, starting to dream, ending a fainting spell, ending a sneeze, and ending orgasm:

1 clear light
2 vivid black mind-sky
3 vivid red or orange mind-sky
4 vivid white mind-sky
5 flame of a lamp
6 fireflies
7 smoke
8 mirage.

These states of increasing subtlety during death, orgasm, going to sleep, ending a dream, and so forth and of increasing grossness during rebirth, post-orgasm, awakening, beginning a dream, and so forth indicate levels of mind on which every conscious moment is built. From the perspective of this system of psychology, we spend our lives in the midst of thousands of small deaths and rebirths.

Conceptual over-concretization of objects prevents realization of the most profound and ecstatic state by generating attachment to superficial, unreal exaggerations. This attachment, in turn, fosters an inability to sustain the basic, blissful state that undermines emotionally imbedded self-deceptions. The suggestion is that ordinary conscious life is concerned with only the gross or superficial, without heed of more subtle states that are the foundation of both consciousness and appearance. We know neither the origin of consciousness nor the basis into which it returns.

It is said that ordinary beings are so identified with superficial states that the transition to the deeper involves even fear of annihilation; when the deeper states begin to manifest and the superficial levels collapse, we panic, fearing that we will be wiped out and, due to this fear, swoon unconsciously. As the late eighteenth- and early nineteenth-century Mongolian scholar Ngak-wang-kay-drup[20] says in his *Presentation of Death, Intermediate State, and Rebirth,*[21] at the time of the clear light of death ordinary beings generate the fright that they will be annihilated.[22] Similarly, the emergence of the foundational state in orgasm is so drastically different from ordinary consciousness that it is usually experienced as a dimming of the mind.

The fact that the mind of clear light—which is so awesome when it newly manifests—is one's own final nature suggests that the otherness and fear associated with its manifestation are not part of *its* nature but are due to the shallowness of untrained beings. The strangeness of our own nature is a function of misconception, specifically our mistaken sense that what are actually distortions of mind subsist in the nature of mind. We identify with these distortions such that when basic consciousness starts to manifest either in orgasm or in dying, we are unable to remain with the experience. The more we identify with distorted attitudes, the greater the fear of the foundational state, which to those who are trained has within it a source of sustenance beyond the dualism of subject and object. The systems of religious education found in the Tibetan cultural region can be viewed as aimed at overcoming this fear of one's most basic nature.

Reason and Orgasm

Although all consciousnesses arise from and return to the mind of clear light, the conceptualization that these grosser levels have their own independent existence causes these states to be alienated from their own source. In this Buddhist system, reason is a form of consciousness that in ordinary life is estranged from its own nature. Far from further fortifying the seeming separateness of reason through theorizing that such estrangement is a virtue, practitioners are called to try to perceive the inner nature of all states

---

[20]*ngag dbang mkhas grub*; 1779–1838. Also known as *kyai rdo mkhan po.*

[21]*skye shi bar do'i rnam bzhag,* Collected Works (Leh: S. Tashigangpa, 1973), Vol. 1, 466.2. Cited in Lati Rinbochay and Jeffrey Hopkins, *Death, Intermediate State, and Rebirth in Tibetan Buddhism* (London: Rider, 1979), 47.

[22]The fear-inspiring aspect of its manifestation accords with the often described awesomeness and sense of otherness that much of world culture associates with types of profound religious experience.

of mind, harmonious with the ground-state that can, through yogic training, be experienced consciously in orgasm. Not only the doctrines of structural psychology in Tibetan Buddhism but also the paintings and statues of male and female in sexual union and of ithyphallic males that abound in Tibetan temples convey the message that the state of the all-good is harmonious with orgasm.

From this point of view, reason is gross in relation to orgasmic bliss, and when reason is considered a disembodied phenomenon, it is arrogant in its sense of distance from its own source-state. Under such circumstances the continuity between orgasm and conceptual consciousnesses such as reason is not being realized. It is my contention that this Indo-Tibetan perspective of continuity could help to alleviate the sense of loathing that some males experience with respect to the power that sexual pleasure has over them, when the surface personality is collapsed in orgasm and the panic of annihilation sets in. Fearing the destruction of the seemingly controlled self, they project their sexual impulses onto others, especially women and gay men—because they seem to wallow in sex and tempt them into their lower selves. Male homosexuals are threatening also because they are seen as males who approach sex, not from an overweening need for control but out of intimacy. Little do these people know that homophobic attitudes that block intimacy are also rampant among gays. As all of us, gay and non-gay, have seen, there is a strong tendency in some males to hate the sexual recipient, whether this be a woman or a man, as the source of their degeneration into an uncontrollable state. They attempt to assert control and dominion over the collapse and annihilation of their usual ego through hating the source of their sexual desire which they project onto others—these others being persons who are attracted to males. They seek domination both of their own sexual craving and also of the process of dissolution—in orgasm—of what is actually their superficial self. Panicking at their own disappearance in orgasm, they look for someone else to blame and to control even in brutal ways in order to distance themselves from their own craving for orgasm. At once attracted to and repelled by their own inner nature, they lash out in distorted disgust, attempting to claim a privileged position over a process that does indeed undermine their identification with superficial states. What is actually an exaggeration of a superficial state tries to pretend control over its profound source.

It seems to me that gay-bashing often arises from the tension of such persons' being faced (sometimes in fact but mostly in their imagination) with males who have not adopted this ridiculous projection. The Indo-Tibetan perspective that conceptual thought and orgasmic bliss have the same inner nature and that, in fact, the state of orgasmic bliss is more subtle than conceptual thought might help to undermine the warped need to attack homosexuals out of fear that they have not assumed the ''proper'' male perspective of dominance.

I do not mean to suggest that in these Indo-Tibetan systems reason is discarded, for it is highly valued as a means to open oneself to greater compassion and increased wisdom and, thereby, to break down the barriers to the conscious manifestation of the mind of clear light. However, the usefulness of reason becomes impossible when it exaggerates its own status into that of an independent, disembodied faculty, a process which promotes projection of other aspects of the personality onto others. Once reason is separated out as an autonomous entity and once persons identify mainly with this disembodied faculty, it is all too easy to view states and impulses that are actually part and parcel of one's own mind as threateningly impinging from the outside. Fear and rejection of sexuality lead to projection of sexuality onto women and homosexuals and result in fear, rejection, and abuse of women and homosexuals. Conversely, the elevation, exaltation, glorification, and deification of women (though seldom of homosexuals) has the same root in denial of sexual passion.

The perspective of Tibetan systems may be useful in counteracting this tendency of self-created separation, for it presents reason as compatible with orgasmic bliss not only because the mind of clear light that manifests in orgasm is the inner nature of all consciousnesses but also because reason can reveal the conflict between appearance and reality and a mind of orgasm can realize this same truth with even more impact. In this way, the veil of the exaggerated concreteness that is superimposed on phenomena is lifted, and the all-good ground of consciousness can manifest. This system of spiritual development that places such a high value on orgasm, viewed as harmonious with reason, beckons us to recognize the inner continuity of these seemingly separate states, thereby helping to undermine the pernicious processes of projection.

Let me be clear that I am not holding Tibetan culture up as a problemless model, a Shangri-La of sexual and social harmony and tolerance. Rather, I am suggesting that the model of consciousness found in Tibetan systems may be helpful in alleviating the estrangement of levels of the personality. Such a revolution in perspective requires recognition of vulnerability and thus is not easy. Perhaps, reflection on this Tibetan presentation of the connection between conceptual, reasoned levels of consciousness and the powerful state of orgasm may be useful for *both* non-homosexuals and homosexuals since the intellectual justifications that support homophobia are not limited to those who identify themselves as heterosexual.

A Brief Practice of the Bodhisattva Malibubarbi*

Christian Huygen

The bodhisattva Malibubarbi embodies and manifests the glamour principle for the benefit of sentient beings. Without any sense of attachment or grasping, she revels in the illusory surface appearance of the world. To realize this principle within yourself, for the good of all sentient beings, study and practice the following with exertion and enthusiasm.

First, assemble many offerings, whatever you can afford. Some persons might assume that nonfattening offerings would be preferable, but in the space of panoramic nondualistic awareness, the distinction between fattening and nonfattening is not made.

The visualization should be constructed as follows: In the sky in front of you appears a slowly revolving glitter ball the size of a mustard seed. This is your mind. Rays of light emanate from the glitterball in all directions, making offerings to the Buddhas of the ten directions and three times; these are returned with the intensity of halogen spotlights.

Instantly the glitterball transforms into the form of Malibubarbi. She appears in the space in front of you, radiant and beautiful, but translucent, like a rainbow or an image in a mirror. She is pink, has one head, one face, two arms and two legs, and stands upright on an eightfold lotus comprised of catwalks and runways which fill the whole of space. Her halo is brilliant, like the flashbulbs of ten thousand paparazzi going off all at once. Her gown is covered with 3,847 tiny mirror sequins, all of which should be clearly visualized. (The iconography of the mirror is a dzogchen aspect of Malibubarbi's manifestation and it would not be appropriate to explain its significance here.)

---

*In Tibetan practice, it is common for sadhanas to be constructed around a visualization of the deity who represents the particular quality or qualities the meditator is attempting to concentrate upon or invoke in his or her consciousness. Often this is a Buddha of a particular color, perhaps holding certain ritual objects or positioned in a specific way, all of which represents a particular quality or attribute. In this brilliant parody Christian Huygen substitutes a doll for the deity to invoke the quality of glamour. Though it might at first glance seem comic, a deeper message is apparent in that with true mindfulness we should attempt to bring the same attention as a sadhana or union with the deity to all of our actions in daily life, including our vanity or attempt to look and be beautiful. Call it drag mindfulness or the mindful cruiser!—*Trebor*

CHRISTIAN HUYGEN (Jigme Thutop) (New York City) was born in 1964 and has been a student in the Nyingma lineage of Sogyal Rinpoche for the past five years. If he could take only one awareness-being with him to a desert island, it would be Green Tara. The practice he wishes he was ready for is chō.

Before Malibubarbi are gathered you and all sentient beings. Like a sea of grass bending in the wind, you all make prostrations to Malibubarbi.

Malibubarbi is very pleased with your offerings. She smiles at you with great kindness and compassion; you should consider that you and Malibubarbi have a sisterly warmth of feeling toward each other, like that between the contestants in a beauty pageant somewhere in the Midwest. Malibubarbi presents you with a stunning diamond tiara. Bow your head and recite the seven-limbed offering.

Malibubarbi places the tiara upon your head. You should clearly visualize light rays entering your fontanelle and also shining throughout the ten directions and six realms, utterly washing away all neurotic clinging and negative self-images everywhere. The moment for the empowerment has arrived. Now Malibubarbi speaks your name, and then says these three words: *"You look fabulous."*

What follows is very important. At the moment when she says "you," all of your bodily misconduct and negative karma becomes the occasion of tremendous physical beauty and positive karma, like a small mole which only makes a face more enchanting. At the word "look," your speech center is purified, and any unbecoming acts of speech you may have committed or thought of committing are cleansed and purified. You think of only nice things to say about everyone you know. Finally, at "fabulous," Malibubarbi's deepest and most profound empowerment enters your heart-mind, utterly transforming it. You no longer need to fret over whether or not this article of clothing goes with that. Your neuroses and passions are all completely dissolved into the play of glamour and fabulosity which fills the vastness of space.

At this stage in the sadhana you should make many auspicious supplications to Malibubarbi, praying that all beings may be touched by emanations of her beauty, and that supercute outfits in vast arrays rain down upon all sentient beings. Because of Malibubarbi's blessing, beings everywhere are able to completely enjoy these miraculous offerings without any sense of attachment whatsoever. They delight in the prismatic self-perfecting display of whatever arises, without any aesthetic judgments or obstacles or grasping.

Finally, you should recite the mantra of Malibubarbi as much as possible. The mantra is her name itself: "malibubarbi, malibubarbi, malibubarbi." While reciting the mantra you should bear in mind that you are not requesting that she come from some place far away to the place where you are, but rather that you are invoking a principle of inherent and ubiquitous beauty that is already fully manifest in the present moment and in your own mindstream.

Malibubarbi returns to her supreme position, standing with effortless poise in the center of her mandala of catwalks and runways. The eight-petalled lotus upon which the entire structure stands begins to fold inward upon itself, and then the entire visualization dissolves into tremendous rays of light which touch all beings and permit them all to realize and manifest their own unique inner beauty. These light rays dissolve inseparably into you.

At the end of the practice session you should dedicate the merit of this practice to the great enlightenment. Remain in a state of spacious, non-dualistic awareness, in which all sounds are beautiful, all visions are beautiful, and all mental experiences are beautiful—whether they're pretty or not.

This completes the description of the brief practice of Malibubarbi. May those who hear and practice it attain absolute liberation in the privacy of their homes in just minutes a day.

Your inexhaustible beauty surrounds me like space
yet regularly eludes my homely mind.
You patiently let me play dressup
in red and saffron robes.
May sentient beings heed the dharma's beauty tips for heart and mind.

Grateful acknowledgment is made to Mark Nomadiou, Bill Cassidy, Cathy Kennedy, and Susan Noland.

The Dalai Lama and Gay Love

Dennis Conkin

In January 1997, Steve Peskind, a gay San Francisco Buddhist leader set in motion a chain of events of truly international proportion when he called on Bhikku Tenzin Gyatso, His Holiness the Dalai Lama, the world-revered spiritual teacher of millions of Buddhists, to clarify his recent contradictory statements about homosexuality.

Peskind asked for the clarification in a statement published in the January 1997 *Gay Buddhist Fellowship Newsletter* six months before the 1989 Nobel Laureate and exiled Tibetan Buddhist political and religious figure was scheduled to arrive in San Francisco in June, to attend "Peacemaking: The Power of Non-Violence," a three-day conference at the Bill Graham Civic Auditorium sponsored by the Tibet House.

Co-sponsored by the California Institute of Integral Studies, the conference included speakers such as Nobel Laureate and East Timorese human rights activist José Ramos Horta, and author Alice Walker and drew an estimated 1,500 social advocates, inner city youth, religious contemplatives, and others for plenary sessions, dialogue, and violence prevention skills development workshops.

"Regarding homosexuality, we know first hand that the Dalai Lama has been personally supportive of sexual relations that include love and mutual consent between homosexual men and homosexual women. He has stressed kindness, non-harm and discernment in all sexual relations," Peskind said in the statement.

Peskind pointed out that when the religious leader was asked his position on homosexual sexual activity in a 1994 *Out* Magazine interview with openly gay Buddhist writer Scott Hunt, questions about the topic caused "noticeable discomfort" for both the Dalai Lama's translator and assistant.

"Blow here," the Dalai Lama initially said, pointing to his mouth and then to his groin "is wrong."

But according to Hunt's comments in the *Out* interview, the Dalai Lama then modified his initial response after some thought.

"If someone comes to me and asks whether it is OK or not, I will first ask if you have some religious vows to uphold. Then my next question is what is your companion's opinion?

"If you both agree"—he laughed heartily—"then I would think I would say, if two males or two females voluntarily agree to have mutual satisfac-

DENNIS CONKIN (San Francisco) is a gay activist and assistant editor of San Francisco's weekly gay newspaper, *Bay Area Reporter*. He practices within the Nyingma Buddhist tradition. This is a revised version of articles he wrote for that same paper in January and June 1997.

351

tion without further implication of harming others, then it is OK," the Dalai Lama said, according to the *Out* interview.

But in two recently published books, including *Beyond Dogma* (North Atlantic Press, Berkeley, 1996), the religious leader seems to indicate that sexual relations between two men or two women is considered sexual misconduct.

After prefacing his remarks to say that Buddhists considered "organs, time, and place" when describing sexual misconduct, the Dalai Lama went on to define "inappropriate parts" of the body during sexual relations.

"The inappropriate parts of the body are the mouth and the anus, and sexual intercourse involving those parts of the body, whether with a man or woman, is considered sexual misconduct. Masturbation as well."

After giving other examples of sexual misconduct, the Dalai Lama went on to say that homosexual sexual orientation "is not improper" in itself.

"What is improper is the use of organs already defined as inappropriate for sexual contact. Is this clear?"

Not really, said Steve Peskind, coordinator of the Buddhist AIDS Project. He pointed out that he's not seeking validation or official permission from the Buddhist religious leader to be gay or to have gay sex.

"Many people, including gay people, come to Buddhism as a refuge from the sexual proscriptions of fundamentalist religions. Unfortunately, these comments by the Dalai Lama encourage external and internal homophobia and the oppression of homosexual behavior," Peskind said in the *Gay Buddhist Fellowship Newsletter*.

"Many who regard this 'simple Buddhist monk,' as he refers to himself, very highly, are confused and distressed by the inconsistency of his statements and their worldwide ramifications," he said.

With a readership of 600, the GBF newsletter serves as a kind of lifeline, primarily for U.S.-based gay Buddhist practitioners—from Castro clones to readers practicing in prison around the country, as well as isolated practitioners surviving in fiercely anti-gay political climates in Malaysia, Nepal and mainland China.

As with other traditions, homosexuality is a controversial topic in many Buddhist sects. While there are a number of openly gay and lesbian Western Buddhist teachers, they are usually found in non-Tibetan lineages, such as in Japanese and Korean Zen traditions, although some can be found in Tibetan practice lines—including ordained and celibate—as well as non-celibate lamas and yogis.

Following the publication of Peskind's letter, San Francisco lesbian and gay religious, political and anti-violence leaders joined in the call for the religious leader to clarify his comments.

"In light of his contradictory comments and his upcoming visit to San Francisco, I think a clarification is called for," said Supervisor Tom Ammiano.

Hate/violence experts echoed Peskind's concern and said that institutional homophobia in religious and other social groups is more dangerous than any other form.

"It's very powerful psychologically for a gay man or lesbian to have someone say that who you are is not acceptable. It creates an atmosphere of permission for violent acts—against oneself or others," said Jill Tregor, director of Intergroup Clearinghouse, a local hate/violence reduction group.

"Statistics show that pronouncements against gays and lesbians do translate out into violence," Tregor said.

Buddhist scholars and human rights activists also expressed concern about the impact of the controversy.

Jeffrey Hopkins, the openly gay long-time University of Virginia Tibetan Buddhist scholar, served as the primary translator for the Dalai Lama from 1979–1989.

Hopkins said that the Dalai Lama's opinion and counsel are not religious or theological edicts, that his personal views may be expressed "in a more casual context."

"I'm sure he's not homophobic," Hopkins said. "And he doesn't have the authority to make broad edicts. He's not like a Pope in that respect," Hopkins added.

A meeting with Peskind and six other lesbians and gay Buddhists, human rights activitists and clergy was arranged for June 11, 1997.

But, at a press conference a day earlier, the Dalai Lama reiterated his views.

"From a Buddhist point of view," lesbian and gay sex "is generally considered sexual misconduct," he said. However such proscriptions are for members of the Buddhist faith and from "society's viewpoint" homosexual sexual relations can be of "mutual benefit, enjoyable and harmless."

After reiterating the same position about Buddhist sexual proscriptions that he did in his books, the Dalai Lama also noted at the press conference that he had previously been asked his views on gay marriage.

Such social sanction of gay relationships "has to be judged in the context of the society itself and the laws and social norms," he said.

The religious leader also said that he did not have the authority to change the religious strictures but said that he would like to consult with other Buddhist leaders about their views on the issue.

The following day, the Dalai Lama met with Peskind, International Gay and Lesbian Human Rights Commission co-chair Tinku Ali Ishtiaq, Buddhist Peace Fellowship activist and Claremont Graduate School professor Lourdes Arguelles, and José Ignacio Cabezón, a gay Buddhist scholar and professor at Iliff School of Theology in Denver.

Also participating were the Ven. K. T. Shedrup Gyatso, a Western fully ordained and openly gay celibate Tibetan Buddhist monk, Eva Herzer, the president of International Committee of Lawyers For Tibet, and Rabbi Yoel Kahn, former Rabbi of Sha'ar Zahav, Reform synagogue.

The meeting was described as "warm and relaxed," and the Dalai Lama candidly acknowledged that he didn't know when or where the Buddha gave these teachings or proscriptions.

Tibetan Buddhist practitioner Scott Hunt said that that acknowledgment was significant and cast the validity of the strictures into "serious doubt," and that being unable to substantiate their benefits is engaging in "dogmatic repetition."

The religious leader also expressed interest in current scientific research on sexual orientation but told the activists that they would have a harder time changing Buddhist scripture than advocating for their human rights.

The Dalai Lama noted that no one can be disqualified from being a Buddhist on the basis of violating any of the precepts, including killing. But, says Peskind, "he did not clarify during this meeting how gay sex as an expression of emotional intimacy, or moderate recreational sex, or gay tantric sex, in any way impedes the path to full awakening, freedom and peace of heart."

The next five paragraphs are taken from the unofficial minutes of the meeting between the Dalai Lama and the gay/lesbian leaders. Statements in quotes represent the Dalai Lama's words.

From a societal and social perspective, His Holiness said, "It is wrong for society to reject people on the basis of their sexual orientation." He recognized that such rejection causes human suffering. He stated that "your movement to gain full human rights is reasonable and logical." There is "no harm in mutually agreeable sexual acts" [speaking of non-Buddhist members of society] and "it is wrong for anyone to look down on people," he added. He further stated that he is opposed to discrimination based on sexual orientation and that Buddhist principles support the struggle of all people for equal treatment and full human rights . . .

His Holiness pointed out that Buddhist precepts take into account the time, culture and society in which they originate. For example, monks wear saffron because at the time it was conventional in India for poor people to wear saffron. Similarly, having sex with a professional prostitute at the time the precepts were formulated was acceptable and is therefore not sexual misconduct unless a third party pays for it. There is therefore, he said, "a possibility of understanding these precepts in the context of time, culture and society. If homosexuality is part of accepted norms, it is possible that it would be acceptable [in Buddhism]. However, no single person or teacher can redefine precepts. I [the Dalai Lama] do not have the authority to redefine these precepts, since no one can make a unilateral decision or issue a decree. Such a redefinition can only come out of sangha discussions within the various Buddhist traditions. It is not unprecedented in the history of Buddhism to redefine issues, but it has to be done on a collective level,'' His Holiness said. He also added that it would be helpful to do more research on the genesis of these sexual precepts . . .

In response to a question by Steve Peskind, co-founder of the Buddhist Aids Project, His Holiness stated that the proscribed sexual activities, for a Buddhist practitioner, constitute misconduct but that a person committing such misconduct can still be a Buddhist. Sexual misconduct is only one of 10 negative activities and a Buddhist practitioner should strive to increasingly avoid these negative activities. He also added that it is better for a Buddhist practitioner to engage in proscribed sexual activities, if suppression of such desires would have more negative consequences, such as aggression or violence due to frustration. Thus, he said, ''it is always important to look to the context of a proscribed activity.''

José Ignacio Cabezón, professor of theology at the Iliff School of Theology and a practicing Buddhist, stated that it seemed unfair that heterosexual (vaginal) sex is condoned while homosexual sex is not. If the purpose of the rules is to decrease all sexual activity, a sexual ethic should be developed to that effect. Professor Cabezón cited Buddhist scriptures which state that a man may have sex with his wife no more than five consecutive times. If the purpose of the proscriptions is to reduce sexual activity, he asked, how does it make sense to allow a man to have sex with his wife up to five times a night while saying that it is sexual misconduct for a man to have sex with another man even once in his lifetime. His Holiness roared with laughter and responded, ''you have a point there!'' He reiterated that the goal for Buddhist practitioners should be to reduce desire, including sexual desire. He stated that for monks any sexual emission is improper. He suggested that one way of looking at these sexual proscriptions is to recognize that the purpose of sexuality, as seen in India at the time, was reproduction . . .

The Dalai Lama closed the meeting by reiterating his support for human rights for all people and by stating that Buddhist principles support the logical and reasonable claims of gay and lesbian people for equal human rights.

As Scott Hunt points out, taking exception to the Dalai Lama's views is neither heresy nor disrespectful. It is the practitioner's responsibility to probe the validity of dogmatic views. The Buddha himself in his statement to the Kalamas made this clear: ''Do not be led by reports or tradition or hearsay. Be not led by the authority of religious texts, nor by mere logic or inference, nor by considering appearances, nor by the delight in speculative opinions, nor by seeming possibilities, nor by the idea 'This is our teacher.' But when you know for yourselves that certain things are unwholesome and wrong and bad, then give them up.''

Winston Leyland, publisher of Gay Sunshine Press and the present anthology, had the following reaction to the San Francisco meeting: "I have the greatest respect and admiration for H.H. the Dalai Lama. Time after time over the past forty years he has shown himself to be a spiritual leader of great depth and insight. But the traditional teachings ('sexual misconduct') to which he refers are nothing more than homophobic reactions within Buddhist cultures of different historical periods, as the Dalai Lama himself obliquely admits by advocating building a consensus for change. But, on one level at least, that consensus already exists. Several 20th century Tibetan spiritual teachers apparently ignored the 'sexual misconduct' theology. H.H. Dudjom Rinpoche (1904–1987), perhaps the greatest Tibetan spiritual master of the century, a great terton (discoverer of hidden teachings), a Dzogchen adept, and head of the Nyingma lineage, was totally gay friendly and accepting of gay, sexual relationships, not seeing them in terms of 'sexual misconduct' (see the John Giorno interview elsewhere in this volume). In 1994 Khandro Rinpoche, head of the Kagyu Nunnery in Sikkim, a lineage holder in the Nyingma/Kagyu traditions and a very high lama, when asked about gay love by Buddhist practitioners during her visit to San Francisco, said: 'Homosexuality is nothing different, nothing new. [It] was there a long time ago—in Tibet, in the East, in the West, everywhere. . . . If you really love another man as a man, no problem. One can grow spiritually through homosexual relations.'

"The Dalai Lama has reiterated his support for equal human rights for gay and lesbian people (see above), for which he should be praised, lauded and thanked. But surely 'equal rights' also means the free use of our bodies in sexual union with our lovers and partners. The credo that gay people can only make love licitly when we do so to avoid otherwise committing violence is a negative, life-denying theology and one which gay and lesbian practitioners absolutely cannot accept. The Tibetan Buddhist theology of sexuality is obviously in need of a major overhauling, with the homophobic 'barnacle' of 'gay lovemaking = sexual misconduct' being jettisoned. It is not the ultimate responsibility of gay people to convince Tibetan, Zen or Theravada monks or lay persons that homophobia (which infuses the 'sexual misconduct' theology) is still rampant in some Buddhist sanghas. Rather, heterosexual or celibate Buddhists through meditation, Dzogchen and other spiritual practices (as well as by initiating humble dialogue with gay Buddhists) have the responsibility themselves to acknowledge that such homophobia is harmful to considerable numbers of Dharma practitioners, and to see that it is eradicated within their own communities, as well as acknowledging the beauty of gay love.

"In the meantime gay Buddhist practitioners of all traditions should continue on their spiritual paths and in their sexual relationships with inward serenity. We need no formal permission from any outside authority to be ourselves, a truth which the Dalai Lama himself fully acknowledges."

V

GAY FICTION ON BUDDHIST THEMES

Scene from the *Chigo Kannon engi* scroll, early 14th century, probably illustrating the moment when the older monk agrees to take the youth home with him. There is something in the slant of the monk's head and the look on his face which suggests his surprise and delight that the youth has asked him for refuge.—*M.C.*

Reproduced with permission of the Kosetsu Museum of Art, Kobe, Japan.

The Story of Kannon's Manifestation as a Youth
[Chigo Kannon Engi]

Anonymous, Early 14th Century

Translated by Margaret H. Childs

The ostensible point of *Chigo Kannon Engi* is to explain the origin of the 11-faced Kannon enshrined in a subtemple of Kōfukuji in Nara. Another facet of the story is an assertion of the reliability of this deity, which the protagonist briefly doubts. Most interesting, however, is the fact that the tale shows a Buddhist deity facilitating a love affair for a lonely monk, who, insofar as he is associated with the Tendai school, should have been committed to upholding the precepts which strictly require celibacy. *Chigo Kannon Engi* and other literary sources reveal, however, that in medieval Japan there was deep ambivalence among monks regarding the applicability of the precept that forbade all sexual activity to intimate relations between men.

A beautifully illustrated version of the tale has been published in Nihon Emaki Taisei, vol. 24, Chūokōronsha, 1979.

Long ago near Hasedera in Yamato Province[1] there was a revered monk. In his meditative practices he never rested from striving to attain ultimate understanding of the universe through his own body. In seeking perfect Buddhahood through the five stages he had for many years enjoyed the support of the Buddha in his practices and had accumulated religious merit. He was now over sixty years old. However, he had no disciple to serve him intimately, to carry on the services in honor of the Buddhist law, or to pray for his salvation in the world to come. Lamenting the paucity of his store of karma, he undertook to make a monthly pilgrimage to the deity Kannon of Hasedera temple for three years.

"Please grant me a disciple who will serve me on intimate terms and who will follow in my place after my death," he prayed. Though he fulfilled his

MARGARET H. CHILDS (Ann Arbor, MI) was born in 1951 and received her Ph.D. from the University of Pennsylvania in 1983. She has written *Rethinking Sorrow: Revelatory Tales of Late Medieval Japan* (1991). She currently teaches in the Department of Asian Languages and Cultures at the University of Michigan. "The Story of Kannon's Manifestation as a Youth" appeared in *Partings at Dawn: An Anthology of Japanese Gay Literature* (San Francisco: Gay Sunshine Press, 1996).

[1]Hasedera is located in Nara prefecture, Sakurai City. It belongs to the Shingon school of Buddhism. The eleven-faced Kannon enshrined there was a popular object of devotion during the Heian period.

three-year vow, he received no answer to his prayer. Despite his resentment, he renewed his vow for three more months of pilgrimage to Kannon. After three years and three months there was still no divine sign. At this time the monk, regretting his fate, complained, "The great Kannon is the heir apparent of the Pure Land Paradise and Lord of the Realm of Potalaka.[2] He is unwavering in his compassionate vow to save every sentient being in the world. I alone am excluded from his vow of impartiality and discriminated against. They say his light shines in every pool of water without distinction, but his reflection is not illuminating the muddy waters of my heart. His power does not extend so far. I regret that the clouds of my past transgressions cannot be dispersed."

At dawn, setting off for home, he descended the mountain. As he was passing through the foothills of Obuse Mountain, he saw a youth of thirteen or fourteen, of complexion pale as the moon and adorned with flower-like magnificence. Over a purple underrobe he wore a garment of white silk and a hakama the color of fallen leaves. He played a melancholy tune on a Chinese flute. He wore a bamboo ornament in his long, sleek hair. Damp with the dew of the dawn of the eighteenth day of the eighth month, he was more graceful than a willow bending in a spring breeze. The sight made the monk wonder if he were not dreaming. Though he thought it might be a demon in disguise, he approached the lad and asked, "It is very strange for someone to be standing here alone in a moor like this so late at night. Who are you?"

The youth answered, "I am from Tōdaiji[3] but I have run away because my master is annoyed with me. Where are you from? A monk's compassion is said to be profound. Oh, please take me with you. I beg you."

The monk was delighted. "You must tell me what happened. If I am to hear all about it, you'll have to come along with me now." He headed for home with the boy in his company.

The monk was overjoyed. Days passed, but no one came looking for the youth, who did all he could to please the monk. The monk in turn, shared his incomparable talents in poetry and music, and passed the months and years in the firm belief that his joy was due to the grace of Kannon.

Three years later, towards the end of spring, the youth became slightly indisposed. Day by day he weakened, until, on the verge of death, he pillowed his head on the monk's knee. The monk took his hand, and brought his face close to the youth. Together they lamented their parting. The youth's last words were deeply touching. "For these three years I have passed my days in a dwelling of compassion, my nights have been spent at the foot of walls of forbearance. Morning and evening you taught me with

---

[2] The Pure Land of Supreme Bliss is a paradise over which Amida Buddha presides. Potalaka is a mythical place in south India.

[3] Tōdaiji, established in 749 in Nara, was for several centuries the official headquarters of Buddhism in Japan.

kindness I shall never forget, even in lives to come. Though they say that the old do not necessarily die before the young, I have thought only of out-living you so that I might hold memorial services for your salvation. My hopes have been in vain, my only regret is that I am going first. A master-disciple relationship is a bond for three lifetimes, so we will meet again in our next incarnations. Now, when I have breathed my last breath and ex-pired, do not bury me in the ground[4] with a marker, nor turn my body to smoke above the moor. Instead put my body in a coffin and place it in front of the altar. Then, on the thirty-fifth day, you are to open it.'' He had barely finished speaking when he breathed his last. His spirit left his body, his life expired like the dew on Mount Hokubō.[5]

The monk was overwhelmed with grief. When a bird faces death, its cry is meek, when a person faces a parting, his words are doleful. The monk sorrowfully remembered the youth's last words and spoke repeatedly of times past. How piteous! To mourn the loss of a loved one is the way of the world, but the intensity of the monk's grief was something not often witnessed. One who delights in the blossoms of spring laments their scat-tering, and the person who sings the praises of the late autumn moon resents the clouds which obscure the sky. Believing it all the divinely de-vised response to his three years and three months of pilgrimages to Hase-dera, the monk's love for the boy had been unparalleled. Suddenly parted after having loved one another for three years and three months, the in-tensity of the monk's grief was natural. It seemed to him that some cloud obscured the youth's moon-like visage, that a breeze had lured away the flower-like figure of his beloved. The tears of despair that a youth had passed on before an aged man repeatedly dampened his robe. When would he be able to forget this parting of master and disciple? How piteous! He who was approaching old age remained, while the youth was gone. He was reminded of fresh buds being scattered and of the cruelty of the turning of the autumn leaves. As the dew on the tip of a branch or the droplets at the foot of a tree both vanish, life, whether long or short, inevitably ends. He wept.

The monk could not go on like that, however, and so he placed the youth's body in a coffin. Following the lad's last instructions, he put the coffin before the altar and diligently performed the memorial services. Peo-ple gathered from nearby villages and distant mountains to copy out the whole *Lotus Sutra* in one day[6] and dedicated their work to the youth's sal-

---

[4]The text irrelevantly alludes to a line from a poem by Po Chu-i (772–846): "Although one may be buried in the ground, one's name will live on.''

[5]Mount Hokubō (Ch. Pe Mang) is a place where members of the Chinese aris-tocracy were buried after the late Han.

[6]The text refers specifically to a practice of many people sharing the labor of copying the sutra in order to produce a copy of the whole text in one day. An En-glish translation of the *Lotus Sutra* is 337 pages long.

vation. When the memorial service sermons were over, and, in an excess of emotion, the monk raised the lid of the coffin, a wonderful scent of sandalwood and *jinsui*[7] incense filled the room. Having transformed from his previous appearance as a beautiful youth, there stood a golden eleven-faced Kannon. His eyes sparkled like the green leaves of the lotus, his red lips were set in a solemn expression, and he held a lotus blossom in his hand.

He addressed the monk with the voice of a bird of paradise. "I am not a human being. The Lord of Fudaraku is called the great Kannon. That is who I am. In order to bring salvation to all who trust in me, I have lived for some time at the foot of Mt. Hase. Because of the earnestness with which you made pilgrimages for many years, I took the form of a youth, one of my thirty-three manifestations[8] and entered into a bond of two lifetimes with you.[9] Seven years from now, on the fifteenth of the eighth month, I will come to escort you to the Pure Land. At our reunion we will be together on a lotus petal in the ninth and highest grade of paradise." Light shone from his body and he ascended into the sky like lightning and disappeared behind a purple cloud.

It was a manifestation of the Chigo Kannon of Bodai'in in Nara. Anyone who makes a pledge, performs pilgrimages, and accumulates merit will be blessed with divine favor and will surely witness a manifestation of the youth. In addition it is said that those who come from near and far to transcribe and dedicate copies of the *Lotus Sutra* experience enlightenment and witness manifestations of Kannon. The true ambition of the Buddhas of the past, present, and future to save all sentient beings is realized in the saving power of the great Kannon.

---

[7] *Jinsui* is incense made from wood submerged in water for an extended period of time.

[8] The list of Kannon's possible manifestations is found in chapter 25 of the *Lotus Sutra*. It includes "the body of a boy or girl." See Leon Hurvitz, trans., *Scripture of the Lotus Blossom of the Fine Dharma* (New York, Columbia University Press, 1976), pp. 314–315.

[9] We might account for the discrepancy between the youth's promise of a bond for three lifetimes and Kannon's reference to ties for two incarnations by noting that the cycle of reincarnation is brought to an end by birth in the Pure Land of Supreme Bliss.

Visiting from Edo, Suddenly a Monk

Ihara Saikaku

Translated by Paul Gordon Schalow

Living in a pathless hut of grass.
Tamagawa Shuzen dips from the well of his heart.
A country girl goes mad with love.

This story comes from Saikaku's *The Great Mirror of Male Love* (1687), a collection of forty short narratives about various male youths whose exemplary practice of male love is highlighted. The first twenty narratives are about youths from the samurai (warrior) class. The life of the warrior revolved around maintaining his personal honor and observing his duty towards his daimyo lord, characteristics that spilled over into the warrior's practice of male love. As a result, most of the samurai narratives end with the death by suicide of the youth or his lover (or both) in a demonstration of their male honor.

The remaining twenty stories turn to the depiction of male love in the kabuki theater, where youths who acted on stage during the day doubled as boy prostitutes at night. Like courtesans in the pleasure districts, kabuki youths found themselves in the exciting but sometimes sordid context of providing pleasure to their patrons for pay. What redeems most of them is their ability to fall deeply in love, which inevitably brings them to a point of crisis in their profession as boy prostitutes. The equivalent of suicide for the kabuki youths is leaving the theater to take the tonsure and lead a life of seclusion as a monk. Taking Buddhist vows allows the kabuki youths to live as though dead to the world, an option not available to samurai youths for whom honor and duty dictate that devotion be expressed in terms of physical death.

The main character in "Visiting from Edo, Suddenly a Monk" is a former kabuki actor in Edo (modern Tokyo) named Shuzen, who takes the tonsure at age twenty in despair over the fact that he is losing his youthful beauty. This act precipitates a crisis for his young lover, a fellow ac-

IHARA SAIKAKU (1642-1693) was a poet and writer of popular fiction in 17th century Tokugawa Japan. He is best known for his fiction exploring the travails of love and sex. His book, *The Great Mirror of Male Love* (English tr. 1990), comprises tales around male lovers in the worlds of the theater, and samurai, and, to a lesser extent, monks. The first story (written 1687) printed here is from that book; the second story is specially translated for *Queer Dharma* from Ihara Saikaku's *A Myriad Discarded Letters* (written ca. 1690). See also: *Partings at Dawn: An Anthology of Japanese Gay Literature* (San Francisco: Gay Sunshine Press, 1996).

tor named Asanojō who has stopped taking customers for pay because of his love for Shuzen. Asanojō tracks down Shuzen and ultimately joins him in his life of Buddhist seclusion, but not before the beautiful fourteen-year-old daughter of a local farmer falls in love with Asanojō and herself comes to enlightenment regarding the futility of love. Years later, another actor visiting from Edo is so inspired by Shuzen's and Asanojō's example that he, too, abandons the world and becomes a monk. Far from praising the youth's spirituality, Saikaku voices the feelings of the young actor's patrons back in Edo when he concludes the narrative, somewhat cynically, with the statement that "it was a pity . . . to lose him at the peak of [his] youthful beauty."

The broad-billed roller sings only at Mt. Kōya, Matsuno-o, and Kōki-ji here in Kawachi Province,[1] and even then only in the utter darkness of midsummer religious retreat. Priests who chance to hear its song find their hearts suddenly purified, especially on this holy ground where Kōbō Daishi founded his temple.

Farther along the same mountain range is another ancient temple in a grove near the village of Tamade. An abbot who was an expert in the sutras lived there, and among his many disciples was a handsome monk by the name of Kaken. I inquired about his past and discovered that he was once the actor Tamamura Shuzen,[2] whose name appeared prominently on billboards throughout Edo. When he played female roles he drove men mad with desire, and his dancing would surely never be seen again, even in the world to come. He was especially skilled in the ways of boy love; no one remained unaffected by his charms.

Time passed, however, and soon people were lamenting the change in his once beautiful figure. At the age of twenty, gazing one night at a moon also on the wane, he decided to hide himself in a certain temple, something he had been considering for a long time. There he shaved off his topknot

---

[1] The broad-billed roller gets its name, *buppōsō*, from its call (actually the call of a species of owl), which sounds like the words for the Three Treasures (*sampō*) of Shingon Buddhism: the Buddha (*butsu*), the Law (*hō*), and the Priesthood (*sō*). It is traditionally linked to Mr. Kōya, the center of Shingon Buddhism. The connection to Matsuno-o in Kyoto comes from *Shinsen waka rokujō* poem 2555 by Fujiwara Mitsutoshi: "The peak of Mt. Matsuno-o looms silent in the dawn; looking up, I hear the cry of *buppōsō*." The link to Kōki-ji comes from a poem in Chinese by Kūkai composed after hearing the bird's song during a stay at the temple.

[2] The name in the headnote, Tamagawa Shuzen, is the correct one. He was an actor of female roles in Kyoto in the years immediately surrounding the banning of boys' kabuki in 1652. In 1661 he moved to Edo and established a theater in Sakai-chō, later forming a joint venture with Ichimura Takenojō. He left the world of kabuki in 1673 and took the priestly name of Kaken, according to *Kokon yakusha monogatari* (1678).

and changed into the robes of a monk. For a time he traveled the provinces as a pilgrim, but he had now settled here in a grass hut of his own making. Vines strangled his scraggly hedge of bush clover, and the window of his hut opened south toward the moon, his only companion. He pursued his devotions morning and night without break. For three years he lived this way without telling anyone of his whereabouts, and soon even thoughts of his birthplace were forgotten.

There was a boy named Asanojō,[3] who was both beautiful and deeply affectionate, whom he had supported while still in the world of the theater. He was the object of innumerable men's desires, but when Shuzen acquired him he won the boy's heart completely. Of his own accord, Asanojō stopped entertaining other men. Although they had promised each other that their feelings would never change, when Shuzen put on the black robes of a monk he did not inform the boy of his plans. Bitter and distraught, Asanojō had traveled the roads from distant Musashino to pay Shuzen a visit.

The moment Asanojō saw him, he felt as if the Shuzen of old had vanished like foam on the water, for with his own hands Shuzen was drawing water from a well using a weighted pole. Asanojō's tears alone were enough to fill the bucket to overflowing.

"What have you done?" the boy cried, clinging to Shuzen's robe. (The fact that he wept shamelessly into the man's sleeve in full view of others showed the extent of his love for Shuzen.)

"Yes, I have taken the tonsure," Shuzen said. "Though still in the world, my abode was unsettled. I feared that we would never meet again. I am grateful you came to visit me here for the sake of our past love. I will always treasure it. But you are after all still in the bloom of youth, of the age that the blossom-viewing public in Edo most appreciates. It would be a shame to turn your back on them. Your parents in Kumagaya would miss you terribly. In light of all this, I think it would be best if you immediately returned east."

Knowing that at the end of this night they would be bidding each other farewell, Shuzen entertained Asanojō by building a fire of dried leaves under a tea kettle, but its meager flame did little to warm his welcome. Aside from two tea bowls, there were no other utensils. He had hung an unmounted piece of paper bearing six words of the sutra above a Buddha shelf made of split bamboo stalks, and on the shelf was a chipped sake bottle filled with summer chrysanthemums. The cool breeze that blew through the hut was their sole source of pleasure. Since Shuzen had no netting to protect them during the night, they stayed awake swatting mosquitos with their fans and spoke of the past until the sound of their voices finally ceased

---

[3]Tamai Asanojō was an actor of female roles in Tamagawa Shuzen's (note 2) kabuki troupe. Theater records indicate he was active from 1661 to 1681.

"Shuzen was drawing water from a well . . ."

and only their tears remained. The ringing of the pre-dawn bell found them thus, caught between slumber and wakefulness.

"When the first cock crows, turn your steps toward the east. In the future, I do not expect to receive any news from you, not even a letter announcing your safe return home. If you should hear word of me, ignore it. Go now, and take this to remember me by." He handed Asanojō a Pure Land rosary, one that he used constantly in his devotions.

Asanojō's tears flowed again like a string of jewels.

Clouds lifted at daybreak and the summer mountains became clearly visible in the distance. Asanojō spoke. "I will do as you wish and return home."

Shuzen watched the boy's figure disappear into the shadows of the lush mountain forest.

It took many days for Shuzen's former peace of mind to return. He secluded himself in his rude hut and turned his attention to intoning the sutras in hopes of forgetting his sorrow. One day, he was startled from his devotions by a knock at the door. He went out to see who it was, and there stood Asanojō shorn of his lovely locks.

"I did as you said and returned east," the boy explained. "Now I have come back to you."

Shuzen regretted the loss of Asanojō's youthful beauty, but there was nothing he could do about it now. He went to speak to the abbot, who agreed to accept the boy as his disciple. "He has realized that life is a mere dream. The world's pleasures no longer hold any fascination for him." Without a trace of regret, Asanojō dyed his robes black and thereafter concentrated his thoughts completely on the world to come. He was a true seeker of enlightenment. Each morning he drew water from the mountain spring and in the evening gathered brushwood for the fire. It was truly rare to see such pleasure as Asanojō evinced performing his ascetic tasks.

In a neighboring village, at a place called Old Market, lived a farmer's daughter of unusual beauty. She chanced to see Asanojō pass by in traveling dress and immediately fell passionately in love with him. Half crazed, she started after him on his way to the temple, but the maidservants dragged her back home. They scolded the girl for her behavior, but she was hopelessly in love and that night crept in secret to the temple. She peered through a window into the hut, illuminated only faintly by a pine torch. Lo and behold, the one she loved had shaved his head and become a monk!

She raised her voice in an anguished cry. "What could have caused that youth to renounce the world?" She wept and wailed as if she would die.

The uproar outside was completely unexpected and Asanojō tried at first to ignore it, but the girl's crazed shrieks soon roused the entire monastery. Many of the monks who gathered around the girl recognized her.

"What a vulgar display," they said in rebuke, but she paid them no heed.

368 / *Ihara Saikaku*

She continued to scream, "Who cut off the boy's hair? Whoever it was, I hate him! I hate him!" She had unmistakably gone mad.

Word was sent to her parents, and soon a close relation arrived to talk to her. "Think how people will criticize you for this. He is a monk. Your desires for him cannot be satisfied. Perhaps someday the time will come when you can meet him once again."

These words seemed to calm her.

"I suppose you are right," she responded. "I was blinded by my own wicked desire when he had no feelings for me at all. It must have been fate that led me to love him in this way. My black hair, which I have treasured each of my fourteen years, I will now abandon as grass on the path towards enlightenment."

With those words, she herself cut off her hair.

Her family had no choice but to allow her to become a nun. A cottage was built for her in the western reaches of the hills. From that time on, the sounding of the morning and evening bells was all that anyone heard of her, for no one ever laid eyes on the girl again. Enlightened by love, she completely turned her back on love.

The two monks, once actors, also completely abandoned the floating world and its ways. They never once strayed from their mountain hideaway, but lived there in total devotion to the performance of their religious duties. Friends from their days of glory in Edo frequently came to visit, nostalgic for the past, but their door was closed to them. The gateway eventually became overgrown with honeysuckle and the path to their door disappeared under a thick growth of bamboo grass.

Some years later, a handsome young actor named Yamamoto Kantarō[4] came to admire the autumn leaves at Tatsuta. He enjoyed the colors immensely. On his way home, he stopped to pay them a visit and was deeply moved by what he observed. Realizing that life was truly but a dream within a dream, he too took the tonsure. His decision was no doubt arrived at after much careful thought, but it was a pity nevertheless to lose him at the peak of youthful beauty.

---

[4]According to *Yarō mushi* (1660), Yamamoto Kantarō was an actor of boys' roles. He moved to Edo in 1661, the same year as Tamagawa Shuzen (note 2), and returned to the Kyoto-Osaka area in 1675 or 1676, after which he disappears from theater records.

The Monk from Kyoto Who Hated Cherry Blossoms*

Ihara Saikaku

Translated by Paul Gordon Schalow

The following story is from Saikaku's *A Collection of Discarded Letters* (1696), published three years after his death. It is the only letter in the collection that treats the topic of male love and, as Saikaku suggests in his brief commentary following the letter, the connection between male love and Buddhist monks was strong enough that the letter's treatment of the topic could be called "typical."

The letter-writer refers to his susceptibility to the beauty of handsome young men as a "chronic" or "incurable" illness (*jibyo*), something one is born with and carries through life as an innate physical or mental disposition. One senses not only the pleasure the monk takes in his latest discovery but also the anguish, given his own humble background, that results from his unreasonable desire for such a high-born youth, who is the son of a local lord.

An abridged form of the story appeared earlier in English translation in *Comrade Loves of the Samurai* (1928) under the title "Letter from a Buddhist Priest telling his Friend that his Lover comes to him," translated by E. Powys Mathers. A complete English translation is presented here for the first time.

I was weary of the cherry blossoms in the capital and decided to leave Kyoto while it was yet spring. Now someone tells me that he intends to see for himself the cherry trees at Higashiyama[1] and join in the music and singing that goes on behind the curtains spread under them, so I have asked him to deliver this letter to you.

First, rest assured that I am well; I was delighted to hear that you, dear monk, have given up the sobriquet "the drunken warrior," and that your commitment to the pursuit of the path of Buddhahood seems steadfast.

IHARA SAIKAKU's biographical note can be found on page 363.
*Translator's note: The translation of this story is based on a modern-print version of Saikaku's text in *Yorozu no fumi hōgu* (A Collection of Discarded Letters) in *Teihon Saikaku zenshū*, vol. 8, pp. 275–279 (Tokyo: Chuo Koron-sha, 1950).

[1]The "eastern hills" that rise to the east of the ancient capital, Kyoto, are even now a favorite place to enjoy the cherry blossoms. The letter-writer's home is in this district of Higashiyama, and his decision to leave the capital was motivated by his desire to escape the noisy revelers who flocked there to view the blossoms in spring.

". . . My reverie was disturbed by the sound of footsteps of an approaching company of people."

"It was a certain high priest who had come to pay a call at the temple. Close by his side was a handsome youth of no more than sixteen years of age, the beauty of whose face was beyond anything I had ever seen in the capital."

My humble home has no doubt become an assembly place for mice in my absence. But since I left behind not even a single dried sardine, the pests must be laughing among themselves at my utter poverty, so befitting my station as a monk.

Chrysanthemums and bush clover are probably blooming all by themselves by now in the gaps in my garden fence. It is sad that no one will be there to mourn them when the night frosts nip the fading blossoms.

I left my key with you so that you would feel free to enter there anytime. Should a handsome youth happen to pass by on his way down Higashiyama, by all means invite him in and show my garden to him. If you like, treat him to some chestnuts and potatoes, which you will find in the root cellar under the bamboo porch on the north side. (Don't tell anyone, but the reason I left them there was because they were a gift from Mr. Takenaka.)

My weakness for handsome youths seems to be an incurable one, for I have once again fallen in love with a young man, whose presence here makes me wonder if I will ever see the capital again.

It all started last spring when I left you in the capital and went to visit an acquaintance in Okayama, Bizen Province. For a time I was treated hospitably enough, but gradually I found it difficult to remain there. So, I boarded a boat that was fortuitously sailing on the very Sea of Seto at dawn that the great priest Saigyō had once so admired in a poem. I threw my fate to the wind, and it eventually brought me to Higo Province.[2] A fellow monk and poet of linked verse I knew at the temple of Kiyomasa[3] invited me to stay and enjoy my leisure with him for a while.

One evening, I rested in the cool breeze of his garden to escape the summer heat. Man-made hills gave the garden a sense of great depth, and water had been made to flow artfully over carefully placed rocks. The effect was most refreshing. I found myself envying the saintly pleasure my friend seemed to derive from the miniature landscape.

From within the thick forest of cedars surrounding the temple came the song of a single nightingale, strangely reminiscent of the capital. This was a moment that ought to be commemorated in verse, I thought, and I struggled to recall the rules of Chinese composition laid out in *The Threefold Rhyme*.[4]

Suddenly, my reverie was disturbed by the sound of footsteps of an approaching company of people. It was a certain high priest who had come to pay a call at the temple. Close by his side was a handsome youth of no

---

[2]Modern-day Kumamoto, located at the southernmost end of the southernmost major island of Kyūshū in the Japanese archipelago.

[3]The temple of Kiyomasa is Honmyō-ji in the city of Kumamoto. It was supported by Katō Kiyomasa, lord of the region, as his familial temple.

[4]*Sanjūin*, a collection of Chinese poems in five volumes designed as an aid in poetry composition. It dates from 1412, but was still widely used in Saikaku's day.

more than sixteen years of age, the beauty of whose face was beyond anything I had ever seen even in the capital. How was it possible, I thought, for such a creature to exist in a place as remote as this western province? The longer one lives, the more surprising one's experiences are.

A shiver ran through my body as I thought of the irony of my plight: I had come to this remote place to escape the disquiet of the flowery capital, and had discovered instead the source of a very special agony. My heart burned inside me. After tea was served to the visitors, I could not bear the thought of allowing the youth to leave without a parting look, and so I stole a peek through a gap in the door. This only intensified my passion, of course.

After his departure, I asked someone the youth's name. He was the second son of a high-ranking nobleman, and his heartfelt desire was to become a monk. It was for that purpose that he had been entrusted to the high priest. I was in a dreadful state, and felt as if my body would burst from the feelings inside me.

"How sad that a simple monk like me should be possessed of such an extravagant love." I admitted to my friend how unreasonable my feelings were, but I could not accept his advice to simply forget the youth. Instead, I was determined to make him aware of the existence of my feelings. This is the letter I wrote to him.

> Yesterday I glimpsed the in-born beauty of your face, and knew that this must have been how, in China, Emperor Wen felt when he saw Deng Tong wearing a purple cap, or how Emperor Ai felt when he saw Dong Xian dressed in imperial robes. Those who see you mistake you for the beautiful Madame Li; those who hear of you yearn for a glimpse of this veritable Yang Kuei Fei.[5]
>
> All who see or hear of you are deeply moved, for the hearts of men are not made of wood or stone. I know that it is impossible to consummate my love, but I feel compelled to spell out in this humble letter exactly how I feel for you.
>
> Ever since the moment I was granted a fleeting glimpse of your face, my breast has smoldered like the smoke billowing from Mt. Aso, and my tears have flowed like the river Shirakawa.[6] Your eyes resemble the circle of the cinnamon tree, and your heart is like the thread of a willow.[7]

---

[5] The youth's beauty is compared to that of legendary imperial favorites from China, two male and two female. True beauty in a youth thus transcends boundaries of sex and gender.

[6] Mt. Aso is an active volcano in the center of the island of Kyūshū; the Shirakawa flows through the northern environs of the town of Kumamoto.

[7] A commentary suggests that "the circle of the cinnamon tree" is the new moon. The metaphor may mean that the youth's eyes are shaped like the new moon, narrow and crescent-shaped, both of which are desirable traits; or, it may be a metaphor for the brightness of the youth's eyes. Commentaries do not offer an explanation for the image of "the thread of a willow." The willow is a common metaphor for a woman's or youth's slender waist.

Upon my arrival at the port of Tsurugasaki, I was straight-away impressed with the peony-like splendor of Kyūshū, a place without rival in the four seas. But it was when I came to Kumamoto that I discovered the greatest beauty of all, one fragment of which is, like a drop of amber, the rarest of gems. Had I not seen it with my own eyes, I would not have believed that a beauty surpassing the cherry blossoms could exist in this world. You are a reincarnation, all in one, of Xi Shi, beloved consort of the Chinese King of Wu, the Japanese beauty Komachi, Yukihira in his youth, and his handsome brother Narihira.[8] Your image not only haunts my dreams but is with me when I am awake.

My only recourse is to offer prayers at the Fujisaki Shrine, or to throw myself into the Kikuchi River.[9] I would gladly give up my life for your sake. The enlightened mind knows that the life of a man, even if he lives a hundred years, is but a moment's dream. I would gladly give up a thousand nights of spring for a single night pillowed in your arms.

In my waking moments, not once do thoughts of you leave me. What sort of karmic bond must it be that links me so powerfully to you?

Thus, I wrote him of my true feelings. And, hard to believe, I just received his warm reply. I cannot begin to tell you how it made me feel. Pen and paper are inadequate to the task. In his reply, he stated that he would like to visit me in my traveler's lodgings one evening soon. I do not know what day it will be, but you can imagine my feelings as I await word from him. I spend my days in an agony of expectation. *This*, I realize, must be love.

The other day I tattooed six letters on my right arm; I hope that they have the desired effect.[10] If only you were closer at hand, I could tell you exactly how things go when he visits me.

His name is Okajima Uneme.

I shall end here. I just wish it were possible to talk all night with you over a cup of saké about this splendid turn of events. I would send the crows of this province to sing in the thickets of the capital at Gion so that morning would never dawn on our conversation.

Please do not tell Gensai's sandal-bearer, Matsunosuké, about this mat-

---

[8]The youth's beauty is again compared to that of male and female legendary beauties, both Chinese and Japanese. Ariwara no Narihira (825–880) was especially famed for his beauty and prowess as a lover of women, although legends of his love of men and youths were in circulation by Saikaku's day.

[9]The Fujisaki shrine was located in Kumamoto and was dedicated to Hachiman, guardian deity of the warrior class to which the youth belonged. The Kikuchi is a river that flows through the northern district of Kumamoto.

[10]A commentary suggests that the six letters are probably the characters "na-mu-a-mi-da-butsu." These words of the sutra are intoned by believers as an expression of faith in the power of Amitābha Buddha to grant their hopes of rebirth in the western paradise. Here, the monk has tattooed the words into his flesh in the hope that he will be granted his wish for sexual union with the youth.

ter. I have written it down just to give you some news about me until my eventual return.

Ninth month, Eleventh day.

Keigan

Saikaku's commentary:

This letter is from a monk disgusted with the noise of cherry-blossom viewing in the capital who went to the western provinces [Kyūshū] where he unexpectedly fell in love with a handsome youth. The letter is sent to a friend in the capital to inform him of the affair, and includes a summary of a love letter that the monk sent to the youth. It is typical of a monk.

A Window in the Wall

Trebor

He was an incarnation. Drinking a bottle of morphine from a paper bag, loafing down San Francisco's Natoma Street after rain, the steam surrounding him as it rose off the sidewalk. A solitary vision in his overcoat and broken-limbed black umbrella, moving past the empty warehouses and closed-down body shops; the treeless, deserted cement world south of Market. Like the wilderness that way. Not unlike the backcountry of Yosemite or the high plain of Tibet.

That was as close as I'd get from now on. No more spontaneous adventures. I was trying to take it slow after all that had happened. All those books, the long crazy trip to Tibet, telling my parents I didn't need the medication anymore. Karma nearly killed me and karma's what kept me alive is all I can figure.

And now here comes some kind of wrathful deity, clumping along in combat boots down the street toward me. I spied him as I left my doorway, moving, a shadow along the wall. One part of me said ignore him, but some other part felt something I'll never know what: Pheromones? Karma? Destiny? Fate? It's all the same. And it made me turn and look straight down the sidewalk at him as I just stood there with my hands in my pockets.

Jimmy was a dark thing. Perhaps that's what struck me about him. Like he'd crawled up out of the earth or hell. He looked dangerous, which always excited me, and which is why I went to Tibet looking for Mahakala. He glanced up from the sidewalk as he approached and asked me if I had a light, pushing the bottle into his overcoat pocket and pulling out a bag of tobacco and some rolling papers. He had the blackest brows and blackest brown eyes I'd ever seen. I didn't know then that heroin did that to your pupils. I was just drawn to him like he was ten feet of shade in front of a tree; somewhere to rest out of the light, somewhere to stay cool.

I didn't have any matches, but I wanted to right then.

"No, I don't, but I live right here. I have some upstairs."

That's what started it. Asking for a light is only supposed to engender a yes or a no. He looked at me and we both said yes with our eyes, recognized some gravity between us. Like we weren't surprised to meet. Like we'd both expected it for a long time somehow.

When I think of that fateful meeting now, I think of what Rumi had

---

TREBOR (San Francisco) was born in 1962 and has practiced within both the Theravada and Tibetan Nyingma traditions. He has authored five chapbooks of poetry and was the co-editor of *Beyond Definition: New Writing from Gay and Lesbian San Francisco* (Manic D Press, 1994). He is currently at work on a novel.

written once: "Lovers don't find one another; they're in each other all along."

He looked away quickly, across the street at a black cat maneuvering tightrope-like along a roof gutter. And he turned back and smiled at me, as if saying "well?"

His eyes made my heart beat and I thought I could certainly offer him a light and maybe burn the whole house down too.

I invited him in.

The dark olive of his skin, the angry little boy curiosity of his furrowed brows as he climbed the stairs behind me, looking around at the new surroundings. I felt a sudden sadness at being a homosexual. That this was how we lived. Sad strangers, sudden intimacies that didn't last, vulnerabilities revealed like a deer in headlights; run down or driven away into lonely forests; lost little boys. I hoped this wouldn't be the same, hoped my suspicions about fate were somehow right.

When I was horny I felt like a blank sheet of paper in need of a story. I felt that way now and his black eyes were dark and deep as ink wells, and his body, pregnant with motion and muscle, had all the potential of a calligraphy brush. I wanted him all over, deep in my fibers that were blasted clean with light; with mania minus lithium my psychiatrist would have said; sick with transcendence.

I dug in a box for matches while Jimmy stood and looked around. The place was nothing but boxes. There were just piles of crates here and there and a futon in the middle of the floor. And I'd come and go, just sleeping there at night. I'd moved in abruptly after they released me, and though I'd been back on medication for several weeks, I wasn't as stabilized as I'd claimed in order to get released early. They trusted me more than the others because I wasn't the suicidal type.

As for Jimmy, I saw scars on his arms as he took off his coat. People who've been institutionalized look for signs on others.

"Did you just move here?" he asked, throwing his coat on the back of a chair that randomly faced a wall.

"I was born here."

"I mean this apartment."

"Oh, two months ago."

"Are you leaving or something?"

"No, I don't think so. Or not that I know of," and I handed him the matches, smiling. He was looking around for a place to roll his cigarette.

I smiled. He was everything I always thought was cute in guys: lanky like a lab puppy, with a lazy mouth that hung half open, a furrowed brow of concentration. And pain. He looked like he was in pain.

"Uh, let's see here," I picked up a wooden wine box full of books and silverware and cups and dumped it in a pile. "If you sit there on the futon, you can use this as a little table," I said as I placed the crate in front of my bed.

He, with some nervousness, complied.

While he rolled his cigarette, I offered him something to drink.

"No thanks," he said. "What's your name?"

"Robb, with two 'b's,' and you?"

"Jimmy, with two 'm's,' " he made me smile.

I sat next to him then. He seemed a little friendlier, definitely something smarter in his almond-shaped black eyes than the usual trick. It wasn't clear that he intended to make this meeting sexual. Yet, I knew he was drawn to me somehow and what the hell could two gay guys do, I wondered cynically. I had little faith in much else and I'd learned my moods stayed steadier when I didn't get wrapped up in grand expectations. And yet, I felt strangely safe sitting down next to him, concentrating as he licked the rolled cigarette and sealed the tobacco inside. It must have been the scars. Fellow traveler.

I picked the matches up off the crate and handed them to him.

"Thanks. Should I smoke outside?" he asked.

I wanted to say "please, don't ever leave," wanting him now desperately to stay and feeling an enormous wave of loneliness move through my chest. I had to laugh at myself or I would have cried.

"No, no, here's OK."

He moved the makeshift table out of the way as he began to puff on the cigarette and picked up a handful of the dumped books like someone who'd poured the milk and now wanted a cereal box to read. *Dharma Bums, Zen Mind, Beginners Mind, The Tibetan Book of the Great Liberation.*

"I don't like Kerouac much, but I like Burroughs."

I said it was just the opposite for me.

Then, abruptly he said, "I'd like to talk to you, but I'm really tired, do you want to take a nap?"

I thought it was a clumsy sexual come-on, and being my horny self, said sure, but he was out in a matter of seconds as we laid back together. Another lesson in junk. I watched him sleep, the slack mouth more open than before, big dark lashes. I couldn't help smiling at his beauty and youth. I remembered the bottle that he'd stashed in his overcoat pocket then, and as I wasn't really tired, I went to find out what he'd been drinking. The prescription label was still on it, with someone else's name and instructions: "Take as needed for pain." Is this a better sign than King Cobra? I wondered, more than a little shocked. But I had a new friend sleeping like an angel on my futon, cause for celebration. I uncapped it, gulped a mouthful and walked back to the futon, feeling a sudden hopefulness as I gazed upon him, and spying Suzuki Roshi's book on the floor next to me, clasped together my hands and bowed my head toward Jimmy, before lying down beside him.

He was staring at the ceiling when I awoke and looked over at him. He turned and smiled. "So, yea, I don't like Kerouac much, but I like the idea of Dharma Bums, hiking around the mountains and gettin' all Buddhist with Gary Snyder," he picked up right where he'd left off . . .

"Yea, after I read that book, I hiked that very mountain," I said, leaning up on one elbow toward him, "Matterhorn Peak in Yosemite. You can follow the same trail they did. . . ."

"So you're a Buddhist?"

"Well, I don't know. I try. . . ." I didn't want to tell him about my trip to Tibet, all lost and crazy, deported by the Chinese, more delusional than I'd ever been. A truly embarrassing case of false-start beginners mind. ". . . I try to get up there to the Zen Center and do the sittings in the morning after I walk."

"Is that where you were going just now?"

"Yea, I walk and then I sit."

"Sorry if I messed up your plans."

"Not a problem," I reassured him.

"I've read that Suzuki Roshi book. It's a real good book. I want to learn more about Buddhism. I like it. It's not so stupid like Christianity."

Assuming his interest was on the level of most guys I'd met, I knew better than to launch into a real conversation on Buddhism. I'd scared a few boys off that way before. And I didn't want to engage in the usual Eastern Religion greatest hits blathering about magical Babaji, Neem Karoli Baba, Ram Dass and reincarnate lamas.

"Wanna get something to eat?" I asked him.

"Yea, but let's meditate together first."

I was taken aback by this. I'd assumed his interest in Buddhism was superficial. Like I say, almost everybody knew about it nowadays, had read Suzuki Roshi's book at least. It was in fact rather cool in San Francisco for young hip queers to be familiar with anything even remotely mystical. But actually wanting to sit was another thing altogether.

I smiled and said, "Yea, that's a great idea."

And we sat there, in that sad empty, disheveled place. Sat there on the edge of the futon, he with his serious brow, concentrating, me with my brows like rainbows, too open for my own good, beginning to wonder about him and losing track of my breath as I saw the morphine bottle, his image in the rain, stripping him in my mind and seeing his naked body with the dark patch in the center of him and imaging his penis, his balls, his flanks and legs. Breathing. Fucking in my fantasies. Breathing. Fucking. Breathing. Fucking breathing. OK, now concentrate.

That was the first of many times we sat together and it's funny now to think we meditated with each other more times than we even had sex. That seemed odd from what I'd experienced of gay relationships. It even made me a little proud, though it was of no credit to my efforts.

We spent a couple of weeks in that room, both being unemployed. It turned out he had nowhere else to go and I knew I didn't.

We didn't have sex at all for those first two weeks. Not because we weren't dying to. Jimmy had a herpes outbreak, and never took his long johns off. We'd kiss and touch for hours, groping. It didn't drive me crazy like I would have thought. We'd fall off to sleep eventually and wake up as aroused as when we'd fallen asleep. It was like being hungry and licking the food you desired but never eating it. Days with him were an ongoing sexual experience. Every turn of his head revealed new muscle movements under the pale olive skin of his neck that fascinated me and cut through me until a lump formed in my throat. I could stare at his hair, or his hand for hours, thrilled. It was the first date that never ended and it was heavenly. We were hot for each other with no cessation and it felt oddly wonderful and electric.

It made me feel that when we did have sex, it should be like never before. If we'd waited, why not make it perfect? I went back to my books. Found everything I could on tantra in the same manic manner I'd discovered Buddhism. Which was by reading a dozen books on the subject, but not once setting foot in a meditation hall. My old romanticism: Maybe Buddhist meditation will make me better because I hate being manic depressive and addicted to lithium. I'll meditate it away, I dreamed. I was young enough to think I could be the exception. I started meditating, stopped taking my medication and ended up on a plane for Tibet with vague ideas of meeting high lamas or being found to be a tulku; perhaps a stint in Milarepa's cave. By the time I was airborne I was so manic, I probably *could have been* mistaken for a saint. I'm surprised I managed to get there at all, through all the hassles of customs, on to the right connecting flight into Lhasa. The hotel. And then just walking. Overjoyed— God I was elated. I hadn't slept in 3 days and I just walked out of Lhasa into the mountains. I don't remember all of it. Just the end. Being hassled by Chinese soldiers near some broken down stupa and yelling at them to leave me alone and getting arrested. Ending up back in San Francisco with my panicky parents taking me back to Langley Porter where I'd been numerous times before as a kid.

But it was a holier mania I experienced now inside that electricity of delayed lovemaking. We told each other everything. He told me about his two suicide attempts, tracing his hand along the scars and letting me feel them too. He'd lived in a group home all through high school because his mother hated him for telling her what her first husband and his father had done to him.

He was doing drugs and gay bars by 15. A heroin addict by twenty.

"I finally found a way to completely forget about sex," he laughed.

He told me he'd been clean for a year.

"What about that bottle of morphine?" I asked, fearing I was prying or maybe even calling his bluff.

"Oh, that. Well, I've had that for awhile. After a friend of mine died, I grabbed it from his bedroom when his lover wasn't around. I figured I wanted it around in case I decided to kill myself again. I want to do it right next time. Third time's a charm, right?"

"So, you're drinking it . . ."

"Oh, yea, well I just decided to. Just this one bottle. It's really nice stuff. I won't get addicted again. And I'm not suicidal. I just felt like it today," he assured me.

At a loss for what to say, I added, "Well, I guess that's better than killing yourself with it."

"My 12-step program would not agree with you," he smiled.

Next to *him* I was only just crazy, and I suppose irrationally stubborn about not wanting to take medication. I was an only child with parents who were absolutely hysterical about my homosexuality, but they never beat me or anything. If anything, they doted on me in an oppressive way that made me steer clear of them.

We laughed a lot between heavy confessions and remembrances because we felt safe enough to tell. The details didn't even mean so much. We were two ruined people. What else was there at this point but the three noble truths—suffering, its cause and a way out. It was like the people I'd met at Langley Porter. Everybody knew and shared the long, slow, painful road to treatment. Buddhism wasn't any different. People ended up there.

When we did go out, we went to bookstores to read about tantric sex. Something different this time that won't hurt him like how his father did and that won't make me feel like the useless, self-centered, indulgent fag my mother really thinks I am, bad because my sex life leads nowhere and to nothing, i.e. a family. Books, a kind of folly, but it was the best we could do then. Without a teacher or a sangha. Jimmy and I were both put off by the meditation centers. Everyone was straight and 40. And here we were, two loopy kids wth funny haircuts, noserings and tattoos. We were going it alone. Hubris, folly, youth. But Beginners mind all the same. When I look back at those two young boys now, I feel their painful alienation, but mostly I smile and feel a deep compassion. It's a practice. They tried.

One day Jimmy said, "Tomorrow it'll be healed over."

I had begun working again, and was ecstatic all day at my monotonous temp job anticipating tantric and ultimate sex with Jimmy. I actually enjoyed and marveled at the workings of the fax and copier machines. Everyone there was angelic and worthy of love. I wondered that if we all knew we'd be enlightened one day, would we all live joyfully anticipating like this? Probably. Most people are depressed I think because they have doubts about death and so have nothing to look forward to. I remembered what Whitman had written: "And to die is different from what any one supposed, and luckier."

Jimmy had begun working at a cafe where he wasn't getting along with anyone. He'd been angry and short with me too. Being kind to him hadn't helped, it made him madder. "Let's sit," was all I could say. "Let's breathe, Jimmy."

And we'd sit. And our breath was like a window in the high, insurmountable cement wall of the prison of daily life. Blue sky, clouds—we too could be birds and fly.

That night he was quiet and we undressed each other slowly. Trying to remember the books and our breathing. Laughing sometimes, because we don't care about Buddhism right now and enlightenment and compassion. We want to fuck each other like dogs! But we stay with it, looking at each other through the giggles. And then he gets serious and says he doesn't know if he can because it's. . . . He thinks of his father. How I remind him of him.

He says he'll try.

We were clumsy, but we did the breathing together, looking in each other's eyes while we fucked sitting Indian style. Everything about him was so beautiful and fragile. His bony shoulders and dark nipples, the way his hipbones stuck out, the hunger of his mouth. We tried to keep it slow, but I had a strange feeling I was going to cry and out of fear and embarrassment speeded up and pulled him with me. We were cumming and forgetting in no time. It's a practice.

Other nights we sat with hard-ons that we wouldn't touch and we'd just look at each other and run our hands across each other's arms and torsos. Jimmy usually got nervous the minute things got orgasmic, so we just stopped having orgasms. We'd just grope around and look each other in the face and then we'd eventually sleep. And though it drove me crazy, like before, it was more erotic, ecstatic, electric to not have an orgasm. I knew his beauty and attraction in a deeper way. I felt his power. I really didn't want to be away from him. The energy unspent held us. Our bodies became precious to each other, like delicate jewels or porcelain.

But only at night. In the day, things got meaner and meaner. He'd lose things, he'd snap at me for asking too many questions, he'd rush around and call me slow. He was impatient. He hated the day as much as I did. He didn't like me watching him suddenly, giving him too much attention.

What could I say? "You wanna sit, Jimmy?" And he'd look at me, almost saying no, never again, but he'd do it. I never knew what drove him to do it so consistently when everything was falling in around him. I suppose, like me, that ultimately it was all he had. That and junk. Because he started again. I found a needle in the wastebasket. His pupils got bigger. He said nothing. We stopped having sex altogether. He kept sitting by my side on the end of the futon, though once he knocked off in such a way that only junk does to you. Slack-jawed, his head bobbing.

I had a feeling he'd get defensive if I asked him about it. He was obviously pushing me away, building walls. My only hope was that he'd keep a window in those walls. We'd become closer than he probably wanted to be with anyone. It wouldn't be the first time that had happened. I look back now and think I should have given him a few hundred dollars for the road, told him not to spend it on heroin, thanked him and wished him well.

But I told myself I loved him. Or didn't love him enough I suppose. To let him go.

So one day I came home and everything was gone. There was no note, nothing. I knew what it was. All my books were gone, the one chair, most of my clothes, the crates. The futon remained.

I was hurt, but not surprised.

I wondered especially about the books. *Zen Mind, Beginners Mind.* "Well someone else gets to read it," I thought. Maybe he'll keep it. I hope he does.

I sat dejected on the end of the futon, beginning to cry. A pleading from somewhere deep inside begged him to come back. Shoot heroin, I don't care. The hell with sitting and trying to make our lives work. We'll just be junkies, see where that takes us. Just come back. Please, Jimmy, don't leave me here alone.

Why had I waited, why was I afraid to confront him? I could have saved things. I'd failed us both. My mind went on until I hoped suddenly that I'd never see him again because I was afraid to forgive him and because what was between us was someone else who I had no right to speak for. And so could not. I only hoped he'd forgive me, but suspected he too could not. Forgive me for loving him. From what he told me, he'd never forgiven anyone. I suppose whoever it was we'd created between us forgives us both.

What could I do but sit? And try to meditate. Though mostly I watched my thoughts and followed quite a few of them. Which isn't always so bad because I realized that night while trying to meditate that I'd found a Buddhist boyfriend on my doorstep after having thought I had to become a tulku and move to Tibet. That we'd been a sangha of sorts, even teachers to one another. That I desired him greatly and of course that would bring me suffering. That the dharma asked, even demanded, things of me that could make me hate it.

I noticed too that when I'd thought about him when he was still here, I thought of us sitting. Well, to be honest, thought of us sitting or having sex. Now it was him I remembered. Him separate from me. As if when he left, the *we* between us broke. His window in the wall was gone. Spackled over by junk. We were two people again as we had been before. We had breathed each other in and now I felt my stomach fall, and the air lightly pass out of my nose, breathing out.

I remembered the last time we'd had breakfast together, the morning before. He was tense. I guess I know why now. He didn't want to talk.

"I just want to eat, can't we just not talk for once?"

I hadn't responded.

As he finished his breakfast, pushing his plate out in front of him, Jimmy took the Drum tobacco and papers out of his coat pocket and set up the ritual space, pushing away the cream roughly, the unused spoon and knife, the pepper and salt shakers. I watched him roll his cigarette like I had a dozen times before. It was so much like a meditation in itself.

He shook a little bit of the tobacco onto the paper, spreading it out expertly. He was like an old man in a deli making sandwiches, he knew just how to move with the materials. He could make the same cigarette a thousand times, without hardly thinking.

I thought of firewood as I watched him arrange the tobacco, dry pine needles on the forest floor, the dead dry wood of tobacco in a heap on the white paper. I thought of calligraphy. Carefully he rolled it up, licked it, turned the ends, looked across at me, got up and went outside. That was the last time we meditated together I suppose. Me watching him going through the ritual motions. Building us a kind of campfire.

I watched him out there in the cold through the window, dragging calmly on the cigarette, his shoulders hunching up his overcoat around his neck, looking out across the street at a stalled muni car. He looked so calm, in control of his world. I wondered if that bus looked like him or me or us. I suddenly wanted to get up, run out to him and hug him close and tell him that I loved him and the broken down muni cars and the street and the way he built a fire. But just then the waitress delivered the bill, I coughed up a well-mannered thank you, and pulled out my wallet.

When I looked back out the window toward Jimmy, he was looking back in with the of-late usual hostility in his eyes. So, I stifled my heart, felt a tear run down the back of my nose and throat and said instead a prayer: "May he be happy. May be peaceful. May he be free from suffering."

I almost wanted to add, "May he fuck off as well," and maybe I did, because he was gone that night. I thought as I left that cafe that I should have been a kingsize Marlboro cigarette right then. As it was, I had nothing he wanted. I felt bitter and unappreciated, like I'd become one of his parents, or maybe both of them. And the heroin? Like some old lover come back around. I was just the other woman now. I knew it had ended in that moment at breakfast when he told me in so many words to shut up, just as I'd known it began that moment in my doorway with a smile and a light. And I watched it burn away as we walked home, one puff at a time through his cigarette. Oxidation. Breathing. In and Out.

When I think of him now, I try to let the anger and sadness and love and all that just pass, though those are slow moving trains. And then I bow to his memory as my teacher, knowing that when you have learned what you came to the teacher to learn, the teacher, no longer necessary, goes away, vanishes, disappears, having learned as well.

And I whisper a thank you to Suzuki Roshi and Jimmy both.

Letting Go

Bob Vickery

Tonight I almost tear out somebody's windpipe on my way to my nightly meditation meeting. All over a parking space. I just found a space and am backing into it, when some guy in an MG zips in from behind and grabs it. I honk my horn, he flips me off, I call him an asshole, he calls me a motherfucker, and I'm out of my car and heading towards him with both fists clenched before I get a grip. *Is this worth going back to jail?* I ask myself. I take two deep breaths and return to my car. When the guy sees I'm not going to fight, he starts jeering at me, calling me a pussy, a faggot. Since he doesn't know me, I guess the last is just a generic insult. Even in the car, with my hands gripped so tight around the wheel that my knuckles are white, I seriously consider that maybe it *is* worth three more months in the slammer to back into that yuppie little shitmobile of his at full acceleration. I don't. I drive off and find a space two blocks away. My stomach is in knots and my throat's so constricted that I can hardly breathe. There's murder in my heart. I go to meditation.

The guy with the beard and beads, whose name I can never remember, is already in the guided part of the meditation. Still steaming, I shuck my shoes off next to the door and park my butt on the nearest empty pillow. Everyone else's eyes are closed. I take a few deep breaths and close my eyes as well. My thoughts are chaos. After a while I give it up and look around the room. I check out the blonde guy with all the muscles, who I've had a hard-on for since I joined this group three weeks ago. Tonight he's sitting right across from me. I let my mind drift into images of what he must look like naked.

Every time I look at this guy, I'm reminded of one of those angels on the Christmas cards I used to see as a kid. It isn't just the blonde hair or the mild blue eyes, it's this air of *calmness* about him. It hangs over him like a shield of light. I feel I could lob a cherry bomb at him and he wouldn't flinch; he'd just turn his steady blue gaze on me and ask me what was on my mind. *What must it feel like*, I wonder, *to be so calm?*

With his eyes closed, I can ogle him openly. He's just wearing a tank top for a shirt, with a yin-yang symbol embroidered on it and the inscription, "Free Tibet" written underneath. He really does have a fine, fine body:

"BOB VICKERY" is the pen name of Clint Seiter (see his essay "Applying Buddhist Dharma to Casual Sex" (p. 299). He has had over forty stories published in various gay magazines and currently has two collections of stories out: *Skin Deep*, and *Cock Tales* (Leyland Publications, 1997). His stories have been anthologized in several multi-author anthologies, the most recent of which is *The Best American Erotica* (1996). This story appeared originally in *Advocate Men* (March 1995).

shoulders like a bull's, biceps pumped up and nicely rounded, a tight waist, muscular pecs. The hands that lie on his knees, palms up, are huge; he could crush a casaba with them. His feet are big too. Next to all the other shoes by the door, his Birkenstocks look like a couple of small rafts. I keep thinking of the line "big hands, big feet, big dick" and wondered if it's true. By the bulge in his draw-string pants, I don't doubt it for a second. I do a creative visualization of him ramming his thick dickmeat hard down my throat, and for the first time since the incident over the parking space I begin to relax.

He opens his eyes and suddenly we're looking at each other eyeball to eyeball. I glance away, but when I sneak another look at him his eyes are still trained on me. *What the hell*, I think. I give him my best barroom eye fuck, throwing in a little leer to make it interesting. His expression never changes, and after a couple of seconds, he closes his eyes again and sinks back into meditation. But after the session's over, he comes up to me and asks if I'd like to catch a cup of something hot with him. I nearly trip over my tongue saying yes.

We go to some cafe nearby. I order a bowl of split pea soup with crackers, he orders red zinger herbal tea. He asks me my name.

"Bill," I say. I ask him his.

"Star," he says.

How precious, I think. New Age pretentiousness really gets on my nerves.

As if reading my mind, he gives a small smile. "It's a sixties thing. My folks were a couple of Haight-Ashbury hippies. They wanted something cosmic sounding for their kids. I got a sister named Moon and another named Earth."

I grin. "What was your dog's name? Pluto?"

Star smiles. "No, Benny. *I* got to name him."

I laugh and Star laughs too. Things start to loosen up between us.

"Have you been meditating long?" Star asks.

I shake my head. "Just since I joined this group three weeks ago."

Star nods. "You looked pretty new at it."

I give a sour smile. "Is it that obvious?" I pick up a pack of crackers and try to open it. For some reason the cellophane won't tear. I struggle with it for a few seconds without making any headway. A small sunburst of rage explodes inside my head. I throw the crackers down and bare my teeth at Star with something I hope can pass as a smile. "How long have you been meditating?" I ask, my voice thin with anger.

Star reaches over and takes one of the cracker packages. "You got to tear it right here," he says. "Right where the red line is." He tears the cellophane easily and hands it to me. His expression is bland, but there's humor in his eyes. The rage wells up inside of me again. *The son-of-a-bitch is laughing at me*, I think.

"Thank you," I say tightly.

"You're welcome," he replies. There's a moment of tense silence, at least tense on my part. Star seems completely at ease. We look at each other. Star wiggles his eyebrows. Suddenly I laugh, and the rage passes off like steam.

Star smiles. "Welcome back," he says.

"Thanks," I say, this time meaning it. I take a deep breath. "You handle tantrums well." I give a wry smile. "You'd make a great kindergarten teacher."

Star shrugs good-naturedly. There's another pause. "Nine years," Star says. I look at him uncomprehendingly. "You asked me how long I've been meditating. It's been nine years."

I give a low whistle. "No wonder you're so goddamn serene."

Star grins. "I have my bad days, too, you know." The thought flashes through my mind that his worst days are probably better than my best. Star takes a sip of tea. Even the way he raises his cup to his mouth is calm, the movement of his hands measured and simple. I watch him, feeling like an orphan out in the storm, face pressed to the window of a warm, well-lit room.

"Why do you meditate?" I ask, with genuine curiosity.

"It's part of my practice." Star catches my uncomprehending stare. "I'm a Buddhist. Meditation is one of Buddhism's cornerstones."

I turn this over in my mind. "A Buddhist? I thought all you guys were bald, wore orange robes and sold carnations at airports."

Star smiles. "Those are Hare Krishnas, Bill. Different religion altogether."

We sit in silence for a few seconds. *Stairway to Heaven* is playing over the sound system. "So what prompted you to join the meditation group?" Star finally asks.

I swallow a spoonful of soup and give him a level stare. *Well*, I think, *here goes.* "It's one of the terms of my probation. To join some kind of stress reduction program." I keep my voice matter-of-fact. "I just got out after three months in jail. For assault." Star looks at me with his calm gaze and says nothing. After a while the silence is more uncomfortable than speaking, so I continue on. "I was shit-faced and got sucked into some stupid fight outside of a bar, where I beat some guy to a pulp. He wound up in the hospital. This wasn't the first time I got in trouble with the law over something like this, so they threw the book at me." I shrug. "I'm a mean drunk. Another condition to my probation is that I join a twelve-step program. I meet with them every morning before work."

"How's it been going for you?" Star asks. His face is like a lake on a summer day, with no breeze to ruffle the waters. Part of me is grateful he's listening to this with no sign of disapproval. Another part is getting a little tired of all this relentless *calmness*.

I shrug again. "I take it from day to day." I give a laugh with precious little humor in it. "The hard part is my temper. I'm such a bad-ass son-of-a-bitch. It doesn't take much to get me started." I give a thin smile. "You didn't realize when you asked me to join you that you were dealing with a psycho from hell, did you?"

Star's expression is thoughtful. "No, I didn't," he says slowly. "It certainly makes things more interesting."

We slip into another silence. I'm beginning to feel more than a little ill at ease. Finally I shake my head and laugh. "I keep expecting you to try to convert me, now."

Star looks genuinely surprised. "Convert you? To what?"

I shrug, uncomfortably. "You know. Buddhism."

Star laughs. "I don't give a rat's ass whether you become a Buddhist or not." He gives me a curious look. "Why did you think I did?"

"I don't know," I say. "I shared a cell with a Jesus freak for a few weeks." I laugh, remembering it. "The sonuvabitch had knocked off a 7–11. He kept trying to fuckin' 'save my soul.'" I pick up my spoon, turning it over in my hand. "It got on my nerves after a while."

Star leans back in his seat and hitches his thumbs under his belt. "Believe me, Bill. I'm not looking for any converts." He drains his cup and places it back in the saucer. He grabs his jacket. "Let's take a walk."

I look at him, startled. "Okay."

We walk around the neighborhood, going no place in particular. It's a typical San Francisco summer evening, which means I'm freezing my butt off. But I like the bite in the air; it keeps my mind alert. Star and I don't say much, but it's nice having him walk beside me. We climb Telegraph Hill and look down at Alcatraz, its red signal light muffled behind the banks of fog rolling in. We pass a dark doorway. I pull Star in and suddenly we're all over each other, kissing, rubbing our bodies together, breathing hot and heavy. Star cups my ass with those giant hands of his and pulls my crotch against his; his dick is hard and urgent under his cotton pants. He dry humps me for a couple of minutes with his mouth fused over mine, his tongue pushing deep enough down my throat to taste what I had for breakfast.

"Let's go back to my place," he whispers.

"No problem," I say.

Star's apartment suits what little I know of his personality: simple, uncluttered, comfortable. There are a few pieces of furniture, not much: a futon, a bean bag chair, a small table and set of chairs, a potted ficus in the corner. In an alcove there's a bench press and set of weights. A single picture hangs on the wall: a series of circles within circles, filled with animals, demons, meditating figures, flowers.

"It's a Tibetan mandala," Star says, noticing the direction of my gaze. "It represents the universe. With the Buddha sitting in the middle." He inserts a CD in his player. Indian sitar music fills the room.

"Nice," I say.

Star comes over and we pick up where we had last left off. I slip my hands under his T-shirt. "This feels very nice," I murmur.

Star grins. "It's all part of my plan to convert you."

I laugh. I plant my mouth over his and we kiss hard. My hands begin kneading the flesh of his torso. It's firm under my fingertips and the muscles underneath have the feel of hard rubber. I run my thumbs back and forth across his nipples. Star closes his eyes. I can trace each abdominal ridge, the cut of each pectoral. I can't wait to see this guy naked. I tug at his shirt, Star lifts his arms, and I pull it over his head. His torso is as beautiful to look at as it is to feel: hairless, ripped, the muscles sharply defined. The skin is the color of pale honey and has a silky resiliency and smoothness under my fingers. I lift his arm and bury my face into his left pit. The musky smell of fresh sweat fills my nose, its sharp taste flavors the saliva in my mouth. I move down to his left nipple and run my tongue around it. Star sighs audibly. I suck on it and give it a playful nip with my teeth. The nipple swells to hardness in my mouth. I trace a wet trail across Star's chest with my tongue and give his right nipple equal time.

I am not by nature a gentle lover. I like my sex rough, I like to wrestle in bed, snarl and spit, spank, plow ass hard and fast or fuck throat mercilessly. But tonight, all bets are off, I feel this irresistible need to be *tender*. The feeling's so new to me it almost seems kinky. I decide to just kick back and let it happen. I slide my tongue down the ridges of Star's abdominals and across the rough fabric of his pants. His dick swells against the white cotton. I kiss it gently, running my tongue against the cloth, darkening it with my spit.

I reach up and untie the drawstring. I glance up at Star's face. He's looking down at me, his blue eyes bright, his lips parted. There's a lamp on the wall behind him, and the blonde hair lit from behind frames his head like a halo. I slowly pull down his pants.

His dick lives up to the promise of his hands and feet; it flops heavily and half erect against his thigh in meaty splendor: red, thick, fleshy, traced with blue veins, the head swollen and blood engorged. I give a sharp exhalation of breath, just shy of a whistle. "Jeez, Star, do you fuck with that or play baseball with it?"

Star laughs. I love this man's laugh; it's open and easy, with a sense of adventure in it. "I just do the usual things with it," he says.

"Well, do them to me, man," I growl. I take his dick in my mouth and move my lips up the shaft, until my nose is buried in his dark blonde pubes. Star sighs, and his dick swells to full hardness in my mouth. I start working it, sliding my lips up and down the shaft, rolling my tongue over it. Star lays his hands on my head, not roughly, just as a guide as he pumps his hips and fucks my mouth with deep slow strokes. I close my eyes and feel his cock move in and out of my mouth, filling it with dick flesh. I open my throat wide, and, with an effort, manage to take it all in each time he shoves his hips forward.

I run my hands across the hard flesh of his ass cheeks, prying them apart, burrowing my fingers into the crack. I find his asshole and massage it, and then let one finger push up inside. Star squirms and he grinds his hips hard against my face. Pulling away from Star's cock, I slide down and press my lips against his ball sac, kissing it softly. Scrotal hairs tickle my mouth. I stick my tongue out and give his balls a good washing. They hang heavy in their fleshy pouch, plump and swollen with cum. I open my mouth wide, to take them both in at the same time, but they're too big. I have to content myself with sucking on the right one and then the left.

Star reaches down and pulls me to my feet. He kisses me on the mouth, my eyes, all over my face. He unbuckles my belt and pulls my jeans and boxers down around my ankles.

"You have a beautiful cock," he murmurs, stroking it slowly with his hand.

"It's not as big as yours," I reply. I can't bleed all of the regret from my voice.

Star shrugs and smiles. "I'm used to that. Bigger isn't always better, you know." And damn if he doesn't say that with enough sincerity that I actually believe he means it.

He leads me to his futon, and in a matter of seconds we're sprawled on top of it, kissing. Star wraps his legs around mine and spreads himself full length on top of me. My body feels like every nerve ending in it is wired to the sensation of his skin against mine. He sits up and wraps his hand around both our cocks; we fuck his huge fist in unison, cock flesh against cock flesh, his balls pressed against mine. I reach up and squeeze his nipples, not gently. Star closes his eyes briefly, but then looks down at me and smiles.

He pivots around and takes my dick in his mouth, deep throating me with a slow, long tempo. From this position, all I can see is his ball sac swinging heavily above my face, and the crack of his ass. From the CD player Ravi Shankar is doing hot licks on his sitar. I do the same on Star's balls, lifting my head and sucking eagerly on his meaty scrotum. My tongue moves higher up and I bury my face between Star's asscheeks, probing into his bung hole. From the way Star's body writhes against mine I can tell the sensations are driving him wild. I wrap my hand around Star's dick and begin to stroke it. We ease into a smooth rhythm, each stroke and lick of mine in sync with Star's slow, steady sucks. The old horizontal dance I love to do so well.

Star comes up for air. He turns his head and looks at me. "I would really love to fuck your ass right now, Bill," he says. "Would that be all right with you?"

I laugh because he sounds so *polite*. "Star," I say, "as far as I'm concerned you can fuck me blind."

Star grins. "What if I just fuck you until you need glasses?" Old joke, maybe, but it's still funny. I laugh again. He reaches into the drawer of a bedstand next to the futon and pulls out a condom and jar of lube.

In no time at all I have my legs over his shoulders and Star is readying himself for the initial plunge. He places his hands on my hips and his cock head probes against my asshole. With excruciating slowness, he enters me. I shut my eyes and grimace from the size of him. "I know, buddy, I know," he murmurs. "I'll go easy." He begins fucking me with a gentle, slow tempo, whispering reassurances, his hands caressing my torso. I open my eyes and see his face right above mine, his eyes watching me carefully. I move my body in pace with his, and everything's all right again, the feeling of him filling me excites me into new hardness. Star smiles. He quickens his pace, thrusting deep, grinding his pelvis against me. I reach down and cup his balls in my hand, squeezing them gently. Star smears a dollop of lube onto his hand and starts jacking me off. He bends down and we kiss, thrusting our tongues deep into each other's mouths.

Star pulls away to an upright position. He starts breathing deeply and steadily, exhaling in a loud sigh with each thrust of his hips. After a while it dawns on me that this is fucking as meditation, that he's using the same breath techniques that I've seen him use during the evening classes. I try to match my breath with his, and eventually I get something of the hang of it: withdraw, inhale; thrust, exhale. Star notices my attempts right away. "Yeah, Bill, that's right," he pants. "Let's see where we can go with this."

Sensations sweep over my body, starting from my asshole and radiating out. I have never felt so intensely the act of being fucked. I groan and close my eyes, letting Star's dick and lube-smeared hand work their wonders on me. "Open your eyes, Bill," Star says urgently. "Don't drift away." I open my eyes and see Star looking down at me, sweat along his forehead, his eyebrows knitted in concentration. I hold his gaze, and we fuck like this, eyes locked, breaths synchronized, bodies thrusting and pulling away in a rhythm that comes more smoothly together with each stroke. I reach up and run my hands over his torso, now slippery with sweat. I seem to be aware of everything around me with a sharpness of detail I've never experienced before: the softness of the futon under my back, the patterns on the leaves of the ficus plant behind Star, each note played on the sitar from the CD. But mostly I'm aware of Star; I feel myself drawn up out of my body and pulled into those blue, blue eyes of his. It no longer requires any effort to match breaths or thrusts with him; we seem to be moving as one body now.

Star's breathing becomes faster, more ragged. His face is drenched with perspiration and his lips are pulled back into a soundless snarl. But his gaze never wavers from mine. I know he's ready to come any moment now, and

I can feel the load being pulled up from my balls as well. It would be easy for me to shoot, but I manage to hold on, to wait for Star; it feels like I have more control over my body than I've ever had before. Star groans. I reach up and twist his nipple, and that seems to be what it takes to push him over the edge. He thrusts deep and hard one final time and then cries out. He bends down and kisses me, his torso squirming against mine, and then I feel his dick pulse inside me as his load squirts into the condom up my ass. At the same time I feel my own load rise up from my balls, and I cry out, my voice muffled by his mouth. My spunk shoots out onto my belly, one spermy gob after another. Star embraces me in a bear hug, pressing his body tight against mine, as I shudder out the last of my load. We lie together in silence, me wrapped in Star's strong arms, feeling his heartbeat against my chest. I want this feeling of flesh on flesh to last forever, to just freeze time right here in the afterglow of a good cosmic fuck, maybe my first. But inevitably Star pulls his dick out of my ass, and rolls over on his back.

I lie there on the futon, staring up at the ceiling. "Jesus, Star," I say, awed. "That was fuckin' incredible!"

He smiles. "Yeah, it's nice when it goes right, isn't it?" He kisses me again, and we lie together on his futon, his arm wrapped around me, my head nestled against his shoulder. I feel myself drifting off to sleep. Reluctantly, I force myself to get up.

"You know you can spend the night here," Star says.

But I have to go to work in the morning and I turn down his offer, with some real regret. Star takes this, like everything else, with equanimity. A thought flashes through my head, a snake in Eden, that it would have been nice if he had shown at least *some* disappointment at my refusal. "Maybe we can do this again?" I say, trying to sound casual. I scan his face carefully for his reaction.

Star smiles. "Yeah, I'd love to." He seems to mean it. *Leave it at that*, I think. *Don't push it.* I get up and start putting my clothes on. I look down at him on the futon as I button my shirt. He looks like a jungle cat relaxing. He looks beautiful. I hold that picture of him in my mind as I walk out the door.

As I drive home, a car suddenly switches into my lane, cutting me off. I have to slam on my brakes to avoid hitting it. It's half a mile later before I realize that I hadn't felt the slightest bit of anger at the driver. I move through the traffic of the city streets towards home like a rock falling towards the center of the earth.

PUT YOUR EAR TO STONE AND OPEN YOUR HEART TO THE SKY

John Giorno 1985

VI

QUEER DHARMA POETRY

Allen Ginsberg, Sea of Japan, July 1963.

Six Poems by *Allen Ginsberg*

GOSPEL NOBLE TRUTHS

Born in this world
You got to suffer
Everything changes
You got   no soul

Try to be gay
Ignorant   happy
You get the blues
You eat jellyroll

There is one Way
You take the high road
In your Big Wheel
8 steps you fly

Look at the View
Right to horizon
Talk to the sky
Act like you talk

Work like the sun
Shine in your heaven
See what you done
Come down & walk

Sit   you sit down
Breathe when you breathe
Lie down   you lie down
Walk where you walk

Talk when you talk
Cry when you cry
Lie down   you lie down
Die when you die

Look when you look
Hear what you hear
Taste what you taste   here
Smell what you smell

Touch what you touch
Think what you think
Let go Let it go   Slow
Earth Heaven & Hell

Die when you die
Die when you die
Lie down   you lie down
Die when you die

New York Subway, October 17, 1975

ALLEN GINSBERG (New York City) was born in Paterson, NJ in 1926 and died in
New York City, April 1997. His signal poem "Howl," overcame censorship and
is now one of the most widely read poems of the century. He was a member of the
American Academy of Arts and Letters and co-founder of the Jack Kerouac School
of Disembodied Poetics at Naropa Institute, the first accredited Buddhist college
in the West. He practiced within the Tibetan Kagyu tradition as a student of
Trungpa Tulku Rinpoche. Among his numerous books see: *Selected Poems 1947–
1995* (HarperCollins) and *Straight Hearts' Delight: Love Poems and Selected Letters
1947–1980*, edited by Winston Leyland (Gay Sunshine Press, 1980).

EGO CONFESSION

I want to be known as the most brilliant man in America
Introduced to Gyalwa Karmapa* heir of the Whispered Transmission
    Crazy Wisdom Practice Lineage
as the secret young wise man who visited him and winked anonymously
    decade ago in Gangtok
Prepared the way for Dharma in America without mentioning Dharma
    —scribbled laughter
Who saw Blake and abandoned God
To whom the Messianic Fink sent messages darkest hour sleeping on
    steel sheets "somewhere in the Federal Prison system" Weathermen
    got no Moscow Gold
who went backstage to Cecil Taylor serious chat chord structure &
    Time in a nightclub
who fucked a rose-lipped rock star in a tiny bedroom slum watched by
    a statue of Vajrasattva—
and overthrew the CIA with a silent thought—
Old Bohemians many years hence in Viennese beergardens'll recall
his many young lovers with astonishing faces and iron breasts
gnostic apparatus and magical observation of rainbow-lit spiderwebs
extraordinary cooking, lung stew & Spaghetti a la Vongole and recipe
    for salad dressing 3 parts oil one part vinegar much garlic and honey
    a spoonful
his extraordinary ego, at service of Dharma and completely empty
unafraid of its own self's spectre
parroting gossip of gurus and geniuses famous for their reticence—
Who sang a blues made rock stars weep and moved an old black
    guitarist to laughter in Memphis—
I want to be the spectacle of Poesy triumphant over trickery of the world
Omniscient breathing its own breath thru War tear gas spy
    hallucination
whose common sense astonished gaga Gurus and rich Artistes—
who called the Justice department & threaten'd to Blow the Whistle
Stopt Wars, turned back petrochemical Industries' Captains to grieve &
    groan in bed
Chopped wood, built forest houses & established farms
distributed monies to poor poets & nourished imaginative genius of the
    land
Sat silent in jazz roar writing poetry with an ink pen—
wasn't afraid of God or Death after his 48th year—
let his brains turn to water under Laughing Gas his gold molar pulled
    by futuristic dentists

Seaman knew ocean's surface a year
carpenter late learned bevel and mattock
son, conversed with elder Pound & treated his father gently
—All empty all for show, all for the sake of Poesy
to set surpassing example of sanity as measure for late generations
Exemplify Muse Power to the young avert future suicide
accepting his own lie & the gaps between lies with equal good humor
Solitary in worlds full of insects & singing birds all solitary
—who had no subject but himself in many disguises
some outside his own body including empty air-filled space forests &
    cities—
Even climbed mountains to create his mountain, with ice ax & crampons
    & ropes, over Glaciers—

San Francisco, October 1974

---

*H. H. Rangjung Rigpe Dorje, the 16th Gyalwa Karmapa (1924–1981) was head
of the Karma Kagyu lineage of Tibetan Buddhism. His first visit to Europe and the
USA in 1974 led to the opening of many Buddhist centres in those regions.

THOUGHTS SITTING BREATHING II

When I sat in my bedroom for devotions, meditations & prayers
my Gomden on a sheepskin rug beside the mirrored closet,
white curtains morning sunlit, Friday *Rocky Mountain News* "Market
    Retreats in Busiest Day"
lying on the table by Nuclear Nightmare issue of *Newsweek*,
Katherine Mansfield's thick bio & Addington Symonds' *The Greek Poets*
lifting a white lamp above my headboard pillow illuminating *Living
    Country Blues'* small print 1 A.M. last night,
with B complex bottled, green mint massage oil, High Blood Pressure
    nightly Clonadine Hydrochloric pills,
athlete's foot Tolnaftate cream, newsclip scissors and a rusty shoe-last
    bookweight standing on xeroxed Flying Saucer papers,
new ballpoint pens, watch, wallet, loose coins keys Swiss army knife
toothpicks, pencil sharpener & filefolder of Buddhist Analytic Psyche
    papers
scattered random across this bedstead desk—
As I breathed between white walls, Front Range cliffs resting in the sky
    outside south windows
I remembered last night's television suitcoat tie debate, the neat Jewish
    right wing student outwitted a nervous Dartmouth pimply liberal editor
knowing that boy who swears to "get the Government off our backs"
    would give my tax money to Army brass bands FBI rather than St.
    Mark's Poetry Project—
He can't read verse with any sense of humor sharp eyed
but then some poets can't either, did Ed Dorn find me fatuous, can I
    breathe in hot black anger & breathe out white cool bliss?
Doomed guilty layman all my life! these pills causing impotency?
Could I move bookcases & clothes out of my bedroom, 8 foot desk file
    cabinets & typewriter
to the small apartment next door N.Y., would that end my hideous
    Public Karma,
Telephones tingling down my spine, pederast paranoid hypnotic burnt
    out teenage fruitcake poets
banging the door for protection from Brain Damaged Electric Guitar
    Police in New Wave Blue Vibration Uniforms?
Be that as it may as blue empty Buddha floats through blue bodied sky,
should I settle down & practice meditation, care for my nervous Self,
    do nothing,
arrange paper manuscripts, die in Lower East Side peace instead of
    heart attack in Ethiopia,
What way out of this Ego? let it appear disappear, mental images

Nothing but thoughts, how solve World Problems by worrying in my
bedroom?—

Still one clear word-mighty poem might reveal what Duncan named
Grief in America

that one hundred million folk malnourish the globe while Civic Powers
inflate $200 billion War Machines this year—

and who gets rich on that, don't all of us get poor heart?—but what do
I know of Military Worlds?

Airfields and Aircraft Carriers, bugle Corps, ice cream concessions,

million dollar Computer rockets—yes I glimpse CIA's spooky dope
deal vanity—but nothing of Camp Pendleton's brainy Thoughts

Norfolk officers' vast housing tracts, messes and helicopters, food
resource

logistics Pentagon committees've amassed—NORAD's Rapture Mountain

Maybe get rid of Cold War, give Russian Empire warm weather access,

inaugurate trillion dollar Solar Power factories on every Continent—

Yes access to sunny blue ocean, not Cold Murmansk & Vladivostok
Ports they need a vast hot harbor

International Agreement big warships forbidden, no battleships from
Russia or America in the azure Greek pond—

What about pirates, storms at sea or kamikaze Hell's Angel North
Africans shooting Jews?

Well a few small Police boats, no Cruiser or Nuclear Subs—

Yes a warm weather port for Russian access South I thought

sitting on my bedroom floor cushion 10:30 A.M. getting hungry breathing
thru shades & curtains on transparent windows, morning sun shining
on white painted walls and gray rug—

So remembering the old story of Russia's claim to a warm weather
harbor I came back to myself, blue clouded Colorado sky adrift
above the Bluff Street Boulder house.

November 8, 1982

ON CREMATION OF CHOGYAM TRUNGPA, VIDYADHARA

I noticed the grass, I noticed the hills, I noticed the highways,
I noticed the dirt road, I noticed car rows in the parking lot
I noticed ticket takers, I noticed the cash and checks & credit cards,
I noticed buses, noticed mourners, I noticed their children in red dresses,
I noticed the entrance sign, noticed retreat houses, noticed blue &
    yellow Flags—
noticed the devotees, their trucks & buses, guards in Khaki uniforms
I noticed crowds, noticed misty skies, noticed the all-pervading smiles
    & empty eyes—
I noticed pillows, colored red & yellow, square pillows and round—
I noticed the Tori Gate, passers-through bowing, a parade of men &
    women in formal dress—
noticed the procession, noticed the bagpipe, drum, horns, noticed high
    silk head crowns & saffron robes, noticed the three piece suits,
I noticed the palanquin, an umbrella, the stupa painted with jewels the
    colors of the four directions—
amber for generosity, green for karmic works, noticed the white for
    Buddha, red for the heart—
thirteen worlds on the stupa hat, noticed the bell handle and umbrella,
    the empty head of the cement bell—
noticed the corpse to be set in the head of the bell—
noticed the monks chanting, horn plaint in our ears, smoke rising from
    atop the firebrick empty bell—
noticed the crowds quiet, noticed the Chilean poet, noticed a Rainbow,
I noticed the Guru was dead, I noticed his teacher bare breasted watch-
    ing the corpse burn in the stupa,
noticed mourning students sat crosslegged before their books, chanting
    devotional mantras,
gesturing mysterious fingers, bells & brass thunderbolts in their hands
I noticed flame rising above flags & wires & umbrellas & painted
    orange poles
I noticed the sky, noticed the sun, a rainbow round the sun, light misty
    clouds drifting over the Sun—
I noticed my own heart beating, breath passing thru my nostrils
my feet walking, eyes seeing, noticing smoke above the corpse-fir'd
    monument
I noticed the path downhill, noticed the crowd moving toward buses

---

Chogyam Trungpa Rinpoche (1939–1987) was an incarnate lama (Kagyu lineage),
who fled Tibet at the time of the Chinese occupation in 1949. He founded meditation centres in Scotland, USA and Canada (Vajradhatu) and was involved in
Naropa Institute in Boulder, Colorado. He was a poet and the author of many
books on Tibetan Buddhism.

I noticed food, lettuce salad, I noticed the Teacher was absent,
I noticed my friends, noticed our car the blue Volvo, a young boy held
    my hand
our key in the motel door, noticed a dark room, noticed a dream
and forgot, noticed oranges lemons & caviar at breakfast,
I noticed the highway, sleepiness, homework thoughts, the boy's
    nippled chest in the breeze
as the car rolled down the hillsides past green woods to the water,
I noticed the houses, balconies overlooking a misted horizon, shore &
    old worn rocks in the sand
I noticed the sea, I noticed the music, I wanted to dance.

May 28, 1987, 2:30–3:15 A.M.

BIG EATS

Big deal bargains TV meat stock market news paper headlines love life
    Metropolis
Float thru air like thought forms float thru the skull, check the headlines
    catch the boyish ass that walks
Before you fall in bed blood sugar high blood pressure lower, lower,
    your lips grow cold.
Sooner or later let go what you loved hated or shrugged off, you walk
    in the park
You look at the sky, sit on a pillow, count up the stars in your head,
    get up and eat.

August 20, 1991

Ginsberg notes that "Big Eats" was a Mahamudra poetics exercise suggested by
the Tibetan Kagyu teacher Khenpo Tsultrim Gyatso in 1991. The first of five verses,
twenty-one syllables each, begins in "neurotic confusion" (Samsara) and the last
concludes grounded in "ordinary mind" (Dharmakaya). From *Cosmopolitan
Greetings: Poems 1986–1992.*

WHY I MEDITATE

I sit because the Dadaists screamed on Mirror Street
I sit because the Surrealists ate angry pillows
I sit because the Imagists breathed calmly in Rutherford and Manhattan
I sit because 2400 years
I sit in America because Buddha saw a Corpse in Lumbini
I sit because the Yippies whooped up Chicago's teargas skies once
I sit because No because
I sit because I was unable to trace the Unborn back to the womb
I sit because it's easy
I sit because I get angry if I don't
I sit because they told me to
I sit because I read about it in the Funny Papers
I sit because I had a vision also dropped LSD
I sit because I don't know what else to do like Peter Orlovsky
I sit because after Lunacharsky got fired & Stalin gave Zhdanov
    a special tennis court I became a rootless cosmopolitan
I sit inside the shell of the old Me
I sit for world revolution

July 19, 1981

Allen Ginsberg on Buddhism and Gayness

I think the more open practice in Buddhism is to be mindful of whatever you do. Whatever you do, do it well and do it mindfully. Whether making it with a man or a woman. Particularly Vajrayana style Buddhism is taking the present situation with all of its shit and transforming it into gold. At least according to the teachings that *my* teacher, Chögyam Trungpa Rinpoche, gave, "make your neurosis your pet." So love is love, whether it's gay or straight. And if you are in love, there is a way of relating to it with majesty, treating it as sacred, treating it sacramentally. So I don't think there's any fixed prevalent practice, at least in the group that I work with, insisting on straightness. It's more working with the way you are already, recognizing the way you are already, and trying to relate to it in a friendly way. Relating to homosexuality in a friendly way would be Buddhist practice, as well as relating to heterosexuality in a friendly way. So at this point I don't have any problem in that Buddhist meditation practice seems to make me less obsessive and clearminded about being rejected. So it's a great help in gay relationships.

A warning about being too attached to *anything*! If there's a sexual mind that is fine, as long as there's also an empty mind simultaneously. Both! *Any* kind of mind is workable as long as there's an empty mind that accompanies it. Or there is recognition that vacancy or disillusionment or basic suffering is involved in any kind of meat activity. Because meat dies. So naturally there's going to be some disillusionment no matter how beautiful and young you are. Unless you're smart; then there's no disillusionment because you're already disillusioned in a very friendly way. So that you don't expect people to act the way you think they *should* act all the time, and you try and accommodate to their spirits and give them space. Accommodate to your own spirit and give *it* space also.

Trungpa Rinpoche said to me and Peter Orlovsky once when asked about gay and straight: one taste.

From 1983 interview with Ginsberg in the Danish gay magazine, *Pan*.

Five Poems by *Trebor*

ODE TO BUDDHA

Oh scantily dressed boygod
teach me your tantra
Deliver me from the samsara of my bed

I've treated a thousand cocks
like lotus flowers
perching myself on them like a throne
but still I feel nothing

Teach me your tantra
look in my eyes

I'm cruising for you buddha
a man with something more to give

I say, if you meet the buddha in a nightclub
pick him up for chrissakes!

Sitting's getting me nowhere
I don't care about the one hand clapping
I'm tired of masturbation

Teach me your tantra
make me your mudra
steal my eyes

Call it the middle way
you're the kundalini kid
guiding it up the middle of me
with your dorje dong
your noble eight-inched path

Teach me your tantra
sing me your song
fuck me right out of being
with your blessed dorje dong!

For biographical information on the San Francisco poet, Trebor, see page 375.

MAKE MY BOYFRIEND A BUDDHA

I keep thinkin' about the day you die
And I gotta believe in reincarnation
I can't live with the thought that you'll never be again
Oh the gods will not know what to do with you
As you sure as hell never knew what to do with yourself
They'll probably make you one of the 10,000 buddhas
confounded by your beauty and your fury

He's so fucking sexy they'll conclude
He'll inspire devotion in millions
Let's give him a pure land
Let's give him a deva realm
with his cock dorje
and his scrotum bell
All his joints are mala beads
and his skin like milk and saffron
            Mandalas for eyes
His words are sacred koans
and his ass is one fine lotus seat

Oh   I keep thinkin' about the day you die

Oh my buddha boyfriend
I could make an altar to you then
keep you here within my arms
But what relics have you left me?
I've not an ounce of your piss or spit,
your fine smooth cum

And I keep thinkin' about the day you die
I know that rainbows will arch up across the sky
like how your back used to do
when you'd spurt
and devas will cry out
in your white rain
falling lotus-petaled gift

Let Manjushri circumcise me then
I'm lost in the sandy unsure ground of grief
the colored pathways of the palace of the Kalachakra
all leading toward destruction with a Tibetan laugh

Oh make my boyfriend a buddha!

CRUSH

I felt about the Buddha
the way I did about Eduardo
I had a crush on him and everything he was about
He of course had no interest in me at all
Not once did he return my calls

Unrequited love
I gave it five years
hopeless romantic that I am
I did what I always do
and what never works
I sat and pined away for him

And then one day the Buddha called
and told me I was hot
That he'd always thought so
He explained that the dharma's just shy

O NOBLY BORN   *For Greg*

It was unlike the usual one-night stand
we sat the next morning on the end of my futon
and for the next 3 weeks too
until he ripped me off
and went back on junk

I sit alone now
ring the tibetan bell
he gave me
—he must have stolen it

I can't help watching for him
on the street
and while I sit—
my spine a great glass window
fogged and running with rain

I keep him in mind
sitting right next to Chenrezig*   [*the Buddha of Compassion]
—a chosen place

And so what about the last blade of grass?
—that part's easy
I vow to deliver him

IF THICH NHAT HANH WAS A FAG LIKE ME

I think it pisses God off if you walk by the color
purple in a field somewhere and don't notice it.
—Alice Walker

In just this moment
I will smoke a cigarette
forget about ulcers, lung cancer and HIV

For just this once
I will walk through the Castro
with a smile on my face
and not because I'm happy
but in the service of love
which was what this was supposed to be about

In just this moment
I will tell a man he is handsome to his face
that his body is beautiful
forever young and strong
and I will not proposition him

In just this moment
I will be the buddhist
I'd promised myself to be
when I was 17
drunk on Kerouac
and Wilder's graveyard answer
to who the hell understands:
—the poets and the saints
—they do some

For just this once
I will take one step
and remember that I am nothing but what I give
humble myself
before the grace and gift of being gay

In just this moment
I will squeeze a tear
one drop of honey
one flower am I
walking in a field of flowers

Two Poems by *Richard Ronan*

BUDDHA'S KISSES

I don't know what it's like really
but it looks like a pink flower
it feels like entrance   though I
don't know who is entered
or by whom
to kiss him

(buddha's mouth was a small cave
that walked into you and pushed
out your walls   carved elephant
gods on the inside of your living
cheek   then masqueraded as a
tiny hollow bead)

he's mostly stoned out and the
rest is just blonde   what else?
I think he thinks he's no longer
a kid and hasn't a thought of
what's left for him then   I would
tell him something is   to come
and join me thence   that I'm
wandering after a thought too:
is there anyone will ever cross
the bar he rests his chin on?
he's thirty   I am too

(buddha's mouth was a pool
that reeled you in to come and
be among its old fish   the tubes
of its lotus   to be among snails
and water walkers and red-throated
frogs   in the snail's limace was
a tiny jewel which wondered as
it turned inward)

RICHARD RONAN was born in 1946 and died of AIDS in San Francisco, 1989. His plays, poetry and prose appeared in fifty plus magazines, including *The American Poetry Review*. Seven of his plays, major contributions to American avant-garde theatre, were produced in New York. His books of poetry include *Flowers* (1979), *A Lamp of Small Sorrow* (1980) and *Buddha's Kisses* (San Francisco: Gay Sunshine Press, 1980) from which the present poems are reprinted.

I like him.   I mean he's the kind
of beat-up sort that I'd take home
and lick back to health or at least
back to where the open wounds
had gelled and he assumed
he was saved because the
swelling had gone down

(buddha's mouth was a speeding
flower car you rode in distributing
oranges and chocolates to the waifs
of war   in the engine of the car
was a tiny heart plump
as a bon bon)

maybe he's an engine jockey
or a wheel turner   he smells
sweetly of disuse   though he
also smells worn from the erosions
that an air passing by brings
to the uncommitted   his name
is richard   mine is too

(buddha's mouth was called
the well of rainbows and it was
a descending play of revelations
and as one fell down the silver tube
one advanced to good red to ochre
to flea green to blue to brine plum
colour and black   then to something
more like the blind taste of colour
the spirit of the bone a swan
had swallowed)

I don't know anything else
and nothing I've said is anything
but too slim   maybe this: I get dizzy
and silvered to kiss him   I sense
a falling   a slippage of landplates
east and west   the pink flower
I think   yes   it has a taste that is
beyond colour   the tongue sits
within it like a pearl in its bed
of shellfish dreaming of the world

AT THE VAJRA CEREMONY

moving west
across the ridges
as winter sets in
through the mountains
down the glacial tracks
the whole caravan
of arks full of scrolls
beaded yaks bearing
handfuls of disciples
a litter with
the lord of dharma
tossing badly
and the young would-be
mystics   the campfollowers
trudging   beating bells
and wondering
who turns the wheel
like this
towards exile and the west

to come to us
here
to me beside michael
who is dressed in goldcoat
and sits in the sun
to gail and maryl
seated against the wall
too young, too old
just outside our sort
of circle
but within others—
one in her own
the other in her own
and her father's

to come to us
aching cross-legged
at the feet of a
sincere intense boy
who sits on a chair
head on arms

moving inward
exiling his hands
and milk skin
his fur chest and
stripped coat
his ten year worn
pullover
bearing his thin beard
and his unthought-of
blackhair
moving his pretty body
toward seedhood
toward protein
toward acids
toward the god he's seen
in others
or maybe in the sun
toward the silence
and loneliness
he will weep for
and bleed for
and which will leave
no one to bind his feet
with linen
or stitch his eyes
with cat gut
a boy
ciphering toward the news
that after the greatest
horror's been met
there is then
the first day
of another caravan
belling its path
elsewhere

Poem by *David Chura*

CLIMBING IN SILENCE

We agree to climb in silence
the way we sit each morning
legs crossed, breathing,
observing our breathing,
when sometimes your breath
reminds me of other sighs,
deeper, warmer,
stirring that serpent of desire
safe beneath the begging bowl
of my hands.

We climb,
and I note each step,
each step
up crumbled rock
wrinkled, hatched, fractious,
past gardens of brilloed lichen
and piled-high cairns,
along mountain's neanderthal brow
and animal-runs lined with green blueberries.

We climb in silence
but there is clatter enough:
Wind batters,
riprap gabbles underfoot,
grasshoppers clack from scrub to scrub.

At Ellsworth Spring
we crouch and pass the silence between us,
gulp water long conspired from this cabal
of birch, moss, fern and rock,
cold as glacier memory,
so cold our green water bottles sweat.

DAVID CHURA (Redding, CT) was born in New York state in 1948. His poetry and essays have appeared in such publications as *Turning Wheel*, *Gay Sunshine*, *Anthology of New England Writers*, *English Journal*, and *The New York Times*. He practices Vipassana meditation, and tries to incorporate Buddhist practice into his teaching of incarcerated youth.

Up again, we hoist our packs
to climb,
and I note my step,
my breath,
mosquitoes' seductive hum.
I note it all:
Yarrow, honeysuckle, stiff-backed pines.
Sheep sorrel, sheep laurel, pale corydalis,
curl of tar black scat.
Orange hawkweed, orange fritillary,
and orange-backed grasshoppers.

But I am a pirate to our silence
and plot to write down
all I see and hear,
treasure to give you
at long silence end,
the way my hand sometimes
strays across to yours
as we unknot from morning's meditation,
serpent of memory and desire
stirred by your sighs,
still stirring.

Two Poems by *Christian Huygen*

YABYUM*

fucking
      every moment
         being fucked

open till there's nothing you can't take
till everything turns the bliss wheel at your heart

piercing
      every moment
         being pierced

on a lotus throne above a lake of fire
till nectar shoots all the way to the top of your skull

Breathing fucks us: out in out in out.
The world sports with us. Find bliss in your lungs.

Now you've entered, opened, made yourself supple.
Lotuses blossom up and down your spine.

Of *course* it hurts. Life *does* that. Just *relax.*

(1995)

*Literally "father/mother," *Yabyum* refers to any pair of male and female archetype deities in sexual union as visualized by Tibetan buddhist practitioners. At advanced stages of the practice, the yogin visualizes himself or herself arising in the form of both deities together, thereby generating a direct, emphatic and nonconceptual experience of the blissful and passionate union of wisdom and compassion, form and emptiness. See back cover of the present volume for a gay version.
   I wrote this poem on the way to my first s/m play party.

FIVE EASY PEACES

1. Stop avoiding pain.
2. Stop clinging to happiness.
3. Say whatever is hardest.
4. Remind yourself that everything is food.
5. Put your burden down.

(1995)

This poem originally appeared in *This is not her*, a companion volume to the exhibition *PIECE: Nine Artists Consider Yoko Ono*, Kiki Gallery, San Francisco, 1995, curated by Rick Jacobsen and Wayne Smith. Reprinted by permission.

CHRISTIAN HUYGEN's biographical note can be found on page 348.

Two Poems by *Jim Everhard*

THE MYSTICAL LIFE

There comes a day when all of us
disappear as completely as
the mystic with his rope trick.
Some of us climb old sheets.
Some climb the wind. No matter
how we get there, we all end up
in the same place. We are more
rootless than life seems, except
in the All. Even the tiny fly
carries part of us into the sky.
We rub off on the rose bush.
We drape across the grass.
We cross that bridge before we
get to it. You may think you know
where you're going, at least which
alternatives you have, but you don't.
When you die you will lose your will.
Being a mystic means accepting
what it is like to be dead
before you are dead, but with your will.
Embrace the mystical life.
Pray for the ability to no longer ask
for anything. Volunteer poverty.
Eat soup from a pot that stays
on a fire of eternal flames,
a soup poor in substance
yet rich and warm.

December 22, 1978

JIM EVERHARD was born in Dayton, Ohio in 1946 and died of AIDS in Washington D.C., 1986. His poems appeared in numerous literary magazines (*Fag Rag*, *Mouth of the Dragon*, *Gay Sunshine*, *The Iowa Review*, *Hanging Loose*, etc.) and in the book *Cute and other poems* (San Francisco: Gay Sunshine Press, 1982). His work was also featured in *Gay Roots* Volumes I & II, and it is from the latter volume that these two poems are reprinted. He was not a practicing Buddhist, but I am including his poems here for their *de facto* Buddhist sensibility. —*W.L.*

to be empty
is to be moral
the angel
is always empty
to be empty
is to be infinitely deep
take off the mask
and see yourself
in eyes
without surfaces
to be empty
is to be swallowed
the angel rises
out of the throat
to be empty
is to have been created
to be empty
is to know of a world
where
when
you did not exist
an angel
stands in your place
until you arrive
and fill its mouth
my life
is the mouth of an angel
a mirror
is an angel
with closed wings
a mirror
is the contemplation
of flight
such beauty
cannot be moral
but like a lake
like the eye
of a dead man
in seeing all
in reflecting the sky
is empty
is empty

February 20, 1978